Education for Hope

Hope

A Course Correction

JOHN E HULL

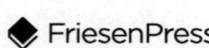 FriesenPress

One Printers Way
Altona, MB R0G 0B0
Canada

www.friesenpress.com

Copyright © 2023 by John E Hull
First Edition — 2023

All rights reserved.

No part of this publication may be reproduced in any form, or by any means, electronic or mechanical, including photocopying, recording, or any information browsing, storage, or retrieval system, without permission in writing from FriesenPress.

ISBN
978-1-03-914534-4 (Hardcover)
978-1-03-914533-7 (Paperback)
978-1-03-914535-1 (eBook)

1. Education, History

Distributed to the trade by The Ingram Book Company

To the forebears: those first-generation Dutch Neo-Calvinist immigrants who had a vision and sacrificed so much to establish an alternative system of education in Canada

"Hope has two beautiful daughters; their names are Anger and Courage. Anger at the way things are, and Courage to see that they do not remain as they are."

—Augustine of Hippo

Artistic rendition of Hope's daughters Anger and
Courage engaged with the ribbon of life
by Evelyn Martin

TABLE OF CONTENTS

Preface ix
Acknowledgements xix

The Neo-Calvinist Tradition of Education in Canada

Part I: The Seeds of Hope (1945–1970) 3
Marching Orders 4
Chapter 1: The Netherlands Context (1800–1970) 8
Chapter 2: The American Context (1845–1970) 18
Chapter 3: The Canadian Context (1945–1970) 28
Exit Slip: Seeds of Hope 49
Endnotes 52

Part II: A Season for Hope (1970–2000) 57
Hope and Its Detractors 58
Chapter 4: Whatever Happened to Joy in Learning? 65
Chapter 5: The Remarkable Story of the Joy in Learning Curriculum Development and Training Centre (CDC) 79
Chapter 6: Vision by Newsletter 106
Chapter 7: The Golden Age of Publishing for Neo-Calvinist Educators 136
Exit Slip #2: A Season for Hope: Summary and Conclusions 176
Endnotes 180

Part III: Clinging to Hope (2000–2022) 187
Education for Cultural Transformation: Keep It, Leave It, or Tweak It? 188
Chapter 8: Christian Education Goes Public in Alberta 192
Chapter 9: Teaching for Transformation 209
Chapter 10: Teacher Preparation at The King's University 228
Exit Slip #3: Clinging to Hope 252
Endnotes 255

Dig Deeper

Topic 1: Curriculum Babble	260
Topic 2: Integration and Integrality	264
Topic 3: The Calvin College Factor	270
Topic 4: The Paradigm of Progressive Education	292
Topic 5: The Curriculum Development Centre's	309
Topic 6: The "Ordering Principle"	324
Endnotes	329

Memoir of an Educator

The Making of a Reformational Educator (1947–1970)	337
Nebraska – My Place of Orientation	339
Iowa – A Place of Disorientation and Reorientation	345
The Remaking of a Reformational Educator (1971–1995)	353
Toronto – Fantasy Meets Reality	355
Bowmanville – Fantasy Becomes Reality	365
The Unmaking of a Reformational Educator (1995–2022)	377
Edmonton: Culture Making	378
Retired: Embracing Hope	389
Endnotes	392

Appendices

Appendix 1: Acronyms	394
Appendix 2: Curriculum Development Centre Publishing Chart	399
Appendix 3: CDC Founding Members, Staff and Board Members	401
Appendix 4: CDC Timeline	403
Appendix 5: The King's University Education Faculty Visioning Documents	407

Bibliography 413

Index 423

About the Author 431

Preface

Why This Book?

Contemporary pundits across the ideological spectrum acknowledge that we live in a time of extraordinary changes. No one knows for sure what the world will look like in twenty years, much less one hundred years. How should we educate our children for a world that is so unpredictable and defined by unprecedented transformation? For decades our education system has crammed ever more information into our children's heads and provided them with a predetermined set of skills or competencies. We used to think this approach best prepared our children to successfully navigate the worlds of work, civil society, and personal meaning, but this vision of education no longer offers hope to the world we live in, if it ever did.

We imagine that we are preparing students to be creative, collaborative, and to think for themselves, but few students describe their time at school in these terms. What our children need is an education that nurtures their ability to interpret their world and empowers them to address the needs of society and the environment, lest they drown in a sea of despair over loss of self, the environment and social stability. At the very least, our children need to be secure about their identity and sense of purpose. The rapid pace of change now upon us has made personal identity a pressing issue, and it will only become more urgent in the years to come. If Yuval Noah Harari and other contemporary prophets are right, the day is near when algorithms will hack us and tell us who we are. If we do not find a better reason to educate our children, soon government and corporate computers will know our children better than they do themselves.

What alternative approach to education should we adopt? How long will it take to implement? Do we have that much time? What narrative and way of life should anchor our educational vision? These are perplexing and complex questions. No individual, no matter how brilliant, can chart a meaningful course into the future for our society. No single philosophy of education can salvage our education system. How well we move into the future will depend on communities of diverse people who share a common set of causes, one of which should be a vision of hope for education.

In this book I suggest we look for guidance from an alternative school movement that currently exists and learn what we can from its successes and mistakes. The tradition I have chosen is, in my view, the most visionary among the alternative school movements that have emerged in Canada, and perhaps the United States as well.

A Bit of History

The oldest school representing this tradition is an elementary school in Holland Marsh, Ontario, which dates back to 1943. Most of the others were established between the late 1940s and the mid 1980s. Presently, the elementary and secondary schools that identify with this tradition number approximately 120 and serve over 30,000 students in three provinces.

A relatively small but resilient group of orthodox Dutch Neo-Calvinists who immigrated to Canada shortly after the end of World War II built this faith-based system of schools. Their motivation for doing so was inspired by a vision of cultural transformation that reflected the social philosophy of Abraham Kuyper, a prominent Dutch theologian-politician in the late nineteenth century, and the theology of John Calvin.

The fact that this alternative school movement is faith based may be off-putting to some readers, but there are four compelling reasons why anyone interested in substantive school reform should be familiar with this tradition of alternative education.

First, the most compelling educational vision of this tradition transcends the dominant perception of what it means to be human, what is most worth knowing, and what constitutes the good life. It goes beyond the worn-out promises tied to social efficiency promoted by those committed to scientific and technological solutions to life's biggest challenges. It also exceeds the unrealized dreams of personal self-actualization and the freedom of individuals to choose their own destiny, the key priorities that we associate with educational humanism and constructivism. This Neo-Calvinist educational vision challenges students to imagine a world where our foundational relationships with the divine, fellow humans, and all other creatures are reconciled by love, justice, mercy, and hope. In such a world, knowledge is commensurate with wisdom, and the good life is defined by shalom: the flourishing of all living things. This vision of reconciliation also distinguishes this tradition from most other faith-based traditions of education.

Second, this tradition has been nurtured by communities that are actually capable of implementing an alternative vision of education, and some have flourished for significant periods of time. The success of these communities is rooted in their faith, unique social structures and intellectual acumen.

Third, like virtually everyone else who has pursued substantive school reform in North America, these Dutch Neo-Calvinist communities eventually settled for a smaller vision of education. The two main reasons why this happened are also instructive. First, these communities were often distracted by internal rivalries; being right took precedence over nurturing relationships. Second, their efforts to implement an alternative educational vision were subtly undermined by the paradigm of progressivism that has dominated North American education for more than a century.

Fourth, throughout its history, visionary educators proposed corrective measures to keep this tradition on course. These initiatives provide a foundation upon which future educators can add their own chapters to the larger narrative and, thereby, perpetuate a living tradition. The trajectory proposed for this tradition and developed in this book builds on these corrective measures. I believe educators from within and without this tradition should at least consider the merits of these course corrections.

The Organization of Neo-Calvinist Schools

To fully appreciate this alternative tradition of education, readers must understand how its schools are organized. Each school is an independent entity controlled by a local school society made up of parents and supporters, most of whom are members of the Christian Reformed Church. Each society elects a board, which, in turn, hires a principal and a teaching staff.

Until 1999, these schools were organized as three regional districts of a well-established American body of Christian schools originally named the National Union of Christian Schools (NUCS). This organization was also started by Dutch Neo-Calvinists, who immigrated to the United States between 1850 and 1920. From the beginning of this relationship, Canadian educators were not completely happy with their American parent organization. It did not take long before each Canadian district had its own layer of administration to provide the support that they felt was not forthcoming from the NUCS head office. These district organizations were named the Ontario Alliance of Christian Schools (OACS); the Prairie Association of Christian Schools (PACS), which represented the schools in Alberta and Manitoba; and the Society of Christian Schools in British Columbia (SCSBC). Readers unfamiliar with this immigrant community should also know it has a habit of assigning long names to the committees and organizations it creates, then referring to them with acronyms. To help readers navigate this landscape of letters, all of the acronyms that appear in this book are listed in Appendix 1.

In an attempt to be more inclusive of its Canadian districts, NUCS changed its name to Christian Schools International (CSI) in 1978. Conflicts persisted, however, and the three Canadian districts finally pulled out of CSI in 1999. Since that time the three regional bodies have operated as independent associations of schools that continue to share a common tradition while following different paths. Today, the Dutch Neo-Calvinist tradition of education in Canada is represented by the Edvance Christian Association of Schools (Edvance), which replaced the OACS, the Prairie Centre of Christian Education (PCCE) (previously named the Prairie Association of Christian Schools), and the Society of Christian Schools in British Columbia (SCSBC).

Soon after their departure from CSI, these three associations formed an alliance that they named Christian Schools Canada (CSC). CSC is a partnership between the three independent associations. It does *not* function as their administrative head like CSI used to. Rather, it provides some key services that need not be duplicated by each regional association. One of the most significant of these is the organization of a national conference.

Technically, no official name applies to the three associations collectively, nor has that ever been the case. I have been told by the leaders of Edvance, the PCCE, and the SCSBC that they simply refer to themselves as "the regional organizations," leaving unsaid, "of the Canadian Neo-Calvinist tradition of education." For the purposes of this book, I decided to refer to these three associations as Christian Schools Canada. This seemed reasonable for the sake of simplicity, and because CSC has a mandate to promote the Canadian identity for these organizations. Furthermore, the easiest way to access all three is to do an online search for "Christian Schools Canada." Due to recent commitments on the part of Edvance and the SCSBC to include schools from other denominational backgrounds, today it is no longer accurate to solely identify them, or CSC, as Neo-Calvinist organizations, although that tradition remains their acknowledged core legacy.

For Whom Was This Book Written?

This may sound overly ambitious, but I wrote this book for multiple audiences. Anyone who has been, is currently, or will one day be involved with the Dutch Neo-Calvinist tradition of alternative education has vested interests in the stories and issues that appear in this book. The narrative not only provides them with an overview of their legacy but also points to a way forward. I also believe educators and supporters who have been, are currently, or will be involved in other faith-based traditions of education can learn much from the strengths and weaknesses of this tradition. Finally, I am convinced that this book has valuable insights to share with those interested in public school reform. Over the course of my career as an educator, I have learned much from the vast literature that deals with the transformation of public schools, and I do not hesitate to say that the tradition of Neo-Calvinist education in Canada has equally important lessons to share in return.

The Structure of this Book

I did not write this book as a disinterested researcher. To the contrary, my whole career as an educator has been intertwined with this tradition of education: its unique worldview, its critique of Western culture, its philosophy of education, its approach to curriculum reform, its vision of life, and, most of all, its people. I unapologetically admit that my construction of this tradition's narrative, my choice of categories, the questions I ask, the analysis I offer, and the conclusions I reach have all been shaped by my own immersion in the tradition. In this book, I offer an insider's account of the bigger story that provided the context for my own teaching career.

After several prods from colleagues who responded to my book proposal and/or read early drafts, I acquiesced to their suggestion that I "put a human face" on this tradition by including my own story. I trusted their judgment on this, but I found following their advice a challenging and risky experience. My memoir as an educator appears at the end of this book and is divided into the same blocks of time as the main narrative.

Some topics that I address in this book begged to be explored more thoroughly. So as not to impede the momentum of the storytelling, I placed these forays in a separate section called "Dig Deeper." These discussions are cross-referenced to the main narrative, so readers can decide if and when they want to explore them. The "Dig Deeper" section is sandwiched between the main narrative and my memoir.

To summarize, this book consists of three components, one major and two in support. The main narrative investigates CSC and its tradition of education. My personal journey as an educator within this tradition runs parallel to this larger story. The "Dig Deeper" section augments the CSC story with a more extensive analysis of a few selected topics. Readers can move between these elements as it suits them.

As noted above, the book is divided into three periods of time. Part I describes the early years of CSC, from the establishment of its first schools in the 1940s to 1970. I did not live in Canada during this time, but the tradition's educational vision still touched my life in a significant way, as the second segment of my personal narrative reveals. What readers will discover in part I is what I learned about this school movement after I moved to Canada in 1971.

I especially want readers to understand how Dutch Neo-Calvinist immigrants in Canada interpreted their vision of education, why that vision came to expression in several different ways, what events highlight this segment of the narrative, and the various contexts that shaped these events.

Part II of the book covers the period from 1970 to 2000. During these decades, the tradition matured into adulthood and achieved notable successes in curriculum reform and overall quality of education. Within this remarkable period of growth, we track the story of a small curriculum-writing organization that epitomized the best and the worst of the tradition. For most of this period, I lived in Ontario and taught in a high school that was a member of the Ontario Alliance of Christian Schools. My primary focus in part II is what happened in Ontario. The narrative that played out there was similar to, but not identical with, the ones that emerged from Alberta and British Columbia. I chose not to write about the people and events that shaped those narratives, leaving it to others to tell those important regional stories.

Part III describes and evaluates the CSC tradition of education in the twenty-first century. Because I moved to Edmonton in 1995 and continue to live there, my focus also shifts to what happened in Alberta. Three events significantly impacted the narrative of Neo-Calvinist education in Alberta during this time.

- The region's most prominent school gave up its independent status to become an alternative faith-based program within the Edmonton Public School Board.
- A small group of educators, primarily from this same school, developed a dynamic, coherent approach to curricular and pedagogical reform that they called Teaching for Transformation.
- The King's University launched innovative elementary and secondary teacher-preparation programs that developed strong, mutually beneficial ties with Neo-Calvinist educators in Alberta and British Columbia and with prominent stakeholders in Alberta's public school system.

The Book's Title

From the beginning of this project, I wanted the title to reflect CSC's educational vision. This vision is rooted in the Neo-Calvinist understanding of the Bible's cultural mandate recorded in Genesis 1:28, where God tasked humans with the mandate to "fill, subdue, and rule over the earth." Neo-Calvinists believe this mandate still holds for Christ's followers. They interpret it as a directive to transform what has become broken in human culture.

CSC educators have long assumed that the best way to facilitate cultural transformation is to cultivate in students a biblical perspective on life; that is, to provide them with a Christian mind. They typically describe Christian education as a Christ-centred education, which to them means every curricular subject is reinterpreted according to a biblical worldview. Thus, when I started to write this book nearly ten years ago, I imagined book titles that showcased terms like "transforming vision" or "education for a biblical worldview."

Although education for a Christian perspective continues to define numerous school vision statements, by now CSC educators and supporters should have learned some valuable lessons about themselves and their vision of cultural transformation. One of the most important of these lessons is the realization that worldview education, as significant as it is, does not go far enough. It can certainly change the way students think, which is no small matter, but a change in worldview alone rarely brings about a transformation of the self, much less the culture.

Throughout most of this tradition's history, visionary educators prodded the tradition to move beyond the provision of a biblical worldview and initiate students into a biblical way of life. This was the more compelling educational vision of the two, so for a long time I favoured the title, "Education for Discipleship."

By the year 2000, even the most ardent advocates of education for discipleship understood that it was an unachievable goal. CSC educators were too entrenched in traditional approaches to teaching to implement such a radical alternative vision. More to the point, its school communities were unwilling to model this way of life for their students. These circumstances ruled out titles that made reference to educating for a way of life.

Today, CSC is once again in need of a serious course correction. In fact, the whole notion of cultural transformation appears to be flawed. Supposing this is true, what is the appropriate aim of a Neo-Calvinist Christian education? What new compass heading must it follow? Can CSC still draw upon its Reformed tradition for inspiration? I believe it can, and what it still has to offer is good news for other traditions of education, including public schools.

The inspiration behind the title *Education for Hope* comes from three sources. My good friend and theologian extraordinaire, Roy Berkenbosch, introduced me to St. Augustine's view of hope. Augustine said hope has two beautiful daughters: Anger and Courage. By Anger he meant the righteous kind that arises from our encounters with injustice, hatred, racism, and persecution in this broken world. Courage is the pluck, the will, and the bravery to see that these evil acts of violence come to an end, especially in the lives of the powerless and marginalized in our orbits of influence.

The term "hope" poses problems, however. Hope is an elusive term. We have cheapened its meaning by our frivolous uses of it to mean "wishful thinking" or the "optimistic feeling that things are bound to get better." To overcome this degraded use of hope, Roy also shared an insight he borrowed from French philosopher Gabriel Marcel, who said, "there can be no hope except when the temptation to despair truly exists. Hope is the act by which this temptation is actively or victoriously overcome." Confronted by despair, we embrace hope.

Could anything be more relevant today than education for hope? We live in a world defined by despair. In addition to a global pandemic that is entering its third year, we face planetary problems that have no foreseeable solutions. Climate change, species extinction, environmental degradation, war, global poverty, millions of displaced persons, and systemic racism quickly come to mind. In every locale we encounter self-serving governments, profit-hungry corporations, and people who are marginalized and suffer injustices on multiple fronts.

If Christians have a cultural mandate from the God revealed in the Bible, then it surely involves sacrificing themselves for the sake of the marginalized. Hope, as St. Augustine understood it, has nothing in common with Christian schools that seek to reinforce the status quo and anesthetize children to pain and suffering. If the Christian life is meant to be a hope-filled life, it must be focused on the reconciliation of what is broken, not achieving success in a consumer-driven culture.

The second source of inspiration comes from within the Neo-Calvinist tradition of education itself. CSC has a long history of embracing both beautiful daughters of hope, but it rarely used such language to convey this fact. I know of at least one exception, and it appears in chapter 7 where I write up the account of the *Man in Society* curriculum and its importance for CSC's development in the 1980s. As one of its authors, I have no trouble remembering why we subtitled that curriculum "A Study in Hope." To a person, we were heavy-duty Christian perspective educators, but intuitively, we knew the ultimate aim of education was hope. Hope, we believed, was rooted in the reconciliation and healing of relationships.

Over the last ten years, a third source of hope has emerged in the "Teaching for Transformation" approach. Promoters of this effort to transform teaching and learning talk of deep hope and deeper learners. What they truly yearn for, I believe, is education that embraces both of hope's beautiful daughters.

CSC's historic emphasis on cultivating a biblical perspective to discern what is wrong in the world and envision what restoration looks like was never intended to stop at theory. Such knowledge was meant to arouse the daughter named righteous Anger and embolden the daughter called Courage. Education for hope is still within reach for CSC, and it serves as a beacon to schools from other traditions as well. All things considered, *Education for Hope* is the right title for a book about the Neo-Calvinist tradition of alternative education in Canada.

Acknowledgements

When a book takes ten years to write, the list of people to recognize and thank for their various contributions grows exponentially. I have tried to keep my list up to date along the way, but it is possible that I overlooked someone. If I did, it is because I am forgetful, not ungrateful.

I am indebted to all those people who agreed to be interviewed when this book was in its early stages. Each one provided valuable information and insights that helped shape the book's structure. Thank you to: Fred Schat for his unique insights; Henry Lise, always decades ahead of the rest of us; Fred Spoelstra and Ary De Moor for their affirmation after reading the material on the *Man in Society* project; Doug Blomberg for his understanding of the big picture; and Ren Siebenga for his wisdom, friendship, and encouragement—he dared to do what the rest of us struggled to imagine.

The story of the Curriculum Development Centre was a major motivation for writing this book. I could not have told this story without Agnes Struik's insights and her provision of the CDC's archives. I hope the story I have told measures up to her expectations. I am also grateful that I had the opportunity to speak with Arnold De Graaf, who graciously and honestly shared his memories about the Curriculum Development Centre and his role in it. I was also fortunate to track down Anne Tuininga and Tom Malcolm, who provided important insights for the chapter on the CDC. I am especially grateful to Harry Fernhout, another key player in the CDC's history. Harry read and offered expert advice on drafts of the book when it was about two-thirds finished and provided some valuable documents.

Interviews also played a key role in my writing of the last three chapters. I received perceptive insights into the last twenty years of education in Alberta from Hans Van Ginhoven, Peter Buisman, Elco Vandergrift, Gayle Monsma, and Jeremy Horlings. Thanks to Justin Cook and Ray Hendricks, who provided similar information about the scene in Ontario. Notable leaders Ed Noot and Darren Spyksma shared their wisdom about the situation in British Columbia.

My former colleague from The King's University, Alyce Oosterhuis, wrote up a short historical piece that I heavily relied upon to retell the story of the origins of teacher education at The King's University. Brian Doornenbal provided a similar detailed firsthand account of the "Teaching for Transformation" story. Both documents were extremely helpful. Thanks also to Louisa Bruinsma and Edith Houtstra, who provided key resources that I needed for chapters 7 and 10 respectively.

In addition to those already mentioned, several people agreed to read different sections of the book and offer their feedback. Melle Huizenga read the manuscript when it was about half complete, and his wise suggestions led to some significant changes. Melle, I wish you were still here to see the final outcome. When the book was nearly finished, Adrian Peethoom graciously agreed to read the manuscript. His feedback on the big issues was particularly engaging, and the text benefitted from his gift for copy editing. My colleague from The King's University, Bob Bruinsma, read the finished book and gave me valuable advice at both the macro and micro levels of editing. His affirmation of the content and writing buoyed me up when I started to doubt the quality of the project.

At various times over the past several years, I have shared my ideas for the book with Roy Berkenbosch or just listened to him talk about the deep meaning of things. He introduced me to the powerful image of the two daughters of hope and much more. Roy mon, you are my main source of inspiration.

Another dear friend, Evelyn Martin enthusiastically provided the image for the two daughters of hope, the book's central theme. Along with Evelyn, several friends and family members gave me valuable feedback on the various book cover designs that I considered; thankyou Jim Visser, Ruth Vander Woude, Matt and Jessica Ver Steeg.

The fine folks at FriesenPress have also served me well at each step in the road to publishing this text. Special thanks to Bret Newton, who guided me through the application process. My team leader Julianne McCallum was a constant encourager and sage advisor; she had answers to all of my questions. Without you, Julianne, the book could not have come together as well as it did. You are the best!

Finally, a big 'I love you' to my soulmate, Glenda, whose support cannot be measured. She encouraged my writing in every way possible, just as she has done for everything that I have aspired to do over these last fifty-odd years. To quote John Prine, "She is my everything!"

THE NEO-CALVINIST TRADITION
OF EDUCATION IN CANADA

PART I
THE SEEDS OF HOPE (1945–1970)

Tradition is the living faith of the dead; traditionalism is the dead faith of the living.

—Nicholas Wolterstorff

Major Story Line: Transplanting a Vision of Education

Marching Orders

Philosopher Nicholas Wolterstorff[1] once observed that to do justice to any tradition, one should understand how it *interprets* its vision, how it *expresses* that vision, and the relevant *highlights* of its narrative. To those three requirements, I add a fourth: one should also understand a tradition in its *cultural context*.

These four requirements serve as my self-appointed marching orders for part I of this book, which explores the formative years of the Neo-Calvinist[2] tradition of education in Canada. This tradition of education emerged in post-World War II Canada through the remarkable efforts of a relatively small group of orthodox Dutch Neo-Calvinist immigrants. In the mid 1940s, Neo-Calvinists made up just ten percent of the population in the Netherlands, but they accounted for roughly forty percent of the Dutch immigrants who came to Canada after the war.[3]

Their unique tradition of Christian education was shaped by three different contexts, which we shall explore in part I. The oldest of these contexts was the tradition's origins in the Netherlands, which provided Neo-Calvinist schools with a faith tradition and a powerful outlook on life and culture. The second context was American, and its formative influence was channeled to this immigrant community in two ways. One involved their institutional relationships with the more established Dutch Neo-Calvinist community that lived in the United States. The churches they established joined the Christian Reformed Church.[4] Many of their children attended Calvin College (now University).[5] All of their schools joined the National Union of Christian Schools (NUCS) with its one-hundred-year history of offering Christian education.[6] The other, more pervasive, American influence defined the overall meaning of education in North America, what I refer to as the *paradigm of progressivism*.⁷ The immigrants' Canadian cultural experience represents a third context. Canada both tolerated and limited their aspirations to establish an ethno-religious identity and pursue an alternative educational vision.

As noted in the preface of this book, the schools that belong to this tradition are currently members of three independent regional organizations: Edvance (Ontario), the Prairie Centre for Christian Education (Alberta), and the Society of Christian Schools in British Columbia.⁸ There has never been an official name for this collection of regional organizations, but since 1999 when they collectively pulled out of Christian Schools International, they formed a partnership that promotes their common identity. The name of this partnership is Christian Schools Canada (CSC) and for lack of a more accurate term, I will refer to them as such in this book. The three contexts just outlined form our investigative boundaries as we seek to understand how Canadian Dutch Neo-Calvinists interpreted and expressed their educational vision during the formative years of their school movement in Canada.

In his seminal work, *Telling the Next Generation*,⁹ Harro Van Brummelen traces the history of Neo-Calvinist Christian schools in North America from their beginnings in the mid-nineteenth century to the late 1970s. This book is a must read for all current and future CSC educators who seek a minimal understanding of the educational legacy they inherited. It is also significant for anyone who is interested in the interaction between faith, ethnicity, and education as fertile ground for school reform. Although he intended to write a North American story, the bulk of Van Brummelen's book describes the history of NUCS as it unfolded in the United States. It is unfortunate that the Canadian story played such a small role in his book, for no one knew better than Van Brummelen the significant differences that distinguished the three Canadian districts of NUCS from their older American counterparts.

As it stands today, little has been published about the narrative of Canadian Neo-Calvinist education specifically. In *Telling*, Van Brummelen provides us with significant, but minimal information covering the years 1945 to 1978. Next to nothing has been published about what happened after that period. Several significant books have been written on key educational issues, such as curriculum design, pedagogy, teacher preparation, and the purpose of education, but they do not distinguish between the American and Canadian expressions of the tradition.[10]

A few academic theses at the master's and doctorate levels have been written about the Canadian Neo-Calvinist tradition of education, but they are difficult to access and remain largely unknown. Prinsen's[11] doctoral thesis and Peetoom's[12] master's thesis rank as the most informative. Like Van Brummelen, both authors researched the origins of Neo-Calvinist Christian education as it arose in the Netherlands during the nineteenth century. Unlike him, they only focus on the Canadian story in this tradition. Peetoom analyzes roughly the same period that Van Brummelen covered, from 1948 to 1970, but Prinsen extends the story to 2000. My aim in part I of this book is to highlight and re-evaluate some key factors in the development of this school movement in Canada that these authors, among others, first brought to our attention. I will carry the story forward to the present (insofar as I know it) in subsequent chapters.

Much work needs to be done at both the micro and macro levels of the narrative if we hope to understand this unique tradition and determine whether it is a living legacy today or an example of dead traditionalism. By micro level I mean the histories of individual school communities with their local heroes, villains, triumphs, and trials. I leave this important work to the capable writers that I know exist in most of these communities.[13] My primary task lies at the macro level where we seek to understand the shared story of the three regional organizations. As noted in the preface, I decided to juxtapose my own story with this larger narrative. In doing so, I address the micro perspective in a limited way. I believe the future flourishing of the Neo-Calvinist tradition of education in Canada depends, to a large degree, on the willingness of its advocates to bring its narrative history to print and voice.

Part I of this book is organized into three chapters. Each one explores one of the aforementioned contexts. These chapters are time sensitive, and each begins with a list of period highlights. In chapter 1 we review the key events that took place in the Netherlands from 1800 to 1920. This period provided the Canadian tradition of Neo-Calvinist Christian schools with the core features of its Reformed educational legacy. The second chapter considers the evolution of their American parent organization, which implemented this legacy in an overpowering American setting. In chapter 3 we focus on the rise of Neo-Calvinist education on Canadian soil. Here we unpack the various ways CSC communities implemented their Reformed legacy of Christian education. Overall, the investigation in part I explores the formative years of a Neo-Calvinist tradition of education in Canada.

CHAPTER 1

The Netherlands Context (1800–1970)

Timeline

1579	The founding of the Dutch Republic.
1795	France overthrows the Dutch Republic, and the state church becomes secularized.
1800–1850	*Het Reveil* (the Awakening) resistance movement flourishes.
1806	Enactment of a school act gives the state centralized control of schools.
1813	The Netherlands regains independence; King Willem I rules until 1840.
1816	Willem I reinstates a government-subsidized national church.
1834	*De Afscheiding* (the rupture) resistance movement forms its own church.
1840	Groen Van Prinsterer (Reveil leader) is elected to Parliament.
1844	First parent-run Christian school is established in the Netherlands.
1848	Non-public schools obtain the constitutional right to operate freely.
1880	Abraham Kuyper establishes the Free University of Amsterdam.
1886	The Kuyper-led *Doleantie* resistance movement founds the *Gereformeerde Kerken*.

Standing up to the Enlightenment Juggernaut

The Neo-Calvinist Christian school movement was conceived at a time when Reformed Christians in the Netherlands were besieged by Enlightenment thinking and the secularization of their society and way of life. The Enlightenment promised to replace centuries of wars waged in God's name with a natural law that freed people from ignorance and superstition and redefined the meaning of virtuous citizenship and the good life. The pressure to redefine the foundations of Dutch society in terms of reason, natural law, and a secular morality was accelerated by a brief period of French rule from 1795 to 1813.

Even after the Netherlands regained its independence, the allure of liberalism remained unabated. Peetoom says this about King Willem I (1813–1840), "He shared with most of his contemporaries the standard Deistic fare: a respectable religion good for one's moral life. God had changed into Supreme Being, Christ into a teacher, man into a rational being, sin into weakness, conversion into betterment, and sanctification into virtue."[14]

Nowhere was the negative influence of the Enlightenment deemed greater than its impact on religion and education. Three years into his reign, Willem, who had lived in exile in England, re-established the *Hervormde Kerk* (Reformed Church) as the State Department of Religion, similar to the England-Anglican model. With the church now organized as "a civil institution ruled by a bureaucratic hierarchy," control of religious affairs was removed from the local level.[15] In this rapidly changing climate Wolterstorff observes, "The state church ... became very intellectualized in its sensibility and in its theology, very liberal, wide open to developments in culture."[16] Schools in the Netherlands fared no better than the church. The state took control of education under French rule, and the arrangement spelled out in the historic School Act of 1806 persisted after the Netherlands regained its independence in 1813. The Act was not updated until 1857.

Under the spell of the Enlightenment, "teachers had to instruct children in all social and Christian qualities so they would become virtuous and useful persons as well as rational beings."[17] The staying power of this liberal legacy is evident to this very day. It still defines the fundamental purposes of public education in North America; namely, to educate students to be rational (critical thinking problem solvers), virtuous (ethical), and useful (workforce ready).

Orthodox Dutch Neo-Calvinists from all strata of society opposed the juggernaut of Enlightenment thinking and its secular way of life, and their resistance was expressed in three separate movements during the nineteenth century. The followers of these movements focused their energies on reclaiming their two primary institutions: the church and the school.

Het Reveil: The Awakening

The first organized resistance to the Enlightenment involved a small group of mostly aristocratic people and leaders from the arts community and the government. Their movement, named *het Reveil* (the Awakening), flourished during the first five decades of the nineteenth century and had some affinity with an evangelical revival movement that originated in Geneva. This movement's adherents had no desire to break away from the state church. Instead, they sought to reform it from within.

Two leaders significantly impacted the formation of Christian education as it emerged in the 1840s: Guillaume Groen van Prinsterer as parliamentarian and Justinus J. L. van der Brugghen, who became prime minister. Van de Brugghen favoured interdenominational schools over public schools while van Prinsterer preferred to divide state-controlled public schools into those of different religious persuasions. Apart from these organizational differences, these two and their supporters agreed that the current state-controlled system of education undermined Christian faith and praxis. Their call for a different type of education reached all levels of Dutch society.

Groen Van Prinsterer was elected to parliament in 1840, where he became a champion of Christian education. This excerpt from one of his speeches portrays the contrast between liberal and Neo-Calvinist interpretations of Christian education at the time:

> When I peel away (the poetic flourishes) from the arguments of my fellow-member . . . then I learn only that the speaker, in good faith, is under the misapprehension that one can have Biblical history without Biblical doctrine, Christian morality without Christian faith, that it is sufficient for Children to know a few proscriptions of the Gospel without knowing anything about the authority on which these proscriptions rest, of the principles whence they are derived, of the purpose to which they point, and of the power through which they can be put into practice.[18]

Van de Brugghen stands at the front of a long line of educators who saw the need for a Christian pedagogy. His search for an alternative form of teaching was triggered by two deficiencies that he observed in government-run schools. In the first place, Van de Brugghen objected to its form of education where children "memorized astonishingly much but knew astonishingly little." In his vision for Christian education, "instead of becoming pre-programmed rolls on a barrel organ, pupils must be led to be independent personalities who create and play their own melodies."[19] Second, he hoped a Christian pedagogy would oppose the narrow moralism that characterized state schools. To achieve pedagogical reform, Van de Brugghen established a normal school for teacher preparation.

Van Brummelen's depiction of the Neo-Calvinist school movement in the Netherlands reveals one of its most enduring characteristics. Van de Brugghen and van Prinsterer (and other leaders) were deeply convinced that an Enlightenment education was not faith neutral. The Enlightenment promoted a secular, scientific dogma that posed a significant threat to a Christian way of knowing and living. The notion that a liberal education is incompatible with Christianity convinced many Calvinist Christians in the Netherlands, and many of those who later moved to North America, that affirmation of a national public school system committed to the Enlightenment worldview was irresponsible, and efforts to change it from within were futile. This understanding birthed the notion that Christian education was a critical player in the resistance movement against the secularization of culture.

De Afscheiding: **The Separation**

In 1834, pastor Hendrick De Cock took 144 members out of his state church congregation and set up a new church. Within six months, sixteen other groups also broke away from the state church in a secession movement known as the *Afscheiding* (the Separation).[20] According to Wolterstorff, the mentality of this breakaway group was "theologically orthodox, intensely pietist, separatist and suspicious of high culture."[21] In contrast to *het Reveil*, this was a movement made up of "little people" or common folk: the labouring classes, farmers, and tradesmen with the aid of a few young clergymen like A. Van Raalte and H. Scholte. Bratt, who has written a significant history about Dutch Calvinism in America, notes that within two years the secessionists had accumulated 150 churches. About the separatist mentality, he writes:

> [they] wanted Christianity to be made full and deep. This entailed, first, a focus upon such themes as human inability and worthlessness and on Christ's death as the only source of salvation ... the converted were obliged to maintain an ongoing intimacy with God through rigorous introspection and daily "spiritual exercises;" to "practice godliness," "rejecting the things of the flesh and of this world," obeying precisely the laws of God as recorded in Scripture ... .[22]

Van Brummelen reports that *Reveil* supporters and *Afscheiding* secessionists took different approaches to Christian education with respect to control and curriculum. Despite its willingness to work for change within the state church, the *Reveil* group generally favoured parent-run schools free from church and state control. The reverse was true for the secessionists. Although they opted to leave the state church for one of their own making, they remained supportive of government- or church-run schools as long as the education reflected Calvinist beliefs rather than a secularized morality. When it came to the curriculum, the *Reveil* group believed Christian perspective had to be cultivated throughout the curriculum and reflected in pedagogy. They were the first in an unbroken line of Neo-Calvinist reformers who saw the need for a distinctive Christian school curriculum and pedagogy. For their part, the successionists remained suspicious of high culture and were content with a more focused vision of Christian influence delivered through the telling of Bible stories and the study of the Heidelberg Catechism.[23]

The *Doleantie*: The Regretful Protest

Near the end of the nineteenth century, Abraham Kuyper[24] spearheaded a third movement of resistance known as the *Doleantie* or "the Regretful Protest." In 1886 this group also broke ranks with the state-run *Hervormde Kerk* and established the *Gereformeerde Kerken*. By 1892 most of the *Afscheiding* churches had joined Kuyper's movement. Although these two resistance groups shared a common enemy in the Enlightenment, their particular outlooks were markedly different. The *Afscheiding* movement was separatist, and the *Doleantie* movement was reformist. Wolterstorff explains:

> Kuyper empathized deeply with the piety of the *Afscheiding* and with its concern for theological orthodoxy. Yet his vision as a whole was profoundly different. What gripped Kuyper was the Pauline vision of a cosmic Lordship of Jesus Christ, and of the calling of Christian people to acknowledge that universal lordship throughout their own existence and to struggle for its acknowledgement in all of society and culture.[25]

The *Afscheiding* impulse to separate from high culture and general society was replaced by Kuyper's desire to bring society under the rule of Christ. However, the pietist inclination to protect children from secular culture by infusing them with Reformed doctrine and a biblically based morality remained active within many communities. Consistent with his vision of cultural transformation, Kuyper and his followers established Christian schools, a Christian university, a Christian political party, a Christian labour union, and a Christian daily newspaper. De Boer and

Oppewal contend that the *Doleantie* movement's biggest contribution to the formation of Christian education was Kuyper's principle of "sphere sovereignty":

> On the occasion of the founding of the Free University of Amsterdam in 1880, Kuyper enunciated a principle later called "sphere sovereignty," whereby he maintained that the basic spheres of life—such as family, state, church, art, agriculture, science, and education have their own nature or character and are subject to their own laws, laws established by God in the creation itself. Each sphere is subject to the all-encompassing sovereignty of God. The spheres are interrelated, yet no sphere has the right to interfere with the sovereignty, under God, of any of the other spheres. Thus, for example, the sphere of academic science, schooling, or education, being a sovereign sphere, has to develop the task assigned to it by God while free of interference from both the state and the church.[26]

While the application of Kuyper's principle of sphere sovereignty removed the school from the control of both the state and the church, Prinsen observes that it led to the "pillarization of society," meaning Dutch society was organized around major groups, "each of which had its own ideology, political organization and schools."[27] Under Kuyper, the role of government was to encourage the efforts of each major social group to express its ideological or faith perspective in all areas of human intercourse: politics, economics, labour, education, arts, and so on. In theory, this method of organizing society would promote a truly pluralistic, democratic social structure where all major groups were not only tolerated but also encouraged to flourish. In practice, the principle of sphere sovereignty was less than ideal as an organizing principle of society. Prinsen notes that "scholars disagree as to how much tolerance existed among these pillared groups."[28]

Five Formative Features of the Dutch Neo-Calvinist Legacy of Education

From this brief summary, we observe that nineteenth-century Neo-Calvinist education in the Netherlands evolved in opposition to the Enlightenment's takeover of Dutch culture. Three different resistance movements contributed to the development of this tradition of Christian education. As a result, Christian educators imagined the purpose of education in two ways. One sought to protect the faith and morality of students while the other educated for cultural transformation. The Kuyperian vision of education dominated the Neo-Calvinist school movement, but the separatist vision continued to flourish in some communities.

By the end of the nineteenth century, Dutch Neo-Calvinist education exhibited five formative features. These extraordinary characteristics defined the legacy of Christian education that Neo-Calvinist immigrants exported to the United States and, later, to Canada.

The first two features define the school's mission. Neo-Calvinists visualize the Christian school as a dissident social institution. One of its key tasks is to repudiate the Enlightenment perspective and way of life. Specifically, this means rejecting the false assumption that modernity and Christianity are compatible shapers of culture. A liberal society may appear to tolerate religion, but it so restricts the practice of Christian living to the so-called "private" spaces in society that a life of faith is gutted of its true meaning. Reason, virtue, and natural law are not impartial, neutral principles that easily harmonize with Christianity. In reality, they function as dogma for modernity just as surely as biblical authority and Calvinist theology provide the firm foundations upon which to build a Reformed Christian way of life. In the context of worldview warfare, Christian education is a weapon of dissent in the Neo-Calvinists' stance against modernity, liberalism, and the secularization of society.

The second formative feature of the Neo-Calvinist educational vision is a corollary to the first. The Christian school has to do more than expose and defeat modernity; it is also tasked to be a transforming social institution. Christian education must interpret reality and the meaning of life from a different "Archimedean point" for the purpose of transforming culture into the Kingdom of God.

Curricular-pedagogical reform represents a third formative feature of the Neo-Calvinist legacy of education. To facilitate the successful pursuit of the Christian school's combined tasks just outlined, educators are expected to base every aspect of education on a biblical worldview. This wholesale infusion of a Christian perspective implies a radical transformation of the curriculum and how it is taught.

The fourth formative feature pertains to school governance. The tradition advocates for parent-controlled schools. The primary responsibility for education does not lie either with the church or the state. In an ideal society governed by the principle of sphere sovereignty, the government is responsible to support each faith community's efforts to educate their own children.

The rich theological-philosophical tradition of St. Augustine, John Calvin, and Abraham Kuyper serves as the tradition's fifth significant characteristic. This heritage defines a Christian perspective in terms of the grand themes of Scripture: the creation-fall-redemption-restoration meta-narrative, the covenant relationship between God and His people, the Kingdom of God on earth, and the lordship of Jesus Christ. Among these, the themes of covenant and kingdom are particularly significant. The Old Testament proclamation that "I will be your God, and you will be my people" implies a covenantal relationship steeped in reciprocal commitment and faithfulness that extends beyond the genealogy that reached its zenith in the birth of Christ to the church of all ages. These themes rationalize the purpose of Christian education as conceived by the Dutch Neo-Calvinist community.

A Legacy of Hope

The tradition of Neo-Calvinist Christian education that emerged in the Netherlands during the nineteenth century is a legacy like none other. It consciously opposes modernity's secular vision of culture as well as the medieval synthesis of the sacred and profane. When we take into account its five formative features, we must acknowledge it as a tradition that embraces both beautiful daughters of hope that St. Augustine named many centuries ago: *anger* at the way things are—modernity's replacement of Christianity as the driver of Dutch culture—and *courage* to see that things do not remain as they are—through the establishment of alternative schools, churches, and other social institutions that serve life in the Kingdom of God.

CHAPTER 2

The American Context (1845–1970)

Timeline

1845-1855 First wave of Dutch Immigrants arrives in the United States.

1856 First Christian School established by Dutch Neo-Calvinists.

1890–1920 Second wave of Dutch Immigration to the United States.

1906 Calvin College is established.

1920 The National Union of Christian Schools is formed.

1949–1960 Curriculum debates take place at Calvin College.

1964 The National Union of Christian Schools commits to publishing curriculum.

1968 The National Union of Christian Schools hires a curriculum coordinator.

1970 The National Union of Christian Schools adopts an eclectic philosophy of curriculum.

Disguised and Invisible

The Dutch Neo-Calvinist tradition of faith and education was transplanted to American soil roughly one hundred years prior to its arrival in Canada. Neo-Calvinist education in Canada was shaped by this American context on two fronts, and in both cases the influence went largely unnoticed. The first involved the community's interactions with four established American organizations: the Christian Reformed Church (CRC), Calvin Seminary, Calvin College (now University), and the National Union of Christian Schools (NUCS). These organizations offered vital services that the Canadian communities could not provide for themselves, none more critical than the preparation of pastors and teachers. Most Canadian Neo-Calvinists were comfortable with their heavy reliance upon these American organizations because they shared a common ethnicity and theological tradition. They generally failed to see the American influences that came attached with these institutions because they were so often disguised as Reformed.

Of these four organizations, Calvin College and NUCS were the most influential by far; however, to accurately assess their impact on Christian Schools Canada (CSC) is not easy. For example, how does one calculate the difference that Calvin's professors made on the thinking and life choices of all those Canadian students who received their degrees from them, many in teacher education, and returned to live and work in Canada? We know that throughout the 1950s and 1960s, several prominent Calvin College professors became seriously engaged in educational philosophy and curriculum theory. Their views shaped many CSC educators, and their thinking, in turn, reflected the major themes that animated American education writ large.[29]

The American influence also came to bear upon the Canadian districts through their parent organization, NUCS. In this chapter, we review the setting that gave birth to NUCS and defined its first fifty years. The last half of this history is of particular interest because it overlaps with the first twenty-five years of CSC.[30]

The second, and by far the most formidable, form of American influence came to CSC communities like the air they inhaled. It was invisible, everywhere present, and so essential to life in the school as to go largely unnoticed. In this regard, Neo-Calvinist communities were, and remain, like all other school communities in Canada and the United States. Everyone's educational vision more or less conforms to the firmly established patterns, principles, and standards that define education in North America. I refer to this ubiquitous expression of the American context as the "paradigm of progressivism" in education.[31]

Dutch Reformed Becomes American Reformed

The first major migration from the Netherlands to the United States took place between 1845 and 1855. A potato famine and other economic hardships associated with a crowded country, in conjunction with religious persecution, motivated many people to seek a better life in America. In 1847, thirteen years after the *Afscheiding* movement began, clergymen A. Van Raalte and H Scholte led two groups of secessionists to the United States as part of this first wave of immigration. The Van Raalte group settled near what came to be known as Holland, Michigan, while Scholte took his group to southeastern Iowa.

Dutch colonists established their first Christian school in Michigan in 1856, just twelve years after the first Christian school was started in the Netherlands. During these early decades of settling into American life, they built many more churches than schools. By 1890 the Christian Reformed Church had 144 congregations but operated just fourteen schools.[32] De Boer and Oppewal, cite three reasons why the early development of Christian schools was so slow within the Christian Reformed Church: "the immigrants were poor, public schools were still tolerable insofar as they permitted the Bible and its teachers were mostly Christians, and third, existing Christian schools were not particularly strong."[33]

A second, larger, wave of Dutch migration to the United States took place between 1880 and 1915. A significant number of these immigrants shared Abraham Kuyper's view that Christ is King over every area of life, and because He is, Christians are called to engage in cultural transformation. Most of these second-wave immigrants joined the Christian Reformed Church, and they rejuvenated the push to establish Christian schools. These newcomers were instrumental in the establishment of both Calvin College and the National Union of Christian Schools in the first quarter of the twentieth century.

Neo-Calvinist educators at this time interpreted curriculum reform in two very different ways. For some the task boiled down to the implementation of a course of study that would "match or surpass public school standards."[34] Their goal was to beat public schools at their own game. To achieve this goal, Van Brummelen concludes, teachers had to endorse

Bobbitt's thinking that schools must have clear, well-defined ends and employ the most efficient means to attain those desired ends.[35] In Van Brummelen's opinion, this desire to outperform public schools is clear evidence that the technical approach to curriculum developed by the administrative progressives was already shaping attitudes about curriculum reform in Neo-Calvinist schools.[36]

A second group of teachers understood curriculum reform in Kuyperian terms. They aimed to build a curriculum where every subject area was based on biblical principles. This re-formation of the sciences called for an altogether different curriculum than the one taught in public schools. Equally important, it required a different set of criteria for judging quality education. This goal posed a major problem for teachers because no one possessed the conceptual framework or the necessary resources to design and implement such an alternative approach. Consequently, at this formative stage in the movement's history, curriculum development drifted toward mainstream practices even though many educators advocated for more radical measures.

Regardless of their approach to curriculum development, Neo-Calvinist educators typically held the "vague, unspecified notion that a teacher who radiated a sound Christian character and had a thorough grasp of Neo-Calvinistic principles would somehow make methodology 'Christian.' Such a teacher would be able to 'teach history, geography, and so forth, in the light of Reformed Doctrine.'"[37] The idea of a Christian teaching method was compelling at this early juncture, but no one could articulate what this actually looked like. The notion that moral character and sound Reformed theology equaled a Christian approach to education flourished for many decades in both the American and the Canadian contexts.

The formation of NUCS coincided with the Americanization of the Dutch Neo-Calvinist community in the United States. This process eventually altered the very purpose of Christian education. By the end of the nineteenth century, the Dutch Neo-Calvinist colonists living in the United States were consciously aware of the fact that they were becoming Americanized, but they disagreed about the seriousness of this problem and what to do about it. Many perceived the inevitability of their children adopting American ways as a threat to the long-term preservation of their

Dutch identity.[38] Complicating this problem was the fact that in most people's minds, being Dutch and being Reformed meant pretty much the same thing. In the end, Bratt reports that almost everyone accepted the solution that "Dutch Reformed" had to become "American Reformed." At that point the priority for Neo-Calvinist immigrants was no longer the conservation of their Dutch ethnicity. The new challenge for the community was to find a way to remain Reformed even as it became Americanized.

Van Brummelen observes that around the turn of the century, the colonists hotly debated the relative merits of public schools and Christian schools, but no one questioned the inevitability of becoming American. In fact, many leaders propagated the idea that the colonists had a moral obligation to become Americans. Kuyper himself endorsed the transition to Americanize because he naively believed the colonists would convert America instead of the other way around. According to Van Brummelen:

> Kuyper reflected that the Dutch colonists must become Americans while maintaining and extending their Neo-Calvinistic influence on the life of the nation. The foremost school leaders accepted this "melting pot" conception. The schools and their supporters were to Americanize while, with true American missionary zeal, transforming the American way of life: "God has given the Dutch to America . . . What for? That the Dutch might be the leaven and salt of a greater people." American Neo-Calvinists were to fulfill their mission as Neo-Calvinists and as Americans in church, state and society. That being both a true American and a true Kuyperian might at times conflict was not considered, not even by Kuyper himself. America, with all its faults, was basically considered to be a Christian nation.[39]

In the years immediately leading up to NUCS's arrival on the scene, the Neo-Calvinist community was desperate to maintain its identity. Church leader B. K. Kuiper argued that the best way to preserve the Reformed identity was to develop a "Calvinistic consciousness." Bratt says others came up with a different defense mechanism. Their way to thwart Americanization and remain Reformed was to encourage "piety" and "confessional loyalty."[40] In these strategies we see a reaffirmation of two long-standing mentalities within the Neo-Calvinist community, one focused on a worldview perspective while the other linked the conservation of a Reformed identity to a life of piety and theological orthodoxy.

In the end, neither of these approaches prevented the process of Americanization from neutering the most formative features of their Neo-Calvinist tradition of Christian education, which called the school to be both a dissident and a transforming institution. When we consider the decades of stiff resistance that Dutch Neo-Calvinists put up against the advance of the Enlightenment in their homeland, it is surprising to see how quickly they capitulated when they were confronted with the American version of the very same ideology.

As a new organization mandated to provide leadership for a collection of schools spread across several states, NUCS faced big challenges on multiple levels. Would NUCS advocate for a vision of culture transformation or a vision of pietist isolation? Would NUCS challenge its member schools to offer a distinctively Christian education or one that sanctified the American Dream way of life?

NUCS, The First Twenty-five Years (1920–1945)

The Neo-Calvinist school movement was sufficiently mature by 1920 to establish a National Union of Christian Schools (NUCS), with headquarters in Chicago. De Boer and Oppewal provide us with a summary of the organization's mission. The purpose of NUCS was twofold: to promote Christian education and to encourage the writing of learning materials. To accomplish these purposes NUCS adopted the following three goals:
- establish a normal school for teacher preparation;
- launch an educational magazine for the enrichment of parents and school boards;
- provide the necessary support for teachers to be professionals and schools to implement their distinguishing features.

This third goal was further broken down into three tasks: "1. the encouragement of teacher associations, 2. the production of a professional journal and 3. the publishing of curriculum materials."[41]

The optimism surrounding the formation of a national organization was tempered by the fact that a number of schools initially stayed out of the union for fear of losing local control. De Boer and Oppewal point out that there were two different opinions about the purpose of NUCS. Some wanted NUCS to be an authoritative body that would set policy for all Neo-Calvinists schools. This view lost out to the majority who held that NUCS should provide services, such as a pension plan and curriculum materials, but local schools should have the option to either utilize the services or not.[42]

Van Brummelen reports that the period from 1920 to 1945 continued to be a "time filled with uncertainty and a lack of direction" for NUCS. Most teachers believed that curriculum reform was the organization's primary challenge, and by "curriculum reform" they meant subjecting every area of study to the application of biblical principles. As early as 1923, this central challenge was metaphorically described as the Gordian knot of Christian education. This was an apt figure of speech, for just as the Gordian knot of Greek legend was impossible to untie because it presented no visible loose ends, NUCS educators did not know where to begin to overhaul the individual sciences. Although NUCS educators rarely questioned their understanding of what curriculum reform meant or their ability to eventuality achieve it, the actual application of biblical principles to the school's course of study confronted them with an unsolvable problem.[43]

When we look backward from WWII and survey the first twenty-five years of NUCS, two observations stand out. First, we cannot help but marvel at the accomplishments of a relatively small group of widely dispersed first- and second-generation immigrants. A saying from the world of boxing is apropos to describe the performance of the Dutch Neo-Calvinist community living in America: it habitually "punched above its weight." Though small in numbers, the community made major contributions to the thinking of the wider Protestant community as well as to its own members. This is particularly true in the areas of theology, philosophy, and education. Its remarkable capacity to establish a nationwide system of

Christian schools was matched by its efforts to engage in post-secondary education and learning.

Second, even though this school movement stood on the combined shoulders of a rich Calvinist theological tradition and a well-developed Kuyperian social theory, this combined heritage provided insufficient insight to untie the Gordian knot of curriculum reform. It was left to NUCS to translate their Neo-Calvinist worldview into a philosophy of education and a matching curriculum model that would implement true school reform. While the school movement waited for NUCS to take these critical steps, it had to rely on its two traditional strengths: a worldview perspective or a Calvinist consciousness, as some thought of it, and a pietist retreat into moral living and doctrinal purity.

NUCS After WWII (1945–1970)

The NUCS story shone brighter from 1945 to 1970. This was largely due to a substantial increase in the overall number of students it served. Student enrollment increased significantly during this time as new schools were built in Reformed settlements stretching from New Jersey in the east to Michigan and Iowa in the Midwest to California and Washington in the far west. The addition of Christian schools opening in Canada also contributed to this period of accelerated numerical growth. Within a few years, the Canadian schools formed three new districts, increasing the total to twelve. "By 1960, 70 percent of North American Christian Reformed families who had access to Christian schools sent their children to them."[44]

Even as the organization experienced unprecedented growth, the all-important work of curriculum development at NUCS remained virtually at a standstill throughout most of this period. Classroom teachers were not expected to engage in grassroots curriculum writing, nor could they while employed with nine-month contracts. Even if they felt the urge to rewrite their curriculum, these teachers lacked the requisite insight and skills to get very far. Most people expected NUCS to produce the necessary Christian curriculum materials, but for a variety of reasons the head office seldom delivered.

Throughout the 1950s and 1960s, NUCS educators continued to work in the absence of a clear philosophy of education. Consequently, the gap between guiding biblical principles and the realization of a distinctively Christian curriculum and teaching methodology was simply too great to span; the Gordian knot remained firmly tied. Worse still, the determination to untie the knot was rapidly waning. Without knowing what actually distinguished a Christian curriculum from a public-school curriculum, NUCS educators could neither effectively critique mainstream educational ideas nor understand the extent to which their movement had been co-opted by their influence.

In the absence of a comprehensive philosophy of Christian education, NUCS leaders were vulnerable to adopting whatever ideas were currently popular. Van Brummelen says NUCS's gradual capitulation to the dominant curriculum orientation of the day was clearly evident in 1959 when it produced a set of ten criteria in an effort to make the publication of curriculum materials more systematic and consistent. The format of this document closely followed the Tyler rationale, a deceptively simple and ubiquitous technical approach to curriculum planning.[45]

In 1964 NUCS finally committed to developing an organized plan for curriculum development, which many considered to be long overdue. To implement this plan, NUCS created three curriculum consultant positions: one each for language arts, social studies, and science. NUCS hired Henry Triezenberg in 1968 to serve as the science curriculum consultant. Soon afterward he was asked to write the NUCS curriculum department operational policy document. Every aspect of this framework document, Van Brummelen reports, reduced curriculum development to a "means-ends, systematized technical undertaking."[46]

At about the same time, NUCS commissioned a retired Calvin College education professor, Nicholas Beversluis, to provide them with a philosophy of Christian education that could guide the organization. The Beversluis document was supposed to pull together the best thinking from the tradition and synthesize it into a coherent philosophy of education. His document captured some essential understandings that characterized the tradition, but in its effort to be inclusive, it failed to provide a coherent philosophical position.[47]

As the 1960s gave way to the 1970s, NUCS finally chose a clear path for its curriculum development agenda when it assigned Triezenberg with the task of translating Beversluis's "philosophy" into a "principles to practice" document. Triezenberg's document contained some familiar rhetoric. For example, it called students "to put their faith to work in all areas of life." But, Van Brummelen argues, what this language implied was for students to live "a personal moral life within the existing (and acceptable) social and academic milieu and structures."[48] Under Triezenburg's leadership, curriculum publishing at NUCS in the 1970s and beyond was guided by the Bobbit-Charters-Bloom approach with its priority of technical efficiency.[49]

Beversluis's philosophy of education provided NUCS with its rhetoric of school reform, but Triezenberg's "curriculum-as-technology" approach functioned as the true driver of curriculum development. As Canadian Neo-Calvinist educators became more aware of this situation, many concluded that NUCS was no longer the keeper of the Neo-Calvinist legacy.

CHAPTER 3
The Canadian Context (1945–1970)

Timeline

1940s	The first four schools are established: Ontario – 1; Alberta – 2; British Columbia – 1.
1951	The *Christian Courier*, a national ethnic magazine, is launched.
1952	The Ontario Alliance of Christian Schools (OACS) is formed.
1953–1958	Herman Dooyeweerd's *New Critique of Theoretical Thought* is translated into English.
1956	The *Christian School Herald* magazine is launched by the OACS.
	The Association for Reformed Scientific Studies (ARSS) is established.
1959	Herman Dooyeweerd meets with ARSS members; ARSS starts to sponsor summer conferences for university students.
1960s	Decade of greatest growth: 31 percent of all current CSC schools are established.
1961	T. H. D. Vollenhoven & H. Evan Runner pen an educational creed for the ARSS.
1962	British Columbia Christian Schools form District 12 of NUCS.
1967	The ARSS becomes the Association for the Advancement of Christian Scholarship (AACS) and establishes the Institute for Christian Studies (ICS).
1968	The Institute for Christian Studies initiates summer curriculum writing workshops (SPICE) for school teachers.
1969	Mass exit of staff from Toronto District Christian High School.
1970	Fifty-four percent of all current CSC schools have been established by this time. The AACS publishes a controversial book: *Out of Concern for the Church*.

Immigration on Steroids

Dutch government statistics show that in the aftermath of WWII, more than 350,000 people left the Netherlands to find a better life in other lands, with close to 140,000 moving to Canada.[50] The Netherlands lay in ruins, and the prospects of a fast return to a normal life in a post-war society were not good. Whereas most participants in two earlier waves of Dutch immigration settled in the United States,[51] the majority of this third wave of immigrants chose to settle in Canada, the Allied country that had liberated the Netherlands from Nazi occupation. These newcomers were predominantly common folk—farmers, artisans, and small business owners; only a few were professionals. They were a resilient, persevering, and hard-working people, and nearly half of them were orthodox Neo-Calvinists who were eager to pursue Abraham Kuyper's vision for social reform in their new homeland. Most of these Kuyperian-minded immigrants had a limited formal education, but they were an intelligent, biblically literate, and theologically sophisticated people.

The majority of post-war Neo-Calvinist immigrants gravitated to various rural communities in Ontario, Alberta, and British Columbia, with roughly half residing in Ontario. Like most new arrivals, their hopes for a better life were tempered by the harsh realities of finding their place in a new homeland. These hardships included, but were not limited to, poverty, language barriers, and social ostracism. The first generation bore the brunt of these hardships, but this immigrant community overcame these challenges with the aid of their Christian faith, a Calvinist work ethic, a willingness to make personal sacrifices, and strong community associations.

These communities consistently maintained their identity, purpose, and social stability regardless of the province where they landed. They achieved all of this through a trinity of mutually supportive core institutions: the church, the home, and the Christian school. In this triad the church provided the biblical and theological nourishment to feed the community's faith life as well as a gathering point for weekly socializing. The home's job was to nurture the loving relationships and strong character required to produce faithful, moral, self-assured, responsible, and wholesome Christian family members. The Christian school mandate consisted of two principal tasks; namely, the reinforcement of the beliefs, values, and identity promoted by home and church and the preparation of students to take up their roles in society in ways that would actualize a Kuyperian vision of societal reform.

Erecting a School Movement

The school building campaign undertaken by these newcomers was nothing short of extraordinary. I know of no other community, immigrant or otherwise, that erected so many schools in such a short period of time and with so few resources. Canadian Neo-Calvinist immigrants spread across three provinces—a distance of over 4,000 km—erected sixty-seven schools and 158 churches in just twenty-five years.

This building program is all the more remarkable when we take into account that not everyone in these communities supported the idea of Christian schools. Some were uninvolved because they could not afford to pay the tuition. Others did not find the quality of education worth the expense. There were also those who were satisfied with the education offered by local public schools. The majority in most communities, however, were ardent supporters, and many of them were willing to sacrifice a great deal to provide their children and grandchildren with a Christian education. The most zealous in the community propagated views that sparked controversy. For example, some called for mandatory membership in the parent-run school society for all members of the church community. Others believed the provision of a Christian education was an obligation implicit in the parental vows taken at their children's baptisms.

We know these Dutch immigrants were able to quickly erect a system of Christian schools on the Canadian landscape, but information about the development of these schools prior to 1965 is scarce. We can garner some insight from commentators like Peetoom, Van Brummelen, and Prinsen. Peetoom, for example, argues that the struggle to develop an alternative Christian school shaped itself into a mythology more than a contemporary educational reality. Van Brummelen alerts us to the serious need for curriculum reform while Prinsen draws attention to the various polarities that divided and subdivided this immigrant community. From these diverse voices, the picture that emerges of Neo-Calvinist Christian education in its early years is rather gloomy.

The available evidence suggests that the education these schools provided was neither particularly distinctive in character nor of high quality during the 1950s and early 1960s. As challenging as it was for these immigrants to establish an alternative system of schools, it was far more difficult to implement an education that lived up to their Neo-Calvinist heritage.

Van Brummelen maintains that, in general, supporters of the emerging Neo-Calvinist school movement in Canada identified with Kuyper's vision to transform culture into the Kingdom of God. In most people's minds this meant the establishment of a parallel system of social institutions in the areas of labour relations, politics, business, the arts, education, and so on. Each of these alternative institutions would execute its peculiar social function in accordance with the appropriate God-given norms, what Kuyper called the principle of sphere sovereignty. Even though local school communities talked the talk of cultural transformation, Van Brummelen believed most schools delivered an education that combined moral teachings and Reformed doctrine with the accepted educational practices and standards of the day.

To be fair the failure of these schools to exhibit the five formative features that defined the legacy of Neo-Calvinist education during their infancy was due in large measure to the inexperience of the parental governing boards, their teachers, and their administrators, all of whom did the best they could in the situation. This first generation of immigrants can be forgiven, I think, for wanting their schools to meet the community's most pressing needs at the time, which many felt were the preservation of its ethnic and religious identity.

Soon after their establishment, these schools joined the National Union of Christian Schools (NUCS), based in Grand Rapids, Michigan. Had this shepherd organization embodied the educational vision of its Dutch Neo-Calvinist past, the Canadian schools might have matured more quickly. Unfortunately, as noted in chapter 2, NUCS was a rudderless mother ship throughout this time.

During the initial two decades of CSC's history, Canadian Dutch Neo-Calvinist immigrant communities demonstrated their capacity to function in one or more of the following three ways: as an interpretive community, as a rival community, or as a revival community. All three continued to impact the CSC narrative throughout the twentieth century. A brief description of each is in order before we explore them more fully.

The label "interpretive community" refers to a group of people who share a way of life and who interpret that way of life by means of a well-developed worldview and a compatible universe of discourse. From this unified stance, the interpretive community expresses its critique of the educational status quo and its alternative vision for educational reform. To the extent that local CSC communities functioned as interpretive communities, they are to be counted among the rare groups that established alternative schools in North America.

Any examination of the Canadian Neo-Calvinist school movement must acknowledge the unfortunate preoccupation Calvinists have with forming splinter groups within their own ranks. These camps, and camps within those camps, rarely cooperated with each other, even when their ultimate goals were virtually the same. Due to their discordant nature, many local communities operated as a community of rivals.

To assign the adjective "revival" to a Calvinist community would be highly ironic to many of its members. Yet, I can think of no better label for the Reformational Movement[52] that swept across the Neo-Calvinist landscape in Canada in the 1950s, 1960s, and 1970s. To be clear, this was an intellectual revival, and its "altar call" challenged converts to adopt an all-encompassing worldview. The local communities that embraced this perspective most embodied the trademark qualities of their educational tradition, but they also triggered some of the deepest divisions in the larger community.

The Interpretive Community

In his compelling lead article in the now classic text, *Handbook of Research on Curriculum: A Project of the American Educational Research Association*,[53]

Philip Jackson convincingly argues that the notion of a "curriculum conception," as popularized by Eisner and Vallance,[54] does not hold the key to school reform, as many educators in the 1970s and 1980s believed.[55] Chief among its weaknesses is the tendency of a curriculum conception to intellectualize something that is dynamic and concrete. Liberating ideas, even a coherent collection of them, are insufficient to bring about substantive change, Jackson concluded. The true trigger for school reform is "a way of life shared by a company of believers who form a loosely knit social network of the kind literary critic Stanley Fish speaks of as an 'interpretive community.'"

> . . . each such community has, as it were, its "party line," which includes a broadly sanctioned set of beliefs; a body of writings, some of which may attain near-canonical status; and a cluster of well-known personages, some of whom may be highly revered and looked on as spokespersons for the group as a whole whereas others are spoken of as "the enemy." These communities almost always have a special vocabulary, if not a full-fledged language, complete with buzzwords that have a special meaning and significance within the community that they do not have outside of it.[56]

Jackson is one of the few mainstream school reform scholars who understands it takes an alternative way of life embodied by a community to substantially change why and how we educate. He believed this way of life is expressed in at least two ways: through the community's social network and its intellectual tradition.

Had Jackson known about the existence of CSC interpretive communities and spent time observing them, I suspect he would have been surprised by how much he could learn from them. For example, they could have taught him the importance that faith plays in sustaining any way of life. He likely would have appreciated the intellectual depth of the Neo-Calvinist critique of the education establishment. Additionally, he might have learned that a way of life and a curriculum conception are not necessarily opposing poles of school reform, but must reinforce each other as deep drivers for sustained change. Perhaps what would have surprised him most of all about these communities was their intent on founding other alternative social institutions as well. They were not content with reforming education; they also aspired to transform the arenas of labour relations, politics, publishing, art, and literature. They felt compelled to do all of this because of their particular interpretation of a Christian way of life.

The Rival Community

The Neo-Calvinist tradition of education has been plagued by the repeated formation of rival camps when serious disagreements arise in the community. Prinsen refers to this regrettable practice as "that old Dutch disease" because as surely as Dutch elm trees succumb to a deadly fungus, Calvinist communities are regularly damaged, and sometimes destroyed, by disagreements over such topics as biblical interpretation, styles of worship, gender roles, or the purpose of education.

Differences over the right way to interpret and express their vision of Christian education divided the Dutch Reformed immigrant community at personal, communal, and organizational levels. It is ironic, if not tragic, that the capacity of these Dutch immigrants to function as interpretive communities contributed so much to their evolution as a community of rivals. Some early manifestations of this "disease" are described below.

As noted earlier, the Neo-Calvinist schools established in Canada quickly joined the America-based National Union of Christian Schools (NUCS). This was particularly true in Ontario where half of all the Canadian Neo-Calvinist schools were built prior to 1970. They looked to NUCS to provide them with critical organizational and administrative support, but they received relatively little in the way of leadership. Many Canadian educators became disappointed with NUCS on three strategic fronts: vision, inclusivity, and curriculum.

On the critical matter of vision, the Canadians felt that only a few American educators in the organization still held on to a culture-transformation perspective. It was obvious to them that NUCS had lost touch with the Kuyperian worldview and instead had accommodated itself to the ideals of American culture. Some CSC educators were also of a mind that NUCS was either unable or unwilling to set aside its national biases; they experienced it as an American organization that seemed reluctant to adopt an international stance.[57]

From the beginning, school leaders in Ontario demonstrated their reluctance to be totally dependent on NUCS. In 1952, they organized the Ontario Alliance of Christian Schools (OACS). Much to the chagrin of the NUCS leadership, this unprecedented move made District 10 of NUCS the only one to have its own layer of administration and organized leadership. The schools in Alberta and British Columbia, Districts 11 and 12 respectively, eventually followed Ontario's example and also formed their own district organizations. Curriculum development was a top priority for the formation of all three Canadian district associations.

The OACS quickly established a school magazine called the *Christian School Herald*. The purpose of the new magazine was to address the needs and concerns of Canadian schools in ways that the *Home and School* publication put out by NUCS did not. The *Herald* also sometimes doubled as a publishing arm of the OACS. Prinsen describes three lengthy booklets that the *Herald* published in the 1960s, which he says, "functioned as an apologetic for Kuyperian Christian education in Canada." Efforts like these demonstrate how determined the Canadian schools were to maintain their Kuyperian vision.

These booklets developed important themes that harkened back to the nineteenth-century Christian-school movement in the Netherlands. The first booklet reiterated the tradition's "long history of opposition to state controlled liberal education." This perception of the Christian school as a dissident institution was not evident at NUCS. This first booklet also affirmed the view that education was a parental responsibility; control over education did not belong to the state or to the church. The third theme it developed was the notion that the Christian community had a mission to fulfill for the benefit of Canadian society. The purpose of Christian education was bound up with their larger task to transform society by bringing all spheres of human activity back in line with the norms that God had embedded into the fabric of natural and cultural life. The second booklet traced the history of Christian education back to the Old Testament

Hebrews while the third addressed the challenge of teaching the various subjects from a Christian perspective.

Although the *Christian School Herald* was the voice of the OACS, it also circulated among the schools located in Alberta and British Columbia. In this way it unified the Christian schools in much the same way as the *Calvinist Contact* (now *Christian Courier*) magazine spoke for the Canadian contingent of the Christian Reformed Church. However, as all three of our main commentators point out, not everyone was critical of NUCS. Consequently, in addition to the growing divide between the OACS and NUCS, camps representing different alliances emerged within the OACS and across Canada.

When Calvin College philosophy professor Nicholas Wolterstorff delivered his landmark speech on curriculum development to NUCS principals in 1966,[58] some Canadians felt ready to tackle the challenge of curriculum reform on their own since there was no help to be had from either NUCS or the Netherlands.[59] The primary question that confronted the Canadians was which of the available educational visions they should follow. Van Brummelen identified three possibilities, which he labeled the monastic vision, the dualistic vision, and the integrationist vision. They corresponded to three stances the community took with respect to "the world": isolation, accommodation, and transformation.

The *monastic vision* for curriculum development reached back to the *Afscheiding* mentality of isolation from and protection against culture. Typically, this approach came to expression as decisions to ban materials from the curriculum that contained profanities or any content that promoted immoral behaviour and unbiblical thinking. On the rare occasion when this approach led to the development of curricular materials, the texts emphasized Bible study and doctrinal instruction. The primary focus of this approach was not on the production of new materials but the eradication of evil influences from the typical curriculum taught in the schools of the day.

The *dualist vision* of curriculum sought a synthesis between two recognizable worlds of knowledge: the objective, neutral world of scientific knowledge and the revealed knowledge that comes to us from the Bible and the Christian tradition. In this approach, contributions that the

Christian faith could bring to bear upon the curriculum were essential but limited to personal spirituality, moral living, and a biblical perspective on certain flashpoint issues like evolution, abortion, and gender. Like the monastic perspective, the dualist approach did not inspire widespread curriculum renewal; curriculum projects mainly dealt with the Bible, church history, and the like. The dualist mentality was quite different, however, in its attitude toward culture. Whereas the monastic approach wanted the curriculum to fend off culture, the dualist approach sought accommodation with it. For the dualists, Christian spirituality, morality, and theology both sanctioned and elevated the academic standards commonly promoted by the public school.

By contrast, the *integrationist vision* of curriculum incorporated the Kuyperian notion that Christian schools educate students for the new life in God's coming Kingdom on Earth. This vision imagined a curriculum where each area of study was shaped by a faith-inspired worldview. To implement this approach, curriculum developers/teachers had to draw on their biblical knowledge when they made critical decisions, such as what to include or exclude from the curriculum, how to interpret the meaning of curricular content, and when and how to use the content. For integrationists, curriculum reform culminated in a reworked program of learning for each subject area.

It is not surprising that the emphasis on curriculum reform in Canadian schools was motivated by those who advocated for the "integrationist stance," as Van Brummelen named it.[60] Their push for a transformed curriculum was coupled with an equally strong emphasis for getting all OACS schools on this track. In their view, if OACS schools did not deliver a curriculum inspired by faith, then why should they exist at all? Bert Witvoet was one of the stronger teacher-advocates for a faith-driven curriculum. He also served as editor of the *Christian School Herald* in the mid to late 1960s. In an editorial he wrote for the *Herald* in 1965, Witvoet minced no words about the direction OACS schools should take.

> We believe that God gave man a cultural mandate ... Our organizational life, therefore, must also be moulded in a Christian way. This, Christian education must teach and

practise or else it has no business calling itself by such a lofty name.⁶¹

Another recognized school leader at that time, Ray Klapwyk, also advocated for a curriculum reformation. In Van Brummelen's portrayal of Klapwyk, we see ideas similar to those propagated by Calvin College professors Jellema and Jaarsma at that time. Klapwyk shared Jellema's notion that the development of a Christian mind involved an analysis of Western ideals. However, his thinking also reflected Jaarsma's understanding of what it means to be human when he said the curriculum should develop a Christian view of human beings and our basic relationships and tasks within the environment.⁶²

As the pioneering period drew to a close, it remained unclear which direction the OACS would take, particularly in the area of curriculum development. Would it share the dualist stance NUCS had adopted or boldly strike out to develop an integrationist approach? OACS educators, administrators, and supporters were divided, and these divisions were manifested in two watershed events that occurred in 1969. Bert Witvoet was at the centre of the controversy in both situations.

In his capacity as editor of the *Christian School Herald*, Witvoet was an outspoken advocate of major curriculum reform. Peetoom observes that Witvoet's editorials led to divisions in local school communities. In one notable piece, Witvoet lamented the fact that just as the school movement had reached the stage where it could begin to tackle curriculum reform, many school boards were preoccupied with administration and policy matters. He questioned whether these boards had sufficient vision to actually give direction to their schools. To tone down the rhetoric of these editorials and lower the level of concern expressed by its readers, the magazine's board decided to appoint an editorial advisory group to oversee Witvoet's editorial content. The fallout of this decision was significant. Witvoet resigned and the board did not hire a replacement. Consequently, the *Herald* vanished after fourteen years of valuable service to the community, and with its departure, the CSC lost a significant voice for curriculum reform.

Van Brummelen recounts the main details of the other noteworthy clash between visions. Witvoet taught English and social studies courses at Toronto District Christian High School, a school where many teachers wanted to implement curriculum-wide reforms. The trouble began when a small but vocal group of parents complained about Witvoet's English unit on Salinger's controversial book, *The Catcher in the Rye*. Even though this unit was consistent with the board's stated vision for literature studies, the board cancelled the unit to pacify the parents. When the dissenters demanded Witvoet's dismissal, the board waffled; they kept him on as a teacher, but they took away his role as vice principal.

Opposition to Witvoet escalated as the school year wound down. Those wanting to see him removed included a few newly elected board members and some parents. This group was led by two American pastors serving in local Christian Reformed Churches. To make a long and bitter story short, Van Brummelen recalls that the board seriously debated cancelling Witvoet's "Christian Life" course, which was very popular with students, and it removed the chair of the education committee who supported Witvoet. In response to these actions, the teaching staff signed their contracts for the coming year but with the condition that the board would engage them in mutual discussions over educational policy. Despite the efforts of nearly a dozen ministers who tried to intervene on behalf of the teachers, the board responded with the declaration that all teaching positions were vacant for the coming year. At the end of the term, the teachers left the school en masse. Depending on one's interpretation of the situation, the teachers were either fired, or they quit.

Van Brummelen portrays these events as more than a clash of personalities, which they certainly were. He claims the heart of the dispute was "the conflict between the monastic and Kuyperian views" of the curriculum. The board wanted to maintain "the narrow way" of their pietist tradition, which means it saw the aim of Christian education as the inculcation of Calvinist beliefs and Biblical morality. The teachers wanted to pursue a much larger vision where students were prepared to engage the world and do battle with the spirits of the age. For decades to come, the three Canadian districts of NUCS schools would employ teachers who advocated for this larger vision of education. These teachers were often leaders in the school system, but they rarely constituted the majority in a local school staff.

The Revival Community

Most Canadian Neo-Calvinist immigrants wanted to live in communities anchored by stable homes, theologically sound churches, and culturally engaged schools. They also wanted cultural transformation for Canada; this was to be their greatest gift to their new homeland. These immigrants may have been naïve, presumptuous, or even a tad arrogant, but they sincerely felt called by God to realign every sphere of Canadian society with God's Word for human flourishing.

Nearly seven years to the day after Dr. Martin Luther King Jr. delivered his historic "I have a dream" speech in 1963, John Olthuis offered up a similar vision on behalf of the Canadian Neo-Calvinist community in a periodical called the *Christian Vanguard*. King's dream envisioned a future in which the descendants of former slaves and slave owners could be brothers, the state of Mississippi would be an oasis of freedom and justice, and his own four children would not be judged by the colour of their skin but by the content of their character. By contrast, the Olthuis dream imagined a society that featured a set of parallel Christian organizations:

> The year is 1985 . . . The Christian political party is now the official opposition and Christian politicians are witnessing to the redeeming and reconciling responsibility of Government . . . (as we walk along Elgin Street in Ottawa, we pass) a church . . . .. the sign reads ELGIN CONGREGATION OF THE CHURCH OF JESUS CHRIST . . . (it is) a joyful, dynamic, worshiping church which seeks the coming of the Kingdom of God rather than the kingdom of the institutional church . . . .. In the parliamentary galleries we meet the head of the CHRISTIAN LABOUR ASSOCIATION OF NORTH AMERICA . . . .. We leave the gallery and pick up a copy of VOICE, the Christian daily newspaper and thank God for the headlines which read: "GOVERNMENT MONOPOLY IN EDUCATION ENDS". . .. We stroll along Bank Street towards the newsstand and pick up a copy of VANGUARD—the

Christian weekly that has replace1d PLAYBOY as the
top circulation North American magazine . . . .[63]

The blueprint for this narrative of cultural transformation came from Abraham Kuyper's model of society where liberal humanists and people of faith would be political equals; government would encourage and enable each of these faith communities to express their particular visions for life in every social sphere. Neo-Calvinist immigrants from the Netherlands were fully prepared to model this social arrangement for their fellow Canadians. Within the first two decades of their arrival, they established a labour union, a political justice organization, a book publisher, a graduate-level interdisciplinary think tank, an art institute, and a literary magazine. All but the last two still exist today.

In the Olthuis vision, the road from dream to reality passed through three landscapes. The first setting featured the development of Christian thought within the community, the second involved the spread of this thought, and in the third the community put this thought into action. I distinctly remember the excitement that his "dream speech" generated in me and my friends. Like most people I knew, we missed the warning that appeared in the pages that immediately followed the speech. Those pages of the *Christian Vanguard* contained a short essay entitled "The Paralysis of the Christian Student," penned by Theodore Plantinga. Plantinga argued that the typical Christian university student was incapable of living and acting the way a Christian student should precisely because they had been taught that the acquisition of a Christian perspective makes all the difference; that is to say, it was the condition that makes Christian living possible. Plantinga made a convincing case that this borrowed assumption from the rationalist tradition was no truer for Christians than it was for humanists.

The Canadian Neo-Calvinist community was ripe for cultural transformation. It had a biblical perspective, so all it needed was a focused movement to drive it. Such a movement appeared early on, and it soon set many people's hearts and minds on fire. Regrettably, it also set many hearts and minds against each other. Some people believed the impetus driving this movement was the biblical call to live an authentic Christian life, but most adherents and opponents of this movement experienced it solely as an intellectual revival. This revival was known by adherents and opponents alike as the "Reformational Movement."

The Reformational Movement began innocently enough as the by-product of an educational reform initiative that emerged within the community. In 1956 a small group of idealistic pastors and lay community leaders led by Dr. Peter Schrotenboer began holding meetings to map out a vision for implementing Reformed Christian higher education in North America. They initially named their group the Association of Reformed Scientific Studies. The organization's unfortunate acronym of ARSS did not diminish its aspirations, for it wanted nothing less than to launch a Christian university patterned after the Free University of Amsterdam. This university would function as the capstone to a system of Christian elementary, secondary, and undergraduate education already under construction by Canadian and American members of the Christian Reformed Church.

Over the next eleven years, the ARSS promoted two projects. Its members methodically laid the groundwork for their university, and they sponsored annual summer student conferences to provide Christian perspective for Reformed students enrolled at secular Canadian universities. H. Evan Runner, a philosophy professor at Calvin College, was the key figure in both projects. To understand why and how a revival movement was born from this association's efforts, we must acquire some background information about Herman Dooyeweerd and Evan Runner.

The roots of the Reformational Movement extend back to the Free University of Amsterdam. There, in the mid 1930s, two brothers-in-law, Herman Dooyeweerd and D. H. Th. Vollenhoven, jointly established the Association for Calvinistic Philosophy, an association dedicated to the development of a coherent Christian body of thought.[64] Dooyeweerd and Vollenhoven were the primary architects of this Reformational philosophy. Dooyeweerd contributed a systematic philosophy, and Vollenhoven designed a method for interpreting and cataloguing the major themes and problems that constitute the history of philosophy. Four of their best students, H. Van Riessen, S. U. Zuidema, K. J. Popma, and J. P. A. Mekkes, led a second generation of Reformational philosophers, and over time they were appointed to philosophy chairs in four major state universities in the Netherlands. This nucleus of first- and second-generation philosophers eventually transmitted a body of thought collectively known as Reformational Philosophy to well-established Dutch Neo-Calvinist enclaves in Canada, the United States, South Africa, and Australia.

From the outset, Dooyeweerd's name was synonymous with the Reformational Movement in Canada. His writings were the first, and almost the only, ones from the core group of Dutch scholars to be translated and published in English. More importantly, he was the main architect of the philosophy of the law idea that formed the backbone of this intellectual movement. His four-volume *A New Critique of Theoretical Thought* was translated into English over the period of 1953–1958. Dooyeweerd's philosophy was a coherent, systematic, and comprehensive perspective consisting of five major themes: religion, creation-fall-redemption-restoration, modal theory, individuality theory, and the process of history. Only serious academics tackled this far-ranging and challenging work. Nevertheless, by 1970 hundreds of North American students had been exposed to the major themes in Dooyeweerd's philosophy while attending the three American colleges affiliated with the Christian Reformed Church: Calvin College in Grand Rapids, Michigan; Trinity Christian College in Palos Heights, Illinois; and Dordt College in Sioux Center, Iowa. Some of these students were Canadians, and when they returned home after graduation, they brought with them Dooyeweerdian ideas and a Kuyperian fervor for transforming culture.

Dooyeweerd made two trips to North America. He delivered a set of lectures on an American tour in 1958 that were later published in 1968 in a volume entitled, *In the Twilight of Western Thought*. This book made his critique of the Western intellectual tradition more accessible to the general public. Dooyeweerd returned to North America in 1959. When he met with the ARSS in Toronto, he advised them to write a new educational creed, "that would affirm Christian principles directly germane to scholarship and higher education."[65] Two years later, the ARSS adopted such a creed written by none other than Vollenhoven and Runner.

If Dooyeweerd, Vollenhoven, and their second generation of student scholars were the brain trust behind Canada's Reformational Movement, then H. Evan Runner was its heart, soul, mouthpiece, chief interpreter, and strategist. How an American with an Irish Presbyterian background played such a pivotal role in a Canadian, immigrant, Dutch Reformed vision of Christianity is an astonishing story.

Runner graduated from Wheaton College in 1936, then pursued graduate studies at four different institutions. His desire to understand the relationship between biblical revelation and scientific learning led him to study under Cornelius Van Til at Westminster Theological Seminary in Philadelphia, Klaas Schilder at Kampen's Reformed Theological School, and Werner Jaeger at Harvard.[66] Encouraged by Van Til, Runner left Harvard to pursue his doctorate at the Free University of Amsterdam. There he studied under Dooyeweerd and Vollenhoven, completing his doctoral thesis in 1951.

When Runner returned to North America in 1951 to teach philosophy at Calvin College, he was a man on a mission. According to Bernard Zylstra, one of his most beloved students, Runner's mission consisted of three interrelated concerns. The first was "a new consciousness about the relation between the revelation of the Scriptures and North American culture."[67] Runner argued that the Bible, properly interpreted, did not support the historic synthesis between Greek and Christian worldviews born of the Middle Ages. The material and spiritual dualisms assumed by most North American Christians when they made distinctions between reason and faith, state and church, philosophy and theology, and public and private were to be rejected in favour of a new perspective that proclaimed "life is religion." This pet phrase of Runner's expresses a central theme in Reformational philosophy: God's law governs all of life, and all human creatures either respond in obedience or disobedience in every facet of their lives.

A second concern in Runner's mission pertained to the new way Christians should understand their role as formers of culture. No longer should their efforts to shape culture be confined to the institutional church. Humanists and Christians shared the modern age in all areas of culture; thus, they should be accorded equal opportunity to shape all areas of society.

To address these first two concerns, Runner's mission included a third element: the cultivation of a new Christian mind. This mind would have to address the well-established but wrong assumption that science is objective and neutral while Christian philosophy is subjective and, therefore, biased. Thus, the development of a new mind was critical for the formation of the next generation of Christian leaders.

Runner primarily focused his mission on his students. In a tribute to his former teacher on the occasion of his death, Al Wolters said this about Runner:

> His impact on the academic world can be explained chiefly through the influence, not of his writings, but of his students. And his teaching of his students was not primarily that of introducing them to the specific academic discipline of philosophy but of inspiring them with a vision of the entire academic enterprise. Another way of saying this is that what Runner taught was not in the first place philosophy but a worldview—specifically, the religious worldview of Dutch neo-Calvinism.[68]

Canadian students attending Calvin College were particularly captivated by Runner's message. They were the sons and daughters of Dutch Neo-Calvinist immigrants who wanted their children to have a Christian higher-education experience. As noted earlier, most of these immigrants had been strong supporters of Kuyper's philosophy and social policies when they lived in the Netherlands. They had firsthand experience of Kuyper's experiment to reorganize society in such a way that every prominent faith community was not only allowed but also encouraged to shape culture through its own collection of social organizations. Because the children of these immigrants who came to study at Calvin College had not been Americanized, they were more receptive to Runner's message.

Runner inspired some of his brightest, boldest, and most capable students to become the leading spokesman for the Reformational Movement. To prepare them for this role, Runner encouraged them to follow in his footsteps and get their doctorate degrees at the Free University while studying under Dooyeweerd, Vollenhoven, and their protégées. The first wave of these elite young scholars returned to Canada in the mid-1960s.

They were eager to take up the challenge of cultural transformation, and they found the ARSS ready to hire them as academic missionaries.

In 1967 the ARSS reorganized itself as the Association for the Advancement of Christian Scholarship (AACS) and launched their "university." They named it the Institute for Christian Studies (ICS). The plan was to start small, then turn the ICS into a replica of the Free University. The first step involved the establishment of an interdisciplinary core faculty that would focus on foundational studies at the graduate level. Once that centrepiece was established, they would add other faculties until the ICS was a full-fledged university. The ICS began humbly with a faculty of one, but within a few years, seven of Runner's former students were teaching as senior members in this interdisciplinary faculty.

At this same time, other former students of Runner's were taking key positions at Calvin College and its sister institutions, Dordt College in Iowa and Trinity Christian College in Illinois. Due to the influence of these professors, dozens of American and Canadian graduates from these colleges travelled to Toronto to study at the ICS in the late 1960s and early 1970s, even though the Institute did not offer a recognized degree. In subsequent years, many of these students also took up positions at all three American colleges, the two Canadian colleges that would be established later as well as at the ICS itself. Reformational scholars also taught in evangelical colleges and secular universities in the United States and Canada at that time. Many people contributed to this ripple effect, which placed Reformational scholars in key undergraduate teaching positions, but Evan Runner stands alone at its source.

By 1970 the Institute for Christian Studies employed a half dozen professors and had attracted dozens of students. Through the combined influences of the Institute, its publications, and a program of family conferences that featured academic lectures geared to the general public, the AACS served as a catalyst for revival within the Reformed community. It also functioned as a source of conflict.

Most people who identified with the Reformational Movement were wowed by the ability of the movement's leaders to expose, critique, and offer alternative perspectives to the major viewpoints that shaped popular thinking inside and outside of the church. They experienced the movement as a purveyor of a better Christian worldview or mind. Some followers did not see Reformational thinking as a final destination but as the first leg of a journey toward the adoption of a radical Christian life. This way of life challenged Christians to step away from their established patterns of cultural accommodation and/or world avoidance to become engaged in a life of biblically inspired culture making. However, the Biblical injunction to administer "a cup of cold water" to an ailing society was primarily understood as resolving systemic problems, not addressing the needs of the marginalized in society. The Reformational Movement generated the best examples of interpretive communities but also contributed to the deepest divisions in the larger Reformed community.

Finding a Place in Canadian Society

The Dutch immigrants who established the Neo-Calvinist tradition of education embraced their new Canadian citizenship, but they identified as Dutch Reformed first. As we saw in the previous chapter, this posed nowhere near the problems for them as it did for their cousins who had immigrated to the United States decades earlier. Canada had no well-defined national identity to impose on its immigrant populations. Consequently, the Neo-Calvinist community's ethnicity, theology, and desire to educate their children outside of the public school system was not perceived as unCanadian. Provincial governments did not just allow them to build their own schools, in two instances, they even provided financial assistance on a per-student basis.

The first twenty-five years of Neo-Calvinist education in Canada represent a dynamic time of building and establishing schools. Christian education was a high priority in the Dutch Neo-Calvinist community, and families were prepared to make significant sacrifices to ensure their children could attend a Christian school. Their motivation to educate their children was rooted in their experience of Christian education in the Netherlands. As noted in chapter 1, the tradition of Christian education was defined by five formative features. So, how well did these Canadian schools measure up to this legacy twenty-five years into the movement?

From their earliest days, the schools in all three regional organizations were operated by parent-run societies, not the church. In this important respect, they remained true to their Dutch Neo-Calvinist heritage. The parents' prior right to educate their children was unanimously upheld by the churches they attended.

Similarly, these schools remained deeply grounded in their tradition's high view of Scripture. Most school supporters agreed that Kuyper's vision of cultural transformation best expressed a Reformed interpretation of Scripture, and the vision and mission statements of their schools reflected this bias. However, throughout this critical gestation period, most school communities were unable to implement this formidable vision. As stated earlier, the more pressing need at the time was to preserve their identity as Dutch, Reformed Christians.

Curricular and pedagogical reform were also important features in their educational tradition. Neo-Calvinist educators accomplished very little on these fronts for the same reasons that prevented the flourishing of a Kuyperian vision of education. The first signs of curricular reform coincided with the rise of the Reformational Movement. As we shall see in part II, teacher involvement in curriculum reform became a distinguishing trait of the CSC in the last decades of the twentieth century. In most cases, however, pedagogical reform was ignored.

Arguably, the most important observation we can make about CSC's first twenty-five years concerns its perception of the Christian school as a dissident and also a transformative institution. To fulfill the first role, the school had to equip students with the ability to understand and critique the secular powers and principalities that threatened a Christian culture. To carry out the second, the school had to initiate students into an alternative way of understanding and living in the world. CSC schools did not effectively fulfill either of these two roles during this time, but a number of teachers and administrators were eager to move in that direction by the late 1960s. Their ability to resurrect these roles is a central focus of parts II and III of this book. They were opposed by members of their own community, but they understood the issues in these rivalries. What every camp in the movement failed to fully understand was the danger that the paradigm of progressivism posed to their legacy. That threat is described in detail in topic 4 in "Dig Deeper."

Exit Slip: Seeds of Hope

In these first three chapters, we set out to understand how Canadian Neo-Calvinist educators interpreted and expressed their tradition's educational vision during its early years of development, a timeframe that I arbitrarily fixed by the dates 1945 to 1970. Each chapter identified relevant highlights within a unique context and described their impact on this educational vision.

Chapter 1 took us back to the nineteenth century, where we investigated the birth and early development of the Neo-Calvinist tradition of Christian education in the Netherlands. That tradition gave birth to two educational visions, one pietist and protectionist and the other culture transformative. The latter was the most espoused vision of the two and it became synonymous with the tradition. It exhibited five remarkable formative features:

- a commitment to the grand themes of Scripture, as expressed in the theologies and philosophies of St. Augustine, John Calvin and Abraham Kuyper;
- a preference for parental control of school governance;
- a priority for curricular and pedagogical reform;
- the school as a dissident institution that exposes and rejects the Enlightenment and its preferred way of life;
- the school as a transforming institution that promotes an alternative vision of the person, society, and a preferred biblical way of life.

Chapter 2 explained how the American context came to bear upon CSC through two avenues of influence, one disguised and the other invisible. The CSC community's dependence upon NUCS and Calvin College made it susceptible to the same process of Americanization that shaped the Reformed sensibilities and thinking of Dutch immigrants in the United States. The chapter identified the paradigm of progressivism as the most prevalent and invisible form of American influence. To keep the school-building narrative moving along, I placed my analyses of the Calvin College influence and the paradigm of progressivism in "Dig Deeper," topics 3 and 4 respectively.

When NUCS finally committed itself to take responsibility for curriculum development in the 1960s, it adopted the dominant technical approach of the Administrative Progressives. For many CSC educators, this development removed any lingering loyalty that they still felt toward NUCS.

Among the commentators on this period that we relied upon, Van Brummelen demonstrates the greatest understanding of, and appreciation for, the CSC legacy of education and the obstacles it had to overcome to implement its larger vision of cultural transformation. In his book, *Telling the Next Generation*, he also expresses more pessimism than hope. He correctly observes that any serious pursuit of cultural transformation requires a school community to be involved in mainstream society, but he believes this involvement always means the school will "be directed by the currents of general educational thought and practice." You will know when the Christian school has capitulated to the public education paradigm, he says, when its "quest for quality education [has] overshadowed the desire for uniqueness."[69] He was more hopeful in his later writings. In fact, he thought CSC could break free from the progressivist education paradigm through the development and implementation of its own alternative curriculum orientation. Our investigations in parts II and III will test the veracity of both predictions.

In chapter 3, we considered the challenges that confronted Dutch Neo-Calvinist immigrants who sought to make Canada their home in the aftermath of WWII. Specifically, we investigated their efforts to establish an alternative education system. By 1970 they had managed to build more than sixty schools in three provinces, but the quality of education offered by these schools for most of that time was generally poor. Toward the end of this period, the situation rapidly improved. Many CSC teachers and administrators were poised to assume personal responsibility for curriculum reform.

During this critical period of growth, the Neo-Calvinist education movement experienced tensions that would escalate into unfortunate rivalries. These rivalries eventually crippled the ability of many CSC communities to function as interpretive communities and implement the more radical Kuyperian educational vision.

Initially, CSC communities managed to establish two of the five features that defined the tradition of Christian education they brought with them from the Netherlands. They remained committed to a vision informed by the grand themes of Scripture, and their schools were governed by independent, parent-controlled societies. The advent of the Reformational Movement inspired many CSC educators to reclaim the other three formative features of their educational heritage: curricular/pedagogical reform, the school as a dissident institution, and the school as a culturally transformative institution.

To sum up the first twenty-five years of Neo-Calvinist education in Canada, a biblical image comes to mind from Jesus' Parable of the Sower.[70] The Dutch Neo-Calvinist community was prolific in sowing seeds of hope across Canada in the form of a system of alternative schools. The seeds fell on a variety of "soils," and the schools that emerged flourished accordingly. After twenty-five years, it was still too early to determine the quality of the harvest, but many knew what a "one hundred-fold" crop was supposed to look like. Such a school would exhibit all five formative features of the Neo-Calvinist educational legacy, and its supporting community would demonstrate a willingness to embrace both of hope's beautiful daughters, Anger and Courage.

Endnotes

1. Nicholas Wolterstorff's fingerprints are all over this book. I consider him to be the philosopher laureate of the Canadian Neo-Calvinist school movement. I had the privilege of hearing him deliver several of the speeches that are quoted in this book. He also put in guest appearances in a course I took at the Institute for Christian Studies taught by Hank Hart. Wolterstorff's illustrious career included thirty years of teaching philosophy at Calvin College (now Calvin University) and thirteen years at Yale University's Divinity School, where he was the Noah Porter Professor of Philosophical Theology and an adjunct professor in the departments of Philosophy and Religious Studies.

2. Neo-Calvinism refers to the revival of Dutch Calvinism in the Netherlands during the nineteenth century. For the Dutch immigrants who relocated in Canada after WWII and much earlier in the United States, Neo-Calvinism referred to "an all embracing worldview or *Weltanschauung* which has a bearing on the whole of human life." Al Wolters, "Dutch Neo-Calvinism: Worldview, Philosophy and Rationality," in *Rationality in the Calvinian Tradition*, eds. H Hart, J van der Hoeven and Nicholas Wolterstorff, (Toronto: UPA), 1.

3. Peter Prinsen, "That Old Dutch Disease: The Roots of Dutch Calvinist's Education in Alberta," PhD diss., (University of Alberta, 2000).

4. The Christian Reformed Church is the North American equivalent of the *Gereformeerde Kerken* in the Netherlands, which emerged in 1886 as a result of a merger involving the Afscheiding secessionist churches and the Doleantie movement led by Abraham Kuyper. Most Kuyperian-minded Dutch immigrants who came to Canada and the United States joined the Christian Reformed Church.

5. Calvin College is the official denominational college operated by the Christian Reformed Church. In 1876 the school split off from the denomination's seminary. Up until 1921 it was known as John Calvin College. Calvin College rebranded itself as Calvin University in 2019; however, I will

refer to the school as Calvin College throughout this book since that is how it was known in the literature I have referenced. .

6   American Dutch Neo-Calvinists opened the first of many schools in 1856. Sixty-four years later, they organized the National Union of Christian Schools (NUCS) in 1920. In 1978 the organization took on its current name of Christian Schools International (CSI). It, too, is headquartered in Grand Rapids.

7   For a detailed discussion see "Dig Deeper," Topic 4.

8   The name of the association of schools in British Columbia has never changed. The Prairie Centre for Christian Education was formerly known as the Prairie Association of Christian Schools. Edvance replaced the organizations for school boards (the Ontario Alliance of Christian Schools), teachers (the Ontario Christian School Teachers Association), and administrators (Ontario Christian School Administrators Association).

9   Harro Van Brummelen, *Telling the Next Generation: Educational Development in North American Calvinist Christian Schools* (Langham, MD: University Press of America, 1986).

10 Harro Van Brummelen and Geraldine Steensma, eds., *Shaping School Curriculum: A Biblical View* (Middleburg Heights, OH: Signal, 1977). Harro Van Brummelen, *Walking with God in the Classroom* (Seattle, WA: Alta Vista College Press, 1988). Harro Van Brummelen, *Steppingstones to Curriculum: A Biblical Path*, 2nd Ed. (Colorado Springs: Purposeful Design Publications, 2002). Gloria Stronks and Doug Blomberg, eds., *A Vision with a Task: Christian Schooling for Responsive Discipleship* (Grand Rapids, MI: Baker Books, 1993). Peter Boer et al., *Educating Teachers for Responsive Discipleship* (Lanham, ML: University Press of American, 1993). These and other important works are analyzed in chapter 7.

11 Peter Prinsen, "Old Dutch."

12 Adrien Peetoom, "From Mythology to Mythology: Dutch-Canadian Orthodox-Calvinist Immigrants and Their Schools," master's thesis (University of Toronto, 1993).

13 Kudos to those who set up Monarch Educare Solutions, an online service that collects photographs and stories from local Ontario Neo-Calvinist school communities in an effort to preserve and celebrate local narratives.

14 Peetoom, "From Mythology," 20.

15 Prinsen, "Old Dutch," 54.

16 Nicholas Wolterstorff, *Keeping Faith: Talks for a New Faculty* (Grand Rapid, MI: Occasional Papers from Calvin College, 1989), 9.

17 Van Brummelen, "Telling," 15.
18 Peetoom, "From Mythology," 26.
19 Peetoom, 13.
20 Peter De Boer and Donald Oppewal, "American Calvinist Day Schools," in *Voices From the Past: Reformed Educators*, ed. Donald Oppewal (Lanham, ML: University Press of America, 1997), 267.
21 Wolterstorff, "Keeping Faith," 9.
22 James Bratt, *Dutch Calvinism in Modern America: A History of a Conservative Subculture* (Grand Rapids, MI: 1984) 4.
23 Van Brummelen, "Telling," 26-28.
24 Abraham Kuyper (1837–1920) more than anyone else personified the Neo-Calvinist movement. Among other things, he was a newspaper editor, a co-founder and professor of the Free University of Amsterdam, a strong advocate of Christian education, the leader of the huge secession movement, and the prime minister of the Netherlands.
25 Wolterstorff, "Keeping Faith," 10.
26 De Boer and Oppewal, "American," 268-9.
27 Prinsen, "Old Dutch," 45.
28 Prinsen, 45.
29 For an extended discussion of these professors and their contributions, see "Dig Deeper," Topic 3.
30 For a detailed history of Neo-Calvinist education in America, read the texts by De Boer, Oppewal, Van Brummelen, and Bratt, which are referenced frequently in chapters 1 and 2.
31 A detailed investigation into this paradigm appears in "Dig Deeper," Topic 4.
32 Peter De Boer and Donald Oppewal, "American Calvinist Day Schools," in *Voices From the Past: Reformed Educators*, ed. Donald Oppewal (Lanham, ML: University Press of America, 1997), 271.
33 De Boer and Oppewal, 271.
34 Van Brummelen, "Telling," 106.
35 Van Brummelen, 109.
36 See "Dig Deeper," Topic 4 for more on the Administrative Progressives.
37 Van Brummelen, 108.
38 Bratt, "Dutch Calvinism," 40.
39 Van Brummelen, "Telling," 86.

40 Bratt, "Dutch Calvinism," 40-41.

41 Peter De Boer and Donald Oppewal, "American Calvinist Day Schools," in *Voices From the Past: Reformed Educators*, ed. Donald Oppewal (Lanham, ML: University Press of America, 1997), 278.

42 De Boer and Oppewal., 277.

43 Van Brummelen, "Telling," 149.

44 Van Brummelen, 171.

45 A description of this dominant approach and those that challenged it can be found in "Dig Deeper," Topic 4.

46 Van Brummelen, "Telling," 185.

47 A summary of this document is included in "Dig Deeper," Topic 3.

48 Van Brummelen, 186.

49 This approach is also known as the Tyler method of curriculum development due to the popularity of Ralph Tyler's *Basic Principles of Curriculum and Instruction*, which was published in 1949. Both names describe the Administrative Progressivist orientation to curriculum. Triezenberg's background in the hard sciences likely contributed to his adoption of this approach and may partially explain his lukewarm attitude toward the integral unit promoted by many CSC teachers. Had Henry Barron, the language arts consultant for NUCS, been given the task of creating the principles document, the relationship between NUCS and the OACS may have been more cordial.

50 Peethoom, "From Mythology," 57.

51 The first wave came between 1845–1855 and the second between 1880–1920.

52 Al Wolters observes that "Neo-Calvinism" was originally coined by the opponents of Abram Kuyper, who was one of the leaders in a revival of Calvin's theological and philosophical views. Kuyper and his followers were comfortable with the moniker. Wolters also clarifies that "Kuyperian" and "reformational" are sometimes used as synonyms for Neo-Calvinism. In my experience at Dordt College and later as an educator in Canada, the term "reformational" generally referred to a Kuyperian interpretation of Calvin's thought, but it specifically connoted the philosophy of the law idea developed by Herman Dooyeweerd and his brother-in-law D. H. Th. Vollenhoven, which they called reformational philosophy. For most Neo-Calvinists living in Canada, the Reformational Movement was inherently linked to the Institute for Christian Studies and its supporters.

53 Philip Jackson, "Conceptions of Curriculum and Curriculum Specialists," in *Handbook of Research on Curriculum: A Project of the American Educational*

Research Association, ed. Philip Jackson (New York: Macmillan Publishing Co., 1992).

54 Eisner, E., and Vallance, E., (eds.), *Conflicting Conceptions of the Curriculum.* (Berkeley, CA: *McCutchan*, 1974).

55 For a comparison of terms like curriculum conception and curriculum orientation see "Dig Deeper," Topic 1.

56 Jackson, *Handbook*, 19.

57 Prinsen, "Old Dutch," 222.

58 Nicolas Wolterstorff, "Curriculum: By What Standard?" in *Educating for Life: Reflections on Christian Teaching and Learning*, eds. Gloria Stronks and Clarence Joldersma (Grand Rapids, MI: Baker Academic, 2002), 17-31.

59 The details of this speech are analyzed in "Dig Deeper," Topic 3.

60 See "Dig Deeper," Topic 2 for a discussion about the confusion over the terms integration and integral.

61 Van Brummelen, "Telling," 188.

62 Van Brummelen, "Telling," 189. A detailed description of the educational philosophies of Jellema and Jaarsma can be found in "Dig Deeper," Topic 3.

63 John A. Olthuis, "Towards the 21st Century: Vision and Direction," *The Christian Vanguard* Vol. 10 (July 1970): 6-9.

64 The organization still exists today as the Association for Reformational Philosophy and continues to publish its esteemed academic journal, *Philosophia Reformata*.

65 C. T. McIntire, "Herman Dooyeweerd in North America," in *Reformed Theology in America: A History of Its Modern Development*, ed. D. F. Wells (Grand Rapids, MI: Eerdmans, 1985). .

66 Bernard Zylstra, "H. Evan Runner: An Assessment of His Mission," in *Life is Religion: Essays in Honor of H. Evan Runner*, ed. Henry Vander Goot (St. Catherines, Ontario, 1981), 5.

67 Zylstra, 1.

68 Al Wolters, "The Importance of H. Evan Runner," *Comment*, 2003, https://www.cardus.ca/comment/article/the-importance-of-h-evan-runner/.

69 Van Brummelen, "Telling," 207.

70 Matthew 13:1-23.

PART II
A SEASON FOR HOPE
(1970–2000)

The one continuing purpose of education, since ancient times, has been to bring people to as full a realization as possible of what it is to be a human being.

—Arthur W. Foshay

Worldviews are best understood as we see them incarnated, fleshed out in actual ways of life.

—Brian Walsh, Richard Middleton

Major Story Line: The Holy Grail of Curriculum Reform

Hope and Its Detractors

Our continuing investigation of Christian Schools Canada (CSC) utilizes the same four-fold criteria we adopted in part I. We again focus on the ways CSC communities interpreted and expressed their educational visions, some highlights from the larger narrative, and the context within which these events took place.

The Dutch Neo-Calvinist community in Canada had many reasons to feel optimistic from 1970 to 2000 as their tradition of education came of age on several fronts. The number of CSC schools doubled, as did student enrollment. They launched two undergraduate liberal arts institutions, The King's College (now University) in Edmonton, Alberta, in 1979 and Redeemer College (now university) in Ancaster, Ontario, three years later. In 1983 the Institute for Christian Studies (ICS) finally received its charter to grant graduate-level degrees.[71] Remarkably, in just thirty-five years this small and resilient immigrant community established a kindergarten-to-doctorate alternative system of faith-based education that stretched from Ottawa to Victoria.

Throughout this period the three historic districts that make up CSC found their own voices. Their educational priorities steadily branched away from the path taken by their American parent organization, even though it changed its name from the National Union of Christian Schools (NUCS) to Christian Schools International (CSI) in 1978 in an effort to be more inclusive. After years of continuous discord, the Canadian districts became independent entities in 1999.

The quality of teachers and administrators improved dramatically across the entire school system during these three decades. By the late 1980s, teachers and administrators were expected to have credentials that met provincial standards. More educators were getting a master's degree and/or developing skills as workshop leaders.

Curriculum reform also stands out during these three decades, but what makes this accomplishment particularly notable is the fact that it was driven by teachers. Teacher-led curriculum development rarely happens, even though reformers have advocated for it off and on since the days of Harold Rugg in the 1920s.[72] Virtually all efforts to encourage teachers to take ownership of curriculum development have been stymied by the well-established Tyler model of curriculum production. In this model experts design, develop, and disseminate curriculum; it is the teachers' job to implement it.[73] One would be hard pressed to find a comparable situation where classroom teachers took upon themselves as much responsibility for the curriculum, and for so long a period, as did CSC teachers. Granted, many CSC teachers were not seriously engaged in curriculum writing, but those who were significantly influenced their respective schools and the direction of their school movement as a whole.

All of these developments contributed to a climate of hopefulness among Canadian Neo-Calvinist communities. But hope also had its detractors. One of the most obvious ones emerged as a rivalry between those who identified with the Curriculum Development Centre (CDC) and those who did not. The CDC was a one-of-a-kind think tank that the Association for the Advancement of Christian Scholarship (AACS) launched and briefly operated. The CDC's work accentuated disagreements over two issues that percolated throughout the CSC community at that time: 1) should the curriculum be organized around the traditional subject disciplines or holistic thematic units, and 2) should pedagogy remain teacher-centred and focused on the transmission of knowledge or shift to a more learner-centred approach where students are actively engaged in their learning? The resolution of these two issues proved to be critical for those who pursued the tradition's most elusive goal: the development of a Christian curriculum orientation.

Questions about curriculum structure and teaching methodology dominated ground-level discussions among CSC educators, but the different ways CSC educators interpreted and expressed their educational vision posed a more critical problem. The majority of CSC educators held to the tradition's long-standing belief that the purpose of Christian education is the cultivation of a biblical worldview in students. A small but vocal group of educators challenged this status quo position. They argued that nurturing a Christian mind in students did not go far enough no matter how biblically attuned their worldview was. By itself a worldview was not an effective catalyst for personal or cultural transformation. The modern notion that ideas precede action, was not well founded, they believed, not even when the ideas came from the Bible. For this group, the purpose of a transformative Christian education was best expressed as a Christian way of life. The phrase "education for discipleship" encapsulated their educational vision.

Whether or not CSC educators had to choose between these two visions was complicated by the fact that most people misunderstood how far apart they actually were. Practically everyone thought that educating for a Christian perspective and educating for a life of discipleship were highly compatible, if not two faces of the same visionary coin. For this reason, our investigation of this segment in the history of CSC requires a solid understanding of this confusion.

Most advocates of a Christian perspective did not consider education for discipleship to be a contradictory goal, because they believed the radical life of Christian living was the natural next step after one acquired a Christian perspective. Similarly, the promoters of education for discipleship were not opposed to the cultivation of a Christian mind, per se. It was, they conceded, an integral part of what it means to be truly human. Furthermore, both groups shared the assumption that the development of a distinctively Christian curriculum orientation[74] represented the critical first step in the implementation of their educational vision. Indeed, the development of an alternative, biblically grounded curriculum orientation was the tradition's holy grail.

Since both sides shared so much in common, it is understandable that many wondered if, and where, there was a rub. Most believed the main difference that separated them hinged on the question of timing. At what point was it reasonable to expect students to adopt a life of discipleship, during their tenure at school or sometime after graduation? For them this difference seemed to be a relatively minor one.

The roles each side assigned to the school, the student, and the teacher, however, were starkly different. Those who expressed their educational vision as the cultivation of a Christian perspective in every subject area pictured the school as an academic institution, not a purveyor of lifestyles. If the community's elementary and high schools did their respective jobs well, their students would acquire a Christian mind. So endowed with this "education," it was reasonable to expect that they would pursue a life of discipleship as adults. In general these educators were comfortable implementing the traditional roles of the school as gatekeeper to social success, the student as passive learner, and the teacher as transmitter of knowledge and manager of classroom behaviour.

The proponents of education for discipleship believed that schools always did more than shape minds; they formed lives. They also thought it was possible, and quite often the case, for Christian schools to simultaneously cultivate in their students a Christian mind and a secular way of life. This unfortunate outcome was due, in part, to their uncritical adoption of the traditional roles of school, student, and teacher and the philosophical/cultural assumptions that gave them status. They intuitively knew the Christian school could not critically reject the values and priorities of a secular society and initiate students into an alternative way of life if its educational practices prepared students to mentally and socially fit into that society and its workforce. They wanted to move in a direction where students would no longer be passive receptors of knowledge but take much more responsibility for their own learning. Likewise, teachers would become architects of learning for a way of life, not mere transmitters of information and managers of behaviour.

The stakes in this struggle to either solidify the Christian perspective vision or reframe it as education for discipleship could not have been higher. The outcome would determine the overall health of the tradition as it entered the twenty-first century. As long as the Canadian Neo-Calvinist community remained committed to education for a Christian perspective, they risked taking their tradition down a dead-end street where worldview became an end in itself. At that juncture, to have the correct point of view meant everything. Should that happen, the community would be tempted to think (though no one would ever admit it) that the acquisition of a vision for life was good enough. Once a community believed it was sufficient to possess the correct view of the Christian life, it was relatively easy to believe that the life of discipleship was too demanding to actually live and to justify the pursuit of the American dream.

The promoters of education for discipleship were vulnerable to their own brand of naiveté when they assumed a theme-based curriculum and a learner-centred pedagogy were sufficient to implement education for discipleship. They struggled to imagine what education for discipleship actually looked like. They flirted with their own version of dead-end thinking when they failed to realize education for a way of life required everyone in the school and its supporting community to model it.

Few, if any, CSC educators understood that the significance of their own quarrels over educational vision and curriculum reform would be eclipsed by an invisible and much more lethal external threat, the paradigm of progressivism.[75] They were aware of this threat insofar as they knew they were engaged in a war of worldviews. Far too many, however, naively believed they had won that war with the establishment of their own school system. To hear them talk, all that remained to be fought were small-scale skirmishes. The teachers most actively involved in curriculum reform knew better. The more substantive their efforts to change their curriculum and teaching strategies became, the more resistance they experienced when they tried to implement them.

The three decades that I characterize as a season of hope could be analyzed from a variety of angles. I decided to focus on curriculum reform and address the key questions that confronted CSC educators at that time:

- How effectively do CSC schools implement a Christian perspective across the curriculum?
- What curriculum orientation best matches CSC's educational vision?
- What does an education for a life of discipleship actually look like?
- Can CSC successfully implement a vision of cultural transformation if its educators remain bound to traditional classroom patterns?
- To remain true to the Neo-Calvinist legacy of Christian education, must CSC supporters relinquish their pursuit of the privileged "American dream"?

Part II is divided into four chapters, with some additional material placed in the "Dig Deeper" section. The opening chapter highlights a remarkable text entitled *Joy in Learning: An Integrated Curriculum for the Elementary School (JIL)*. This was the first, and arguably one of the most significant, attempts to make a course correction in the tradition through curricular and pedagogical changes (albeit limited to the K-3 level). *JIL* inspired tremendous hope in many teachers, but its potential to make a system-wide impact was hampered by its own shortcomings, some key failures on the part of those who published it, and the unwillingness of district leaders to promote this approach.

The second chapter draws our attention to the most unusual story in the history of Canadian Neo-Calvinist education, the rise and demise of the Curriculum Development Centre (CDC). The CDC emerged as an anti-establishment curriculum-writing organization at a time when the three regional administrative bodies of CSC either did not exist or were incapable of coordinating the efforts of their teachers to rewrite school curriculum. The CDC had no formal ties with any level of Christian school administration, but it embodied the greatest aspirations of the tradition. Tragically, the CDC disappointed most people in the end. The CDC's story mirrors the best and the worst of the Canadian Neo-Calvinist education tradition; its story was a major impetus for my decision to write this book.

The next chapter highlights the CDC newsletter, which served as an effective vehicle for articulating and spreading educational vision among CSC teachers. Over its seven-year history, the newsletter showcased some of the best thinking in the Neo-Calvinist education universe and in a format that was easily accessible to classroom teachers. In the absence of any CSC-sponsored educational magazine or journal, this newsletter offered a rare perspective on curriculum reform.

The last chapter investigates the golden age of Neo-Calvinist educational literature. Although most of these texts addressed the broader North American Neo-Calvinist education movement, they provide us with the most profound insights into the two main ways that CSC educators interpreted and expressed their transformative educational vision: education for a Christian perspective and education for discipleship. This body of work also contains the tradition's best efforts to construct an alternative curriculum orientation.

The community struggled to understand the true nature of hope's two beautiful daughters. Most directed righteous Anger at the secular perspectives that shaped the curriculum, and channeled Courage to the construction of an alternative curriculum orientation. Some called for a course correction. Their Anger addressed the disconnect between education for Christian perspective and education for transformed living; they called for Courage to follow the rebel Christ.

CHAPTER 4

Whatever Happened to *Joy in Learning*?

Timeline

1967 The Association for the Advancement of Christian Scholarship (AACS) sponsors the Summer Program in Christian Education (SPICE) for teachers.

  SPICE participants imagine a new program of learning for Christian schools from K-12.

1970 *Joy in Learning, Vol. 1 (JIL)* is available in a stenciled format. Arnold De Graaff is appointed to teach at the ICS.

1973 *Joy in Learning, Vol. 1* is published as a loose-leaf binder.

1979 *Teaching with Joy* is published as a follow-up document to *JIL*.

Grassroots Curriculum Reform

In the late 1960s, some CSC teachers began to see themselves as curriculum developers. Over the next twenty to twenty-five years, a dedicated cohort of these teachers worked to rewrite the curriculum they taught. This teacher-led curriculum-writing movement stands out as one of the most distinctive features of the Neo-Calvinist education tradition in Canada.

CSC teachers who were actively involved in curriculum writing at this time received their inspiration from several sources. They were motivated by their legacy of alternative Christian education that had long assumed that curriculum reform was integral to teaching. Ironically, mainstream school reformers also spurred them on insofar as they popularized the idea that teachers should consciously adopt their own curriculum conceptual frameworks. The main driver of curriculum reform, however, came from the Reformational Movement[76] and its foundational critique of contemporary culture and clarion call for culture transformation.

From the beginning, CSC teachers who seriously took up the task of curriculum reform understood the magnitude of the task. To rewrite a program of studies was a huge undertaking on its own, but they knew they also needed an alternative philosophy of curriculum that could guide the process of curriculum content selection, organization, and design. This philosophy would provide them with coherent answers to these foundational questions:
- What is most worth knowing?
- How should the curriculum be organized?
- What teaching strategies are most conducive to learning?
- Who is a good student?
- What defines teacher excellence?
- How should student learning be evaluated?

In addition to these challenges, CSC teachers had to pursue curriculum reform in a context devoid of the most basic supports. For starters, they lacked the requisite skills and time to develop curriculum. Their schools did not provide them with dedicated days or even hours to do curriculum writing during the school year, and professional development of any kind was still years away. Teachers who wanted to engage in serious curriculum writing had to take the time from their precious two months off between school years and learn by experience.

Some also had to pursue curriculum reform in the face of opposition from one or more of the following: their administrators, fellow teachers, or their parent community. Local opponents to curriculum reform were typically content with the benign resources provided by NUCS, materials that did not actually confront their children with the challenge of cultural change.

CSC teachers received no financial incentives for their efforts. The fact that they worked on twelve-month contracts made it possible for them to develop curriculum during the summer. However, they often had to pay out of pocket for travel, workshop fees, or the resources they needed. Eventually, some school boards provided their teachers with a few hundred dollars each year for professional development.

Given these restraints, curriculum reform for most CSC teachers was limited to the improvement of the lessons, units, and courses they actually taught. Some collaborated on the development of a coherent and distinctive philosophy of education that rationalized their tradition's approach to curriculum development. A select few set out to construct a distinctively Christian curriculum orientation that reimagined the purpose of education, the organization of content, and the focus of pedagogy, so all of it coincided with a biblical worldview.

A teacher-led curriculum reform movement of any size needs support from both the school and district levels of administration if it is to flourish. Initially, there was little backing to be had from any quarter. When teachers in all three districts insisted on developing curriculum on a continuing basis, the question of who would provide leadership arose. NUCS was the obvious candidate, but as noted in chapter 2, this America-based parent organization was fundamentally out of step with many Canadian teachers, especially those in Ontario. NUCS was unprepared to support a teacher-led curriculum development movement on three counts.

First, NUCS officials could not imagine teachers as curriculum developers. On the American side of the border, NUCS teachers were typically hired on nine-month contracts. This prevented them from engaging in serious curriculum development because they had to work second jobs during the summer months just to make ends meet. Second, by this time NUCS was committed to the Tyler model for curriculum development, which relegated curriculum writing to hired experts. But the biggest reason NUCS could not support CSC teachers was the latter's preference for writing "integrated units,"[77] as they were known in CSC circles at the time. Such units, Van Brummelen reminds us, were infused with a Christian perspective that not only determined the selection, interpretation, and uses of content but also aimed to "build a totally new way of life in Christ." NUCS preferred a curriculum "designed to impart the knowledge and skills normally set by current curriculum standards and to teach moral and spiritual values for living a life in Christ."[78]

Without help from NUCS, the facilitation of a grassroots movement of curriculum reform in Canada fell to the districts themselves. However, in the early years a district level of administration either did not exist, or if it did, it was not prepared to take up this critical responsibility. The Ontario Alliance of Christian Schools (OACS) failed to support curriculum reform for a number of years, due in part to its allegiance to NUCS. This lingering loyalty frustrated many reform-minded teachers. Throughout the 1970s, issues pertaining to curriculum reform sparked tensions between the OACS and the Ontario Christian School Teachers Association (OCSTA). By 1980 all three Canadian districts had a full-time curriculum coordinator who was responsible for facilitating what was fast becoming a robust tradition of teacher-led curriculum development. In the intervening period, the administrative void was partially filled by an unexpected source. That source will be the focus in the remainder of this chapter and the two chapters that follow.

From SPICE Comes *Joy*

In the summer of 1967, the Association for the Advancement of Christian Scholarship (AACS)[79] launched the Institute for Christian Studies (ICS) and sponsored a set of workshops for Christian school teachers called the Summer Program in Christian Education (SPICE). SPICE was a natural extension of the student conferences that the AACS had organized for several years. Initially, the OACS co-sponsored SPICE, much to the chagrin of the NUCS head office in Michigan. Had this initial cooperation between the AACS and the OACS flourished, the history of teacher development and curriculum reform in Canadian Neo-Calvinist circles would have turned out differently than it did. But, as we shall see, personality clashes and differences in educational philosophy quickly got in the way.

Arnold De Graaff was the most influential leader of SPICE workshops. When he first conducted workshops for SPICE, he was a psychology professor at Trinity Christian College in Chicago. De Graaff received his first taste of Reformational philosophy[80] from H. Evan Runner at Calvin College as an undergraduate student. His understanding of pedagogy, the nature of the child, what determines the underlying direction of culture, and Kuyper's notion of sphere sovereignty were fleshed out later when he studied at the Free University in Amsterdam under professors Waterink, Janse, Dooyeweerd, and Vollenhoven. De Graaff's teaching duties at Trinity included an educational psychology course. When Trinity's academic dean refused to allow De Graaff to offer a summer curriculum-writing workshop for education students out of concern this would offend NUCS officials, De Graaff took advantage of a standing invitation from the AACS in Toronto to lead SPICE workshops.

De Graaff immediately became the leader of a group of teachers at SPICE who wanted to produce nothing less than an alternative course of studies for Christian elementary and secondary education. De Graaff was a creative thinker and a charismatic personality. He had an amazing ability to rally people around his vision for a distinctly Christian education. Regrettably, he also had an equally amazing capacity to alienate people. This group's dream was to publish a series of nine manuals that demonstrated what a curriculum infused with a biblical perspective actually looked like. It would feature content organized around themes rather than the traditional subject disciplines. It would also encourage experiential learning rather than a more cerebral education that "turned students into little scientists." A draft in stenciled format of the first of these manuals emerged from the SPICE setting in 1970, and it bore the title *Joy in Learning: An Integrated Curriculum for the Elementary School*. That same year, De Graaff left Trinity Christian College and took a position as senior member in psychology at the ICS.

Three years later, during the fall of 1973, *Joy in Learning, Vol. 1 (JIL)* was published as a 620-page loose-leaf binder aimed at grades 1–3. De Graaff and teacher Jean Olthuis were listed as the editors of the manual, but as the introduction to the binder reminds readers, it represented the work of "a considerable number of teachers, college students and graduate students in education." We will pick up the unique story of *JIL*'s publication in the next chapter, but for the remainder of this chapter we will examine the project's considerable strengths and weaknesses.

What *Joy* Was Meant to Be

The contributors to *JIL* believed that CSC had not gone beyond changing the atmosphere of the classroom and adding Christian values to commonly held facts within the curriculum at any point in its twenty-five-year history. They believed their movement was due for a major course correction; it was time to reorient it to the biblical vision of what it means to be human and live a godly life. This vision was rooted in Scripture's grand narrative of creation-fall-redemption-restoration. For these teachers, the "restoration of education" meant teaching a completely redesigned program of studies for grades K to 12. *JIL* was to be the first of many texts that would make up this new program.

In the minds of the *JIL* authors, philosophical reform preceded, or at the very least had to be developed in conjunction with, curricular reform. Consequently, a major function of *JIL* was to articulate a Reformational conceptual framework for curriculum redesign. De Graaff was neither a schoolteacher, a curriculum writer, nor a philosopher, but he was an astute observer and a committed student of Reformational philosophy. It was this intellectual tradition that provided him with the key components for a new framework. One such component was the declaration that science is not the source of truth, as moderns claim, for the simple reason that the veracity of the scientific method cannot itself be proven by the scientific method. In reality, all theories were rooted in a faith, that is to say, in a pre-scientific religious commitment. The proposition that science is our best source of knowledge was true only when people believed it to be so. All knowledge begins with a confessional statement.

Another key component in Reformational thought asserted that mainline educational theories mistakenly absolutized aspects of human experience, such as the rational, the psychological, the behavioural, the social, or the material. These reductionist views of reality always produced dualistic anthropologies and worldviews that were incompatible with Scripture's holistic view of the person as a religious being and its understanding of the cosmos as a good work of the Creator.

We can summarize *JIL's* educational vision under three broad headings: its *purpose*, its *process*, and its *project*. The expressed *purpose* or aim of education in *JIL* is to "help children take up their calling in life," and there is but one ultimate calling: the call to be human. To be truly human, we must live the life that Jesus modelled, a life characterized by love, justice, care, service, and so on. At the core of that life, humans fulfill a single overarching task: to serve the Creator through the development of creation's potential for the benefit of all creatures. This overarching task consists of the many common activities that make up daily life, the stuff of all of our vocations, responsibilities, and relationships. In other words, the sphere of human service is commensurate with the second great commandment (alike unto the first), namely, "love God and our neighbours as ourselves." What kind of education "helps students take up their calling?" An education that provides them with a *confessional knowledge*, the knowledge that tells them who they are, who God is, and what service they owe to their Creator.[81]

This vision of education stood in sharp contrast to the one that dominated Christian education circles at that time, which defined the Christian life in terms of worship, moral purity, and theological orthodoxy. It also rejected mainstream education in North America, which had its own agenda to help children understand and take up their calling to be human. In that setting, human nature was fulfilled by a life of consumption in an ever-expanding economy. Students were encouraged to adopt twin but conflicting pursuits. They were to become independent, self-actualized, competitive, problem-solving, constructing, ethical, and tolerant individuals who were also expected to be law-abiding, well-adjusted, productive members of a status quo social structure created in the image of the American dream of prosperity.

The *process* spelled out in *JIL* is both *formative* and *self-formative*. Consistent with its distinctive purpose, the manual's approach to pedagogy carved out a unique space for Neo-Calvinist education. The authors were well aware that the authority of the teacher and the freedom of the student represented conflicting ideals in mainstream North American education. To prevent anyone from thinking *JIL* advocated for either side of the teacher-centred vs. student-centred polarity, the editors clarified what they meant by formative and self-formative. Teachers, they believed, must exercise formative power in order to lead students to take up their calling to be human. But in their use of power and authority, teachers must not be coercive, manipulative, prescriptive, controlling, or overpowering. Instead, they must be invitational, vulnerable, and guiding. Teaching must always serve learning because, ultimately, the goal of teaching is to enable students to find their way in/of life.

The complementary side of the teacher's formative power was the student's responsibility for his or her own learning. What this responsibility looked like varied at each stage of a student's development, but student self-formation always implied that the student had a real say when decisions were made about what was to be learned and how. To have meaningful input into these decisions, a student must have the actual freedom and power to make choices. Teacher authority and student responsibility went hand in hand. In fact, true pedagogical formation always leads to a student's self-formation.

The authors of *JIL* wanted to prevent both teachers and students from becoming self-serving masters in the classroom. The brakes needed to be applied to teacher authority and to student freedom because both teaching and learning were *acts of service*. The master to be served in the classroom was neither the teacher nor the student but the Creator and the Creator's purpose for humanity. This greater purpose must stand above the vested interests of all other stakeholders in the educational enterprise, including the government and its curriculum, industry and its economic concerns, and parents and their aspirations for their offspring.

Given this understanding of purpose and process, what was the most suitable *project* of education? Simply stated, it was the exploration and interpretation of creation; all of it. Everything in our experience had to be interpreted through a biblical worldview, not just moral and theological issues. The authors of *JIL* believed that worldview determines how we organize, parse, and interpret the meaning of reality. Knowing that textbooks were the primary purveyors of worldview, their first step in the development of a radically new curriculum orientation was to replace them.

For students to "develop a meaningful view of life," they had to "see things in their integral unity." Students experienced life as a whole; therefore, they should study it as a whole, not as so many different subjects. *JIL*'s vision did not go into a lengthy critique of the subject disciplines, but the message was clear. Education geared to our calling as humans was best served by a thematic curriculum.

Contrary to what many believed or desired, *JIL* was not a textbook, and neither was it a curriculum resource. The authors wanted to produce an integral approach to curriculum, in this instance, for grades 1–3. They consciously tried to articulate a worldview, a philosophy of education, an anthropology, a psychology of education, a curriculum design with matching pedagogy, and a model program of studies that exhibited internal coherence and consistently reflected the Bible's grand narrative. What they tried to construct was an alternative curriculum orientation.[82]

JIL reminded Neo-Calvinists that the reason they built their own alternative school system was to provide their children with a different kind of education. The authors assumed that to help students take up their calling, they not only had to reimagine curriculum design, teaching, and learning in light of this alternative purpose, they also had to break free from the assumptions that currently defined the traditional classroom.

With 20/20 hindsight, and a more sophisticated set of critical categories to guide our analysis, we can better understand the significance of this singular text. What comes to light now is the important revelation that the authors of *JIL* intuitively understood the relationship between the deep drivers of education and the regularities of classroom practice.[83] That is to say, they recognized that in order to significantly change the one, they had to make equally weighty changes to the other. Because of this breakthrough, *JIL* anticipated, by years, many innovations that have become commonplace in both mainstream and faith-based education circles, such as worldview-driven education, thematic units, project-based learning, differentiated instruction, communities of learning, and developmentally appropriate pedagogy.

The Problem with *Joy*

JIL was a conceptual framework document that contained a well-constructed, twenty-two-page exposition of educational aims, curriculum design, pedagogy, and overall rationale, plus about 600 pages of themes, topics, and activity ideas loosely organized around four broad categories, all packaged together in a three-ring binder. It was a text replete with vision and activity ideas.

Given the popularity of *JIL*, it seems safe to conclude that Christian educators from within and without the Neo-Calvinist tradition of education were on the hunt for an alternative Christian curriculum at this time. Few of them, however, anticipated how difficult it would be to implement the vision embodied by *JIL and* expressed through its unique purpose, process, and project.

Historically, the most significant aspect of *JIL* was its interpretation of education's purpose as a way of life. The "human calling" from God to "let there be humans," to live a life of service, was cited as the deepest meaning and context for all learning. This represented a significant but subtle shift away from the more popular understanding of Christian education as the cultivation of a Christian mind. *JIL*'s emphasis on rooting all learning in confessional knowledge—knowing who you are in relationship to God and the task God has called you to take up in life—was not what occupied the attention of most teachers who bought the text. All their energy was directed at the successful teaching of a theme-based curriculum using a learner-sensitive pedagogy. The ultimate goal of educating students into a life of service was simply out of reach for all but the most innovative and reform-minded teachers.

The fact that *JIL* was not meant to be a textbook intensified the challenges for the teachers who used it. First, there was the challenge regarding the material to be learned. The writers of *JIL* set out to "restructure the contents of the children's learning experiences themselves, so they might look at life from a biblical perspective." To accomplish this goal they introduced a promising new way to reorganize the entire curriculum for grades 1–3. They arranged all curricular content around the four created realms: the physical realm of the earth/universe, the realm of plants, the realm of animals, and the realm of human society/culture.

Each realm was divided into easily recognized subtopics, and within these the authors provided list upon list of briefly described sub-themes and activity ideas but nothing more. The authors could have fleshed out their content model, but they chose not to organize the material according to grade level or provide sample units and lesson plans. Their reluctance to be more prescriptive was driven by their conviction that student ability cannot be ascribed to arbitrary grade levels. In theory, it made perfect sense to leave teachers with the responsibility to construct plans that met the needs of their specific group of students. Unfortunately, many teachers who were intrigued by the CDC's approach were unable to make this leap. The program of learning contained in *JIL* came to them like a giant jigsaw puzzle without any picture on the box. Many teachers could do little more than insert selected activity ideas into their normal classroom routines. Even seasoned teachers struggled to make the quantum leap from teaching a traditional subject-based curriculum to the reframed, thematic program of learning that they were encouraged to adopt using *JIL*.

The authors of *JIL* eventually realized that teachers needed more than a roughly hewn curriculum framework made up of loosely connected themes, topics, and activity ideas in order to reimagine their programs of learning. Teachers needed deeper insights into theme-based content as well as actual examples of activity-based and project-based unit/lesson plans. Equally important, their success depended on the support of a collaborative learning community in their school setting. To sum up, the first big challenge that teachers faced was the content problem: the *JIL* binder did not provide everything that teachers needed to implement the redesigned curriculum it envisioned.

But there was as second major challenge as well. As indicated earlier, the authors correctly assumed that to properly implement the manual's redesigned curriculum, teachers would have to move away from their traditional, teacher-centred approach and adopt a pedagogy that balanced teacher control with student responsibility. Here, too, the bar was set too high for many teachers, even though *JIL* outlined the broad contours of this pedagogy and featured many activities where students clearly had more ownership of their learning. Most teachers who tried to implement *JIL* could not completely let go of their traditional, formal, teacher-centred style of teaching. The adoption of an informal, more student-friendly pedagogy proved to be an even greater challenge than the task of reframing curricular content. On this front, too, teachers desperately needed in-class coaching and a sympathetic school culture to help them switch over to a fundamentally new way of teaching and learning.

The challenges described above embody a recurring conundrum for curriculum reform visionaries. If their reforms are too radical, even sympathetic teachers are unable to take the necessary giant step forward to achieve them. Alternatively, when reformers propose the kind of incremental changes that classroom teachers can manage, substantive reform never seems to arrive.

Six years after *JIL* was published, Jean Olthuis put out a follow-up text in an effort to help resolve the difficulties teachers encountered with the original manual. She titled her book *Teaching with "Joy": Implementing Integrated Education in the Classroom* (TWJ).[84] Her manual came too late for those teachers who, by this time, had either gone back to their former ways of teaching or had adopted portions of *JIL* without making any wholesale changes in their approach. In the preface to this second manual, Olthuis admits that the introduction to *JIL* had not been specific enough on two fronts: it had failed to give teachers an adequate overview of the manual, and it had failed to show them how to flesh out an integrated unit within the classroom. These frank admissions were something of an understatement since her "clarification volume" runs to 180 pages.

On the bright side, *TWJ* provided teachers with an expanded set of planning categories. The text still stopped short of offering a model for planning, but Olthuis named and partially described planning elements that would eventually become commonplace in CSC. For example, her overview included a discussion that featured the development of a rationale and major themes, much like the notion of the conceptual statement that Geraldine Steensma[85] and Harro Van Brummelen popularized at about the same time. There was also a section for writing out aims and goals as well as a list and description of topics that is reminiscent of a scope and sequence. The overview made much of planning activities, for it is here that the teacher specifically planned ways to encourage student responsibility for learning and tracked how the perspectives of the various subjects would be integrated. The overview also included topics on planning skill development and student assessment.

To conclude, it is significant to note that *TWJ* makes exclusive use of the term "education for discipleship" to describe the preferred way of life that Christians are called to live. In *JIL* discipleship appears as one of four or five biblical terms that one could use to identify this life. Given the fact that CSC educators in the 1980s and 1990s often used education for discipleship to describe the aim of Christian education, a case could be made that *JIL* was the second source of its inspiration, Wolterstorff's 1966 speech being the first.[86]

There are, however, compelling reasons not to identify *JIL* as a source of education for discipleship. Arnold De Graaff told me that he would never have promoted a term like "education for discipleship" because discipleship is one of those concepts that conjures up a specific set of behaviours that easily lead to yet another dualism in our thinking. Anne Tuininga, another major contributor to the development of *JIL*, remembers many things about the significance of this text, but she has no memory of the term "education for discipleship." Jean Olthuis is no longer with us, so she cannot speak to the matter. One year prior to the release of *TWJ*, the Curriculum Development Center released its first *Joy in Learning* newsletter. That newsletter featured an educational vision called Education for Discipleship written by the CDC's new executive director Tom Malcolm. It is quite possible that this vision statement influenced Olthuis's decision to use that term to represent "the life God calls humans to live."

The key phrase in *JIL's* purpose statement says, "help students take up their human calling." What exactly did "help" mean? Minimally, "help" meant giving students a deeper confessional knowledge of the scope and depth of their service to God. "Help" also meant the provision of "a view of life." The question is, did it also mean "help them to live that life" inside and outside of school? That connotation cannot be determined with certainty. Wolterstorff used the phrase "equip the child for the life of discipleship" in his 1966 speech. *JIL* used "help" in the same way that Wolterstorff used "equip"; both referred to the acquisition of a particular kind of knowing. But Wolterstorff plainly said education for discipleship implied more than a view of life; it was a life that students were to embody in the present as well as the future, both in school and outside of school.

Finally, one is tempted to think that *JIL* was so wrapped up in its effort to articulate an alternative way to organize curricular content and define the roles of teacher and student that it lost track of the fact that the life Jesus modelled is the whole point of education. If the human calling to live this life was meant to be the new organizing principle for structuring the curriculum and defining the roles of student, teacher, and school, then why was there no attention paid to justice, mercy, and care which define that life?

JIL's attributes certainly outweighed its faults for many educators. Nearly four hundred binders were sold within three months of its release in 1973; the remaining six hundred copies of the first printing were gone within three years. Five hundred more copies were sold in a second printing. CSC teachers bought the bulk of these binders, but copies were also obtained by teachers and schools in Mennonite, Pentecostal, and Lutheran school systems in Canada and the United States and by schools from as far away as India, Australia, Bolivia, and Venezuela. Clearly, there was a worldwide hunger for a more authentic experience of Christian education. We can only imagine what influence this singular text and its grandiose vision might have had on CSC if it had received more widespread support.

CHAPTER 5

The Remarkable Story of the Joy in Learning Curriculum Development and Training Centre (CDC)

Timeline

1973 Fall	The CDC is created by four contributors to *Joy in Learning, Vol. 1*.
1974 June	The AACS takes ownership of CDC, appoints Arnold De Graaff as director, and hires three long-term/part-time curriculum research/writers.
1975 Jan	The CDC receives a substantial gift to pursue its work.
1976 June	Arnold De Graaff leaves the CDC to teach full time at the ICS.
1976 Oct	The AACS officially drops the CDC but continues to offer it space and office support.
1976 Nov	The CDC's big donor refuses to fund further projects.
1976 Fall	The CDC adopts a board of directors and continues as an independent organization.
1978 Sept	The CDC hires Agnes Struik and adds classroom consulting as a service.
1981	The CDC and the Canadian Curriculum Council fail to form a partnership.
1982 July	Founding member Jean Olthuis leaves.
1985 Fall	Founding member Anne Tuininga leaves.
1990	The CDC is officially dead.

What You Don't Know about Your Tradition Could Kill It

The Joy in Learning Curriculum Development and Training Centre (CDC), which existed from roughly 1970 to 1990, authored the most extraordinary chapter for curriculum reform in the history of Neo-Calvinist education in Canada. This claim will no doubt puzzle many current Canadian Neo-Calvinist school (CSC) teachers because they have never heard of the CDC and know nothing about its publications. They may be even more astonished by my additional assertion, that unless they both understand and build on the CDC's legacy of curriculum reform, CSC and its vision of alternative education stands in grave danger of stagnating into a dead traditionalism. I make these provocative statements because I am convinced that the current generation of CSC educators cannot chart a purposeful course into the future for the Neo-Calvinist school movement if they do not know where their tradition has already journeyed and what it has and has not accomplished.

The CDC's story, more than any other, provided the impetus for my decision to write this book. It was also the most emotionally difficult chapter to write. As I look back on the history of Neo-Calvinist education in Canada and the CDC's place within that tradition, I am deeply saddened by our inability to communally develop a Reformational approach to curriculum and pedagogy in the service of an education for authentic Christian living.

I knew most of the people who worked at the CDC, and for many years I served on its board of directors. As I conducted the research and reflected on the CDC's history, this phrase kept popping up as a theme for the CDC's narrative: "The thrill of victory and the agony of defeat." These words have been stuck to the walls of my mind ever since they were used to introduce ABC's *Wide World of Sports*, which aired on American television back in 1978. I still wince every time my mind's eye sees that ski jumper's brutal crash at take-off when the announcer said, ". . . and the agony of defeat." The CDC's brief history was punctuated by significant triumphs and brutal setbacks; the memories of them still cause me to swell with hope and shudder in despair. Current and future CSC teachers could learn so much from its story, precisely because of the magnitude of the CDC's successes and setbacks. The same holds true for school reformers of every stripe.

In my view, the CDC stood at the top of the Neo-Calvinist podium for advancements in curriculum reform for many decades, and it may still do so. It set a number of records that no individual or group associated with the CSC tradition has surpassed. For example, the CDC gave the Neo-Calvinist school movement:
- its boldest vision statement and rationale for an integral Christian education;
- its clearest articulation of a pedagogy that harmonizes teacher authority and student responsibility;
- its only reimagined program of studies that reflects a biblical understanding of creation;
- a highly effective model for teacher mentoring.

These substantial contributions were matched by a number of agonizing failures on the part of the CDC and other key stakeholders in the Neo-Calvinist education movement at the time. For example, the CDC staff chose not to follow the precedent set in the development of *Joy in Learning* and involve classroom teachers in their curriculum-writing projects. Second, they could not develop partnerships with other stakeholders in the Neo-Calvinist school movement, thereby limiting the CDC's legitimacy and financial stability. The Ontario Alliance of Christian Schools (OACS) and the AACS must share the blame for this second failure. The leadership of the OACS lacked the insight, vision, and grace to join forces with the CDC and pursue their tradition's most dynamic vision. Although the AACS possessed the vision and the courage to take ownership of the CDC, it could not muster the will or the resources to sustain it. Third, the CDC too often published curriculum materials that were not serviceable to classroom teachers for one or more of the following reasons:
- they assumed a pedagogical prowess that teachers did not possess;
- they did not easily fit into the local school's program of study, and
- they were not always age appropriate or even classroom ready.

This chapter presents the CDC narrative in four sections. The first recounts the actual birth of the CDC and its brief adoption by the AACS. We next reflect on some strategic decisions that the CDC staff made regarding finances and vision that significantly impacted their future. In the third section we briefly sketch out the CDC's history as an independent organization and pay particular attention to the people who worked there. The concluding section reviews the CDC's publishing record. My presentation and critique of the CDC's educational vision appears separately in chapter 7.

An Orphan, Four Mothers, and a New Home

To understand how the Curriculum Development Centre came into being, we must return to the *Joy in Learning* story and look at the extraordinary way it came to be published. In an astonishing display of vision, passion, and entrepreneurship, four contributors to *JIL*—Jean Olthuis, Anne Tuininga, Deborah Steele, and Mary Gerritsma—incorporated a "company" in the fall of 1973 to facilitate the administration, financing, publication, and distribution of 1,000 copies of *JIL*. They named their company the Joy in Learning Curriculum Development and Training Centre (CDC). This fearless foursome did not intend for the CDC to become an actual centre, at least not initially; it was simply a legal entity that provided short-term solutions to some immediate problems, such as the ability to offer tax-deductible receipts. The formation of the CDC also allowed these women to approach supporters, publishers, distributors, and, eventually, purchasers without being perceived as a "fly by night" outfit.

In January 1974 the four "CDC mothers," as I shall affectionately call them, faced financial difficulties, even though 315 of the 1,000 copies of *JIL* had already been sold. To put what happened over the next few years into perspective, I have placed the current value of 1970 dollars in parentheses. In a letter addressed to the board of directors of the AACS and dated January 21, 1974, the CDC mothers requested a short-term loan of $5,000 ($32,000) to pay their bills. They informed the board that the costs to produce and publish *JIL* totalled $13,000 ($86,600). The expected income on the sale of 1,000 copies was $11,000 ($73,250). Consequently, the women were looking at a $2,000 ($13,300) personal loss for all their efforts.

Every time I recall the details of this story, I have to pause, first to acknowledge what dreamers these women were and second to wonder how many teachers today would be willing to make similar sacrifices and commitments for their educational vision. For me, these women are true sources of inspiration because they eagerly embraced both of the daughters of hope that St. Augustine named: righteous Anger at the way things are (the current state of curriculum and pedagogy in their school system) and Courage to see they did not remain that way (by rewriting and partially financing a program of studies).[87]

The fact that these four women sought financial help from the AACS made perfect sense. The AACS had already sponsored or co-sponsored curriculum-writing workshops for at least five years and had contributed considerable resources toward the production of *JIL*. Not only did ICS[88] senior member Arnold De Graaff write large portions of *JIL*, Ada Oegema, an AACS staff member, typed the final draft of the manuscript. In their letter the women acknowledged that had it not been for the support provided by the AACS, *JIL* would never have been completed.

The letter also informed the board about a dream they shared with other SPICE participants concerning a curriculum mega project. *JIL*, they explained, was the first text in a nine-volume curriculum that would reimagine the traditional elementary and secondary program of learning for Christian schools all over the globe. In an appendix attached to their letter, the *JIL* women outlined this ambitious program of integrated learning:

Vol. 1 *Joy in Learning – Integrated Curriculum for Elementary*, grades 1–3
- A curriculum organized by realms: physical, plant, animal, human
- A comprehensive list of activity suggestions

Vol. 2 *Ways of Life – Integrated Curriculum for Elementary*, grades 4–6
- In-depth cultural studies of eight countries: Canada, USA, China, Russia, and one country each from Africa, South America, Asia, and Europe

Vol. 3 *The Number and Shape of Things – Integrated Mathematics Curriculum for Elementary*
- Experiential approach to typical topics: K to Jr. High

Vol. 4 *Artfully Done – Art Curriculum for Elementary*
- Already in experimental form, so no description provided

Vol. 5 *The Nature of Things – An Integrated Science Curriculum for Jr. High*
- Themes: Motion, Energy, Chemistry, Biology

Vol. 6 *A Long Ways to Go – A History Curriculum for Jr. High*
- Past ways of life in the West: from Sumerian to current North American

Vol. 7 *God, Man's Partner – An Integrated Bible Curriculum for Elementary* (part 1)
- Already in experimental form, so no outline given

Vol. 8 *A Holy God and a Holy People: An Integrated Bible Curriculum Elementary* (part 2)
- Joshua, Judges, Leviticus

Vol. 9 *Man in Society – An Integrated Curriculum for the Secondary* School (Part 1)
- Christian perspective developed in nine areas: intimate relationships (marriage, family, friends, sexuality), the Church, education, government, economics, media, health, arts, and urban planning

The CDC mothers told the AACS board that it had taken many contributors five years of summer curriculum-writing workshops to produce *JIL*, and it would take another eight years to complete the remaining eight volumes in this manner. They believed the one-volume-per-year rate of production was feasible due to the fact that volumes two through nine were already in various stages of development. But, they argued, this eight-year time frame was unacceptable because Christian schoolteachers desperately needed a biblically based curriculum as soon as possible. They next proposed a timetable of five years to complete the mega project. The total cost to produce these eight volumes over five years, they estimated, would be $80,000 ($533,000).

The letter also included a rough two-stage plan for the production of the second volume on cultural studies by May 1975. Stage one could take place in July and August of 1974. The CDC mothers planned to gather as many teachers as possible to research the eight selected cultures to be studied in volume two, *Ways of Life*. This work would again be coordinated by Arnold De Graaff and Jean Olthuis. Stage two would run from September to March or April. During this time a small team of three would continue to research, write, and edit the manuscript until it was print-ready. The members of this team would include Jean Olthuis at two-thirds time, Anne Tuininga at one-third time, and Mary Gerritsma at one-third time. The plan proposed that all of the summer participants would receive remuneration from their school boards. They offered no suggestions about who would pay the writing team the $12,000 ($80,000) to complete stage two.

Finally, the letter informed the board of directors that the four women intended to approach them and the board of trustees in the near future to ask them this critical question: who should parent this orphan project moving forward? Even though the women believed this decision belonged to the AACS trustees, they had the chutzpah to define the board's options for them and indicate which one they most preferred. They said the AACS could a) take over the mega project, in which case the CDC would become irrelevant and cease to exist, b) give full responsibility for the project to the CDC, which would then become an independent organization, or c) provide the CDC with half of the funds or $40,000 ($267,000) for the mega project, spread over a five-year period. After this period of subsidy, the CDC would become fully independent.

The CDC mothers clearly preferred the third scenario. Their vision was not just bold; it was also novel. They imagined a curriculum-development centre that was neither a department in a large publishing firm committed to making a profit on generic textbooks nor a service operated by a school board or teachers' union to meet the specific needs of teachers. The CDC would be an independent, non-profit organization owned by visionary teachers and committed to the design of an alternative program of studies shaped by a Reformational worldview.

Not long after they received their loan, the CDC mothers penned their second letter, on February 11. As promised they sent the letter to the board of trustees as well as to the board of directors. In it they reiterated their position that it was up to the AACS to decide who should adopt the mega curriculum-writing project. They also restated their preference for the option where the AACS would give the CDC the ownership of the project and provide it with a gradually decreasing level of support over five years.

The matter was decided in June 1974 when the AACS officially adopted the CDC as its second project, the Institute for Christian Studies being the first. The board appointed ICS senior member Arnold De Graaff to be the CDC's director at one fifth of his position. They also hired Jean Olthuis and Anne Tuininga from the original four women entrepreneurs as long-term, part-time curriculum developers. Their combined contracts equaled just over two full-time positions. Various other people would be signed to short-term contracts as they were needed to work on the remaining eight projects.

With the stroke of a pen, the CDC became a centre for curriculum development and training with its own paid staff. There is no record to reveal what the AACS boards thought they were doing when they acquired the CDC! Did they imagine this was a five-year commitment to complete a particular project, or had they made a long-term commitment to curriculum reform? What role did they think the CDC would play vis-a-vis NUCS and the OACS? Did they see the CDC as a service organization that would step into the breach of a leadership vacuum in NUCS and chart the way forward for curriculum development for CSC, or did they picture the CDC as a radical purveyor of a curriculum orientation that resonated with teachers who were sympathetic to the Reformational Movement? In the end what they envisioned did not actually matter because the arrangement came undone in a mere twenty-eight months.

To Leap Tall Buildings in a Single Bound

Arnold De Graaff had a clear vision for the CDC, which Jean Olthuis and Anne Tuininga whole-heartedly adopted. To pursue this vision, De Graaff led his colleagues to the crossroads where all serious curriculum reformers must make a critical choice: should they take the high-risk path that leads to substantive change or the low-risk route that results in curricular improvement? If they choose the former, they commit to leap-frogging conventional practices in one giant jump, but they risk failure to make any lasting difference. If they decide to play it safe, they are likely to generate incremental reforms, but not the hoped-for bigger goal. This dilemma has also been described this way: must reformers step outside "the box" in order to implement a major change, or can they achieve their goals by working within the given structures?[89]

The Reformational perspective held the answer within itself. It assumed that an integral, alternative Christian education could not be implemented in a context shaped by secular assumptions. Consequently, they had to tackle two daunting challenges. The first was to critique the foundational assumptions that upheld every aspect of contemporary education. The second was to reimagine and replace them with an alternative.

No one else in the Neo-Calvinist education universe was willing to walk down this path of radical reform, even though it was the most congruent with the assumptions that defined their tradition. This is why the CDC staff held out the most hope for this tradition of education. They alone aspired to embrace both beautiful daughters of hope: Anger and Courage. They were courageous enough to cast aside established practices and reimagine a new educational experience. However, as we are about to discover, an overdose of confidence and a string of ill-advised strategic decisions greatly inhibited their ability to carry out this daunting mission.

Two factors contributed to the CDC's short tenure as a project of the AACS: money and isolation. There was never enough of the first, and there was too much of the second. Let us first consider why money matters led to the premature dissolution of the relationship between the AACS and the CDC. Afterward, we will explore how the CDC's strategic planning contributed to its isolation from other stakeholders in the Neo-Calvinist education movement and limited the relevance of the materials it would eventually publish.

The AACS initially set an annual budget of $30,000 ($200,000) for the CDC, which was very generous in light of the CDC mothers' projection that the writing of the second volume in the mega project could be done in a year at a cost of $12,000 ($80,000), and the price tag to develop the remaining eight volumes over five years would come in just under $90,000 ($600,000).

This budget contained critical caveats, however. The AACS expected the CDC staff to raise as much of this money as possible and from sources outside those already supporting the association. This expectation was wishful thinking at best. At worst, the AACS board saddled the CDC staff with an impossible combination of tasks, namely curriculum development, fundraising, and program administration. The budget also suggests that the AACS was willing to risk spending money it did not have.

Within months the CDC's financial situation greatly improved when an anonymous donor gave the AACS $25,000 ($166,500), so the CDC could publish the follow-up volume to *JIL*.[90] This donation amounted to more than double the money that the CDC mothers estimated it would cost to produce the *Ways of Life* volume. The gift also drastically reduced the AACS's costs to $5,000 ($33,500) for one budget cycle, and it effectively delayed the need for the CDC staff to fundraise. This infusion of money could have led to the timely publication of the second volume in the series, but instead it tempted the CDC staff to bite off more than they could chew.

The gift prompted the CDC staff to request a revised budget for the 1975/76 fiscal year, so they could expand their work. The AACS board of directors approved their request in January 1975. De Graaff immediately hired Harry Fernhout and Don Sinnema to work full time on the Bible curriculum volume. Trudy Baker was hired part-time to work on the mathematics volume.

This new budget covered the period from January 1975 to June 1976 and totalled $78,000 ($520,250). Responsibility for raising the $53,000 ($353,500) not covered by the donation was to be shared 50/50 by the AACS and the CDC. The new budget had significant implications for the CDC staff, who put themselves on the hook to raise $26,500 ($176,750).

Eleven months later, and just prior to the beginning of the new fiscal year, the CDC staff officially shared two festering concerns with the AACS board of governors regarding their working conditions. First, they reported that their administrative, clerical, and fundraising duties seriously impacted their curriculum-development work. They appealed to the AACS to significantly reduce, if not eliminate, these responsibilities. Second, they expressed frustration over their lack of basic administrative supports, such as an office telephone, filing system, mailing list, secretarial help, a newsletter, and a fundraising campaign.

In this same submission, the CDC outlined two scenarios for moving ahead. Both were overly optimistic because they significantly increased the AACS's financial contribution to the CDC. In one the AACS/CDC partnership would continue, but the annual budget would jump from $30,000 ($200,000) to $70,000 ($466,200). On top of this whopping increase, this scenario stated that any growth in the AACS's financial situation should be applied to the CDC as well as to the ICS. The other scenario cast the CDC as an independent organization, responsible for its own administration and fundraising, while the AACS would provide a gradually decreasing annual grant for a number of years until the CDC could become financially self-sufficient. This option resurrected the preferred arrangement outlined by the CDC mothers in their letters to the board two years earlier. Incredibly, the AACS agreed to the first scenario and adopted a budget of $70,000 ($466,200) for the CDC in the coming fiscal year. Given the well-known challenges of raising donations, it appears everyone had high hopes that the donor who had previously given the CDC a large gift would do so again.[91]

The CDC's concerns and scenarios were submitted to the board of governors for a second time on September 1, 1976, in anticipation of an October meeting where the AACS board of trustees planned to review the AACS/CDC relationship. On October 6, the trustees informed the CDC staff that the AACS could no longer maintain its relationship with the CDC. Neither could the AACS provide the CDC with an annual grant to gradually wean it off its primary source of income. The one and only reason for this parting of ways, the board declared, was the AACS's inability to fund the CDC. The decision, they insisted, had nothing to do with the CDC's vision and purpose. To demonstrate their goodwill toward the CDC, the trustees offered the CDC office space and some modest administrative support in perpetuity.

Money matters clearly played a dominant role in the AACS/CDC relationship, and the lack of money eventually ended their relationship. But a second major theme also defines this period in the CDC's history, and it concerns the evolution of the CDC's educational vision and strategic plan.

The CDC mothers believed that the Canadian Neo-Calvinist tradition of education needed a redesigned program of learning, where every area of study was interpreted through a biblical worldview. This need was immediate, and they had a five-year plan to address it. Although they understood that the development of an alternative program of learning required a retooling of the philosophical foundations of the curriculum, they did not think this prior task was a significant hurdle. Perhaps they felt the philosophical framework developed in *JIL* was sufficient.

De Graaff took a different position. Any strategy to quickly crank out Reformational curriculum materials put the proverbial cart before the horse. That is, it wrongly placed current teacher needs ahead of vision. In De Graaff's view, no matter how desperate teachers were for a curriculum inspired by a Reformational perspective, the CDC had to first reconstruct the philosophical and anthropological underpinnings of a Reformational philosophy of education. Only when this framework was in place could the CDC develop a new program of learning. The framework that appeared in *JIL* was just a beginning; much more had to be done to reimagine the organization of curriculum and the roles of learner and teacher. De Graaff understood what few others in the Neo-Calvinist tradition at that time did not, that a new framework for curriculum reform had to include *pedagogical reform*.

De Graaff's educational vision significantly raised the bar for Neo-Calvinist educators. A Christian perspective was no longer enough, nor was a reformation of the sciences or even an alternative curriculum design. For De Graaff a Reformational philosophy of education had to demonstrate the coherence between curriculum design, the human calling to live a godly way of life, and engaged learners. The pursuit of De Graaff's vision effectively ruled out the possibility of the CDC becoming a service organization tasked with publishing much-needed curriculum materials, but few supporters ever realized this. Under his leadership, the CDC would take on the role of a research and development organization, whose principal job was to construct an alternative philosophy of education. Even though it would be necessary to flesh out this philosophy in curriculum exemplars, the immediate relevance of them for the classroom was not a top priority for De Graaff.

As a first step down the path of radical reform, the CDC staff significantly redefined their overall task. They decided to only develop three of the remaining eight volumes in the alternative program of learning. In addition to the already published volume one, *Joy in Learning*, they planned to complete volume two, *Ways of Life*, volume three, *Biblical Studies* (formally vol. 8) and volume 4, *The Number and Shape of Things* (formally vol. 3). The strategic decision to drastically downsize the program of learning was consistent with De Graaff's vision. Once completed, these four volumes would address all grade levels of elementary education and provide a variety of exemplars that demonstrated how to implement the alternative philosophical framework.

The CDC staff made a similar decision regarding the contents of the cultural studies volume. As noted earlier, this volume was supposed to investigate different ways of life from all over the world: Canada, the United States, China, Russia, and one country each from Africa, South America, Asia, and Europe. The CDC staff decided to reduce the number of cultures to three. That decision was consistent with their mission to develop a philosophical framework as their first priority. They did not need nine examples to validate their approach. Unfortunately, all subsequent important decisions they made concerning this volume defy explanation.

We learned earlier that just weeks before the AACS board took ownership of the CDC, the four CDC mothers provided them with a two-stage plan and a budget for completing the cultural studies volume in one year. Their plan mimicked the process they used to develop *JIL*. The first stage was to be carried out by a group of teachers working under the guidance of De Graaff and Olthuis. This group would do the initial planning and data gathering during a summer session reminiscent of a SPICE workshop. A CDC writing team would then synthesize all of this material and write up the final project.

When Olthuis and Tuininga actually started work on the cultural studies volume as CDC employees, they inexplicably departed from this plan. First, they cut out the participation of teachers. This decision set an unfortunate precedent; the CDC staff would never solicit the participation of teachers to help them design and write curriculum.

Two other critical decisions are equally puzzling. It would have made imminent sense for the CDC staff to develop the Canada unit as their first cultural study, since the Canadian way of life was the most familiar to them and work on this unit had already begun. A curriculum project that focused on Canada would have also resonated well with any donor willing to fund the development of a follow-up text to *JIL* and would be immediately beneficial to teachers. The CDC staff, however, decided not to make the Canada unit their first priority. Instead, they inexplicably chose to simultaneously develop units on Japan and Kenya, two obscure and randomly chosen cultures that they knew virtually nothing about, had never visited, and would be a challenge for most teachers to incorporate into their programs of study.

The size of the cultural studies units also changed dramatically. We can safely assume that the original volume, which would have contained nine cultural studies, was meant to be comparable in size to *Joy in Learning*, which dedicated about twenty pages to unpack the conceptual framework and nearly 600 pages to content. Even if the space needed to articulate the philosophical, anthropological, and pedagogical underpinnings a cultural studies volume required fifty pages, the nine study guides would have been roughly sixty-five pages in length. That number seems more than adequate to provide an overview for each unit, the criteria for content selection, a rationale for the unit's relevance, summaries of the important topics and relevant issues, a set of key questions for students to engage, suggestions for major assignments and projects, and a description of recommended teaching and assessment strategies.

The actual work done on the second volume led to something quite different. The Kenya and Japan units took on huge, textbook-size proportions. When completed, the Kenya text alone totaled 360 pages while the Japan unit came in at 330 pages. These "units" emerged as hybrids. They were part research paper, part teacher guide, and part student textbook. Curiously, the framework sections in the Japan and Kenya units were similar in size and content to the one that appeared in *JIL*. The large size of these texts does not, therefore, reflect a deepened and expanded philosophical framework but rather expansive coverage of content details. It appears that the

Japan and Kenya units took on lives of their own as cultural studies rather than serving as exemplars of a maturing curriculum orientation.

So far we have taken a high-altitude view of the CDC's life as an AACS project. The time has come to get closer to ground level and focus on the principal staff members. Several sources provide us with insight into the personal experiences of the people who worked at the CDC. These sources include staff-meeting minutes, memories shared in recent interviews, and an unpublished paper[92] written by Agnes Struik, who joined the CDC staff in 1979 as a teacher consultant.

De Graaff was clearly the visionary force behind the CDC, but he had to lead his staff as a one-fifth, part-time executive director. His primary role was to conduct research into the foundations of psychology and develop graduate-level courses at the ICS. Obviously, this arrangement did not provide him with many opportunities to further develop the CDC's educational philosophy. These restrictions on De Graaff partially explain why the development of a new philosophical framework did not advance much beyond what appears in *JIL*.

Olthuis and Tuininga worked on the Japan and Kenya units as researchers and writers. They were educators, not philosophers; they could apply a vision, not craft one. By their own admission, they were young, brash, and idealistic as they pursued a Reformational transformation of education. They imagined themselves as participants in a bigger movement to turn the world upside down and proclaim the Lordship of Christ over all things. They confessed to their colleague, Struik, that they believed they had all the answers. "It was like we had discovered the truth for the first time. It was liberating. It was empowering."[93] The following quote summarizes their experience:

> It seemed as if not one stone could be left unturned. We studied the history of education, contemporary education, we visited schools, went to England and checked out the British primary schools. We were always trying to sort out the underlying belief that motivated a way of teaching and learning and how it lined up with a reformational world and life view. All assumptions were brought under the scrutiny of the reformational perspectival glasses.[94]

Tuininga remembers her time working on the Japan and Kenya units with a great deal of fondness and personal satisfaction. She recalls it as a wonderful daily opportunity to learn fascinating things about distant lands and the people who lived there. At no time in our interview did she mention feeling obligated to the generous donor who provided her with this opportunity and fully expected the CDC to provide useful curriculum for CSC teachers.

A second disagreement over vision took place inside the walls of the ICS in the late spring of 1974, and the CDC paid a huge price as a consequence. The senior members of the ICS were embroiled in a debate over the ICS's identity and the role of its senior member professors. De Graaff's one-fifth position as the CDC's director was a focal point in the debate. The majority of senior members believed the practical work of curriculum development was out of step with a research Institute. De Graaff and fellow senior member James Olthuis believed there could be no good theory without practice and no good practice without theory. They argued that in addition to the ICS's task to rethink the foundations of the various academic disciplines, it should prepare Christian teachers, lawyers, artists, therapists, and businesspeople. In the end, De Graaff and Olthuis lost the fight, and De Graaff was forced to decide whether to remain as the full-time senior member in psychology or fully commit to the CDC.

De Graaff chose to pursue his work at the ICS. Consequently, the CDC had to find a new executive director as well as a new source of income. Even though he was no longer an employee of the organization, De Graaff remained just off stage for future CDC operations. He continued to be the guiding light for Anne Tuininga and Jean Olthuis. In his interview with me, De Graaff revealed that he now regrets his decision to focus his career on psychology, and he wished he had chosen education instead.

The two years and four months that the AACS operated the CDC were characterized by several stark contrasts. In the beginning, the CDC had financial backing from two sources; at the end there were none. The CDC staff possessed a profound understanding of what was wrong with the current paradigm of education, and they were willing to embrace both of hope's beautiful daughters when others were not, yet they underestimated the task they had chosen for themselves and overestimated their ability to achieve it. They were idealistic and zealous, but they somehow got sidetracked from their primary objective to develop an alternative philosophical framework. They chose to work outside the CSC structures provided by NUCS and the OACS, but they made the strategic mistake to pursue curricular and pedagogical reform with no specific students, teachers, classrooms, or schools in mind. Much was written, but nothing got published.

The loss of a parent organization that could fund its operations proved to be the undoing of the CDC, although it somehow survived for another fourteen years as an independent entity. The next section surveys that period of time.

One is the Loneliest Number

In the aftermath of the AACS decision to let the CDC go, the CDC staff faced some big questions. How could the CDC carry on? Should the CDC carry on? If the CDC could somehow survive, what role should it play? Incredibly, it transitioned rather easily into an independent organization. It adopted a structure similar to that of a Neo-Calvinist school run by a school society. The CDC (like a school) became the responsibility of a dues-paying membership (like a parent society that elected a board of governors from among its ranks). CSC teachers sympathetic to curriculum reform made up the bulk of this membership. Their modest membership fees, coupled with many small donations received from people of diverse occupations, provided the CDC staff with an annual income of around $30,000 ($192,000). This was a significant amount of money, but it was not enough to meaningfully support the work of three part-time employees. Still, the CDC managed to stay afloat.

Even as an independent entity, the CDC's credibility was always suspect because of its affiliation with the AACS/ICS. Those in the Dutch Neo-Calvinist community who thought the views of those who taught at the ICS were theologically unorthodox at best, and possibly heretical at worst, were also suspicious of the CDC's approach. The CDC could not survive the combined lack of money and credibility.

During the CDC's fourteen-year life as an independent organization, approximately thirty different people served on its board of governors, and at least twenty people worked on its staff as researcher/writers, administrators, editors, or development officers.[95] The mainstay employees were Tom Malcolm, Anne Tuininga, Jean Olthuis, Harry Fernhout, and Agnes Struik. Who were these people? Were they mavericks? Rogues on the loose? Some within the Neo-Calvinist education tradition thought so, but this caricature is grossly inaccurate. The CDC staff were people of vision who had a passion for Christian education. Each was willing to make significant personal sacrifices for the sake of advancing the cause of educational reform. They were people of character, and they were also "characters," who persevered through the most challenging work conditions, which sometimes meant not receiving a paycheque. They embodied, to an extreme, the commitment to cultural transformation that characterizes the Canadian Neo-Calvinist school movement as a whole. The brief summaries that follow offer just a peek into the personal narratives that constitute the CDC story.

Tom Malcolm was hired to replace De Graaff as executive director shortly before the AACS cut the CDC loose. Malcolm had been introduced to Reformational thinking as a student at Geneva College in Beaver Falls, PA, where he took courses from Pete Steen. Steen was a faculty member at Trinity Christian College in Chicago, the same school where De Graaff began his teaching career. Known for his charismatic personality, Steen was also an itinerant professor who taught unlisted courses in rented spaces at several small Christian colleges like Geneva. Malcolm was one of the many American students who, in response to Steen's influence, came to study at the ICS in the early 1970s and settled in Canada as a landed immigrant.

Malcolm recalls that the AACS board provided two options for ending its relationship with CDC. CDC staff could "shut the lights out right away" or "soldier on until the projects under way were completed." They chose the latter option. He recalls De Graaff telling him that his job as director was to keep the ship afloat until the CDC could put out everything that had been written in some usable format. De Graaff's view by that time, Malcolm remembers, was "that the responsibility for developing curriculum lay with the associations of Christian schools and education departments of colleges. CDC materials would go out as examples of what could be done which others could build on or not."[96] Unfortunately, for CSC teachers, their district associations were ill prepared to take up that mantle. At one point the CDC tried to form a partnership with the Canadian Curriculum Counsel, a NUCS-appointed body responsible for funding selected curriculum projects that arose from CSC teacher ranks.[97] Their failure to collaborate epitomized the tradition's biggest weakness, which Prinsen dubbed as that old Dutch disease.[98]

Malcolm did not disappoint. During his four years as director, he oversaw the publication of six major projects. The CDC also began to publish a quarterly newsletter at this time. The first three issues of the newsletter featured a restatement of the CDC's philosophy of curriculum that first appeared in *Joy in Learning* five years earlier. According to Agnes Struik, Malcolm was the one who recast this vision. The details of this vision statement are analyzed in the next chapter.

Harry Fernhout and Don Sinnema were hired to write Bible curriculum shortly after the CDC received a major gift. Both were second-generation Dutch immigrants to Canada and members of the ICS's first graduation class. De Graaff was not concerned about the fact that neither had any teaching experience; what mattered foremost was their Reformational acuity. Both men, had flourished under the tutelage of professors John Vander Stelt and John Van Dyk at Dordt College and their time studying with ICS senior member Jim Olthuis. Fernhout and Sinnema had the theological background to write specialized commentaries for teachers that reflected the covenant-history perspective of exegeting the Old Testament.[99] They were tasked with the further development of the Bible study program, which had emerged from SPICE. Since work had already been done on Genesis and Exodus, they were asked to write study guides for the books of Joshua and I, II Kings. Both projects were ready for publication when the AACS let the CDC go.

After they completed their projects for the CDC, Fernhout and Sinnema went on to complete their doctorates. After receiving his, Sinnema took a position teaching theology at Trinity Christian College, and he anchored that program for many years until his retirement. Fernhout eventually returned to teach at the ICS as the senior member in education foundations. Later in his career, he served as the president at the ICS and at The King's University in Edmonton.

Fernhout did not immediately pick up his academic career upon the completion of his graduate studies in 1983. He first served for three years as the CDC's director. This was largely a rescue mission as the CDC staff was in deep turmoil. Jean Olthuis, the CDC's principal researcher and writer, had left a year before. The new director, Sally Armour-Wolton, did not get on well with the remaining two staff members, Tuininga and Struik. The CDC's board replaced Armour-Wolton with Fernhout, but his arrival did not prevent the worn-down Tuininga from finally calling it quits. This left Fernhout and Struik as the principal staff members. During Fernhout's tenure as director, the CDC published its last two curriculum projects and the final issues of its newsletter. Fernhout also penned the third, and most expansive iteration of the CDC's vision in the fall 1984 issue of that newsletter. The contents of this historic document are also analyzed in the next chapter.

Jean Olthuis was one of the four women who brought the CDC into existence. Of the four, she had the most teaching experience. Olthuis was the principal researcher and writer on the CDC staff. She was the lead editor of *Joy in Learning*, and she authored the follow-up text, *Teaching with Joy*. Together with Anne Tuininga, she researched the Japan and Kenya units and did the bulk of the writing. She also wrote large sections of the Canada portion of the *Way of Life* project, which was never published. In addition to her curriculum-development work, Olthuis also offered the occasional workshop for classroom teachers interested in using CDC materials, particularly *JIL*. Exhausted, Olthuis took a year leave of absence in July 1982, but she never returned.

Anne Tuininga was also one of the original four mothers. Hailing from Alberta, she attended Chicago's Trinity Christian College, where she studied under De Graaff. Tuininga taught in five different schools in three provinces over a nine-year period, which included a two-year hiatus when she lost her voice. While teaching in the OACS, she participated in De Graaff's SPICE workshops and became excited about his educational vision. Her role at the CDC was to research and write, but she much preferred the research work. Tuininga was the one who usually took responsibility for fundraising. Over the years she also picked up many dangling administrative jobs that were begging for attention. Tuininga worked tirelessly for a decade, most often under extreme conditions and for minimal pay. Yet, when I asked about her CDC days, she never once mentioned the hardships she endured. What stood out in her memory was the fun she had working with Struik and the CDC's educational vision to liberate students in the classroom.

Agnes Struik joined the CDC staff in September of 1978, after the staff accepted her proposal that they hire her as a classroom consultant. It is ironic that Struik became the CDC's longest-serving employee. For most of that time, she was also the face of the organization. Struik brought a much-needed new perspective to the CDC. She agreed with the CDC's call for radical changes in education and society at large, but she was critical of how little attention the CDC paid to "the emotional, social, financial and psychological costs that such changes would require," both for teachers and for CDC staff members.

Struik's understanding of curriculum reform was shaped by her close ties with Geraldine Steensma[100] and Doug Blomberg.[101] Their influences opened her eyes to the weaknesses in the CDC's concept of an "integrated curriculum."[102] She acknowledged that in *JIL*, the CDC had addressed the faith/learning dualism that plagued Christian education, but her colleagues had little understanding of the implementation challenges. She understood that teachers do not learn how to teach thematically and experientially by reading a manual. Neither can someone teach others how to teach a radically different way if they have never done it themselves.

Struik spoke of consulting as a way of walking with teachers. As she worked shoulder to shoulder with teachers in their classrooms, she strived to be as non-threatening, understanding, caring, and compassionate as possible. She believed, if she were to have any success in helping teachers transition away from a traditional to an alternative way of teaching and learning, she would have to "take them where they were at, encourage, validate whatever steps they were taking to make changes . . ."[103] After spending a day with a teacher, Struik would sit down for long hours to write up extensive feedback that she could share with the teacher the following day. Struik called her model of consulting "action/reflection/

redirection." It was a model that, in her words, "put the change process in the hands of the teacher."[104]

Throughout the 1980s, Struik helped dozens of teachers all across Canada and as far away as the United States and Australia. Most were elementary school teachers, but some, (including me), taught at the high school level. She worked not only with teachers from Neo-Calvinist schools but also with teachers from other traditions. Struik's mentoring work gave legs to the CDC's vision. She showed teachers how to take their first steps away from their traditional approach to teaching and adopt a more child-centred pedagogy in conjunction with a thematic organization of the curriculum. When they look back and reminisce about their careers, these teachers consistently refer to the time when Agnes Struik worked with them in their classrooms as the most significant in their development as teachers. There was no leaping over tall buildings, but Struik ignited powerful sparks of hope.

Most CSC classrooms were closed to Struik, however. Some CSC educators disliked De Graaff, and they still thought of the CDC as his organization. Others had no personal axe to grind with De Graaff or the AACS, but they felt threatened by the CDC's notion that the student also had an "office" or a particular God-given task/responsibility. In Reformed thinking, an office implied a domain of authority as well as responsibility and accountability. The traditional notion of in loco-parentis was deeply engrained in the CSC tradition of education: the school was an extension of the home, and the teacher an extension of the parent when it came to educating children. In this model, teachers received all of their authority from the parents, and students had no authority whatsoever; they were passive recipients of their education. Any notion that students had a determinative role in their education was perceived as progressivist nonsense.

Barriers came in other forms as well. Some teachers wanted Struik's help, but they did not have the support of their administrators. Even when they did, often there was no money available to pay Struik's modest fees. There were also principals who wanted Struik to work with their teachers, but the teachers saw no compelling reason to change the way they taught.

Somehow, Struik also found time and energy to write curriculum materials. She contributed significantly to the various segments of the Canada section of *Vol 2 A Way of Life*; her most ambitious project, however, was to update *Joy in Learning*, which was already fifteen years old. Tragically, no one ever benefited from her efforts because the CDC folded before either of these projects could be finished.

By mid-1987 the CDC was little more than a name. It employed Struik part time, but there was no office, and there were no projects in progress and little money. The dream to publish texts that embodied a new integrated educational vision was all but extinguished. The CDC died quietly in 1990. Struik sent the cheque that paid off the CDC's final creditor, and all that remained of the CDC fit inside a couple of boxes that she kept stored in her basement. These valuable archives include folders full of reports and minutes from the board, staff memos and reports, financial statements, correspondence, unfilled book orders, and even some uncashed donation cheques. She graciously let me use these materials when writing this book.

Publish and then Perish

The CDC published a total of twelve texts during its lifetime. Of these, seven combined to form the four surviving volumes of the alternative program of learning that the CDC mothers had described to the AACS board of governors. In addition to *Vol 1 Joy in Learning*, the CDC published the Kenya and Japan units of *Vol 2 Ways of Life*, the studies of Joshua, I & II Kings, and I & II Samuel that formed *Vol 3 Biblical Studies*, and a volume on elementary mathematics, entitled *Vol 4 The Number and Shape of Things*. A complete list of CDC publications is provided in Appendix 2.

The CDC did not publish a single text while it was the project of the AACS, although several were in the final stage of editing. The first five years of the CDC's life as an independent organization were relatively good ones because it managed to release seven publications. The next five years were terrible. Only one curriculum project was published, and the CDC came unraveled on multiple levels. Four additional projects that contained roughly 2,000 pages of material were never published. These included book-size studies of Canada's ecology, transportation, and tundra region, plus a major revision of *Joy in Learning*.

The CDC's list of publications comprises a strange body of work. Even if we ignore the outlier texts and only consider the seven curriculum projects, the collection is neither an abbreviated alternative program of studies imagined by the CDC mothers nor a set of exemplars that embody an alternative educational vision, which De Graaff hoped for. Each project exhibits a unique combination of innovations and shortcomings.

The biblical studies projects were well received in CSC and beyond. The writing was strong, rich in detail and exegetical perspective. Those who used these texts considered them far superior to the Bible materials put out by NUCS. The popularity of these texts was enhanced by the fact that they could be easily incorporated into the existing Bible programs and be taught using a traditional pedagogy. The authors were theologians who had never taught, so it is understandable that these projects lacked the interdisciplinary focus and student-centred pedagogy that the CDC promoted. Student activities designed by Olthuis and Tuininga were included in two of these projects, but they did not magically turn these texts into exemplars of a new educational philosophy.

After years of publisher problems, the cultural studies of Japan and Kenya were finally published in 1980 and 1981 respectively. These texts did not advance the development of an alternative educational philosophy either. Their introductory sections basically repeated what had already been stated in *JIL* years earlier. To their credit, the studies on Japan and Kenya offered a holistic approach to understanding a culture and its preferred way of life. The texts suggest that "the study of other cultures presents its own pedagogical requirements . . . to do justice to the way of life of a particular nation . . . we must, first of all, study its society as a whole."[105] As an example, the text encouraged students to not study the physical features of a land in isolation, but in conjunction with the ways people utilized and developed the land.

Both texts develop the key insight that culture exhibits a communal vision of life, which at its foundation is a "confessional vision of life." What people believe in their hearts they confess in their speech and live out in daily life. This view is consistent with the Reformational mantra that "life is religion," meaning humans are created to serve God. However, there is a flaw in the CDC's understanding of culture as an expression of a confessional stance.

The notion of "giving expression" to what a people believes emerges as an "expressed view." Culture is depicted as the collective expressed views of a people concerning a whole host of relationships, such as family life, politics, education, the economy, and so on. Two issues arise from this understanding of culture. First, can we really assume that what people believe in their hearts (what they love most and are committed to) is consistent with what they say they believe? Second, can we state with confidence that a confessional vision of life is identical to a people's actual way of life? It seems rather obvious that people regularly confess one thing and either love and/or live another.

The CDC's intent to offer a holistic approach to the study of a culture and to identify faith as the deep driver of culture is very significant. However, the idea that individuals and communities of faith "give social and cultural expression to their inward mind (or heart)" is a suspect assumption borrowed from the Romantic tradition that plagues the Neo-Calvinist philosophical tradition.[106]

It must be said that even though the CDC's published texts exhibited significant strengths, they did not effectively showcase an alternative orientation to curriculum. Struik's work with teachers made the biggest differences. She helped dozens of teachers shift to a more student-centred pedagogy and a more theme-based curriculum. It was the CDC's newsletter, however, that broadcast the CDC's vision to the widest audience. That story is unpacked in the next chapter.

The Last Word Belongs to Struik[107]

No one can speak with more authority about what the CDC had to offer or the factors that brought it to ruin than Agnes Struik. In her unpublished paper, "The Life Story of CDC," she offers personal and insightful reflections on both topics. We begin with her review of the factors that brought about the CDC's demise.

Struik observes that the CDC staff was stacked with visionaries who had limited to no teaching experience. No one on staff had any business or marketing experience either. The CDC staff knew how to produce curriculum projects, but they had no clue how to sell them. A second factor that brought about the CDC's demise was a lack of funding. After the AACS "cut the apron strings," the CDC did not have the confidence from others in the community who had the means to support it. The CDC's decision to remain unaffiliated with NUCS (later CSI) meant it could not access the funding for Canadian curriculum projects generated by CSC.[108] The staff also lacked an understanding about how change occurs in a school. In this sense, they were insensitive to the CDC's primary audience. Finally, she says, the CDC took an ivory-tower approach to its work and cut itself off from teachers.

Struik says the CDC's best gift to the Neo-Calvinist tradition of education, and to anyone else eager to reform education, was a Reformational approach to pedagogy and curriculum design. This approach broke free from the traditional views of the student and teacher that dominated the CSC. Struik stands firm in her belief that the CDC's educational vision was more than ideas because she saw it embodied in numerous classrooms. The CDC was able to provide this gift of a non-traditional approach, she recalls, because its staff was willing to sacrifice so much and receive so little in return. Had its staff not been people of vision and dedication, the CDC would never have had the impact that it did.

The CDC also showed the Neo-Calvinist education tradition that the kind of transformation it desired was only possible to actualize in a context of risk; teachers needed the freedom to make curricular and pedagogical mistakes.

Publications represent the fourth contribution that the CDC offered. These publications were few in number and contained some major flaws, but, Struik reminds us, they shared a transformative vision of education with educators from all over the world, including England, Germany, the Netherlands, Russia, Africa, Japan, Korea, Australia, New Zealand, the United States, and Canada. In the absence of any kind of leadership from NUCS and the Canadian districts, the CDC offered workshops on unit writing and pedagogy based on the model expressed in *JIL*.

Last, and likely most importantly, the CDC provided consulting services to teachers "at whatever stage they were in their development and encouraged [them] to evaluate themselves and their teaching so they could make the changes they found necessary." The CSC associations are only now making provisions for mentoring programs.

Struik also acknowledges that the CDC made its share of mistakes. She admits the staff had serious issues, but if the CDC had never existed, "our understanding [in CSC] of curriculum, pedagogy, the role of the teacher and the child would not be where it is today." Struik is understandably biased in her assessment of the CDC's significance, but she does not exaggerate.

CHAPTER 6

Vision by Newsletter

Timeline of Key Articles

1978	*Joy in Learning Newsletters No. 1–3,* Education for Discipleship by Malcolm/Staff
1979	*Joy in Learning Newsletter No. 4,* Looking to the Eighties, Wolterstorff
1980	*Joy in Learning Newsletter No. 6,* Strategy for the Eighties, Steensma
1984	*Joy in Learning Newsletter No. 15,* Reaffirming the Vision, Fernhout
1985	*Joy in Learning Newsletter No. 16,* Dialogue on Christian Education, Stronks, Beck, Van Brummelen, Masselink

The Quest for Authenticity and Integrality

The CDC published a quarterly *Joy in Learning* newsletter from the spring of 1978 to the spring of 1985. During that seven-year stretch, it scraped together enough funding to print seventeen out of a possible twenty-eight issues. This newsletter:
- informed readers about the coming and going of staff, and the status of their curriculum projects;
- served as a platform to advertise CDC texts;
- featured analysis of important topics by staff and respected educators in the Dutch Neo-Calvinist community;
- gave voice to the CDC's educational vision.

The newsletter's most important function was to focus the attention of readers on educational vision and its implications for curriculum and pedagogy. The first three issues reiterated the CDC's vision, which initially appeared in the *Joy in Learning* curriculum binder five years earlier. Many readers likely encountered the CDC's vision for the first time in these issues. The most developed and compelling version of the CDC's educational vision appeared six years later in issue fifteen, which came out in the fall of 1984. At least three other newsletters showcased the educational visions of respected colleagues in the Neo-Calvinist tradition. These newsletters are important historical documents because they provide snapshots of the perspectives that defined the CSC tradition during the last quarter of the twentieth century.

Malcolm Interprets De Graaff

Executive Director Tom Malcolm, with advice from his staff, wrote the vision document featured in the first three issues of the CDC's newsletter. His main resource was the introduction to *Joy in Learning*, which De Graaff had written more than five years earlier. As noted in our previous assessment of *JIL*, De Graaf's vision consisted of four interlocking assumptions or principles:

- Our human calling from God to live a life of service is the ultimate purpose of education.
- The impact of this decision on the curriculum appears in two significant ways: 1) all learning is rooted in a confessional level of meaning that clarifies who we are in relation to God, our fellow humans, and other creatures, and 2) content is organized around themes instead of subject disciplines.
- Students are self-forming persons who must respond to this calling in developmentally appropriate ways.
- Teaching as formation must be harmonized with student learning as self-formation.

Mirroring the approach that defined *JIL*, Malcolm built his interpretation of CDC's educational vision upon the foundation of biblical answers to two questions: "What does it mean to be human?" and "How then shall we live?" This vision interpreted Scripture's view of human nature as a call-and-response relationship to the Creator. God calls humans into being, so they might "live a particular way of life," the one Jesus modelled for his disciples.

De Graaf emphasized several key characteristics of this "human calling." It is an "unavoidable calling," that is, it applies to everyone. Contrary to the modern perception, "being religious," is not a choice. What we can choose to do is disobey this calling and adopt a different way of life, but we cannot escape relationship with God. It was also a "calling for people of all ages." De Graaf argued that our human calling did not kick in when we reach some notable point in our lives. We must respond to this calling from the moment we are born until the day we die. Third, this was a "life-encompassing calling." A godly life was not limited to worship, theological orthodoxy, and moral purity. Instead, God called humans to adhere to His Word in every area of life. In summary, we do not live our lives in two domains, one religious and the other secular, but we choose to take our whole lives in one of two directions: obedience or disobedience.

De Graaf's interpretation of human nature and the good life had three significant implications for education. All learning was deepened by the confessional knowledge of who we are in relationship to God, our fellow humans, and all other creatures. Teachers had to treat students as self-forming learners. The curriculum should be organized around themes instead of scientific disciplines.

The CDC's vision statement echoed these principles, but it contained some notable additions and omissions. The most noteworthy of Malcolm's contributions was naming the vision; he called it "Education for Discipleship." This name might have reminded some CDC supporters of Wolterstorff's inspirational speech delivered to NUCS educators in 1966, which marked the first occasion that anyone characterized the purpose of Christian education as the life of discipleship.[109] For most readers of the newsletter, however, this was probably their introduction to the term, as well as to the concept that Christian education went beyond the reinterpretation of every subject area through the lens of a biblical worldview. How many readers realized the CDC's vision expressed a major shift in purpose for their tradition is impossible to know, but it was certainly evident to many.

In addition to naming the vision, Malcolm's document dedicated considerable space to the developmental nature of the human calling. De Graaf argued that students must be allowed to take up their calling at every age, but he did not flesh out what this looked like at different stages of their development.

Malcolm also introduced another new term in the CDC vision statement when he asserted a Christian way of life was the *ordering principle of the curriculum*.[110] This term captured De Graaf's implicit belief that the aim of education must function as the deep driver of the curriculum. This was not exactly a novel idea. For many years, Neo-Calvinist educators had believed their biblical worldview transformed the sciences, even though they only had the vaguest idea about what a reformation of the sciences actually looked like. To explicitly make a way of life the ordering principle of the curriculum was a game changer.

The CDC's decision to do exactly that has historic significance because, through that act, it distanced itself from and stood opposed to both poles of progressivist education. At the humanist end of the spectrum, the desires and preferences of the student served as the ordering principle of the curriculum. At the opposite technicist end, the curriculum was ordered by concerns for social efficiency and the logical structure of the academic disciplines.

Education for discipleship also went beyond the pietist and Christian mind visions that flourished within CSC at the time. The CDC's vision challenged CSC educators to do more than cultivate a morally pure and theologically correct school atmosphere or reinterpret the sciences through the lens of a biblical worldview. Education for discipleship required them to reimagine the purpose of education, the teaching/learning relationship, and the traditional organization of the curriculum. The school had to champion a life of service. Students had to be given the freedom and responsibility to be self-forming, responsible humans at their particular stage of development. Teachers had to put aside their role as sole authority and knowledge dispenser in the classroom and become architects of learning scenarios that utilized thematic units.

The CDC's vision also contained an internal flaw that curtailed its ability to chart a new course for CSC and other Christian education traditions. For reasons that I only partially understand, both De Graaf and Malcolm took an unusual approach when they set out to explain the significance of a biblical vision of life as the ordering principle for the curriculum. They did not, as one might expect, delve into the Bible's portrayal of this way of life. Throughout Scripture this life is characterized by totality terms like *love, justice, mercy, hope, peace,* and *faith*. Each of these terms represents a unique way of summing up this life. To be explicit, the Bible equates a godly way of life with the one exemplified by Jesus Christ. The defining responsibility of every Christian community is to tease out the patterns and principles that characterize this way of life and apply them to their contemporary cultural situation.

Instead of exploring that alternative way of life and its ramifications for education, De Graaf and Malcolm focused on the nature of the calling to be human. They pointed out that the call is unavoidable (it applies to everyone), it is lifelong (it applies all the time), and it is life encompassing (it applies to all human activity). Why did they do that? Why did the attributes of the calling to be human take precedence over the way of life to which the call pointed?

The only explanation that makes sense is to conclude that De Graaf and Malcolm remained captive to their tradition's habit of casting educational visions within a setting of worldview warfare. Two ways of life were undoubtedly pitted against each other at some deep level, but the first priority in the implementation of their educational vision was to win a philosophical battle. Their enemy in that battle was the sacred/secular dualism that had bifurcated Western thinking since the Middle Ages. As reinterpreted by the Enlightenment, this dualism kept Christian education locked in a corner away from the world of education and virtually all other areas of culture making. Although important philosophically, CDC's overriding concern to root out dualist thinking only resulted in a swap of perspectives or views. In other words, education for a "biblical perspective on the curriculum" gave way to education for a "biblical perspective on a way of life." This strategy prevented CDC from moving the Neo-Calvinist tradition of education from a pursuit of "perspective" to "a way of life."

Vision for the 1980s

Issue four of the newsletter came out one year later than scheduled, and it did not bring closure to the CDC's vision statement as originally planned. Instead of illustrating the vision as portrayed in the CDC's curriculum publications, the newsletter featured the text of a speech that Nick Wolterstorff delivered to the CDC's annual membership meeting on September 14, 1979. The speech was entitled "Looking to the Eighties: Do Christian Schools have a Future?" Wolterstorff began by saying the available evidence did not convince him there was a future for Christian schools as purveyors of an alternative brand of education. He briefly cited a couple of situations that gave him hope, such as the flowering of evangelical Christian schools in the American south that were not racist but "authentic Christian schools." He was far less optimistic when he considered the current, complacent condition of "well-established schools," such as those in the Neo-Calvinist tradition.

The future of Neo-Calvinist Christian schools, he contended, depended on their ability to offer an alternative education in the midst of a non-isolationist, secular society. He informed the audience that he did not intend to "engage in prophecy and prognostication," but he intended to set forth the conditions under which this tradition of Christian education might flourish. To begin, he defined the terms "alternative education" and "non-isolationist education."

Wolterstorff reminded his audience that their tradition of education was established for the specific purpose of offering an alternative education, which meant giving their students a Christian worldview. This Christian worldview was radically different from the one typically promoted in public schools, and it went far beyond other traditions of Christian education that stressed theological orthodoxy and moral purity. From the beginning the Reformed community exhibited a "passionate concern with wholeness, with integrity, with the totality of things . . ." What they were saying was this: "The Christian gospel does not speak just to our theological thought. It does not speak just to our ethical thought. It speaks to all our thought about the world and life."[111]

Wolterstorff next observed that the Neo-Calvinist school tradition never intentionally sought to isolate itself from culture. It assumed it could pursue its primary educational goal in a non-isolationist setting. Furthermore, it was convinced that it had a vision of cultural transformation to share with its secular culture. He then wondered aloud whether or not this transformational vision had already been compromised by the Christian school's exposure to the dominant culture, implying that it had been for the most part.

Wolterstorff went on to say that the noble goal to imbue students with a certain view—a view pertaining to all of life—had become problematic insofar as it was perceived as a *cognitive* goal. The Lordship of Jesus Christ took us beyond saying the goal of Christian education is to "impart a view" or "way of thinking" to the more demanding conclusion that it shaped a way of living. The Christian way of life included a way of thinking, but there was so much more. This more, Wolterstorff contended, was implied by the term "life of discipleship."

The Neo-Calvinist educational tradition recognized God's lordship over all things and over all manner of thought. The tradition had become complacent, Wolterstorff claimed, in a second way. It had succumbed to the idea that teachers were the only ones who had to model Christian thinking and the life of discipleship.

> In short, the Reformed community constantly asks of its teachers that they work out an alternative mode of thought, and conduct education in an alternative manner. But it seldom makes the same demand on others. The lawyers of the community act pretty much like other lawyers, and little is said by way of challenging them to act as rebels and reformers of American law. So too for MDs and farmers and businessmen. But of our teachers it is asked that they work out a genuinely Christian alternative.[112]

If the community that surrounds the Christian school was unwilling to challenge all of its members *to think* Christianly, Wolterstorff argued, what was the prospect it would expect them *to live* the life of discipleship? The unlikelihood of this happening made Wolterstorff suspect there was no future for a Christian community that sought to offer a truly alternative education.

To end on a hopeful note, Wolterstorff stated that the Christian community could succeed in educating students into a life of discipleship if it met two conditions. First, this way of life had to be modelled by teachers and adults from the school community regardless of occupation. "We know that children tend to model themselves after people whom they love or respect." Second, "to counteract the . . . dissonant models in the surrounding society, the Christian school . . . home . . . [and] church must . . . give the child reasons for acting in the right way."[113]

Wolterstorff did not offer a strategy to meet these conditions. He tackled educational issues as a philosopher because philosophy was what he did best. Through speeches, workshops, and books, he periodically redefined the issues for Neo-Calvinist educators, a service they desperately needed. Then he left it to these educators to figure out the curricular and pedagogical implications of his philosophizing.

As the Neo-Calvinist school movement entered its fourth decade, it could point with pride to its establishment of an alternative system of Christian schools across three regions of Canada, but it could not boast about its ability to implement an alternative educational vision. Whether its individual schools sought to implement a transformative worldview or a way of life, these visions, more often than not, flourished in the domain of rhetoric rather then the classroom. Surely, these were sobering words for the CDC's staff and supporters.

Strategy for the 1980s

Geraldine Steensma spoke at the CDC's annual meeting the following year, and her "Strategy for the Eighties" speech was featured in issue six of the newsletter. Steensma said her task was to pick up where Wolterstorff left off and clarify how teachers could make education for discipleship concrete in the classroom. To that end she addressed three conclusions that she culled from Wolterstorff's speech: 1) Christian education is for Christian life, not just Christian thought, 2) Christian life is shaped by the entire conduct of the school, not just the curriculum, and 3) the curriculum gives the child articulate, sound reasons to live a Christian life. In each instance, Steensma uncovered "something that had been concealed" and offered a remedial course of action.

She first addressed Wolterstorff's conclusion that Christian education is for Christian life, not just for Christian thought. Christian educators regularly fail to acknowledge this, Steensma observed, because they are under the illusion that providing students with abstract knowledge is enough. Two false assumptions support this illusion, she argued. One asserts that teachers "give" students an education, and the other declares abstract theoretical knowledge leads to understanding beliefs, which, in turn, results in a commitment to these beliefs. Consequently, teachers wrongly assume that "knowing about" or "knowing that" or "knowing how" on their own leads us to live by that which we know.[114]

Steensma felt that Wolterstorff's speech did not help his audience understand the true nature of Christian education. She proceeded to clarify this herself, taking her cue from Isaiah 50:4, which says that the purpose of learning is to know "how to speak a word in season to one who is weary." This text inspired Steensma's observation that "a disciple learns, not to acquire good grades, a diploma, a college degree, or a respectable, well-paying profession . . . a true disciple's learning leads to living in such a way that true words and actions will sustain another in need."[115]

Steensma thought Christian educators had become comfortable separating Christian thought from Christian life because they found it difficult to establish what "ought to be." The reality is, she argued, teachers cannot educate for a life of discipleship if they do not nurture discipleship in themselves. Teachers cannot take students further than they are willing to go themselves.[116] Consequently, Steensma's first strategy for the 1980s challenged teachers to nurture discernment and true discipleship in themselves, with the clear understanding that discipleship implied a life dedicated to serving those in need.

The second of Wolterstorff's conclusions stated that the Christian life must be shaped by the entire school, not just the curriculum. What Wolterstorff understood intuitively, Steensma demonstrated from her experience. Teachers fail to discern why curriculum reform is not enough, she argued, because the factors that shape the classroom remain hidden to us. She based this insight on her experience as a grade-five teacher, when she was given complete freedom by her administrator to be as innovative as she wished. In that unfettered setting, Steensma encountered seven "forms" that shaped life in the classroom and made innovation extremely difficult. The first and foremost shaper of classroom life, she discovered, are textbooks and other published materials. These texts typically treat the teacher as a technician and the student as an object of learning. They tend to be discipline specific rather than thematic, and they place a heavy emphasis on information transfer. Steensma's strategy for the 1980s encouraged teachers to chuck the textbooks and build a curriculum around multiple resources that served the teacher's priorities. She identified the products for student learning as a second formative feature of the classroom. Typical products include worksheets, answers to questions from a text, a written report, a quiz, or a test. These products are often prefabricated, predictable, individual, and require a minimum amount of creativity. Steensma advised her audience to switch to products that required creativity, deeper knowledge, and student collaboration.

Other formative factors included the type and arrangement of classroom furniture, the bell schedule, and classroom rules and routines. All of these are designed to maximize efficiency and compliance, Steensma argued. She encouraged schools to provide furniture that enhanced collaboration, schedules that allowed for flexibility, and procedures that promoted learning rather than control.

Steensma also recognized the formative influence of the teacher-student relationship. Teachers typically have all the power. They do most of the talking, and they are the centre of attention. Her strategy to move forward implored teachers to empower their students and give them more responsibility for their learning.

The final shaper of classroom learning that she named was the testing-evaluating process. Teachers assume learning can, and ought to be, quantified and measured. They believe test results accurately tell us what a student knows. Steensma recognized that doing away with our unfortunate system of summative, quantified assessment was virtually impossible, but she described a variety of formative practices that bring much-needed balance to the matter of assessing student learning.

The last of Wolterstorff's conclusions stated the need for Christian educators to develop a curriculum that consistently presents students with sound Christian reasons for them to act/live a certain way. Steensma believed that Neo-Calvinist educators had for too long been blind to the fact that the possession of the correct view of life does not automatically lead someone to live that life.

Steensma's strategy on this point was particularly interesting. She observed that on at least two occasions she had attended one of the CSC teachers' conventions, and these experiences had left a lasting positive impression on her. Essentially, her response to Wolterstorff's third conclusion was to somehow bottle the inspiration, vision, insight and camaraderie that characterized these conventions and have parents, school boards, and school administrators "drink" the contents.

Steensma's speech was particularly compelling because she spoke with the authority of one who was a teacher and a philosopher. With the exception of Struik, she was likely the only person in the room who had actually tried to implement education for discipleship. Like Wolterstorff, she understood the blind spots and the complacency that plagued the Neo-Calvinist school movement, particularly in CSI's American districts. Unlike Wolterstorff, she was well aware of the external forces of resistance. Long before the literature on school reform recognized the formative power of the so-called regularities of the classroom, Steensma testified to the way they disfigured the teaching/learning experience. She also recognized that unless the whole community committed itself to living the life of discipleship, there was no way educators could take Christian education beyond the cultivation of a Christian perspective.

Steensma uncovered some of Wolterstorff's blind spots, but she had one or two of her own. She intuitively understood, but apparently did not see, that the "forms" that shaped life in the classroom were just the tip of an iceberg. Beneath them was a "deep structure of schooling" that sustained their practice. This deep structure was made up of the foundational assumptions and beliefs about education that our society holds most dear. As long as this deep structure remained hidden, she could not fully understand that the success of teachers to implement her strategy hinged on their ability to replace the criteria/rationale that determined current practice.

The CDC's staff and supporters had good reasons to believe the speeches delivered by Wolterstorff and Steensma affirmed the CDC's vision of education for discipleship. However, neither of these speakers were fixated on the development of a non-dualist philosophy as a precursor to educating for life. Wolterstorff clearly warned against substituting a "view of life" for a "view of curriculum reform;" both interpretations of Christion education reduced its purpose to a cognitive goal. Steensma went beyond talking about the life of discipleship in general terms. She understood it as a life of service for the sake of those in need. Both speakers were adamant in their insistence that education for discipleship was impossible to implement if this way of life was not lived in the school and its supporting community. These conclusions did not bode well for an organization that worked alone and was committed to designing a philosophical framework as its first priority.

Fernhout Interprets Malcolm and De Graaff

The CDC's situation became critical in the fall of 1984. Revenues were drying up, and community support was waning. The staff had just come through a particularly difficult time, which had resulted in the departure of its director. Harry Fernhout, who had recently rejoined the CDC after the completion of his graduate studies, replaced the outgoing part-time director and joined Agnes Struik who continued to work as a teacher consultant/curriculum writer. A series of temporary helpers filled the part-time clerical position that rounded out the skeleton staff.

The CDC's board of directors believed that the organization still had much to offer the world of Christian education, so in a last-ditch effort to revive support, it asked Fernhout to update the CDC's vision and develop a strategic plan for moving forward. Shortly thereafter, Fernhout submitted a document composed of three parts: a reaffirmation of the CDC's educational vision, a plan for the reorganization of the CDC's activities, and a strategy to form relationships with other organizations. The board decided to publish the educational vision in the fall issue of the newsletter and mail the other two parts to CDC members only.

Fernhout's rendition of the CDC's vision was not only its most compelling, this document also stands out as one of the premier vision statements to emerge from the Neo-Calvinist education movement. Notwithstanding his occasionally ill-advised and sloppy use of terms, Fernhout crafted one of the most insightful rationales ever written in support of an education for discipleship. For this reason it deserves more than a cursory investigation.

Fernhout opened his document with a brief history of the CDC's vision of integrated education.[117] It had evolved through three stages: the pre-*Joy in Learning* stage, the *Joy in Learning* stage, and the post-*Joy in Learning* stage. The vision that animated the CDC mothers, and most other CSC educators in the 1960s stated that the purpose of Christian education was the reinterpretation of each area of academic study through the application of a biblical worldview, "lest secular views capture students minds unchallenged." This transformative vision was sometimes referred to as education for the development of a Christian mind.

Joy in Learning made two important alterations to this vision. First, it redefined the purpose of education. It said that, at its core, education should "help students take up their human calling," to live a life of service to God. The *JIL* vision also restored students to their rightful place as learners by recognizing the "office of student." Students had their own legitimate task before God, as responsible learners. To ensure that students took up their role as self-forming learners, the vision required a pedagogy that was sensitive to students' developmental needs.

Fernhout said this enhanced vision came to its fullest expression in the "integrated unit." By this term he meant one that used an interdisciplinary or thematic approach to content organization and employed a pedagogy that empowered students to be self-forming. He correctly observed that the CDC's emphasis on students as responsible, self-forming learners distinguished its understanding of the integrated unit from the one generally promoted by CSC teachers.

According to Fernhout, the third phase of the CDC's educational vision came to light in later CDC materials. As the CDC staff continued to think about the implications of providing students with a vision of life or worldview, they concluded more was needed. Christian education must also "inform a way of life." Fernhout did not clearly explain how "informing a way of life" improved upon a "vision of life" nor did he clarify which CDC publications demonstrated this. He simply said, "Education should not only provide children with a view of the world but equip them for radical discipleship manifesting a Christian way of life in a post-Christian culture."[118]

Many readers were likely confused by this brief account. Fernhout obviously wanted to convey the fact that the CDC's vision had expanded over time, but exactly how it had changed was fuzzy. The shift in education's purpose from a transformation of the sciences to taking up the human calling to live a Christian life was not difficult to imagine, but what Fernhout meant to convey by the moves from a "vision of life" to "informing a way of life" to "equipping for life" was not immediately clear. Was this a transition from worldview to specific concepts about lifestyle, or was this a process that started in theory and ended with lived practice?

After this brief but not sufficiently clear review of the three-stage evolution of the CDC's educational vision, Fernhout proceeded to flesh out the contours of his updated version of the vision in four landscapes of "integrated learning." By this term he meant vision-infused learning.[119] The first landscape brought together *vision* and *education*. Within that general context, he explored three specific settings: the integration of the curricular program, the learner as a person, and the integration of education with life.

Fernhout's portrayal of vision-infused education was rooted in a rich understanding of the key term "vision of life." A vision of life, he observed, "refers to the way we . . . see ourselves and the world we live in."[120] Our "sight" has multiple sources. Our eyes present us with the reality that is right in front of us, but the "sight" we get from the "eye of our heart" interprets the ultimate meaning of our world. Furthermore, what we see with our physical eyes and interpret with the eyes of our heart is shaped by our experience living in a particular family, society, and community. When a "vision of life" embodies these three sources of knowing, it becomes more than an intellectual construct or world and life view. Fernhout astutely pointed out: "People don't just intellectually possess their vision, they *live* it."[121] He argued that a true vision of life speaks "through the entirety of our being and through all of our deeds, [and] helps us distill our experiences of good and evil, joy and pain, love and fear in the deep wisdom of the Scriptures."[122]

His description of a vision of life stands out as one of the most profound to emerge from the Neo-Calvinist tradition. With the exception of the Teaching for Transformation[123] initiative that arose in Alberta during the first two decades of the twenty-first century, Fernhout's reaffirmation of the CDC's educational vision is the only source that has acknowledged three deep drivers of education: head knowledge (worldview), heart knowledge (interpretation of meaning),[124] and hand knowledge (experience). Vision and worldview were no longer synonyms in Fernhout's statement.

To complete his analysis of the general landscape of integration, Fernhout identified several implications that this vision for life had for students. The vision would, he claimed, "help students develop the tools necessary to evaluate themselves and their world confidently . . . [so] they may be spiritually empowered to speak to their society in terms of their vision." As students took ownership of this vision, they would be enabled to forge "a Christian lifestyle that encompasses all of life's basic responsibilities."[125]

Fernhout also pointed out the difference this vision would make on the kind of knowledge that schools valued. Like their public-school counterparts, Christian schools typically concentrated on intellectual, factual knowledge. Schools that embodied a biblical vision of life "could not rest with this limited view of knowledge." Any knowledge (that connotes being educated) must be recontextualized by "a much deeper, richer sense of what it means to know God, self and God's world, and live in [the] light of this knowledge."[126]

This overarching landscape of vision and education provides us with a rare glimpse into what education for a life of discipleship actually looked like, but in the process, Fernhout left new questions unanswered. What tools did he imagine students needed to "evaluate themselves and their world confidently?" What did this evaluation process even mean? Was he still thinking of biblical answers to worldview questions, like what it means to be human and what is the nature of the good life? Or did he have something less cerebral in mind? What did it mean for students to "speak to their society in terms of their vision?" Did this still have something to do with the Reformational Movement's priority to name and undress the spirits of the age? Or did this "speaking" connote actual acts of culture making? Finally, how would taking ownership of this vision result in the formation of a lifestyle for students? Was this just another way of expressing the modern notion that worldviews shape ways of life, or did "forging" a Christian lifestyle imply that students would experience the life of discipleship at school?

Fernhout's first discussion on integration concludes with this telling observation: "the further development of the practical implications of a biblical view of knowledge and vision of life is one of the most important items of unfinished business on the agenda of Christian philosophy of education."[127] It is ironic that after all his ground-breaking efforts to sketch out a holistic picture of knowledge and finally bring the CDC to the point of saying education for discipleship had to be lived in the school, Fernhout assumed the fulfillment of this vision in a school setting was a matter of philosophy. What is most troubling, however, is the fact that the business he referred to remains unfinished to this day.

Fernhout next addressed the landscape of curricular integration. The key question of curriculum design asked: what organizing principle should shape all curricular content?[128] Like De Graaf, Fernhout wanted to situate the CDC outside of the dominant paradigm of progressivist education and its two organizing principles of the curriculum. He was very aware that the most established of these was the logical structure of the academic disciplines. This organizing principle was the driving force behind the "strong tendency (of schools) to divide the content of learning among separate subject areas, and to identify learning with factual mastery of these areas."[129] He also understood the humanist origins of the antithetical position within progressivism, which organized the curriculum around the preferences and desires of the student. In this section of the document, Fernhout affirmed the CDC's long-standing commitment to stand outside this spectrum of progressivist options and promote the life of discipleship as an alternative organizing principle.

According to Fernhout, to maintain congruence with its alternative organizing principle, the CDC had to adopt an integrated curriculum structure:

> Inspired by biblical images of the nature of God's creation in general and human beings in particular, we assert that Christian living involves relating to all things and all people in their wholeness. Our care of God's creatures renews itself when we experience those creatures as whole beings that exist in many different ways.[130]

To authentically reflect this holistic understanding of reality, the curriculum had to portray all creatures and their relationships in their totality and authenticity. What curriculum design was best suited to this task? From its beginnings, the CDC staff had assumed it was an interdisciplinary or theme-based curriculum.

The traditional academic subjects were greatly diminished in the CDC's understanding of an integrated curriculum because they presented students with an incomplete and fragmented understanding of the world. Fernhout conceded the traditional subjects had a role to play but only as long as they were "linked with the common thread of a Christian vision of life." They could not be "seen as independent, disconnected human inventions, but rather as reflections of the patterns of God's creation as interpreted by humans."[131]

To conclude his discussion on the integration of the curriculum, Fernhout outlined an integrated unit on trees. By "integrated" he meant the unit was both vision-infused and interdisciplinary. It is worth mentioning that his example was a multidisciplinary rather than an interdisciplinary unit.[132]

Fernhout next unpacked the CDC's long-held assumption that curriculum reform apart from pedagogical reform made no sense. The integration of the learner as a person was, in fact, even more important than the integration of the curriculum. In every iteration of the CDC's vision, pedagogical matters received at least twice as much attention. To implement a biblical vision of the learner, Fernhout argued, we must know "who persons are" and "what they are to become."

The Bible tells us that human beings are the image-bearers of God, but what this truly means we only ever know in part. We are spiritual beings because it is the life breath of God that animates us. We are relational beings because "we are created to live in communion with God, our fellow humans, and the rest of created reality." The "good life" we are called to live is a life of committed service to God through our stewardly care for all our earthly relationships. The Bible also reveals that we are broken because of our inability to uphold our end of these foundational relationships; this is the reality the Bible names sin.

What we are supposed to become, says Scripture, is a new creation in Christ. In Christ we engage in a process of relationship restoration that is simultaneously guaranteed and in the making. This process of becoming what we were created to be cannot escape the reality of brokenness, but neither is it rendered meaningless by that reality. This vision of the person lies at the root of the CDC's view of the learner as a responsible person. People live in communion with God at every stage of life. "Being a learner," therefore, is a worthy calling before God. This biblical understanding of the learner as a person has big implications for pedagogy. If we acknowledge that learners have a responsibility to learn all they need to know in order to become what they are meant to be, we cannot turn them into objects to be manipulated. Our teaching methods may not treat them as "passive information receptacles." On the contrary, teachers must teach in ways that encourage students to exercise their responsibility; they must transform discipline into discipling.

In addition to this recognition of the learner's responsibility, Fernhout's integration of the learner as a person included two more elements. He called one the *multidimensional and personal nature of learning*. When we see learners as persons, we can no longer reduce learning to cognitive mastery of bodies of information.[133] Because people exhibit a diversity of gifts, abilities, and interests, the only education that can foster their development into whole, integrated persons is one that takes these differences into account. The other key element in his view is the *development of persons*. Because our journey to become responsible persons is a time-sensitive process, Fernhout believed education must always take the student's developmental stage into account.

The third and final landscape of integration linked *education* and *life*. Education in school was not an end in itself, Fernhout declared, and the classroom was not "an isolation ward where people are prepared for the future." "Learning is not just a matter of 'getting an education'; learning is *about* life, takes place *within* life, and is directed *toward* life."[134] With this understanding, Fernhout developed three final points.

First, educators must not allow their classrooms to become artificial worlds or limit learning to abstractions. Students must constantly connect with the world outside of the classroom. What students learn in school should be integrated with every other form of education they experience.

Second, Christian education should "nurture students to embrace life in all its joys and sufferings" in ways appropriate to their age level. As a function of the Christian community, education "seeks to help students forge an integrated life pattern." In other words, education "assists them in developing their sense of self and their sense of discipleship in conscious awareness of the conflicting spirits shaping ways of life in our culture."[135]

Third, Christian education cannot be confined to schooling. We are lifelong learners, and the aim to learn for a way of life is an intergenerational concept."[136]

In its final stage, the CDC's educational vision not only called for the transformation of students' thinking but also an initiation into a biblical way of life.

A careful reading of Fernhout's reaffirmation of the CDC's vision reveals his desire to take the final step in the evolution of the CDC's vision. He imagined an education where students not only thought about discipleship but also were initiated into it. However, like the other visionaries just mentioned, he seemed to expend all of his energy just crossing the bridge to arrive at the desired shoreline. Once there, the exploration of educating for a way of life ended.

To conclude, we look at three aspects of this vision statement that negatively impacted its effectiveness. Fernhout's misuse and overuse of the term "integration" likely distracted some readers and limited their ability to appreciate where he wanted to take the CDC's vision. This was clearly the case for Van Brummelen given his critical response to the document.[137] Fernhout's use of "integration" was unfortunate, but it clearly conveyed his noble intention to make education for discipleship the compass setting for every aspect of education.

The document is also weakened by his reliance on unfamiliar, vague, or overlapping categories. For example, the meaning of a "vision of life" is confusing. Most people, I believe, assume the term connotes an "imagined life" or an "idea about life." Typically, 'a vision' refers to something we possess prior to acting. This is exactly what Fernhout did not want to convey. He wanted to move past educating for a "view" of life or teaching "about" a way of life. He insisted that people didn't just intellectually possess a vision of life; they lived it. Fernhout wanted "vision of life" to imply "living a life." Why not just say, "educate students to live a way of life"? This section of the document would have also benefitted from an acknowledgement that people often live a life that is incongruous with their vision of life.

Fernhout's efforts to associate discipleship with an actual "way of life" are enhanced by phrases like "live the knowledge" and "live the vision." His message was muddied, however, when he also said that a vision of life "informs" a way of life, "speaks" to society, or "equips" for life. To finally move the CDC beyond the Neo-Calvinist fondness of educating for a particular perspective, Fernhout could have simply referred to discipleship as a way of life instead of a vision of life.

Finally, Fernhout's document is weakened by an aspect of his presentation of the learner and pedagogical reform. To his credit, he followed the precedent set by De Graaf and Malcolm, who characterized education for discipleship as a "developmental calling." The problem was not, as some critics believed, a dependence upon humanist educational psychology. Neither did it pertain to how much space he allotted to this topic (twice as much as he gave to curriculum organization). The problem is that all his attention is directed to "how" learning takes place (it is developmental), and none is focused on "what" the life of discipleship looks like at any given point in life, and how teachers might draw students into it.

I Agree with the CDC in Principle, but . . .

The next issue of the CDC newsletter featured remarks from four panelists who were invited to the CDC's annual membership meeting to share their responses to Fernhout's updated CDC vision statement. John Stronks and Harro Van Brummelen were education (read curriculum) coordinators from the OACS and the SCSBC respectively. Both had a history of criticizing the CDC's work. Aukje Masselink had formerly been the principal of the Toronto District Christian High School but was currently a special education teacher and head of guidance for the Scarborough Board of Education. Clive Beck was a professor of philosophy of education at the prestigious Ontario Institute for Studies in Education (OISE) at the University of Toronto. All four were familiar with the CDC's work, and the CDC's board hoped the evening would stimulate dialogue and sharpen everyone's "understanding of some key issues relating to CDC's educational perspective."

After the four panelists had spoken, Harry Fernhout was given an opportunity to address the panelists. Regrettably, his remarks were not included in the newsletter. The stated reason for this omission was limited space. This was a rather flimsy excuse given the fact that the newsletter included two pages dedicated to news and a book review, neither of which carried the significance of this exchange. The article's introduction also mused that the absence of Fernhout's rejoinders to the criticism of the panelists allowed readers to evaluate the speeches on their own terms. This explanation has more merit, but it is regrettable that Fernhout's contribution to the discussion was never published later.

John Stronks

John Stronks began his speech on a conciliatory note by stating he agreed with many ideas in the CDC's vision document. He also assured the audience that he considered himself to be in a room full of colleagues in Christian education. He likely felt obliged to begin his remarks this way because of his long-standing opposition to Arnold De Graaff and

his gradual withdrawal of support from the ICS. Stronks then named the vision statement's confessional assumptions with which he agreed:
- God as the creator of all things;
- the centrality of God's word;
- the creation-fall-redemption-reconciliation meta-narrative of Scripture, and
- the mission of humanity to be good stewards of the creation.

He also identified four aspirations of Christian education that he shared with the CDC: "to nurture a biblical vision of life," to foster a biblical view of knowledge, to embrace the fullness of life, and to aim for personal integrity and individuality. To summarize, what he agreed with were the assumptions that virtually all Neo-Calvinists held. After this quick review of common ground, Stronks launched into his strong disagreements with the vision statement's understanding of the curriculum and the learner.

Stronks criticized the statement for saying so little about the contents of the curriculum and directing all of its attention to its ordering principle. The vision was lacking on the content side, he argued, because it "doesn't contribute to current debates on core curriculum, literacy standards and achievement accountability." The vision of life as an ordering principle was misguided, he stated, because it displaced the traditional subjects that normally filled that role, a reality that most OACS schools readily accepted.

Both arguments lacked credibility, however, because Stronks failed to acknowledge an important context. It was true that the document did not address "content issues" of the kind he considered to be important, but this was not the intent of the vision statement. More importantly, he failed to acknowledge that the CDC's ordering principle was rooted in the very confessional assumptions that he himself adhered to, whereas, his own ordering principle of subject disciplines did not. In fact, both of his concerns were consistent with the educational vision promoted by the administrative progressives, whose position dominated North American education.

The CDC's view of *curriculum* was problematic for Stronks on at least two additional fronts. He felt that the stress on nurturing the learner encroached on the domain of the home. In his interpretation of the roles properly played by church, home, and school, the school's job was primarily academic. He also believed that the CDC's advocacy of the "integrated unit" was exaggerated. He suggested that no OACS school would adopt a theme-based curriculum. Yet immediately after he made that observation, Stronks stated that the example of an integrated unit on trees contained in the vision statement was "remarkably similar" to work done by OACS teachers.

Stronks's critique of the CDC's view of the learner and the learning situation repeated the pattern outlined above. He provided a fairly accurate description of the CDC's view of the learner, but he failed to acknowledge that it was rooted in the same biblical view of what it means to be human, which he held himself. Instead, he accused the CDC of falling victim to "the humanistic learning theory," even though the vision statement consciously rejected that position. Incredibly, Stronks said, "Personally, I would like to see a greater emphasis on the more recent developments in the cognitive learning theory."[138] Why Stronks assumed an approach to learning theory rooted in the work of Jean Piaget was compatible with a biblical vision of education while that of a Carl Rogers was not he did not say.

Clive Beck

The OISE's Clive Beck was next to speak. He must have felt completely out of his element addressing a room full of Dutch Neo-Calvinists. Like Stronks, he opened with an attempt to identify with the audience. He informed the audience that he had been raised as a Baptist, and one of his research interests was world religions. Beck's philosophical starting point was vastly different from the one that animated the CDC's vision statement, but he tried to find common ground in the document's "emphasis on integration," which he rightly interpreted as a concern for integrality of worldview and the rest of life. Beck held to a dualist view that split reality into spiritual and natural realms, an ontology that most people in the room rejected. He agreed with the thrust of the CDC's vision because it brought "the spiritual" into play, but he did not comprehend the extent to which an education for discipleship was meant to transform the educational experience. Like Stronks, he expressed concerns over the CDC's rejection of the academic subjects as the ordering principle of the curriculum.

Harro Van Brummelen

Harro Van Brummelen next delivered his assessment of the CDC's vision. Once a strong supporter of the CDC, Van Brummelen had recently suggested to Struik that the CDC had outlived its usefulness, and he advised her to set up her own consulting business. In his introductory remarks, he said he felt comfortable with much of what was said in the CDC statement, but he only specifically mentioned his appreciation for its emphasis on educating for responsible discipleship. Having said that, he launched into an extensive list of concerns.

Van Brummelen's lengthy speech would have likely been even longer if he had addressed all of his concerns. Since the speakers had agreed in advance not to repeat each other, he chose to primarily talk about the statement's overuse and misuse of the term "integration." In doing so, he also took several opportunities to "school" the audience about aspects of his own educational vision and philosophy of curriculum.

Van Brummelen rightly observed that the term "integration" had a long history in the Neo-Calvinist school movement. He suggested that it had so many meanings and interpretations that it was practically useless. This state of affairs made the precise use of the term a must. On this score, he believed, the CDC's vision statement had failed miserably because it applied the term to too many contexts. Misuse of the term showed up immediately when the statement referred to the integration of vision and education.

I find Van Brummelen disingenuous to say integration was misused in this instance because Neo-Calvinists educators, including himself, had used the term "integration" of vision (worldview) and education for a long time. In fact, Van Brummelen was primarily responsible for popularizing this misuse of the term by Neo-Calvinists. Everyone else in education used the term "integration" with reference to content organization.[139]

About curricular integration Van Brummelen acknowledged that the CDC's vision aligned with a long-standing CSC belief that the curriculum should stress the coherence, harmony, and interrelatedness of the creation. However, he did not buy the CDC's argument that to achieve this integrality the academic disciplines must disappear in favour of a theme-based or interdisciplinary curriculum. He accurately pointed out that efforts to implement a thematic curriculum were perennially short-lived. However, he failed to acknowledge that the primary reason why this happened had to do with the dominance of a curriculum orientation that favoured a disciplinary approach. Van Brummelen also failed to acknowledge that the examples of thematic units that appeared in his own work were identical to the one outlined in the CDC's vision statement, namely, they were multidisciplinary in nature, not interdisciplinary or thematic.

Setting aside for a moment whether the ordering principle of the curriculum should be a way of life or the logical structure of the academic subjects, Van Brummelen's understanding of an "integrated unit" had merit.[140] He believed such a unit should exhibit both internal and external unity. Internally, the unit "must have a clearly stated conceptual theme which states the key ideas towards which all thinking and activities will be directed." Externally, "the unit must clearly be related to the goals of the course."[141]

With respect to the CDC's understanding of the integration of the learner as a person, Van Brummelen opened by saying he agreed with the CDC's vision that we must educate for responsible action, namely, that students should learn how to act as persons in a biblical sense. However, he warned the CDC that its understanding of the integrated person was dangerously similar to the notion of "personalized learning," as practiced by the Accelerated Christian Education (ACE) programed learning approach. This was a rather far-fetched conclusion for a scholar like Van Brummelen to make. On the surface, CDC's view of the self-forming child could be misunderstood as a borrowed notion from the child-centred wing of progressivist education, but it had nothing in common with programmed learning.

As a strong advocate of education for discipleship, it is odd that Van Brummelen failed to appreciate the historic significance of the link that the CDC carefully developed between God's calling for humanity to live the life of discipleship and its view of the student as a self-forming person.

He seemed overly eager to educate his audience about the four phases of learning, which he believed did a better job of drawing out the learner as a responsible person. His patronage of this position is ironic because it is rooted in the process philosophy of Alfred North Whitehead, the experiential learning theory of David Kolb, and popularized by instructional design expert Bernice McCarthy, who identified four styles of learning. Had the Neo-Calvinist communities' best minds in education philosophy been willing to work together, perhaps they could have better understood the strengths and weaknesses of their positions, which, in fact, had much in common.

The final expression of integration in the CDC's document brought together education and life. Van Brummelen called this application of integration a misnomer. He also believed that, taken to its logical conclusion, the CDC's vision statement effectively did away with the need for schooling and replaced it with the school of life. On this and most other fronts, Van Brummelen cast what he read in the worst possible light. The CDC's vision statement did not do away with school, but it did reimagine its role as a strictly academic institution. Fernhout had raised concerns about learning being an artificial experience, cut off from the real world. To implement educating for a life of discipleship, schools had to "nurture students to embrace life in all of its joys and sufferings." Such embracing cannot be done in the abstract. Van Brummelen developed these very initiatives four years later in his book, *Walking with God in the Classroom*.[142]

Van Brummelen sought to end his speech on a positive, collegial note when he acknowledged that "during the last twelve years the CDC has made us all much more aware of the issues we have to face in education . . ."[143] One has to wonder about the sincerity of this compliment when he failed to cite a single positive example. Van Brummelen's lasting take-away from the CDC's legacy was, in his words, its emphasis that "education must be so directed that it truly does not hinder children to come to Jesus." It is difficult to imagine how such a universal priority of Christian educators from any tradition, could be considered a unique contribution to the Neo-Calvinist tradition of curriculum reform.

Aukje Masselink

The last speaker, Aukje Masselink, took a completely different approach. Rather than critically react to the CDC's vision statement, she offered a model of "integrated education" that she had developed during her days as an OACS teacher. Her strategy was to build on the CDC's vision, not attack it. Her model was elegantly simple: an integrated education exhibits harmony and coherence between four key players who share a common vision of Christian education: children, parents, teachers, and the community. The respective roles of each group were defined by this commonly held vision, and her model demonstrated how, when blended together, they formed an integrated educational experience.

Christian *parents* were responsible to God to teach their children to love and fear the Lord. They were ultimately responsible for their children's education; therefore, they must be engaged in that process. To the extent that parents gave the education of the children over to the school, they had to trust that the education offered there matched their own vision and way of life.

Teachers had to possess personal integrity and a true sense of who they were because what they taught and how they lived modeled learning and life for their students. Teachers had to know their students and create an environment where integrated learning could take place. This involved everything from the arrangement of classroom furniture to cultivating in students the appropriate skills they needed to learn. Finally, and here she sided with the CDC, teachers had to personalize learning as best as they could.

When she addressed the role of *students*, Masselink offered her only criticism of the CDC's vision. She believed the CDC naively assumed all students were motivated and willing learners. More work had to be done to account for the wide range of ability in students the teachers actually encountered. The bulk of her exploration of educating students was rooted in Geraldine Steensma's portrayal of the four foundational relationships in creation: person to creation, person to God, person to person, and person to self.

According to Masselink, an integrated education prepared students to do the good works they are called by God to do while living in the world. Through their education they internalized the command to love God and neighbour. Finally, she observed, an integrated education gave students the perspective to know themselves, what they believed, where they were strong, and what made them weak. All of this had to happen in the context of a *community*, for it was from the community that teachers emerged, and it was to the community that students returned.

Legacy and Lessons Learned

The opening line of Fernhout's reaffirmation of the CDC's educational vision sums up the organization's legacy: "From the very beginning, CDC's work has been motivated by a sense of educational vision rather than by mere response to curricular needs."[144] The incompatibility of these two aspirations in the minds of CDC staff stands as one of the great tragedies of the Neo-Calvinist education movement. The other great tragedy was the inability of the CDC and CSC leaders to work together to implement their tradition's most compelling vision.

Educational vision was the CDC's strong suit throughout its existence. It came to expression in the introduction to *Joy in Learning* and in two official vision statements published in its newsletter. Ironically, education for discipleship was largely missing from the CDC's other publications. It mainly found its way into the classroom through the consulting work of Agnes Struik.

The CDC staff stood shoulder to shoulder with the other recognized leaders in CSC circles, including reformers like Nicholas Wolterstorff, Geraldine Steensma, and Harro Van Brummelen. They all promoted a vision of "education for discipleship." They were equally unanimous in their rejection of the "banking concept of teaching" that reduced learning to a technical process where teachers deposited cognitive, factual information into the heads of passive students, who were expected to regurgitate this "knowledge" on tests. All of them also advocated for authentic learning and deeper knowledge, which, in turn, prompted them to promote integrated units and pedagogical reform.

The architects of the CDC's vision were the only ones, however, who made a vision of life the ordering principle of the curriculum.[145] Wolterstorff's analysis always stopped short of unpacking his vision at the curricular and pedagogical levels. He left these details to classroom teachers. Influenced by the thinking of Philip Phenix,[146] Steensma and Van Brummelen maintained the "unity" within the logical structure of the traditional academic disciplines as their ordering principle.

The CDC was virtually alone in its recognition of the office of student and the development of a pedagogical model that balanced the formative function of teaching with a self-formative role of the student. Steensma held compatible views on teaching and developmental learning.

In its day, the CDC's educational vision provided the most comprehensive alternative to those promoted by the administrative and pedagogical progressives. It recognized the need to establish coherence and consistency among the vision's constituent parts: the confessional understandings, the purpose of education, the philosophical-anthropological framework, curriculum design, pedagogy and classroom practice. Without this wholesale congruity, there could be no victory over the culture's entrenched dualistic understanding of human nature and reality.

There are important lessons to be learned from the CDC story as well, and most of them are difficult for educators from various traditions to internalize. For example, our first takeaway from this narrative is a principle of community development: do not choose between "being right" and "being in right relationship." Whenever these become mutually exclusive objectives, communities inevitably become divided. When being right prevails, each side tenaciously clings to its version of the truth, and rare is the occasion when one side's truth is honored by those on the other side. If the priority of both sides is to maintain their relationship, the process of reform will, no doubt, slow down. This slow pace may eventually be the death of reform; however, the trust that hopefully emerges over a commitment to work together provides the community with its only chance to move ahead together.

The second lesson reminds us that curriculum reform only materializes when it moves beyond the abstract world of theory and rhetoric to the environment of an authentic classroom. Curriculum reform requires more than a philosophical framework to be actualized, even if this framework is clearly rooted in confessional principles that accurately answer our questions of ultimate concern. The addition of compatible theories of curriculum design and pedagogy are not enough either. Curriculum reform only materializes when a conceptual framework is made manifest in the classroom.

For teachers to carry out curricular reform, they require all of the following: content knowledge, philosophical knowledge, pedagogical expertise, minimal distractions, adequate financial backing, administrative support, and permission to transgress the established practices of classroom life. This is the third lesson CDC's story provides us.

Finally, the CDC narrative reminds us of the need for community. School reform cannot be achieved by a think tank working alone. A think tank working with teachers and administrators will achieve much more, but it will still ultimately fail to bring about lasting reforms. If educational reform implies educating for an alternative way of life, those initiating the reforms need buy-in from the school's supporting community. If the alternative way of life is not modelled within and without the school, students will learn, as the saying goes, "to talk the talk and not walk the walk."

CHAPTER 7

The Golden Age of Publishing for Neo-Calvinist Educators

Timeline

1971	*Christian Philosophy of Education* by N. H. Beversluis.
	To Those Who Teach: Keys for Decision-Making by Geraldine Steensma
1973	*Joy in Learning: An Integrated Curriculum for the Elementary School,* eds. Arnold De Graaff & Jean Olthuis
1977	*Shaping School Curriculum: A Biblical View*, eds. Geraldine Steensma & Harro Van Brummelen
1980	*Man in Society: a Study in Hope* by Ary De Moor, Henry Contant, John Hull, Robert Koole, Gordon Oosterman, Fred Spoolstra, Peter Van Huizen, and Stuart Williams
	Educating for Responsible Action by Nicholas Wolterstorff
1981	*Shaping Christian Schools: A Conference*: conference presentations published by the Society of Christian Schools in British Columbia
1984	*The Transforming Vision: Shaping a Christian World View* by Brian Walsh & J. Richard Middleton
	"Beyond 1984 in Philosophy of Christian Education," by Nicholas Wolterstorff, keynote speech at the Ontario Christian School Teachers Association'sannual convention
1986	*Telling the Next Generation* by Harro Van Brummelen
1988	*Walking with God in the Classroom: Christian Approaches to Learning & Teaching* by Harro Van Brummelen
1989	*12 Affirmations: reformed Christian schooling for the 21st Century*, by Steven Vryhof, Joel Brower, Stefan Ulstein, and Daniel Vander Ark

1990	*Christian Schooling: Education for Freedom* by Stuart Fowler, Harro Van Brummelen, and John Van Dyk
1992	"Task and Invitation" by Nicholas Wolterstorff (keynote speech at the first international conference for Reformed Christian education)
1993	*Christian Education and the Deep Structure of Schooling* by John E. Hull.
	Educating Christian Teachers for Responsible Discipleship by Peter DeBoer, Harro Van Brummelen, Robert Koole, and Gloria Stronks
	A Vision with a Task: Christian Schooling for Responsive Discipleship, eds. Gloria Stronks and Doug Blomberg
1994	*Steppingstones to Curriculum: A Biblical Path* by Harro Van Brummelen
1995	*Truth is Stranger than it Used to Be: Biblical Faith in a Postmodern Age* by Richard Middleton and Brian Walsh
1997	*Voices from the Past: Reformed Educators*, ed. Donald Oppewal
2000	"Transformation: Dynamic Worldview or Repressive Ideology?" by Brian Walsh

The Arc of a Changing Vision

The quantity and quality of published materials produced by an alternative tradition of education are indicators of its overall health. In this chapter we take a quick tour of the scholarly work produced by educators who identified with the Dutch Neo-Calvinist education movement in North America, particularly those texts that most impacted Christian Schools Canada (CSC). Prior to 1970, CSC educators had access to only two resources that addressed the purpose of a Neo-Calvinist Christian education and a vision for curriculum reform. The *Christian School Herald* magazine founded by the Ontario Alliance of Christian Schools (OACS) published some booklets in the early 1960s that dealt with these topics, and the National Union of Christian Schools (NUCS) printed and distributed the now iconic speech that Nicholas Wolterstorff delivered to its annual meeting of principals and board members in 1966.[147] The minimal output of publications from the Neo-Calvinist community in Canada is not surprising given its short life up to that point. Why the much more established community on the American side did not publish more is puzzling, for there was plenty to write about. There was, for example, the lengthy curriculum debate mentioned in chapter 3 that animated numerous professors at Calvin College but was largely confined to classroom lectures and on campus documents.[148]

This situation changed dramatically during the next three decades when a significant body of published work emerged. Most of these texts appeared after 1983, and Canadian authors did more than their share of the writing. Surprisingly little has been published about the Neo-Calvinist school movement since 2000. The reasons behind this second publishing drought would be a worthy thesis topic for someone currently active in the system. Today, it is easy to demonstrate that there was a "golden age" of publishing that focused on the North American Neo-Calvinist education tradition; however, we cannot, on that basis alone, also conclude the heyday of the tradition is now in the past, although there may be other reasons to think so.

The twenty-one published texts named in the timeline above include thirteen books, two speeches, two curriculum resources, two conference resources, a doctoral thesis, and one journal article. These texts, in addition to the CDC newsletter articles mentioned in chapter 6, do not comprise an exhaustive list of Neo-Calvinist writings about Christian education that appeared during these decades, but they capture the tradition's best thinking. Nearly all of them focus on the larger questions of educational vision, worldview, philosophical foundations, and educational aims. Some also deal with topics closer to classroom life, such as curriculum design, pedagogy, student assessment, the classroom environment, and discipline. Several texts made a big difference across all three regions of CSC. A couple were barely noticed. Others piqued general interest but had little impact. A few had the potential to wield considerable influence on the larger public education stage, but they were not widely read.

Harro Van Brummelen either authored or made a major contribution to eight of these texts. He and two Americans, Nicholas Wolterstorff and Geraldine Steensma, stand out as the leading voices for the advancement of the Neo-Calvinist Christian school movement in Canada. Wolterstorff's

1966 speech and Van Brummelen's first book, *Telling*, are discussed at length in other parts of this book,[149] so they are not dealt with here. Each text in the above list made an important contribution to the collective knowledge of the North American Neo-Calvinist education community. Rather than summarize the importance of each one, a process that could fill a book all by itself, this chapter follows the more streamlined strategy sketched out below.

A Christian perspective or worldview was central to all of these writings, but most texts only made assumptions about it and did not bother to exegete its meaning. Two speeches by Wolterstorff and two books and an article by Walsh and Middleton are the exceptions. The time spans that separate Wolterstorff's two speeches and the Walsh/Middleton books are almost identical: 1984 to1992 and 1984 to 1995, respectively. An additional article written by Walsh that appeared in 2000 adds clarity to what appeared in the 1995 book. This abbreviated collection of writings provided CSC educators with a clear understanding of the strengths and weaknesses of their tradition's dependence upon a worldview perspective. It also offered insight into the trajectory of the Neo-Calvinist school movement and compelling reasons why a serious course correction was necessary.

The following portrayal of the waxing and waning of worldview education serves as the backdrop for an analysis of classroom focused texts written by Geraldine Steensma, Harro Van Brummelen, and the authors of the *Man in Society* project. Coupled with the *Joy in Learning* curriculum, these texts represent the tradition's best efforts to articulate an alternative curriculum orientation. By employing this strategy, I hope to convey an accurate portrait of the way Neo-Calvinist educators interpreted and expressed their educational vision in published form.

What Wolterstorff, Walsh, and Middleton Said in 1984

In October of 1984, Nicholas Wolterstorff delivered the keynote speech at the annual teachers' convention hosted by the Ontario Christian School Teachers Association. His speech was called "Beyond 1984 in Philosophy of Christian Education." Earlier that year, Brian Walsh[150] and J. Richard

Middleton[151] co-authored one of the most insightful and accessible books on worldview to arise out of the Dutch Neo-Calvinist education movement.[152] Their book was titled *The Transforming Vision: Shaping Christian World View*, and it was widely read by faith-based educators of various backgrounds.

Before we mine the major points of these texts, two differences in approach should be clarified up front. First, Walsh and Middleton addressed worldview at a cultural level and for a wide audience, whereas Wolterstorff's speech focused on the implications of worldview for a specific group of educators. Second, and more importantly, Walsh and Middleton believed "Worldviews are best understood when we see them incarnated, fleshed out in an actual way of life."[153] To determine a community's operative worldview, they advised their readers to first look at the community's way of life and inductively work backwards to arrive at its worldview. Wolterstorff followed the more conventional route: he first defined a worldview, then deductively arrived at the way of life that consistently reflected it.

Wolterstorff

The Ontario Christian School Teachers' Association invited Wolterstorff to give the keynote speech at their annual teacher's convention in 1984. He was asked to address a current hot curriculum issue: should the curriculum be organized around subject disciplines or interdisciplinary themes? As he so often did, Wolterstorff took a step back and tackled the prior issue of educational purpose instead. He firmly believed that curriculum problems could more easily be resolved once philosophical misunderstandings about the purpose of education had been removed.

Wolterstorff informed his audience that he believed one philosophy of education had actually dominated the North American Neo-Calvinist school system for the past one hundred years. He further assumed that most educators in the tradition only partially understood this philosophy. To address this deficiency, he used his speech to summarize this philosophy, identify its strengths and weaknesses, and recommend changes.

In Wolterstorff's opinion, his philosophy professor at Calvin College, William Jellema,[154] had articulated this philosophy better than anyone else. Jellema stood firmly in a Christian liberal arts tradition. He advocated for the development of a "Christian mind" as an alternative to the other major minds that defined the Western intellectual tradition, Greek, medieval, modern, (and later, postmodern). Education, Jellema believed, always "manifested" the way of life of the "kingdom" or culture it served, and it "initiated" students into that life. Wolterstorff summarized Jellema's vision of education this way:

> The goal of Christian education is not just the formation of a way of thinking. Nor is it that plus the development of moral character. Nor is it that plus the cultivation of a mode of piety. Nor is it that plus the transmission of one and another part of humanity's knowledge. Education is for the totality of life in a kingdom.[155]

Jellema's position was built on four connected theses. The goal of Christian education is to "equip students for active citizenship in the Kingdom of God" (Neo-Calvinist speak for "a way of life"). This equipping involves "whatever knowledge and skills are necessary for this citizenship" (the stuff we normally expect to learn from a formal education) and "a grasp of and a commitment to the Christian worldview." To equip students for their citizenship in this manner, the school must provide students with a Christian understanding of reality and engage them in a foundational analysis of human social and cultural products.[156] Most CSC teachers at that time would have simply said, "the goal of Christian education is to provide students with a biblical perspective on every area of life."

By this time in his career, Wolterstorff saw inherent problems in his mentor's position, and two were substantial. The first pertained to the nature of the life for which we educate.

Neo-Calvinist had the habit of speaking about "life in the Kingdom" without any mention of suffering and injustice. The tradition made much of humanity's mandate from God to develop culture, but it rarely spoke "of the call to bring good tidings to the afflicted, to bind up the broken hearted, to proclaim liberty to the captives, to liberate those who are bound, to comfort those who mourn."[157] Wolterstorff was hesitant to name the root cause of this weakness, but he planted the idea that Neo-Calvinism functioned "as an ideology of the Christian bourgeoisie" who had never experienced much suffering themselves.

The nature of learning in Jellema's philosophy, and the tradition generally, posed a second problem. The program of learning in the Christian school only sought "to develop abstract science in Christian perspective, and not also to develop praxis-oriented science of service to Christian social action . . ." The tradition banked on the ill-conceived notion that students who were equipped with a Christian mind would take up the radical life of discipleship later in life. In the school setting, initiation into a way of life suitable for the Kingdom of God was strictly a mental process.

For his part, Wolterstorff wanted to reclaim Jellema's vision of education for a comprehensive Christian life but with two important correctives. First, student learning had to move beyond the abstract world of science to the concrete world of lived experience. Second, learning that initiated students into a Christian way of life must involve seeking after justice, showing mercy, binding up wounds, and establishing peace.

Wolterstorff's speech did not resolve the OCSTA's curriculum debate, but it addressed a more urgent problem. He told those who had the ears to hear it that their tradition of Christian education had drifted off course. Education for a way of life, not worldview, had always been the bottom line. Education for a Christian perspective failed to achieve this goal insofar as it remained an abstract learning experience. It also misrepresented that life to the extent that students were not existentially confronted with the suffering and injustices of the world. The implications of his speech for curriculum development were clear, even though he did not state them explicitly. The debate about how best to organize curricular content paled in comparison to the challenge of designing curriculum that encouraged students to bring justice, peace, hope, and healing to concrete situations of suffering and injustice.

Walsh & Middleton

What inspired Walsh and Middleton to write their book? Interestingly, we find out from Wolterstorff, who wrote its foreword. He observed that:

A deep disappointment and a profound longing, motivate this book. The authors, themselves Christians, observe that vast numbers of their fellow North Americans count themselves as Christians. Yet Christianity is ineffective in shaping our public life. What effectively shapes our public life and our society generally is our adulation of science and technology and economic growth.[158]

The problem that Walsh and Middleton confronted was specifically this: why is the Bible's comprehensive and dynamic worldview so ineffective in shaping public life? They believed there were two main reasons: Christians generally fail to see the bigness of this vision, and they are reluctant to put it into practice in a secular culture. Their two-pronged solution to this problem was straightforward but not simple. They called on the Christian community to *enlarge* and *integrate* a biblical worldview to the rest of life in a secular age. By "enlarge," Walsh and Middleton challenged Christians to "see" that the Christian life is not limited to practices we typically associate with the church; rather, the Christian life speaks to all areas of our so-called public and private lives. The integrality of Christian living depended upon the willingness of Christians to step into the biblical story and allow its worldview to make a difference in the way they lived.

The Transforming Vision was really a worldview primer written to help Christians overcome their dualistic manner of thinking about and living in their world. The book explored five topics: the general nature of a worldview, how to judge the quality of a worldview, the boundaries of a biblical worldview, the main features of the modern worldview, and what putting a biblical worldview into action looks like. All five are useful for evaluating the development of the CSC movement.

Minimally, a worldview is a way of seeing. It provides a community of viewers with a model of the world and how they should live in this world. For Walsh and Middleton, it is a critical mistake to think of a worldview as a vision *of* life; it is a vision *for* life. "If a worldview does not actually lead a people in a particular way of life, it is no world view at all."[159] This eliminated the need to distinguish between an espoused worldview and an operative worldview. The only worldview that merits the name is the one we are living.

Worldviews are "perceptual frameworks," Walsh and Middleton said; they are not systems of thought like theologies or philosophies. They agreed with others in the Neo-Calvinist tradition who said worldviews are "pre-scientific" by nature. That is to say, they are not theoretical like the sciences nor are they a product of a science. Instead, they are the shapers of science. Al Wolters stated it this way: worldviews arise from the domain of "one's common-sense perspective on life and the world and the 'system of values' or 'ideology,' which in one form or another is held by all normal adult human beings regardless of intelligence or education."[160]

Walsh and Middleton believed that everyone has a worldview, which is always shared with a community. The primary purpose of this worldview is to provide answers to four fundamental questions: Where are we? Who are we? What is wrong? What is the remedy? People are rarely conscious of their answers to these questions, and many find it difficult to articulate these answers if pressed to do so. Nevertheless, our (conscious or subconscious) answers to these questions give direction and purpose to our lives. Because they do, we can determine what they are by looking closely at how people live. To demonstrate, Walsh and Middleton sketched out life scenarios of real people who were rooted in Japanese, North American, and Dene cultures. The North American answers to the four worldview questions bear no surprises. Where are we? We "stand in a world of natural potential and our task is to utilize that potential to economic good." Who are we? We are free and independent individuals; we are the masters of our own destinies. What is wrong? We are hindered from fulfilling our potential "by ignorance of nature and lack of tools for controlling it." What is the remedy? Our "hope rests in the good life of progress wherein nature yields its bounty for human benefit."[161]

Worldviews are bridges between faith and life. Walsh and Middleton expressed the Neo-Calvinist belief that "faith determines which world view we will adopt." It is our faith, what we believe in and assume to be true, that dictates how we answer the four worldview questions. These answers, in turn, drive our decision-making in all areas of life. Here as well the authors did not distinguish between espoused beliefs and lived beliefs; only the latter fit their description.

We can identify multiple worldviews in our society, Walsh and Middleton argued, but one dominates and defines the culture. Many Americans and Canadians, past and present, think of their respective countries as Christian nations, but a biblical worldview has never been fully manifested in North American society because of a "split-vision worldview" that holds sway among Christians of all denominational backgrounds. This dualist way of perceiving the world blurs the reality that humans either serve the Lord or some idol because it "identifies obedience, redemption and the kingdom of God with only *one* area of life. It sees the rest of life as either unrelated to redemption (or the sacred), or worse—under the power of disobedience, sin and the kingdom of darkness."[162]

Their book, *Transforming*, also explored ways to evaluate a worldview. Since we encounter different worldviews all the time, and our response to them ranges from outright rejection to wholesale adoption, Christians need criteria to judge the quality of a worldview.

Walsh and Middleton acknowledged their empathy for worldviews that "coincide with their own or offer insights which deepen (their) own." For example, they had affinity for the Dene worldview's respect for the land or the worldview behind critical pedagogy, which seeks justice for the oppressed. They next outlined four criteria for judging a worldview's merits.

First, a worldview should offer a view of the whole world, not just part(s) of it. It should open up all of life to those who adhere to it. The dominant North American worldview fails to meet this criterion because of its overriding concern for economic development. Second, a worldview should sensitize its followers to love and justice. Third, a quality worldview exhibits internal coherence; all its parts must agree. Middleton and Walsh cite the worldview of contemporary Japan as an example that fails this test because it emphasizes "both a oneness with nature and the superiority of the Japanese over all other peoples of the world." Lastly, a worldview should open people to flourishing and life, not bring on suffering and death.

Middleton and Walsh then spent three chapters outlining the contours of a biblical worldview. Consistent with their Neo-Calvinist tradition, they associated this worldview with the Bible's grand narrative of creation, fall, redemption, and restoration. In these chapters the authors demonstrate their considerable skill and knowledge as biblical scholars as they assemble this worldview.

The world understood as God's creation is the Bible's starting point. This world has a purpose and is not a random act of spontaneous evolution. However long it took and by whatever means, the Bible says creation came about by the power of God's Word or Wisdom. This choice of the world's origins is significant because the Word and Wisdom do more than call creatures into being; they imprint design on what is created. That is, they inscribe on each created thing its meaning and purpose.

The biblical account of the world as God's creation reveals important knowledge about who God is and what it means to be human. As creator, God is worthy of worship from all creatures. As creator, God remains faithful to creation through the covenant promises God initiates. To be human is to bear God's image, vis a vis the creation. In one capacity, humans are to "rule over" all other creatures. In another, humans must choose "to serve" God or an idol. Middleton and Walsh believe the biblical notion of humankind as stewards balances our roles as authorities. In the grand narrative of creation, fall, redemption, and restoration, the first two worldview questions are answered in the Bible's understanding of creation. Where are we? In a world created by God for the purpose of flourishing, as defined by Wisdom and the Word. Who are we? Creatures created by God to be stewards of all creation on God's behalf.

The biblical worldview also acknowledges "the fall." "It is our covenantal responsibility to serve the Lord our Maker, and yet we are not forced to do so. It is possible to disobey, to depart from who we are called to be. And this possibility became reality in the fall."[163] Walsh and Middleton again stand firmly in their tradition by assuming humans are by nature religious beings. That is, we cannot live without a god; we need a centre for our being. As Bob Dylan would say, "we gotta serve somebody."

It is the nature of an idol to usurp God's place and our own place. The authors point out that it is one thing for humans to reject God and God's design for our lives, but replacing God with an idol implies a commitment to a destructive way of life. Just as humans bear the image of God when they serve God, they bear the image of any alternative god they choose to serve. The fall answers the third worldview question. What is wrong in our world is the human failure to serve God and bear God's image in all of our relationships.

Redemption defines the third component of a biblical worldview. The Bible interprets human history as a redemptive history, a story of God repeatedly making a covenant with humankind and all of creation. It is a promise to bring about God's Kingdom on earth, an event that will end the time of disobedience and its destructive consequences. All this redemptive hope is centred on the life, death, and resurrection of Jesus Christ, God incarnate. Christ is the remedy to everything that ails our world.

The authors argued that the biblical worldview of creation, fall, redemption, and restoration is a holistic and comprehensive vision for life; no part of reality that escapes its boundaries. However, Christians have historically understood it in dualistic terms due to a variety of outside influences. The distinctions between body and soul in Ancient Greek philosophy, temporal and eternal in Augustine's thought, and nature and grace in medieval philosophy have all contributed to a dualist interpretation of creation, fall, redemption, and restoration. Walsh and Middleton also suggest that the secularization of Western culture would never have occurred had Christianity not adopted a restricted view of a godly way of life. This brings us to the book's fourth topic.

The secular, modern view of the world dominates North American culture. In that world humans are autonomous, free individuals who are busy building their own utopia on Earth. There is no god, and religion amounts to superstition. Despite its distaste for deity, Walsh and Middleton name three idols that demand to be served in our modern culture: scientism, technicism, and economism. They liken them to the parts of Nebuchadnezzar's statue (idol), as described in Daniel 2.

Scientism serves as the legs of our modern idol; it embodies the foundational view that "human reason, especially in the form of scientific method, can provide exhaustive knowledge of the world of nature and mankind." Technicism rests on top of scientism like the belly of our modern idol. It "translates scientific discovery into human power." Through this power humans engage in the "efficient, productive, formative and technological mastery of nature." Economism represents the head of our idol; it glorifies wealth and commits us to an ever-expanding economy and a more affluent standard of living. The three gods together combine omniscience, omnipotence, and "full and glorious material prosperity."

The all-important final topic in the book outlined what it means to embody a biblical worldview. There is no blueprint or recipe that lays out the contours of a Christian way of life. Cultural life is dynamic, not static. Therefore, what we need is a clear vision and sense of direction. Walsh and Middle provided several directives or Kingdom signposts. The cultural vision of the Christian community must be comprehensive rather than selective. For example, it makes little difference if Christians respond to abortion but not gun violence. It makes no sense to oppose one kind of death and support another kind. Christians must renounce all their idols, which, admittedly, is a tall order. They will have to stop trusting in science, technology, and economic interactions for their salvation. The embodiment of a biblical worldview also entails a recognition of the multidimensionality of life. All aspects of life must be put in their proper place, and none can be given absolute priority. Christians also need to redefine what is considered "normal" by searching out God's norms for life. Finally, as Christians, we must regain our sense of community and belonging in every relationship that we share with others.

What Wolterstorff, Walsh, and Middleton Said Later

Wolterstorff

In 1992 Wolterstorff was the keynote speaker for the first-ever international conference of Christian schools that belonged to Christian Schools International. Christian educators from Australia, England, New Zealand, the Netherlands, and South Africa came to Toronto to attend this conference with their colleagues from Canada and the United States. Wolterstorff once again stepped back from his assigned topic on curriculum and focused instead on the goals of a Christian education, which he analyzed from various points of view. Rather than deliver a linear argument, Wolterstorff jumped from one familiar entry point to another. He cleverly employed an imaginary kaleidoscope to accomplish this. With each "spin" of the cylinder, Wolterstorff added another view to an emerging picture. It was an ingenious way to make a singular and rather simple point.

It is significant that in a speech about the goals of a Christian education delivered to an international gathering of Neo-Calvinist educators, Wolterstorff never once mentioned the words "worldview" or "perspective." Instead, he focused on the tradition's emphasis on *task*. He noted that Neo-Calvinist educators had given much thought to the proper task of the school, the teacher, the student, and the curriculum. They thoroughly understood the biblical notions of calling, responsibility, and office. In a word, the tradition understood the purpose of a Christian education as a duty. Wolterstorff did not refute this legacy, but he set out to convince his audience that Christian education should also focus on *invitation*. Students should, he claimed, also be invited to experience joy, delight, and shalom in the execution of their task. Wolterstorff did not reduce the meaning of "task" to the joy and delight of learning. He meant a Christian education should invite students to experience the joy, delight, and peace of the Christian life inside as well as outside of the school.

The tradition's fixation on task, Wolterstorff explained, was rooted in its interpretation of God's "cultural mandate," as recorded in Genesis 1:28. There God commissioned humans to be fruitful, increase in number, fill the planet, and rule over all other creatures. Neo-Calvinists thought of this mandate in terms of development. In a world where the realities of the fall and redemption overlapped, the cultural mandate implied a realignment of social institutions and structures to conform to God's norms for peace, justice, and love. Wolterstorff argued this understanding of "task" was deficient because it did not include the call to bring healing and reconciliation into the culture. God did not just command humans to perform a task, but God offered them blessing and flourishing.

Christian educators require two kinds of eyesight, Wolterstorff explained, one eye that focuses on the task of development and another eye that fixes our attention on the task of healing. He acknowledged that we can't teach students to be joyful, delighted, or justice seekers, but our teaching strategies and curricular content can set up situations that offer students the opportunity to see the miseries and injustices in the world and the challenge to act on them. After one of his spins of the imaginary kaleidoscope, Wolterstorff ventured briefly into the world of curriculum theory. He sketched out the four major orientations and emphatically rejected any combination of them as a viable context for delivering a Christian education. Without being explicit, he advocated for a distinctively Christian curriculum orientation that focused education on our transformational task to redirect culture and bring healing and reconciliation. This is as close as he ever came to offering a theory of curriculum.

Walsh and Middleton

By 1995 it was impossible to ignore the fact that postmodern attitudes and views had laid siege to the modern worldview and supplanted it on various fronts. North Americans were no longer confident in modernity's answers to the four worldview questions. In response, Walsh and Middleton published a second book, *Truth Is Stranger Than It Used to Be: Biblical Faith in a Postmodern* Age. The problem that confronted the authors was no longer why the Christian worldview was so ineffective but what value it had as a socially constructed interpretation of reality. Christians still faced the challenges that the authors outlined in *The Transforming Vision*; they needed to enlarge their vision of the Christian life and integrate it into their daily activities. Now they also had to "respond with integrity to a culture that discounted the truth of all worldviews in a way that maintained a vibrant fidelity to Scripture and brought personal and social healing."

Middleton and Walsh wrote their second book to help Christians understand the cultural shift from the modern to the postmodern condition, especially the changed status of worldviews. Consequently, they spent the first third of the book carefully comparing and critiquing the modern and postmodern answers to the four worldview questions. The Christian community, however, needed more than these insights if it wanted to be faithful to the gospel and take up the life of Christian discipleship. The second part of the book addressed that challenge head on: how then shall Christians live in a postmodern world? The authors' approach likely took many of their readers by surprise. They addressed this challenge in dialogue with the postmodern critique of metanarratives. They stated the problem in part two of the book in this unique manner: "Is the Christian faith, rooted as it is in a metanarrative of cosmic proportions, subject to the postmodern charge of totalizing violence?"[164]

Let us take a closer look at the first few chapters of the book. Here the authors outline the shift from modernity to postmodernity using their respective answers to the four worldview questions: Where are we? Who are we? What is wrong? What is the remedy? In this reorientation of cultural perspective, worldviews take a huge hit. Worldviews made sense in a modern world; they were the vehicle that carried our understanding of everything that world contained. In the postmodern world, worldviews were perceived to be the root of much evil.

The modern worldview assumes that "we are in a world of natural resources that can be known objectively by means of the scientific method and controlled by technological power."[165] We function in that world as homo-autonomous; that is, we are "the self-normed masters not only of our own destiny but of the destiny of the world."[166] Anything that impedes our autonomy, inhibits our progress, and threatens our sense of world mastery is wrong; the main culprits being ignorance, tradition, and superstition. We can create our own remedy to these hindrances by scientifically grasping and technologically controlling and transforming the world.

Middleton and Walsh explain that postmodernity undercuts the modern worldview using its highly suspicious mindset. It assumes we now live in a world where reality has become unfamiliar. Reality is no longer an objective given for us to discover; it is whatever our socially constructed worldviews tell us it is. In this world, we are *"homo linguisticus"*; we are the creators of reality through our words. Things go wrong in this world when communities attempt to make their worldview a totalizing system and meta-narrative for all. In this way worldviews are inherently violent because they seek the destruction of all alternative stories. The remedy is to dispose of all metanarratives and grand systems of truth, leaving room only for a plurality of "local tales," narratives that hold true for specific communities.

To summarize our culture's reorientation from modernity to postmodernity, reality (where we find ourselves) shifted from an objective world that we can know truthfully to a world known by multiple, subjective interpretations whose claims on truth are all suspect. Before, our human selves were centred in an objective world that operated by natural laws. In that world we understood and manipulated nature. Now our selves lack a centre, and we no longer know who we are or what our purpose is. In the modern world, ignorance, tradition, and superstition threatened scientific truth and our salvation. The postmodern world revealed that all claims to universal truth do violence to those who disagree. At one time the truth and promises of science and technology meant something. Now we are suspicious of all meta-narratives.

In part two of their book, Middleton and Walsh set out to demonstrate that the Christian faith has the resources to withstand the postmodern challenge and even learn from it. They were convinced that Christian communities who were open to learning from the postmodern critique of modernity and all metanarratives would not only remain faithful to the Scriptures but also be empowered to live out their faith as they move into the twenty-first century. To demonstrate that Christianity and its biblical metanarrative are not predisposed to violence against those who hold other narratives, the authors engage in a serious study of the Scriptures.

Middleton and Walsh make a compelling case for Christianity's relevance in a postmodern context. They argue that the Bible works against totalization because of two inherent qualities that prevent it from promoting violence. First, the biblical narrative contains a radical sensitivity to suffering. Second, the narrative is rooted in God's overarching creational intentions, which apply to everything God made, not just a portion of it. Far from promoting violence against those who reject and/or replace this metanarrative with a different one, the Bible calls people to align themselves to God's purposes for shalom, compassion, and justice.

The biblical worldview comes in the form of a story. In this narrative, humanity is given an identity and a purpose. We are made in the image of God for the purpose of caring for everything in the world. Called to a position of authority in God's creation order is vastly different from the imperial self that is imagined by the modern world. Being tasked with the stewardship of all earthly relationships is a far cry from the disoriented, purposeless self of postmodernity.

The second book from Middleton and Walsh ends on the same note as their first. What is most needed from Christians is not a better worldview but a willingness to "step into the Christian story." The risk one takes to engage the life of discipleship involves giving up on the false promises of progress and prosperity promoted by modernity and avoiding the postmodern temptation to be cynical or fall into despair. The life of discipleship is a reoriented life. Eventually, it will change the way we think, but initially the challenge is to find opportunities where people need justice, mercy, comfort, hope, and peace and to be courageous enough to act.

Five years later, Walsh published an article that put the books he wrote with Middleton into context. He titled the article "Transformation: Dynamic Worldview or Repressive Ideology."[167] He reiterated the point made in both books that he wrote with Middleton: worldviews are best understood when they are incarnated. Want to know someone's worldview? Don't ask him or her to answer the four worldview questions; check what is in their garbage.

The biblical worldview can change the way we think, and the results can be empowering, but the ultimate aim of Scripture is to change how we live. Worldview education must go well beyond an intellectual comparison of answers to worldview questions. It must also go beyond the adoption of a view of life. Christian education must match a biblical perception of the world to a life lived. Walsh believed that as long as their biblical worldview remained limited to a theoretical vision of life, Christian communities ran the risk of repressing others. When this worldview was incarnated as a way of life, Christian communities acted as peacemakers and justice seekers.

In this article, Walsh hinted at the pedagogical and curricular possibilities for initiating students into a life of Christian discipleship. In doing so he took a step in a direction that held out hope for the CSC movement. Walsh knew that the adoption of a preferred way of life involves making choices on many fronts. Choosing wisely requires appropriate criteria. Each area of the curriculum, he argued, is rife with possibilities for engagement. These decisions lead to themes that tie the various strands of education together. Education for Christian discipleship can be transformative in countless ways. For example, students can perceive and experience the land as home rather than frontier or commodity; culture can promote community and service rather than self-sufficiency and independence; and our idols of scientism, technicism, economism, sexism, hedonism, "sportism," militarism, and consumerism can be renounced instead of worshipped.

Summary

This small collection of texts from Wolterstorff, Walsh, and Middleton delivered a consistent message about worldviews generally and a biblical worldview in particular. Worldview education remains important. Christian educators and their students must be able to understand and evaluate the dominant worldview in their cultural context. Likewise, they need to understand the dynamic nature of a biblical worldview. However, as vital as worldview education is on both counts, Wolterstorff, Walsh, and Middleton do not believe it is the ultimate goal of Christian education. The purpose of Christian education is to initiate students into a way of life, the life modeled for us by Jesus Christ. This life engages culture, particularly those areas where people experience suffering and injustice. In a word, it is a life bearing hope.

These texts warned CSC educators that their Neo-Calvinist tradition of education had veered off course. The Christian school was intended to be a dissident and a transforming institution on two fronts: the development of a biblical perspective and the cultivation of a way of life. For reasons good and bad, everyone's attention had focused primarily on the development of a Christian perspective. For the tradition to get back on track, the authors identified three corrective measures: 1) CSC educators must move beyond education for a Christian perspective and initiate students into a way of life, 2) this way of life must be inclusive of all areas of culture making, and 3) the task of realigning all social structures with God's norms (the cultural mandate) must be twinned with bringing healing, hope, mercy, and justice to those who suffer.

It is relevant to note that all three authors were well versed in philosophy and theology, but they were not curriculum designers. They appeared to understand that the way educators organized the curriculum mattered, but this issue was of secondary importance. None of them acknowledged the debate between a subject-based vs. a thematic-based curriculum, much less advocated for one of the positions. For them the most important curricular issue to resolve was how to initiate students into a biblical way of life. Walsh offered some initial guidelines for curriculum planning: identify the choices that make up a lifestyle, clarify the criteria for making lifestyle choices, and plan learning tasks that present students with the challenge to enter the story of reconciliation. Wolterstorff also challenged educators to construct learning situations that challenged students to see and respond to those who suffer unjustly. In addition to that, he urged educators to cultivate learning where students experienced the joy and peace that acting in love generates.

Having sketched the arc of change in the Neo-Calvinist's educational vision, we will next turn to an evaluation of some of the most influential texts in our list of publications. The purpose of this exercise is to determine what curriculum orientation these popular texts promoted and to what degree this orientation represented a course correction for the tradition.

Geraldine Steensma: An American Crusader

Geraldine Steensma was a pioneer in the Neo-Calvinist project to reimagine what education could and ought to be when a school community primarily looks to the Bible for its vision. In "Dig Deeper," Topic 3, we reviewed some of the views that her father, Professor Cornelius Jaarsma, promoted at Calvin College. In important ways, she took up her father's mantle when she advocated for an education that stands on Biblical foundations and recognizes students as responsible and whole persons rather than passive minds.

Steensma was a daughter of the Neo-Calvinist education movement, but she received her undergraduate degree from Slippery Rock State College and earned a master's degree at Teachers College, Columbia University. Her time at Teachers College coincided with that of Philip Phenix, a brilliant professor, who at the tender age of nineteen impressed Albert Einstein with his mathematical ability. Phenix wrote numerous books on education, and nearly all of them emphasized his vision for the integration of the academic disciplines. Although Steensma's philosophy of education was born of different intellectual parents that propelled her toward a different end point, her concept of curriculum design and subject integration bears the unmistakable DNA of the views that Phenix propagated.[168]

Steensma was a teacher and administrator in both Christian and public schools during her first career. She had a reputation for innovative teaching, deep understanding, compassion for students, and a passion to fix what she saw as broken in North American education. She was a person who embodied an Augustinian brand of hope, she was zealous about the need for authentic Christian education, and she dedicated her life to its flourishing. She was a professor of education and director of the teacher education program at Covenant College in the early 1970s.[169] The qualities that defined her reputation as a schoolteacher/administrator deepened during her stint at Covenant.

Over a span of approximately twenty years, Steensma influenced the Canadian wing of the Neo-Calvinist school movement in several noteworthy ways. She led workshops and gave speeches for teachers, she consulted with them in their classrooms, and she authored several important texts, including an address that appeared in a CDC newsletter.[170] Steensma and her husband, Richard, set up Signal Publishing Company to distribute literature that promoted Christian education. In 1971 she used Signal to publish a short book of about one hundred pages, entitled *To Those Who Teach: Keys for Decision-Making*. Steensma described this work as a "pedagogical statement" written primarily for the benefit of her students at Covenant College. In the early 1970s, it was virtually the only visionary book on teaching available to CSC teachers.

The book contained eight "keys," and each one was meant to unlock a perennial educational problem. This set of keys provided an abbreviated framework that especially beginning teachers could use to set a course for their careers as Christian educators. Steensma cut these keys from her deep well of biblical knowledge and classroom experience, but it was up to her students to use them to unlock these problems in their own classrooms and schools.

The first three keys addressed the role of the student, the role of the teacher, and the nature of their relationship. A traditional understanding of all three was one-dimensional and fragmented, Steensma believed. For example, it variously misrepresented the student as a mind, a personality, a noble savage, a worker, or a problem-solver. These reductionist perceptions were based on the ways notable Western thinkers understood the essence of humanity: as rational (Plato), as psychological (Freud), as natural (Rousseau), as economic (Marx), and as social (Dewey). The role of teacher was equally limited in scope. Steensma was particularly concerned about the dominant image of the teacher as technician. She also disagreed with the traditional classroom where the teacher held all the power and made all of the important decisions while students were passive and rarely given responsibility.

Steensma reimagined the roles of student and teacher and their relationship. Students must be seen as fully functional and relational creatures. Like their teachers, students are image-bearers of God, which means they must be encouraged to respond meaningfully in their foundational relationships to God, to fellow humans, and to creation, both inside and outside the school.

She defined the role of teacher using a nucleus of three biblical offices: prophet, priest, and king. To faithfully fulfill the office of prophet, teachers must know who they are with respect to the creator, their neighbours, and the creation. They must be knowledgeable about the world and be able to interpret the spirits of the age. In the office of priest, teachers must surrender themselves to service; in ultimate terms, their lives are not their own. They are expected to be agents of healing who intercede where there is brokenness. To execute the office of king, teachers must exercise self-control and channel their power and authority for the good of others. Authority must give form to an educational setting that serves justice, mercy, peace, and understanding. Given these reimagined roles, the teacher-student relationship must be transformed into one of mutual flourishing where teachers foster student responsibility and students respond to the teacher's authentic nurturing.

The second set of keys addressed learning: what it looks like, its appropriate context, and what should be taught and how. In the traditional classroom, learning was limited to the cognitive recall of factual knowledge. Abstract subject disciplines provided the context for this learning and determined what skills students should acquire. Steensma thought learning should be personally meaningful and take the form of authentic and concrete acts of culture making. Her views anticipated by thirty-five years the important work of Andy Crouch.[171] The context for learning is concrete experience, not abstract academic disciplines. Students should always see the unity that binds diversity. She believed the skills of reading, writing, and mathematical computation should be taught at all levels of education in conjunction with the integration of disciplinary skills.

At times Steensma appeared to reject a subject-based curriculum, but what concerned her was teaching that kept the disciplines isolated and disconnected from each other. She revered the academic disciplines, which she believed helped students focus on what needs to be known. The academic disciplines offered students essential content, a particular method of inquiry, and different ways to organize knowledge. The normative features unique to each discipline did not necessarily lead to the fragmentation of knowledge. To consciously integrate the disciplines, she took her cues from the thinking of Philip Phenix.

The final two keys dealt with building community in the classroom and the larger context of teaching. The status quo situation reflected a systemic lack of harmony in the classroom. Students felt powerless in the presence of their teachers. Similarly, teachers often felt dominated by their administrators. Respect and open communication were hard to find in most school settings. The task of teaching was often equated with transmitting content and behaviour management.

Steensma believed that success in utilizing the first six keys mentioned above ensured the development of a classroom community of learning. Mutual respect and understanding were sure to prosper when teachers and students respected each other's calling and office, shared decision-making responsibilities, and gave priority to learning that was meaningful and relevant.

The true context for teaching was "ministry." This ministry was characterized by reconciliation, commitment, authenticity, and community. Through reconciliation students learned to forgive and to be forgiven. When teachers nurtured commitment, they empowered their students to transcend the temptations to conform and respond with their personal convictions. Authenticity encouraged students to know and respect themselves and others. Finally, the ministry of community impressed upon students that no one is self-sufficient, and our well-being hinges on the quality of our relationships.

Many CSC teachers were inspired by this little book. They had virtually nothing else to draw from until *Joy in Learning* was published in 1973. After *JIL* appeared, they had to wait another four years before the next significant book emerged, this one also initiated by Steensma. She was well aware of the limitations of her first book, and she immediately started to plan a second, more substantial project. She imagined a book that would articulate a fully formed biblical framework for curriculum development.

By 1974 Steensma was no longer teaching at Covenant College but was working as a full-time consultant for Signal. That year she invited Canadian Harro Van Brummelen to help her launch her project. Three years later they published *Shaping School Curriculum: A Biblical View*.[172] Thirteen educators from Canada and the United States also contributed to this text. Steensma and Van Brummelen functioned as editors, but they also wrote the all-important framework and vision sections for the text as well as two of its chapters. The other contributors applied the Steensma-Van Brummelen framework, as each understood it, to a discipline for which they had some recognized expertise. Thus, the book not only spelled out a conceptual framework for curriculum planning but also applied it to a wide range of academic disciplines.

According to Ary DeMoor,[173] the curriculum coordinator for CSC schools in Alberta at the time, *Shaping* influenced curriculum writing in CSC schools during the late 1970s more than any other published source. This book's curricular framework nurtured hope within CSC's grassroots curriculum-writing movement in at least five ways.

First, Steensma and Van Brummelen set forth an inspiring yet demanding framework for curriculum development. They affirmed the Neo-Calvinist legacy that Christian education "is to equip students to live lives of response to their Creator, Redeemer and Lord."[174] This vision is rooted in the biblical revelation that God called humanity into being to actively reconcile "all the aspects of His creation so that Christ may be preeminent (Col 1:18.)"[175] This work of reconciliation clearly referred to

God's cultural mandate: the human responsibility to structure society in accordance with God's norms. The authors, however, also pointed out that reconciliation involves healing what has become distorted and ruined by sin on a personal level.

Second, the framework spelled out a biblical view of knowledge that challenged the dominant perception of knowledge as the acquisition of information and intellectual know-how. The biblical way of knowing, they argued, is not a matter of the head but the heart; it embodies "a formative function." When we "know," in the biblical sense, we not only acquire information, we also engage in a personal relationship that commits us to act in accord with what we know. In other words, we don't truly know something until we have acted on it in the context of a relationship. The implications of this element in the Steensma/Van Brummelen approach were huge: minimally, it meant the intellectual acquisition of a view of life is insufficient; students must live it to really know it.

Steensma and Van Brummelen also resurrected two other elements in the Neo-Calvinist legacy. They acknowledged that students need to recognize that Christians stand in the world as dissenters and reformers. A Christian approach to curriculum must, therefore, equip students with the sensibility and the ability to critique what is broken in their culture and empower them to be agents of healing and justice.

Fourth, this book provided elaborate designs for both elementary and secondary curricula. These models reflected multiple levels of knowledge and, within each level, various areas of study. The authors also used them to demonstrate how to balance academic study with perspectival learning.

Lastly, the book outlined a much-needed approach to construct and implement an integrated unit. The key component in this unit-building process was the "conceptual statement."[176] Teachers were encouraged to articulate a conceptual statement prior to planning a unit of study. "This statement should contain the key idea(s) toward which all thought and activity will be directed."[177] If at all possible, biblical norms and thinking were to be incorporated in the conceptual statement. Prior to this innovation, CSC teachers had no tools or design principles to use in curriculum planning; they simply had to rely on their own intuition and understanding of Scripture to filter what content was included and excluded from their curriculum.

Overall, *Shaping* provided CSC teachers with inspiration for, and a method of, developing curriculum units. CSC teachers were understandably drawn to the specific strategies outlined in the book and the new tools it made available. The book also contained some significant weaknesses, but its benefits distracted CSC educators from these shortcomings.

The approach to curriculum planning in *Shaping* was conflicted by the fact that it recognized two different ordering principles for the curriculum: the human calling to live a life of reconciliation revealed in the Bible and the structural unity of the subject disciplines, as described by Philip Phenix. Harry Fernhout drew attention to this conflict in a paper he presented at a conference organized by Harro Van Brummelen in 1981.[178] Fernhout raised concerns that at a critical point in the development of their curriculum framework in *Shaping*, Steensma and Van Brummelen adopted Phenix's rationalist position.[179] Phenix certainly held convictions that resonated well with the biblical approach that Steensma and Van Brummelen promoted, but Eisner and Vallance[180] pegged his approach as an outstanding example of a curriculum for self-actualization or consummatory experience.[181] In the end, the logical structure of the disciplines functions as the organizing principle of the curriculum in *Shaping*, which biased curriculum planning toward perspective development rather than life-style engagement.

The issue of who or what forms the hearts of students is important, but Steensma and Van Brummelen get tangled up in theological red tape when they assume students had to be converted to Christ by the Holy Spirit before they could meaningfully take up the life of discipleship in a school setting. Their position is problematic on at least two levels. First, all confessing Christians live conflicted lives; conversion does not represent a clean break from one way of life to another. Christians (too) easily move back and forth between the life of discipleship and the comfortable, consumption-centred lifestyle that dominates our culture. Similarly, people of different faith traditions, even those who profess no faith at all, have been known to embody in their way of life, the qualities the Bible associates with discipleship. Second, if teachers assume their students cannot meaningfully engage a Christian way of life until such time as the Holy Spirit leads them to embrace it, then they are likely to focus on "equipping" their students for this life, as Steensma and Van Brummelen suggest, rather than challenging their students to try this life on for size.

Shaping offers an approach to curriculum development that is meant to prepare students to live in response to their creator. The heart of this preparation is the acquisition of a deeper understanding of the unity and diversity of creation. Steensma and Van Brummelen believed a subject-based curriculum, as imagined by Phenix, made these insights readily available. Taken to its logical end, their approach altered the face of education, but it did not change its basic nature as an academic examination of ideas.

The curriculum models that appear in *Shaping* also detract from its vision of education for a way of life. They bias education toward learning about the disciplines and their interconnections rather than learning how to live a life focused on reconciliation and healing. These models suggest that the academic disciplines function as the ordering principle of the curriculum, not the life of responsible discipleship.

The conceptual statement tool developed in the framework had great potential for advancing the quality of unit planning among CSC educators, but it also biased education toward an academic experience. It reinforced the traditional view that ideas precede action and the reconciliation of relationships. Van Brummelen and Steensma also predisposed the writing of conceptual statements toward theological clichés, "God talk," and variations of the creation-fall-redemption-restoration meta-narrative when they said:

> If Biblical norms and thinking are reflected in the statement, the possibility that the student will commit himself to live by that which he has acquired academically will be enhanced. In doing this the teacher sees beyond the acquisition of the concept; he [sic] will look for personal commitment that will lead to loving action in the student's life.[182]

In actual practice, most of the conceptual statements written by CSC teachers failed to demonstrate the coherence between faith, worldview, aim of education, curriculum philosophy, unit content, pedagogy, student evaluation, and actual acts of culture making. Too often their units featured God talk at the beginning and end, leaving the content in the middle largely untouched. Because of this "bookends" approach to integrating Christian perspective, the gap between the conceptual statement and the life of response to God remained wide.

Steensma and Van Brummelen promoted the development of "integrated units," and their reasons for doing so overlapped with the Curriculum Development Centre's (CDC) approach. Like the curriculum developers at the CDC, they believed the academic disciplines only provide students with a limited understanding of reality, as separate entities. Both *Joy in Learning* and *Shaping* endorsed the use of intradisciplinary or multidisciplinary forms of integration, and each had their own reasons for stopping short of advocating for inter- and trans-disciplinary approaches.[183] Consequently, curriculum integration as practiced in CSC has generally not been truly thematic but has featured a rotation of familiar disciplinary perspectives engaged one at a time while focused on a particular topic.

It is safe to assume that Steensma's intentions with *Shaping* anticipated the corrective measures advocated by Wolterstorff, Walsh, and Middleton many years later. She and Van Brummelen envisioned a Christian life that addressed broken relationships and suffering on both the cultural and personal levels of experience. They ventured into uncharted waters when they worked backwards from a way of life to curriculum development, but these forays were limited in number and not well developed. In the end, their curriculum framework did not break loose from the traditional notion that a school provides an academic experience.

Harro Van Brummelen: A Canadian Champion of Curriculum Reform

Harro Van Brummelen was born in the Netherlands and emigrated to Canada with his parents in 1953 at the age of eleven. He graduated from McGill University with a BEd, specializing in mathematics. He went on to get a master's in education at the University of Toronto and a PhD in education from the University of British Columbia. His career in Christian Schools Canada included the teaching of high school mathematics, serving as a principal, and holding the position of education coordinator. During his second career in higher learning, he excelled as a professor, faculty chair, and assistant dean at Trinity Western University in Langley, British Columbia. Van Brummelen was a careful scholar, a beloved teacher, an insightful mentor, an effective administrator, and a tireless promoter of Christian education. His influence within CSC circles is unapparelled, and his reputation extends well beyond the Neo-Calvinist tradition. It would take a book to properly account for and celebrate Van Brummelen's singular impact on the development of the Neo-Calvinist school movement, particularly in Canada. Hopefully, someone will write that book soon.

In part I, I drew heavily upon Van Brummelen's first major solo publication, *Telling the Next Generation*. In that book he reveals the Dutch roots of the Neo-Calvinist school movement in North America and traces the tradition's development from 1848 to 1977, particularly as it unfolded in the United States. At the end of that work, Van Brummelen expressed his dismay over the general direction NUCS had taken, and he said the jury was still out with respect to the willingness and ability of its Canadian school districts to implement the tradition's educational vision of cultural transformation.

As an acknowledged leader on both sides of the Canada/US border, Van Brummelen did what he could throughout his career to keep the Neo-Calvinist tradition of education on track. Notable among his many efforts were two major publications, *Walking with God in the Classroom* and *Steppingstones to Curriculum*. He also made significant contributions to several other important books. For the purposes of this chapter, I will briefly address what I consider to be Van Brummelen's legacy as a visionary, a scholar, a curriculum theorist, and a game changer.

Most of Van Brummelen's contemporaries considered him to be the voice of the tradition's educational vision. He was, after all, the person who gave names to the various ways that CSC educators interpreted and expressed their vision. What he called the *monastic approach* sought to protect students from the influences of the surrounding culture. This protectionist vision rekindled the mentality of the nineteenth-century *Afscheiding* movement in the Netherlands, which still defined some elements of the CSC community.[184] The *dualist approach* made Christian academics look attractive and attainable. However, this vision represented an unholy synthesis of Christian morality, doctrine, and social theory with secular assumptions and standards for education. By contrast, the *integrationist approach* reimagined an education wholly shaped by a biblical worldview and committed to the transformation of culture. Van Brummelen was recognized as the leading advocate of this vision.

Van Brummelen was a visionary on other fronts as well. He saw the need to advance the overall quality of Christian scholarship about education. In response to this need, he was the principal organizer of several major academic conferences. These events built up a broad community of scholars, most of whom were active educators. He also advocated for the development of learning communities that extended beyond the walls of the school. These communities provided the optimal context for learning and were essential for the implementation of education for discipleship.

Scholarship was another of Van Brummelen's strengths. His books capably addressed a wide range of topics, including philosophy of education, learning theory, pedagogy, leadership, student assessment, and, of course, curriculum theory and design. His analysis was at once compelling and punctuated with examples taken from the classrooms of teachers that he knew personally. In *Walking* he sketched out a Christian approach to teaching and learning that addressed a plethora of topics, such as the purpose of the school, the nature of teaching, a model for structuring a classroom, a theory of knowledge, curriculum planning, student evaluation, and the school as a learning community. This was the only text to emerge from the Canadian Neo-Calvinist tradition that could effectively serve as a textbook for university-level education students and as a resource for Christian educators regardless of the school system in which they taught.

Van Brummelen's last published book, *Steppingstones*, was equally notable. It is the most complete example of an alternative curriculum orientation to emerge from the Neo-Calvinist tradition of education. Although he would never say so, many CSC educators thought this book ended the quest for the holy grail of Neo-Calvinist curriculum reform.

Steppingstones represented the alternative curriculum orientation the tradition had long pursued.

In addition to Van Brummelen being a visionary and a scholar, he understood the challenges of curriculum design. His insights as a curriculum theorist were invaluable to the teacher-led curriculum-writing movement that emerged in CSC in the 1970s and flourished for many years afterward. Neo-Calvinist teachers had long struggled to effectively integrate their biblical worldview of creation-fall-redemption-restoration into the school curriculum because they lacked the requisite philosophical insights and a method for designing curriculum.

Van Brummelen provided the tradition with several effective conceptual tools. For example, he showed teachers how to take their first baby steps to connect worldview to biblical perspective. Step one drew parallels between a standard set of worldview questions and the grand narrative of Scripture: "Who am I?" (God's image bearer) "Where am I?" (creation) "What has gone wrong?" (the fall) "What is the remedy?" (redemption) "What does the future hold?" (restoration). He next demonstrated how these questions could be rephrased and reinterpreted in such a way that the biblical grand narrative provided a new perspective and context of meaning for the curriculum.[185]

Van Brummelen also popularized the conceptual statement, a tool that first appeared in *Shaping* and which he preferred to call a thematic statement. This tool helped teachers construct their own curriculum units, which, in turn, made them less dependent upon textbooks written from a secular perspective. Teachers used the thematic statement to describe the big picture of an original unit of study. In *Walking*, Van Brummelen used the thematic statement to describe what the unit was supposed to teach. He distinguished three categories of content:
- The unit's general themes (hence the name "thematic statement")
- All the concepts and skills that students were to learn
- The attitudes, dispositions, and commitments the unit was meant to foster in students

The thematic statement evolved considerably in *Steppingstones*. In addition to the three types of content outlined in *Walking*, Van Brummelen added *enduring understandings* and *guiding questions*. An *enduring understanding* or big idea "goes beyond the description of content to be learned." It referred to what is most worth remembering about a unit: that is, the perspective gained or the understanding achieved in the process of learning the content. *Guiding questions* (or *essential questions,* as they are sometimes called) are the first-order, open-ended questions that help students discover and engage the enduring understandings. These questions often begin with the word "why."

Van Brummelen expanded the role of the thematic statement in a second way, with the addition of a rationale section. The teacher had to give a compelling justification for the unit's place in the curriculum. To build a persuasive case, the teacher had to understand how the unit fit in with the rest of the school's program of studies, why it was relevant to students' lives, and how it engaged them with relevant local, regional, and global matters.

Of all the elements that make up Van Brummelen's legacy, the most significant for me was his role as a game changer. Like Wolterstorff, Steensma, and the curriculum designers at the CDC, he wanted the Neo-Calvinist tradition of education in Canada to move beyond the cultivation of a *worldview* to the pursuit of a *way of life*. He referred to that way of life as the life of responsible or responsive discipleship. Therefore, the most challenging question that Van Brummelen ever had to answer was, how do teachers educate for discipleship?

Van Brummelen's legacy in the Neo-Calvinist tradition of education is unmatched. So, why did his efforts not accomplish everything he hoped for? The tradition failed to measure up to his expectations because many CSC educators struggled to achieve the high standards that he set. I count myself in that group. It is also the case that his approach had some built-in shortcomings, and I will next focus on three of them.

More than once, Van Brummelen stated that teachers must plan activities where students are put in situations that challenge them to make authentic decisions that are congruent with a biblical way of life. On these pivotal occasions, Van Brummelen took the Neo-Calvinist tradition to the very doorstep of education for discipleship. However, he consistently refused to cross the threshold into the space where students are *initiated* into a life of discipleship. Van Brummelen would only go so far as to say

Christian education *equipped* students for that life, a position that kept him locked in the land of perspective development.

The difference between "initiating into" and "equipping for" may sound trivial, but it is significant. In our earlier analysis of the book, *Shaping School Curriculum*, we took note of Van Brummelen's view that only the Holy Spirit could initiate students into the Christian life. He also believed that a curriculum orientation that "equipped" students for a life of discipleship functioned as a "frame for learning," but it was not "the building." It gave teachers a light for their path, but it was not a strategic plan.[186] He believed that a curriculum orientation (necessarily) stopped short of engaging teachers and students in the life of discipleship. Van Brummelen once observed that *Steppingstones* dealt with the planned curriculum, not the experienced curriculum. These views set him slightly apart from those educators who believed their task was to initiate and immerse students into a life of discipleship.

A second shortcoming pertains to Van Brummelen's understanding of the major curriculum orientations. Van Brummelen provided his readers with an accurate but cursory knowledge of the major curriculum orientations in *Walking*. He fleshed them out more fully in *Steppingstones*. Despite his abundant knowledge about these orientations, he underestimated their formative power over the regularities of the classroom and their ability to obstruct the implementation of alternative visions of education. He recognized that curriculum orientations provided a general sense of direction for teaching and learning, but he believed teachers took that common point of reference in different directions depending on their own basic beliefs about life and education. He compared this reality to a group of authors using the same opening chapter to write different books.[187]

Over the course of his career, Van Brummelen argued that a community of learning was the only context within which an education for discipleship would become manifested. He assumed this community had to extend beyond the walls of the school, but, unfortunately, he did not elaborate on what this community looked like or how it could be developed.

The Neo-Calvinist tradition has always made curriculum reform a top priority, believing it is the vehicle that ultimately transports an alternative vision of education into reality. Van Brummelen provided the tradition with its most well-equipped vehicle. He stood shoulder to shoulder with Steensma, Wolterstorff, Walsh, and Middleton, who all believed the ultimate aim of Christian education is a way of life. His curriculum orientation brought the tradition to the very doorstep where education for perspective meets education for a way of life; however, it stopped just short of achieving the desired course correction.

Seven Canucks and a Yankee

An unprecedented event in CSC's history took place in 1980, when Christian Schools International (CSI), formerly the National Union of Christian Schools (NUCS) published *Man in Society: A Study in Hope*.[188] What the *Joy in Learning* (*JIL*) curriculum did for CSC elementary teachers in the 1970s, the *MIS* curriculum duplicated for CSC secondary teachers in the 1980s. Both projects were conceived in the Summer Program in Christian Education (SPICE) curriculum workshops held in Ontario and were developed over several years by teachers who were willing to give up a significant portion of their brief summer holidays to construct an alternative curriculum. Both also embodied a bold vision for reframing the curriculum by consciously interpreting the content from a biblical perspective and organizing it in an interdisciplinary fashion.

The *JIL* and *MIS* publication stories, however, could not be more different. In chapter 5, we chronicled the efforts of four women who used their own money and an imaginary organization to launch *JIL*. The teachers who wrote the *MIS* curriculum managed to get it published through their American parent organization. This accomplishment has historic significance because *MIS* was the first and, to my knowledge, only curriculum project that CSI ever published that was designed for and written by CSC teachers.

The *MIS* project did not fit the CSI mold for curriculum development. For starters, its authors were teachers, not pay rolled researchers. More contentious was the fact that the curriculum philosophy behind the project was not congruent with CSI's Principles into Practice[189] guidelines; indeed, the two documents were rooted in conflicting curriculum orientations. So, why did CSI feel compelled to sponsor the *MIS* project?

The decision was politically motivated. Throughout the 1970s its three Canadian districts accused CSI of harboring an exclusively American bias. A major point of contention was the fact that all the money the home office collected on a per-student basis from its Canadian schools to fund the publication of textbooks was allocated to projects that primarily served the needs of the American districts. To demonstrate its willingness to be more inclusive, the organization changed its name in 1977 from the National Union of Christian Schools to Christian Schools International. The *MIS* curriculum proposal served as the first major test of CSI's new inclusive posture. If CSI refused to publish *MIS*, it risked alienating all three of its Canadian districts.

The *MIS* curriculum was not an Ontario project, even though it evolved from the "Christian Life" course that Bert Witvoet[190] taught at Toronto District Christian High School in the mid-1960s and was developed in the womb of SPICE workshops. During the mid-1970s, teachers from all three districts worked on the *MIS* curriculum in these summer work sessions and piloted the units in their own classrooms. By the time I joined the project in the summer following my first year of teaching, the project's creators had moved on to other endeavors, and the project torch had been passed to a new group of teachers

The seven of us who worked on the *Man in Society* course during the summers of 1977 and 1978 were committed to its development for use in our own classrooms and to the task of publishing it, so others could use it as well. All of us were young and in the early stages of our teaching careers. We had limited classroom experience and no background in curriculum writing. We might have been more concerned about our collective deficiencies had we not been so buoyed up by a shared vision of infusing our school curriculums with a Christian perspective of reconciliation and hope. In our enthusiasm to complete the *MIS* project, each of us accepted the responsibility to be the principal author for one or two of the units in our second year of working together. Some of us worked alone while others worked in pairs.

We assembled the final version of the project during a one-week planning/editing session in Edmonton in July of 1979. CSI had agreed to publish the text, but with conditions. The most contentious of them required the addition of their representative, Gordon Oosterman, to our writing team. To our surprise, Oosterman was not threatened by our approach, and he did his part to bring the project to fruition. At the end of our Edmonton meetings, we turned our respective documents over to Ary De Moor and Oosterman, who saw the project through to its publication at CSI. Although De Moor was one of our "group of seven," many of us still felt uncomfortable relinquishing control of the project to CSI because we were not convinced that its publication of the *MIS* manual would meet our approval.

Before we consider the relative strengths and weaknesses of the project, we need a mental picture of the *MIS* text. Like *JIL*, *MIS* was published in the form of a large three-ring binder, so teachers could personalize the course with the addition and subtraction of material over time. The published document totalled 550 pages and was divided into 8 units of study. These units were meant to function equally well as a resource for teachers and a textbook for students.

The first unit dealt with perspective—what it is and why it is important. For us the notion of a disinterested, objective presentation of "the facts" was a myth. Textbooks always promoted a bias, and we felt it was crucial to clarify ours and the pivotal role it played in shaping the text. The next three units focused on living in community, the healthy development of a self-image, and the personal relationships of friendship, courtship, marriage, and family. The remaining four units addressed major areas of human activity in the larger society: politics, education, work, and mass communication. Each unit was organized around several main topics. Each of these topics was further divided into subtopics. A set of student readings appeared at the end of every unit.

The authors of each unit primarily focused on two tasks: the selection of the most relevant content and the development of a biblical interpretation of that content's meaning. Our main resources for executing these tasks were our intuitions and a collective reservoir of knowledge. The central biblical theme of creation-fall-redemption-restoration served as the ordering principle for our units. We applied this motif to each unit by unpacking our answers to these four perspectival questions:

- What does the Bible teach us about this area of society?

- How have history and tradition shaped our ideas and the development of each of these areas?
- What is the present condition of this area in Canadian society?
- What changes and alternatives can Christians propose and implement that will contribute to the reconciliation of this area of society with God's purposes?

The *MIS* project had two notable strengths, the first being its vision. The stated purpose of the course was to *educate for hope*. The inspiration for this vision came from the apostle Paul, who observed that in Christ all things are made new. God reconciled Himself to us through Christ and gave us the work of reconciling the world to Himself. In our carrying out of this task, we act as "ambassadors for Christ."[191]

As a group of authors, we believed that to faithfully journey down the pathway of hope, Christians must heal what has become broken in our four foundational relationships: We to God, I to self, I to my neighbour, and We to all creation. This vision initially came to expression in our work as an alternative perspective for learning. It challenged teachers and students alike to reimagine the nature of human relationships in various areas of social intercourse. We also believed the vision came to full expression in the actual work of reconciliation. Therefore, the ultimate aim of the course was to engage students in faithful living, not to simply think about it.

The manual's second strength was closely connected to the first. To fully implement the vision of the course we assumed teachers had to employ non-traditional ways of teaching, learning, and evaluating student work. Like most CSC teachers, we initially thought it was possible to develop a biblical perspective in students utilizing a traditional classroom setting, but the more we pursued an education for reconciliation, the more we realized the *MIS* curriculum required a more holistic and student-friendly orientation to curriculum design, pedagogy, and assessment.

I would be remiss if I did not say up front that these two strengths would have been more pronounced in the manual had they actually been embodied in the teaching of those who wrote it. To be honest, we struggled to live up to the demands of our own vision. If we had been further along in our own adoption of non-traditional forms of curriculum organization and pedagogy, the manual would have contained more compelling examples and clearer guidelines for teaching the course. Notwithstanding our shortcoming as teachers of the course, the *MIS* project was historically significant because its vision reoriented high school educators to go beyond the formation of a Christian worldview perspective.

The *MIS* curriculum had some serious weaknesses too. For starters, the project suffered from a crisis of identity. This crisis emerged on several levels, and in each instance, we expected the project to be too many things all at once. First, we expected the text to be a resource book for both students and teachers. We did not fully appreciate the challenges that this decision presented to us. We had no idea what constituted a minimal set of resources for teachers or for students of different abilities, nor did we plan what material was best suited for teachers or students. Having no strategy, we did not clearly indicate which elements in the units were primarily meant for teachers or students and which could be meaningfully shared. To further complicate the situation, the units were laid out in textbook fashion. This format suggested that students should read everything.

At the time it seemed to us a text that could double as a resource for teachers and a textbook for students was both admirable and desirable. We gave little thought to the down sides.

This confusion was rooted in a deeper identity problem. The *MIS* curriculum evolved as a course that the seven of us had to teach in our own schools. The only time we worked on this course together was during short summer sessions for planning and writing. Our efforts naturally focused on unit development; there was simply no time to design and write out a curriculum design framework or rationale for our work. We consciously employed the creation-fall-redemption-restoration theme as the ordering principle of the curriculum, but we did not flesh it out very well. The text embodied many undeclared assumptions that teachers outside of our group would not know. If our sole purpose for designing the course was to enable others to teach it, the manual would surely have turned out differently. In the end our "in house" course had to double as a published "resource/textbook," marketed to be purchased as a class set.

The identity and place of the course within the larger school curriculum was also overly complicated. In their earliest years, CSC high schools offered a four-year Bible study curriculum. The *Man in Society* course grew out of a concern that graduates from the school lacked a biblical perspective on life. This perspective was supposed to be cultivated in every course, but the idea emerged that the grade twelve Bible course should be converted into a concentrated perspectives course. The *Man in Society* course was not meant to absolve other courses and their teachers from the responsibility of fostering a Christian worldview; rather, it was to serve as the capstone course for a Christ-centred education. The introduction to the *MIS* manual offered options for utilizing the course. We said it could be a one-year stand-alone course or be combined with another subject like English or Bible as a two-year course. Our desire to make the manual as versatile as possible resulted in a manual that lacked a clear identity and sense of purpose.

The second area of weakness concerned curriculum organization and pedagogy. Even though we strongly believed our vision of education or hope demanded the implementation of a non-traditional approach to both, we waffled on our messaging. At most we encouraged prospective teachers of the course to step outside of their traditional comfort zones and assign individual work and group work, balance written work with class discussions and community research, add student presentations to teacher presentations, solicit student ideas, and find resources that had local significance and/or relevance to students. In an attempt to make the manual universally acceptable, our introduction went so far as to say the book was intended "to be of maximum service to most styles of teaching and learning." This statement effectively let teachers off the hook.

The curriculum was also burdened by a third weakness: it was overly biased toward the development of perspective rather than fostering opportunities for students to engage in reconciliation. This bias was engrained in the CSC, so it comes as no surprise that it showed up so prominently here despite our efforts to move past it.

The development of perspective dominated the project because all formative influence flowed from ideas to action: biblical faith gave birth to worldview, and worldview informed philosophy and theory, which, in turn, shaped learning, and learning led to action. The course preoccupied teachers with the fleshing out of the students' understanding of social structures, the history of their development, the current status of these structures, and the systemic changes we needed to repair them. For us, worldview was the only deep driver of the curriculum. We could not imagine designing the course by working backwards from concrete, broken situations that needed reconciliation, a strategy that would have been more consistent with our vision.

Looking back, I believe the greatest strength of the *MIS* curriculum was its focus on reconciliation and hope. Its authors understood these as central qualities of the life Jesus modelled for us, and we held them out as goals for our students. On this score we anticipated the corrective measures that Wolterstorff, Walsh, and Middleton called for a few years later. However, we remained entrenched in worldview education for a variety of reasons. We struggled to set aside our traditional approach to teaching. Once the manual was published, we stopped meeting as a group. Had we continued to work together, perhaps we would have fostered more hope in our respective classrooms.

Exit Slip #2: A Season for Hope: Summary and Conclusions

The last thirty years of the twentieth century represented a period of hope for Canadian Neo-Calvinist education. Dutch immigrants built a kindergarten-to-graduate-degree system of schools in record time. The elementary and secondary schools that made up the three regional districts of Christian Schools Canada served thousands of students and attracted highly qualified teachers and administrators. CSC schools had come of age and were primed to take up the dual roles of dissident and transformative social institution.

Most parents and educators working in the CSC system at that time assumed the school's contribution to cultural transformation was the cultivation of a biblical worldview in their students. They also believed the school's success in implementing this perspective required a retooled curriculum.

A grassroots movement led by teachers inspired all of the significant initiatives to rewrite the curriculum. Though remarkable for its duration and quality, this movement's accomplishments were limited due to a perennial lack of time and resources. Working alone or in small groups, primarily in summer workshop settings, CSC teachers managed to crank out dozens of new unit plans or, in a few cases, revise an existing course. They did this without the benefit of a well-defined philosophical framework or curriculum orientation. Two major projects stand out, the *Joy in Learning* curriculum for lower elementary grades and the *Man in Society* curriculum for senior high school students. Both projects were intended to push the envelope of Christian education beyond the formation of a Christian mind toward a way of life. Both also emphasized the need to move away from traditional patterns of teaching and learning in the classroom.

The *JIL* project gave birth to the Curriculum Development Centre, which tried to develop an alternative curriculum orientation while working outside of the NUCS/CSI system. The teachers who wrote the *MIS* curriculum sought to bring about curricular change from within the system. Both curriculum documents created significant ripples across the waters of CSC during the first half of this period, but despite these efforts, the overall vision of educating for perspective remained dominant.

During the second half of this thirty-year period, a body of literature emerged that addressed two critical issues: educational vision and curriculum reform. The authors of these texts were either philosophers and theologians who taught at the university level or visionary schoolteachers. Those most removed from the elementary and secondary classroom made the strongest case for educating for a way of life, but they offered little insight into the strategies required to implement this goal. Visionary educators who had plenty of classroom experience, brought the movement to the doorstep of implementing an alternative curriculum orientation. However, no one clearly described a combination of curriculum activities and teaching strategies that initiated students into a way of life.

CSC's ability to implement its vision of cultural transformation was stymied by several obstacles. Three of them emerged from within the movement itself, and one was an external threat. CSC's aspirations were restrained from within by its American parent organization, divisions within its own ranks, and the unwillingness of its communities to commit to the radical life of Christian discipleship. The intractability of the traditional roles for teachers, students, and schools rooted in the paradigm of progressive education also held them in check.

This period in the CSC narrative has some important lessons to teach us about educational reform. The main lesson to be learned is this: it is even more difficult to implement an alternative educational vision than it is to build a system of independent schools. Four additional lessons bear this out. Classroom teachers must be heavily involved in the implementation of curricular and pedagogical reforms. The traditional roles of school, teacher and student undermine the establishment of alternative educational visions. To make the switch from traditional to non-traditional forms of teaching and learning, teachers need administrative support, peer collaboration, classroom consulting, and lots of time. A system-wide program of reform needs buy-in from the people who wield the most power and influence in the organization as well as from the school's support community.

This period also revealed major insights into CSC's educational vision. Worldview education is vitally important for changing the way students think, but it does not transform their lives or their culture. Even when implemented effectively, which is rarely the case, education for biblical perspective usually results in an academic education with Christian trimmings, what Van Brummelen referred to as a dualist vision of Christian education. By contrast, education for a life of discipleship saddled the schools that pursued it with a "gap problem."[192] The distance between this goal and actual practice was so great that educators lost sight of the goal. When that happened, education for a way of life was no longer a meaningful pursuit.

Because worldview education proved to be ineffective and education for discipleship was beyond attainment, CSC was saddled with a vision problem as it moved into the new millennium. Its options were limited: continue along the same trajectory, commit to a less demanding but more achievable vision, or latch on to a key element of their legacy that has the potential to keep the tradition alive. In my view the third option is the only one that made sense.

With the benefit of hindsight, it appears that CSC had a solution for its vision problem brewing within its own ranks. I refer to the *Man in Society* curriculum's notion of an education for hope. The concept lacked clarity in the *MIS* document, but it had the potential to meaningfully draw upon the twin goals that energized CSC educators: transformed knowledge and transformed living. This is where St. Augustine's vision of hope's two beautiful daughters become most helpful. The daughter of righteous anger over the way things are needs a well-developed biblical perspective for discernment. The courageous daughter who desires to heal what is broken requires meaningful opportunities to act. From its inception, education for hope had the potential to keep CSC educators tethered to the dissident and transforming roles of the Christian school. It required outlets for perspective to make a real difference in people's lives both inside and outside the school, and it did not carry the impossible burden of adopting a new way of life or transforming Canadian culture. As we shall see in part III, the daughters of hope did rise up to animate certain sectors of the Canadian Neo-Calvinist school movement, but hope came from the most unexpected sources.

Endnotes

71 The ICS received its initial degree-granting charter in this year for the Master of Philosophical Foundations. Harry Fernhout explains the nomenclature of this degree was a compromise "that satisfied the Ontario government because it was not a 'standard' MA, and (it) satisfied the ICS because it was not a theological degree and actually described the nature of the program. The charter also permitted the ICS to offer a program of doctoral studies provided that the actual degree was granted by a university approved by the Ontario government under a Ministerial Consent. This was the basis of the conjoint program with the VU (Free) University in Amsterdam. The charter was amended to add the Master of Worldview Studies in 1992. The charter was amended again in 2005 with approval of the MA and PhD."

72 Harold Rugg (1886–1960) was, according to the *Encyclopedia of Curriculum Studies*, one of the most prominent and controversial figures in the history of US education. He was a pioneer in the establishment of the social reconstruction wing of progressive education. He created an innovative social studies textbook series, titled *Man and His Changing Society*, that promoted the combining of history, geography, economics, and political science into an integrated, coherent program that encouraged students to approach social studies from a social justice perspective.

73 The role this model plays in the larger paradigm of progressivism is described in "Dig Deeper," Topic 4.

74 My preference for using the term "curriculum orientation" is explored in "Dig Deeper," Topic 1.

75 See "Dig Deeper," Topic 5 for an analysis of this paradigm.

76 See the discussion of the interpretive community in chapter 2.

77 For a discussion about the use and misuse of the terms "integrated" and "integral" curriculum, see "Dig Deeper," Topic 2.

78 Harro Van Brummelen, *Telling the Next Generation: Educational Development in North American Calvinist Schools* (Lanham, MD: University Press of America, 1986), 208.
79 Originally named the Association of Reformed Scientific Studies.
80 The origins of Reformational Philosophy are outlined in chapter 2.
81 Many years later, proponents of Teaching for Transformation called this Deeper Knowing (see chapter 9).
82 For more about curriculum orientations, see "Dig Deeper," Topic 1.
83 For a detailed discussion of this relationship see "Dig Deeper," Topic 4.
84 Jean Olthuis, *Teaching with "Joy," Implementing Integrated Education in the Classroom* (Toronto, ON: Curriculum Development Centre, 1979).
85 Geraldine Steensma and Harro Van Brummelen, eds., *Shaping School Curriculum: A Biblical View* (Terre Haute, IN: Signal, 1977).
86 See page 40 for the highlights of this speech.
87 See preface, vii.
88 The Association for the Advancement of Christian Scholarship (AACS) established the Institute for Christian Studies (ICS) in 1967..
89 This conundrum is dealt with in "Dig Deeper," Topic 5.
90 A summary of the CDC's relationship to this donor is provided in "Dig Deeper," Topic 5.
91 This expectation also shows up in "Dig Deeper," Topic 5.
92 Agnes Struik, "The History of the Curriculum Development Centre," unpublished manuscript, (author's possession).
93 Struik, 3.
94 Struik, 2.
95 See Appendix 3 for a list of names.
96 Excerpted from written responses to interview questions, received May 20, 2014.
97 A summary of this story is provided in "Dig Deeper," Topic 6.
98 Prinsen likened this "Dutch" tradition's propensity for debilitating divisions to that killer disease of Dutch elm trees (see Chapter 3, Rival Community).
99 The covenant-history approach to understanding the Old Testament assumes the meta-narrative of creation, fall, redemption, and restoration and becomes focused on a covenantal relationship that God establishes with a chosen people. This perspective offers a richer interpretation of the Bible than those

approaches that assumed the purpose of the biblical text was to highlight a moral lesson or theological doctrine.

100 Struik did consulting work with Steensma. Steensma's contributions are described in chapters 6 and 7.

101 Struik met Blomberg on her trip to Australia. Blomberg eventually replaced Harry Fernhout as the senior member of educational foundations at the ICS. His views on curriculum reform can be read in Doug Blomberg's *Wisdom and Curriculum: Christian Schooling After Postmodernity* (Sioux Center, IA: Dordt College Press, 2007).

102 For a discussion of this term, see "Dig Deeper," Topic 2.

103 Struik, "The History," 5.

104 Struik, 5.

105 Arnold De Graaff, Jean Olthuis, and Anne Tuininga. *Kenya: A Way of Life*. (Toronto: Joy in Learning Curriculum Development and Training Centre, 1981), 25.

106 Wolterstorff's argument on this point shows up in "Dig Deeper," Topic 3, Jellema.

107 Paraphrased from Struik, 7-8.

108 The CDC's efforts to partner with the Neo-Calvinist establishment in Canada is discussed in "Dig Deeper," Topic 5.

109 An analysis of this speech appears in "Dig Deeper," Topic 3.

110 A more detailed discussion of "ordering principles" can be found in "Dig Deeper," Topic 6.

111 Nicholas Wolterstorff, "Looking to the Eighties: Do Christian Schools Have a Future?", *Joy in Learning* no. 4 (Fall 1979): 2.

112 Wolterstorff, "Looking," 4.

113 Wolterstorff, 6.

114 Geraldine Steensma, "Strategy for the Eighties," *Joy in Learning* no. 6, (Fall:1-3, 1980): 1.

115 Steensma, 2.

116 Steensma.

117 Fernhout uses the term "integrated" to convey the integrality of vision in education or curriculum. See "Dig Deeper," Topic 2 for a discussion about the uses of integration and integrality

118 Harry Fernhout, "Reaffirming An Educational Vision," *Joy in Learning* no. 15, (Fall 1984): 1.

119 Fernhout uses the term "integration" to convey multiple concepts in his vision statement. See "Dig Deeper," Topic 2 for a discussion about the use of integration and integral.

120 Fernhout.

121 Fernhout, 2.

122 Fernhout.

123 The Teaching for Transformation movement is summarized in chapter 9.

124 Jamie Smith believes we are more motivated by what we love than what we think; this is how he understands the heart as a deep driver of education. Smith, James K. A. *You Are What You Love: The Spiritual Power of Habit* (Grand Rapids, MI: Brazos Press, 2016.)

125 Fernhout.

126 Fernhout.

127 Fernhout.

128 Wolterstorff asked this very question back in 1966. See Dig Deeper, Topic 3.

129 Fernhout.

130 Fernhout.

131 Fernhout, 3.

132 The various forms of curriculum integration are reviewed in "Dig Deeper," Topic 2.

133 Fernhout, 4.

134 Fernhout, 5.

135 Fernhout.

136 Fernhout, 6.

137 His response is summarized in the next section of this chapter.

138 John Stronks, "A Dialogue on Christian Education," *Joy in Learning* no. 16 (Winter 1985): 2.

139 See "Dig Deeper," Topic 2.

140 See "Dig Deeper," Topic 6 for a discussion about the ordering principle of the curriculum.

141 Harro Van Brummelen, "A Dialogue on Christian Education," *Joy in Learning* no. 16 (Winter 1985): 4.

142 Harro Van Brummelen, *Walking with God in the Classroom: Christian Approaches to Learning and Teaching* (Seattle, WA: Alta Vista College Press, 1988), 7-10.

143 Harro Van Brummelen, "A Dialogue on Christian Education," *Joy in Learning* no. 16 (Winter 1985): 5.

144 Fernhout, 1.

145 See "Dig Deeper," Topic 6 for more on this topic.

146 Parallels to the views expressed by Philip Phenix in his book *Realms of Meaning* (New York: McGraw-Hill Book Company, 1964) can be readily found in the influential text assembled by Geraldine Steensma and Harro Van Brummelen, eds., *Shaping School Curriculum: A Biblical View* (Terre Haute, IN: Signal, 1977). .

147 The key points of Wolterstorff's speech are outlined in "Dig Deeper," Topic 3.

148 The main positions involved in that debate are reviewed in "Dig Deeper," Topic 3.

149 References to Van Brummelen's *Telling the Next Generation*, show up frequently in the introduction to part I and in chapter 1. Wolterstorff's speech, "By What Standard?" is reviewed in "Dig Deeper," Topic 3.

150 Brian Walsh studied at the Institute for Christian Studies and received a PhD from McGill University. For many years he has served as the Christian Reformed campus pastor at the U of T and adjunct professor of theology at Trinity College and Wycliffe College in Toronto.

151 J. Richard Middleton was born in Jamaica and emigrated to Canada, then the United States. He received his doctorate degree from the Free University of Amsterdam. He served as a campus pastor in Canada and the US. Since 1996 he has been a professor of biblical worldview and exegesis at Northeastern Seminary at Roberts Wesleyan College.

152 For a more scholarly but easy to read analysis of worldview from the Neo-Calvinist tradition, see this book and book chapter written by Al Wolters: *Creation Regained: Biblical Basics for a Reformational Worldview.* (Grand Rapids: Wm. B Eerdmans Publishing Co., 1985, 2nd ed. 2005). . "Dutch Neo-Calvinism: Worldview, Philosophy and Rationality," in *Rationality in the Calvinian Tradition*, eds. H. Hart, J. van der Hoven, and Nicholas Wolterstorff (Toronto: UPA, 1983), 113-131.

153 Brian J Walsh, J Richard Middleton, *The Transforming Vision: Shaping Christian World View* (Downers Grove, IL: Intervarsity Press, 1984).

154 A summary of Jellema's philosophy of education is provided in "Dig Deeper," Topic 3.

155 Nicholas Wolterstorff, "Beyond 1984 in Philosophy of Christian Education," in *Educating for Life: Reflections on Christian Teaching and Learning*, eds.

Nicholas Wolterstorff, Gloria Stronks, Clarence Joldernsma (Grand Rapids, MI: Baker Academic, 2002), 66.

156 Wolterstorff, "Beyond," 74-75.

157 Wolterstorff, 75

158 Walsh, Middleton, *Transforming,* 9.

159 Walsh, Middleton, 32.

160 Wolters. *Dutch Neo-Calvinism,* 2.

161 Walsh, Middleton, Transforming, 36.

162 Walsh, Middleton, 95.

163 Walsh, Middleton, 61

164 J. Richard Middleton, Brian Walsh, *Truth is Stranger Than It Used to Be: Biblical Faith in a Postmodern Age* (Downers Grove, Intervarsity Press, 1995). 83.

165 Middleton and Walsh, "Truth," 19.

166 Middleton and Walsh, 20.

167 Brian Walsh, "Transformation: Dynamic Worldview or Repressive Ideology," *Journal of Education and Christian Belief* 4, no. 2 (September 1, 2000): 101-114.

168 The down side of this relationship is explored in "Dig Deeper," Topic 6.

169 Covenant College is located in Lookout Mountain, GA, on the border of Tennessee. The college has existed on this site since 1964. Prior to that the college shared a campus with Covenant Theological Seminary in both Pasadena, CA, and St. Louis, MO. After a history that involves at least one church split and one merger, the college is currently an agency of the Presbyterian Church in America.

170 See chapter 7 for a discussion of the CDC's newsletters.

171 Crouch, Andy, *Culture Making: Recovering Our Creative Calling* (Downers Grove, Ill: IVP Books, 2008).

172 Geraldine Steensma and Harro Van Brummelen, eds., *Shaping School Curriculum: A Biblical View* (Terre Haute, IN: Signal, 1977).

173 Ary De Moor. "Curricular Concerns in the Eighties." Paper presented at the *Shaping Christian Schools Conference*, Surrey, BC, April 8-10, 1981: 2.

174 Steensma and Van Brummelen, *Shaping, 15.*

175 Steensma and Van Brummelen, *Shaping,* 15.

176 Later Van Brummelen referred to it as a thematic statement.

177 Steensma and Van Brummelen, 148.

178 Harry Fernhout, "Summary of Critique of *Shaping School Curriculum*." Paper presented at the *Shaping Christian Schools Conference*, Surrey, BC, April 8-10, 1981).

179 Philip Phenix, *Realms of Meaning* (New York: McGraw-Hill, 1964).

180 E. Eisner and E. Vallance, Eds., *Conflicting Conceptions of Curriculum* (Berkeley, CA: McCutchan Publishing Corp., 1974).

181 See "Dig Deeper," Topic 6 for more on this issue.

182 Steensma and Van Brummelen, *Shaping*, 148.

183 The types of subject integration are discussed in "Dig Deeper," Topic 2.

184 See also p. 7.

185 Harro Van Brummelen, *Steppingstones to Curriculum: A Biblical Path* (Colorado Springs, CO: Purposeful Design Publications, 2nd Ed., 2001), 50, 176.

186 Van Brummelen made these exact points in a rejoinder to an article I wrote on education for discipleship that appeared in the *Journal of Education and Christian Belief* Vol. 13, no. 2, 2009.

187 Van Brummelen, rejoinder.

188 Demoor et al, *Man in Society: A Study in Hope* (Grand Rapids, MI: CSI Publications, 1980) 77.

189 See the related discussion on page 46 of part 1.

190 Van Brummelen, *Telling*, 216.

191 2 Corinthians 5:17–21.

192 I distinguished between a "gap challenge" and a "gap problem" in an article titled "Aiming for Christian Education, Settling for Christians Educating: The Christian School's Replication of a Public School Paradigm," which appeared in *Christian Scholars Review* XXXII: 2 (Winter 2003): 203-224. That discussion and its context is provided in "Dig Deeper," Topic 7.

PART III
CLINGING TO HOPE (2000–2022)

We are not to simply bandage the wounds of victims beneath the wheels of injustice, we are to drive a spoke into the wheel itself.

—Dietrich Bonhoeffer

We only tap into hope when we are able to face the reality of how broken our world is.

—Ruth Padilla-DeBorst

Major Story Line: Stepping onto Education's Main Stage

Education for Cultural Transformation: Keep It, Leave It, or Tweak It?

I have previously acknowledged that the Neo-Calvinist tradition of education is sustained by the biblical injunction known as the "cultural mandate." Like Christians from other traditions, Dutch Neo-Calvinists use the term to designate the role God gave to humankind in the story of creation (Genesis 1:26–28). Humans were created in God's image and granted God's blessing to multiply, fill the earth, and oversee the development and care of all other creatures. The grand narrative of Scripture reveals that humans rejected the terms of this mandate, and God responded to their disobedience with the restoration of all things through the life, death, and resurrection of Jesus Christ. As they await the "fullness of time" when Christ will return to reconcile all relationships, Neo-Calvinists believe the cultural mandate still holds. They adhere to Abraham Kuyper's interpretation of the cultural mandate as a call to transform culture from its broken state into the Kingdom of God.

The cultural mandate is so prominent in Neo-Calvinist theology that it overshadows the "great commission" recorded in Matthew 28:16–20 where Jesus instructs his followers to go and make disciples of all nations. In fact, the latter has been regarded as the New Testament's way of expressing the cultural mandate. The task of making disciples starts with evangelism (conversion and baptism), but it quickly extends to a life dedicated to making all things right.

Neo-Calvinism understands cultural transformation to mean the re-formation of all social institutions in accordance with God-given norms. The Christian school plays a vital role in cultural transformation. To fulfill that role the Christian school needs to be a dissident and a transformative social institution. It must not only generate a fundamental critique of the status quo worldview and way of life but also promote a biblical alternative on both counts. The most pressing question that faces CSC in this new millennium is what should be done about their Neo-Calvinist legacy of cultural transformation. Should they hang on to it, trade it in for something new, or refocus it?

This is not a question that most CSC communities have consciously asked themselves, if we are to believe the vision and mission statements of their schools. According to these statements, it seems safe to say that the majority of CSC communities have decided to soldier on with worldview education. I base this conclusion on the recurrence of the term "Christ-centred education." Historically, this term has connoted a curriculum permeated with a Christian perspective. Until such time as this term is clearly redefined, we must assume that CSC communities refuse to accept the fact that worldview education does not typically transform lives or culture.

Collectively, the current vision and mission statements of CSC schools reveal a system with multiple identities. The second most popular educational aim in these statements is the "development of gifts," which likely reflects the influence of a popular book published in the early 1990s called *A Vision with a Task*.[193] The "unwrapping of gifts" was one of three ideals embodied by the phrase "education for responsive discipleship" developed in this text. It is revealing that the other two ideals promoted in this text, "sharing each other's joys and burdens" and "seeking shalom," rarely appear in current CSC vision and mission statements. Explicit expressions of educating for a way of life rank about third in frequency, as do references to offering a quality education.

Although allegiance to their Neo-Calvinist tradition remains unwavering in the rhetoric of vision and mission statements of most schools, well-informed sources from all three CSC regions believe their school communities are leaving the Neo-Calvinist tradition behind by incremental steps. This process occurs rather thoughtlessly, and many communities would likely deny it is happening. By contrast, a few communities have consciously set out to leave the tradition and pursue other goals.

The Neo-Calvinist vision of cultural transformation has proven difficult, if not impossible, to implement. To their credit, CSC communities have not given up on cultural transformation simply because they have found it difficult to bring about. However, it is time they face the worst of all questions: what if this vision is wrong-headed?

In part II of this book, we noted the concerns raised by Wolterstorff, Walsh, and Middleton who said the Neo-Calvinist community's emphasis on Abraham Kuyper's vision to raise up a parallel system of Christian cultural organizations distracted their attention from addressing local and more personal examples of injustice and suffering. More recently, James K. A. Smith echoed this concern in a speech when he observed that people absorbed with the idea of transforming culture have no imagination for self-sacrifice and martyrdom.[194]

Not so long ago, Robert Koole published a perceptive article on cultural engagement in *Christian Educators Journal*.[195] He cited several sources who believe the whole notion of cultural transformation is unreasonable. James Davison Hunter, for example, believes the claim is unrealistic and potentially dangerous. He says talk of cultural transformation "carries too much weight, and implies intent to conquer and dominate."[196] Equally disconcerting are the conclusions in Andy Crouch's important book, *Culture Making*.[197] Crouch identifies four postures that describe how Christians engage with culture, and none of them involves its transformation. A key chapter in his book is titled "Why We Can't Change the World."

If cultural transformation (via worldview and/or lifestyle) is a misguided way of understanding the cultural mandate in Scripture, then it is high time CSC communities let it go. But what then? Where should the tradition look to find new direction and meaning, and what vision should replace cultural transformation? The answers to these vexing questions are not as elusive as people may think. A course correction has been brewing within CSC ranks for many years. I believe a homegrown alternative approach to teaching and learning, called "Teaching for Transformation," provides the tradition with its greatest source of hope. The appearance of the term "transformation" in the title is unfortunate because, as we shall see, the approach sometimes tempts educators to remain chained to unproductive patterns with long histories. At its best, however, Teaching for Transformation channels education toward the reconciliation of relationships that exist within the social orbits of the school. It promotes a vision of education for hope and peace through community/cultural engagement.

Part III of this book contains three chapters. Given my move to Alberta in 1995, my account of the larger CSC narrative since 2000 revolves around the major events that occurred there. The first chapter describes and evaluates one of the most controversial events in CSC history, the agreement reached between the Edmonton Society of Christian Education and the Edmonton Public School Board, which turned Edmonton Christian School into an alternative Christian program within the public system. The next chapter tells the Teaching for Transformation story and its potential to revitalize a school movement with many languishing communities. The final chapter in this book describes the development of the teacher-preparation program at The King's University and its significance for the two western regions of CSC as well as public school education in Alberta.

These three chapters reveal a tradition in transition, and communities are moving in multiple directions. A course correction toward an education for an Augustinian kind of hope is arguably the most compelling for the Neo-Calvinist school movement in Canada today, and it is gratifying to see it thriving.

CHAPTER 8
Christian Education Goes Public in Alberta

Timeline

1949	The Edmonton Society of Christian Education (ESCE) opens a grade 3–6 school in a downtown church basement.
1955	The ESCE opens East Elementary School in the Beverly neighbourhood.
1957	The first campus is moved to the McQueen neighbourhood and renamed West School.
1967	The ESCE opens Edmonton Christian High School on a lot adjacent to the West School.
1969	The ESCE opens North Elementary School on Fort Road.
1988	The School Act gives school boards in Alberta authority to offer alternative programs based on language, culture, religion, subject matter, or teaching philosophy. The Edmonton Public School Board offers the Logos program of Christian education.
1994	The ESCE closes East School campus and merges the East and North schools to Create Northeast Christian School on the Fort Road Campus
Fall 1998	The ESCE board initiates talks with the Edmonton Public School Board (EPSB) to explore the possibility of its schools becoming an alternative Christian program.
1999	
Feb. 19	The ESCE receives a letter from the Society of Christian Schools in British Columbia that expresses deep concerns about its negotiations with the EPSB.
Feb. 25	The ESCE and the EPSB negotiating teams reach an agreement.
Feb. 26	The ESCE board endorses the agreement.
Apr. 26	The ESCE membership votes in favour of the agreement.

May 25	The EPSB trustees vote in favour of the agreement.
Sept.	Edmonton Christian School (the high school and the West and Northeast elementary campuses) operate as an alternative program within the Edmonton Public School Board. The buildings remain the property of ESCE.
2004	Edmonton Christian High School campus is completely renovated and expanded.
2008	Northeast Christian School moves into a new state-of-the-art building in the Hollick-Kenyon neighbourhood.
2021	West Christian School is renovated and expanded into a state-of-the-art facility.

Be Careful What You Pray For

When I was elected to serve on the board of the Edmonton Society of Christian Education in 1997, the good old days of Edmonton Christian School were a distant memory. During the late 1970s and early 1980s, the society operated a school system that consisted of three elementary campuses and a secondary campus with a combined enrollment of over 1,000 students. As the third generation of Dutch Neo-Calvinist immigrants gave way to the fourth in the 1990s, signs of decline were painfully evident. Many parents who lived in the Beverly neighbourhood felt betrayed by other members of the society over the loss of "their school" when the board merged the East and North schools to form a Northeast school on the newer North school campus. This drastic downsizing did not curtail rising costs and the need to hike tuition rates. The price of a Christian education was becoming prohibitive, and an alarming number of families began to opt out for cheaper options like the Logos program in the public school system or one of the three other independent Christian schools in the city. Smaller enrollments exacerbated the embarrassing problem of low teacher salaries. The society's educational vision was also under siege. A fellow board member told me that any random group of ten parents could yield a half dozen different interpretations of Christian education.

During my first year on the board, we dealt with two main issues: the implementation of a new board governance model and strategies to tame the multi-headed dragon of high tuition, low salaries, loss of clientele, and diluted vision. An unavoidable but highly undesirable future for the society was lurking just over the horizon, namely, a significantly downsized operation that provided a Christian education to those who could afford it and were committed to the society's historic vision.

No one on the ESCE board had the stomach for turning Edmonton Christian School into an elitist operation, but what other future did it have? We prayed and worried! In early 1998 our school superintendent, Hans Van Ginhoven, reported that Strathcona Christian Academy (SCA) in neighbouring Sherwood Park had just signed an agreement to become an alternative program in the Elk Island Public School Board. This was shocking news on two fronts. The idea that an independent Christian school would willingly become a public school was unthinkable. Second, we had already lost several families to SCA because of its lower tuition. How many more of our parents would switch when the school had no tuition?

As board members of a struggling operation, we understood why SCA's arrangement with a public school board was tempting. With the stroke of a pen, SCA eliminated tuition for their parents and greatly increased teacher salaries. We were curious to know what their agreement looked like, so we obtained a copy. We were not impressed with its details. In our view, SCA had given up all control over the operation and direction of their school. They were content with the arrangement, we concluded, because their vision for academic excellence and purity of Christian morality and theology was not put at risk. We could not imagine entering into a similar arrangement with the Edmonton Public School Board (EPSB) because our vision of Christian education went far beyond moral and spiritual purity. To preserve our vision of Christ-centred education, we would need guarantees that the principals and teachers in our schools both understood our vision and were wholly committed to it.

Times were desperate, so we felt compelled to pursue every possible option for moving forward, even those that seemed doomed to failure. The board instructed Van Ginhoven to check out the willingness of the

Edmonton Public School Board to explore alternative program status for Edmonton Christian School. In our wildest dreams, we did not think these talks would lead to anything, if they happened at all. In the meantime, we did our homework on the history of alternative programs in Alberta.

Like most provinces in Canada, public schools in Alberta during the 1950s and 1960s were Christian friendly. Most of the population identified as Christian in those days. No one objected to the recitation of the Lord's Prayer, Bible instruction, or the celebration of Christian holy days in public schools. Canada was a much more secular society in the 1980s. By then, many trappings of Christianity were on their way out of public schools. Some people in Alberta longed for a return to the days when Christianity was front and centre in public education, and they voiced their concerns to Alberta Education. Other groups lobbied the ministry for programs that emphasized different cultures, second languages, the fine arts, sports, military training, or different approaches to teaching. In 1988 the provincial government changed the school act and gave public school boards the authority to offer alternative programs based on a variety of criteria, including religion. These programs augmented the mandatory provincial program of studies.

The logos program emerged as an alternative program based on religion. It was nondenominational by design and emphasized activities like morning prayers, Bible readings, and spiritual songs. There was some talk about a Christian perspective in learning, but the teachers who signed up to teach in this program had no background or experience related to the development of a Christian perspective on the curriculum. At the end of the day, the Logos program provided a segregated public school education with a Christian frosting.

Among the forty-plus public school boards in Alberta, the EPSB always led the way in developing alternative programs. The undisputed champion of alternative programming in the province was Emery Dosdall, who served as the superintendent of the EPSB from 1995 to 2001. Dosdall's dream was to build a world-class public school system in Edmonton. The alternative program option was tailor made for his vision that every parent should be able to find a public school program that suited the needs of their children.

We Are Not Enemies

The ESCE board sent a committee of four people to meet with EPSB officials in the fall of 1998. The group consisted of past chair Dr. Alyce Oosterhuis (one of my colleagues in the education faculty at The King's University); our superintendent, Hans Van Ginhoven; board member Ben Elsen; and me, the newly appointed board chair. I distinctly remember the four of us discussing the possible motives behind the EPSB's willingness to talk with us about alternative program status. We did not rule out a "divide and conquer" mentality, a secular strategy to finally rid the province of independent Christian schools by picking them off and absorbing them. We clearly did not trust the public board. In our Neo-Calvinist mindset, the EPSB was an enemy of Christian education; it stood on the opposite side of "the antithesis," Abraham Kuyper's term to signify the great divide that separated those individuals and institutions that submitted to God's laws from those who did not.

The EPSB team was led by two highly professional and accessible women named Faye Parker and Gloria Chalmers. They were not the sort of people we expected to encounter. In fact, they consistently presented themselves to us as friends, not foes. To our amazement, they understood our vision of Christian education when we explained it to them, and they expressed genuine appreciation for its depth and the ESCE's long history in the province. The idea of an independent school with decades of history becoming a self-contained alternative program within the EPSB did not strike them as crazy, but they clearly understood the challenges that such an agreement presented to our board and theirs. We brought an unexpected report back to our fellow board members at the ESCE, although we could not foresee any actual agreement arising out of our talks with the EPSB, we had encountered nothing but encouragement and enthusiasm to explore a possible relationship.

A surprising yet troubling pattern emerged in these early negotiations. We would present what we thought were deal breakers to an agreement, and Parker and Chalmers would resolve them. I think it was at our third or fourth meeting when Parker stunned and shamed us with a summary of what we had experienced up to that point but struggled to process for ourselves. She informed us that the EPSB was impressed with the depth and extent of our vision, not threatened by it. Furthermore, when the EPSB made a commitment to an alternative program, it did everything possible to ensure the success of that program. She wondered out loud why we seemed to think the EPSB wanted an ECS alternative Christian program to eventually fail. It was a game-changing question. Indeed, why did we harbour this suspicion? After that meeting we stopped assuming the worst about our counterparts and their organization. Mutual respect and friendship flourished from that point onward.

Not long after that pivotal meeting, we addressed the elephant in the room: who had the final word about the hiring (and firing) of the principal and teachers? We knew it was the public school superintendent's responsibility to select the principals, and they, in turn, hired the teachers in accordance with a personnel department that was beholden to union policies. Our strategy was to lobby for the ESCE to have veto power in the principal selection process. Parker and Chalmers could work no magic here, however, confirming what we already suspected. Veto power for our society was not only unacceptable, it was illegal. We left that meeting with a strange sense of sadness and regret because we had reached the point of believing alternative status in the EPSB could be very good for all concerned. Yet, we knew all too well that the ESCE's membership would never give up their control over the school's administration.

Our deflated negotiating committee met prior to our next scheduled board meeting in February to debrief about our experience negotiating with the EPSB and to construct a report that informed the board of our failed negotiations. As our meeting got underway, Ben Elsen shared an ingenious way to keep the negotiations alive. He suggested that we try to enshrine our vision and mission statement into the agreement. If the school's vision and mission statement was "set in stone," so to speak, then only those administrators and teachers who were committed to it could be appointed by the superintendent. It suddenly occurred to us that this provision was of equal, if not greater, importance than who actually appointed the principals and teachers. We immediately set up another meeting with Parker and Chalmers to see what they thought.

At this point in the narrative, it is worth mentioning that vision and mission statements are typically short, pithy slogans formulated to be easily remembered. They identify the school's priorities in shorthand, but they are prone to be misinterpreted, or at very least, interpreted in a variety of ways. Such abbreviated statements need to be thoughtfully unpacked by teachers and administrators if they are to be effective shapers of a school's direction, purpose, and policies. Fortuitously, a few months prior to our negotiations with the EPSB, the ESCE's board set up a long-range planning committee with a mandate to refine and flesh out the society's vision and mission statements. Given my background in educational foundations and curriculum theory and design, the board appointed me to chair this committee.

Over a two-month period of research and talks with various teachers and administrators, our committee developed a six-page vision and mission document. The document outlined the respective roles and expectations for students, teachers, the curriculum, the school environment, the community, the board, and the facilities. The statement was in its penultimate draft stage when it was sidelined by our negotiations with the EPSB. In light of Elsen's suggestion, we quickly wrote a final draft, had it approved by our board, and presented it to Parker and Chalmers at a meeting that we again assumed would likely be our last.

True to form, Parker and Chalmers expressed no concerns about enshrining our expansive vision and mission document in an agreement, but they needed Superintendent Dosdall's approval before we could proceed. Within days we learned that an agreement with the EPSB could include our vision and mission document in its entirety. After thinking our negotiations with the EPSB were dead, we found they were back on. With the most challenging matter seemingly resolved, our negotiating committee had to work on a host of lesser but still sticky matters. Some of these issues also had the potential to be deal breakers for some members of our board, staff, and the society.

As our negotiations with the EPSB continued, our committee had to help our fellow board members, school staffs, and society members make the same paradigm shift that we had made during the course of our negotiations. Our change of mind and heart was precipitated by our engagement with EPSB personnel. As we worked together to resolve challenging issues, we earned each other's respect and trust. Our board, school staffs, and the ESCE membership had to arrive at the point we had but without the benefit of the process we had engaged or the relationships we had cultivated. To facilitate their journey, our committee doubled its efforts to be as transparent and as informative as possible.

To help the ESCE community get a sense of the negotiation process, the board asked me to write several open letters to the membership. Here is a segment from the first of these letters which reveals our board's approach:

> Initially, our strategy looked for ways to protect our school from a suspect partner. We entered the negotiations with an adversarial mentality. In doing so we underestimated our counterparts and misjudged their motives. We were blind to the possibility that Edmonton Public would agree to enshrine our educational vision in the agreement document and make an overt commitment to protecting it. We first sought guarantees that would prevent the superintendent of Edmonton Public from messing with our school's vision. We had not anticipated that Edmonton Public would be equally concerned about protecting this vision from a group of "renegade parents," for example. Now that our vision of Edmonton Christian School will be enshrined in the agreement, our main negotiating task has shifted to clarifying the mechanisms by which Edmonton Public's superintendent and our school society will work together to maintain the integrity of the school's program and staff.[198]

The ESCE board and its negotiating committee met with each sector of the school community to listen to their concerns. The board demonstrated considerable wisdom and transparency in this endeavor. Over a period of four months, from January to April, representatives of the board met with the teaching staff three times. One of these meetings also involved ECS personnel. Superintendent Dosdall and chief negotiator Faye Parker also met with the ESCE board. The board sent out a total of four open letters to the ESCE membership reporting on the negotiations and clarifying issues. The negotiating team even met with the ministerial of the Christian Reformed Churches in Edmonton.

The teachers and administrators at ECS had much to gain if ECS became an alternative program. All of them would receive a huge increase in pay and be enrolled in a much richer and more secure pension plan. These perks were particularly attractive to the younger people on staff. However, financial gain was not the bottom line for ECS teachers and administrators. Many said they could not support the agreement if the most senior members on staff, especially those on the verge of retirement, would lose any money in the shift from their current pension to the new one. Many also expressed concerns for the job security of ECS teacher assistants, substitute teachers, and custodians. Some said they could not imagine being a member of the Alberta Teachers Association, which officially opposed the government's funding of private schools and had policy statements that expressed a bias against Christian education. Due to the tireless efforts of Parker, Chalmers, and others from various departments within the EPSB, all of ECS staff's issues were resolved satisfactorily except one: membership in the contentious Alberta Teacher Association was nonnegotiable.

The ECS administration team consisted of a superintendent, three principals, and some part-time vice principal support. As an alternative program, our superintendent would become the overall school administrator, and the principals would become campus vice principals. From the perspective of our negotiating team and our board, the administration of ECS would remain relatively unchanged. We would still have one person (the principal) who oversaw the whole operation and three (vice-principals) who ran the day-to-day operations of the three campuses. Each person on the admin team would have roughly the same responsibilities but with a lower title and much greater pay.

The main concern for the society and its board was to remain true to its historic vision and to keep faith with the larger CSC community. Many people could not wrap their minds round the idea of ECS becoming an EPSB alternative program. Accusations like sleeping with the enemy, selling out the store, and betraying the tradition circulated in private and public conversations. These concerns were strongly expressed in a letter to the ESCE board from the board of the Society for Christian Schools in British Columbia. Respected leaders in the Alberta Neo-Calvinist community were also alarmed by the possibility of their flagship school becoming a public-school program. The ESCE board tried to assure everyone that it had no intention of leaving the Prairie Association of Christian Schools (now the Prairie Centre of Christian Education), where it had always played a leading role.

On February 26, 1999, the ESCE board had to decide if it would endorse the negotiated agreement or not. We decided to forgo our normal voting policy. If we could not unanimously agree to endorse the agreement, then the matter was dead. After a long, soul-searching discussion, everyone gave their consent. The next step was to put the agreement to a vote by the society's membership.

A Tale of Two Votes

Transparency meant everything in the lead-up to the night the ESCE voted on the board's recommendation to adopt the negotiated agreement with the EPSB that would make ECS an alternative program under its jurisdiction. In addition to all of the information sharing initiated by the board to that point in time, it set up a special meeting on February 12, 1999, where everyone could put their views on the table. This meeting took place two weeks prior to the society's vote. More than 800 people showed up. The board wisely invited the two most prominent critics of the proposed agreement to speak first. Faye Parker also addressed the crowd on behalf of the EPSB.

After all the speeches were given, the board used a modified jigsaw teaching strategy[199] to facilitate the discussion. The large crowd was divided into approximately twenty groups and sent off to various classrooms. A board member, administrator, or teacher facilitated the discussion in each classroom and took notes. In these more intimate settings, many more society members were able to raise their concerns and get answers on the spot or in written form later. When the board met and reviewed the feedback from these group meetings, it was clear that some individuals were strongly opposed to the proposed agreement, but a majority community members seemed optimistic. What most surprised the board was the affirmation that the proposal received from the oldest members of the society.

On the night of the vote, even more people attended. The board took unique steps to ensure, as best it could, that the community came away from this historic vote united rather than fractured. As was the custom with society meetings, the agenda began with devotions but with a twist this time. A brief meditation based on an Old Testament story preceded a service of prayer. In the story the prophet Nehemiah called upon a community of returned exiles to remain united in their efforts to rebuild Jerusalem's wall despite all manner of obstacles. The implications were clear: the ESCE community should remain united regardless of the impending vote's outcome. The prayer asked for a climate of grace and understanding from those who would "win" and "lose" the vote. No matter which future the community decided to pursue, everyone in the room had to help build it.

The ESCE board kept one of their recent decisions to themselves that night. They decided that their motion to adopt the negotiated agreement with EPSB had to have seventy percent approval from the society to pass instead of the usual fifty percent plus one. It made no sense to the board to move ahead on such a historic decision one way or the other unless there was a significant majority. This was a risky strategy, however, and likely one that would not have stood up, if challenged. How could the board over-ride the constitution and nullify a decision that received a majority win of fifty-one to sixty-nine percent, especially if the number was in the high sixties?

The board excused itself from the meeting to count the votes. To their great relief a majority in excess of seventy percent approved the proposal. They returned to face an anxious crowd. It was announced that the society had passed the motion by a large margin. In keeping with the spirit of the devotions shared earlier, no one clapped or cheered for joy, nor did anyone show any sign of disgust. Everyone quietly filed out of the auditorium to ponder what they had just done.

The reality of ECS becoming an alternative program now rested with the nine trustees who made up the Edmonton Public School Board. Their vote took place a month later, on May 25. The outcome of this vote was difficult to gauge in advance. EPSB personnel told us two of the nine trustees were likely to vote against the proposed agreement, and at least two others could go either way. This was worrisome because public opinion toward the negotiations was mostly negative. Leading the charge was *Edmonton Journal* reporter Lianne Faulder, who used her column as a platform to voice critical concerns. The Alberta Teachers Association (ATA) and the Canadian Union of Public Employees (CUPE) also spoke out against religion in education.

Several dozen ESCE supporters showed up to witness the vote, which was preceded by Faye Parker's compelling presentation and defense of the agreement to the board. A late-spring thunderstorm rumbled outside, and someone joked that the trustees had better pay attention because God was talking. The trustees voted seven to two in favour of the proposal. Consequently, at the start of the 1999–2000 school year, Edmonton Christian School became an alternative Christian program operated by the Edmonton Public School Board.

Early Fallout from the Agreement

News of what happened in Edmonton spread quickly throughout the three regions of Christian Schools Canada. Most people disapproved of the news, and many were shocked. This was particularly true in Ontario. Critics of the decision accused the ESCE community of selling out its historic vision and the CSC movement. In Alberta a few CSC communities were deeply disturbed by the ESCE's move, but many eventually followed its lead and negotiated agreements with their own public-school boards. The agreement between the ESCE and the EPSB was often used as a template for these negotiations.

Initially, the news was not well received by the mainstream unions. The ATA's president, Peter McNabb, was reported to have said that "private schools should not be funded by public money because Christian schools are not dedicated to democratic and humanistic education."[200] Doug Luellman, president of CUPE Local 474, chimed in with another biased sentiment when he accused the EPSB of creating a "two-tier" system of education. He claimed "religious schools" were receiving preferential treatment because they could still charge extra tuition, they controlled their buildings, and they had autonomous control over their religious curriculum.[201] These negative reactions quickly died out, however, as other stories dominated the news.

Two years out from the vote date, few ESCE members or ECS personnel had concerns. Every aspect of the school was flourishing. The only discontented people were the vice principals, who felt they had been demoted in more than name. Even though they were still in charge of the day-to-day operations of their campuses, parents were used to asking for the principal when they wanted something to be done. Too often, matters the VPs used to handle when they were principals, went over their heads. The ESCE board was frustrated that the admin team could not sort out the matter. The team was upset with themselves and with the board.

From the outset of this extraordinary relationship between a Neo-Calvinist school society and a public school board, educational vision was front and centre for ESCE members and ECS teachers and administrators. Everyone knew it was the school's lifeline to its legacy, and its preservation rekindled the spark of curriculum reform.

Two Decades and Counting

Edmonton Christian School has been an alternative Christian program within Edmonton Public School for more than twenty years now. With each passing year, the question of whether or not the ESCE made the right decision in 1999 has become less relevant. Most society members have no regrets whatsoever. Edmonton Christian School is affordable, the teachers are well paid, students with learning challenges can access a variety of services, total enrollment is approaching 1,500 students, and the society now operates three beautiful, state-of-the-art facilities. By all outward accounts, Edmonton Christian School is thriving.

Much has changed over the years, and now is a good time to assess the school's evolution as an alternative program. The most obvious difference in the school pertains to its students. Prior to becoming an alternative program, the ECS student body was largely made up of the offspring of the Dutch Neo-Calvinist community. Today, ECS has a very diverse student body, particularly at the Northeast campus. According to recently retired ESCE executive director, Peter Buisman, ECS students now come from 180 different churches representing twenty-five denominations. Although members of the founding Dutch community continue to dominate the ESCE's ranks, the proportion of their students in the overall student body has decreased to about thirty percent. This outcome is a matter for celebration and concern.

That people from a variety of ethnic communities now have access to a Christian education is a wonderful consequence of the 1999 decision. This outcome is consistent with the society's historic vision of making a positive impact on Canadian culture. However, diversity has a down side. New parents do not fully understand the school's vision, neither do they contribute to the society. Consequently, the community is not as unified as it once was. There may come a time when the student body's diversity reaches a point that it negatively impacts the school's direction and purpose, but the more immediate concern is the health of the society. The society functions as the "silent partner" in the ECS story, and so far, it has been embraced by each new generation of the founding community. The society and the EPSB are the mutual keepers of the school's vision. If either one loses its heart for it, the school's legacy will be in serious jeopardy.

What has been the most important outcome of ECS becoming an alternative program in the ESPB? Former ECS administrative head, Hans Van Ginhoven, believes it is the positive image that Christian education now has on the main stage of education in Edmonton.[202] As the principal of one of Edmonton's most prestigious public high schools, Van Ginhoven is well positioned to make this assessment. Even the Alberta Teachers' Association has done an about face. It is crucial to know what lies at the root of this positive image. If Christian education is no longer perceived as a substandard, anti-democratic, and biased form of education, then what or who changed? Has Christian education become less threatening because it now measures up so well against secular standards, or have the major players in the education system come to appreciate the value of ECS's biblical vision for the larger society? Depending on who one asks, either reason is true.

For Peter Buisman, who was the principal of the ECS high school campus for many years and finished his career as the ESCE's executive director, the most important result of the 1999 decision were the freedoms that financial security bestowed upon the society and what the society did with that freedom.[203] Without the burden of punishing tuition fees, the society had the resources to keep the school's furnishings and equipment up to date. Staying abreast of innovations in computer technology was particularly critical. As noted earlier, the society was also able to raise millions over the past two decades to rebuild its three campuses. As important as the acquisition and updating of equipment and facilities were, Buisman believes the most important outcome of the school's newfound financial security was its ability to develop the vision of ECS teachers. Buisman played a key role in the emergence of Teaching for Transformation (TfT), an integral approach to teaching and curriculum development.

Teaching for Transformation is so important historically that the next chapter is solely devoted to it. What is important to remember in this discussion is the context of its origins and implementation. TfT was inspired by the need to keep the school focused on its historic vision. It also reignited the long-standing tradition of teacher-led curriculum reform, which perennially suffered from a lack of resources. Buisman observed that prior to 1999 the society had to rely on individual teachers to use their own wits to teach from a Christian perspective. There was no time and few resources to facilitate their growth. As noted in chapter 5, the CDC's Agnes Struik was the only classroom consultant active in the whole CSC system during the 1970s and 1980s.

After 1999, the school had the money to free up visionary teachers to develop what became known as TfT. It was now possible to take teachers out of the classroom for several days per year to train them in TfT principles. According to Buisman, TfT clarified for all the teachers and administrators in ECS what integral Christian teaching meant. Who could have predicted that the long-awaited solution for developing a

Christian approach to curriculum planning and teaching depended upon membership in a public-school jurisdiction?

One last question remains: what is the status of ECS's vision after two decades in the public school system? The vision/mission statement that was enshrined in the agreement with the EPSB is still there. It is a vision that reflects the main currents of thought that defined the CSC community up to the year 1999, as well as a few local priorities. The Neo-Calvinist emphasis on discernment (i.e., perspective or worldview) is clearly present, but ECS was not solely in the business of educating Christian minds. The discernment students need to understand the God-ordained normativity that underpins all societal relationships must also equip them to live a Christian life. The statement assumes that students will experience this life at school, not in some future life. The statement, therefore, embodies the two main impulses of the CSC legacy: worldview education and discipleship education.

ECS's vision and mission statement also reflects a course correction for the movement that was emerging at that time, namely, cultural engagement. The purpose of Christian education is to confront students with real-life problems. In their engagement with these problems, they must make informed, ethical choices that will develop in them a sense of social responsibility. In addition to all of this, the statement promoted the development of individual gifts, the recognition of student differences, and a rigorous and diverse academic program.

All the evidence suggests that ECS has not lost contact with its Christian vision and mission after twenty years in the Edmonton Public School Board as an alternative Christian program. If anything has changed, it is stronger now due to the development and implementation of the Teaching for Transformation (TfT) initiative. However, much work still needs to be done to fully implement TfT in individual classrooms. To my knowledge, ECS staff seldom talk about worldview education or education for discipleship, the two historic expressions of education for cultural transformation. Instead, they are focused on cultural engagement that leads to reconciliation and the restoration of relationships. This is an encouraging sign, for it suggests a course change toward a realizable education for hope.

It is the greatest of ironies for CSC educators, especially those in Ontario and British Columbia, that the school they wrote off as a sellout has provided the strongest leadership for revitalizing the tradition's educational vision, and it has done so at a time when many CSC communities have lost touch with their legacy while in full control of their schools.

CHAPTER 9

Teaching for Transformation

Timeline

2000–2003   Educators at Edmonton Christian School (ECS) seek a more effective way to implement a distinctively Christian curriculum.

2004–2010   The Prairie Association of Christian Schools (PACS) sponsors an ad hoc committee to further advance the ECS approach into a curriculum-writing template.

2010   The emerging model is named Teaching for Transformation (TfT). Darryl DeBoer, Director of Learning at Surrey Christian School in British Columbia begins to collaborate with D. Monsma to promote TfT.

2011   Doug Monsma becomes Director of Learning at the Prairie Centre of Christian Education (PCCE), a reorganized PACS and the recognized leader of TfT development.

2013   Monsma, DeBoer and ECS principal Peter Buisman attend an Expeditionary Learning conference in Boston.

2014   TfT shifts from a template for curriculum writing to a framework for changing classroom practice, and takes root in PCCE schools.

2015   The SCSBC signs a formal agreement with the PCCE to offer TfT training facilitated by Darren Spyksma.

2017   The Centre for the Advancement of Christian Education at Dordt University is contracted to develop the TfT approach for American schools under the leadership of Darryl DeBoer.

The Evolution of TfT[204]

Teaching for Transformation (TfT) was conceived in the aftermath of the historic agreement that made Edmonton Christian School an alternative program within the Edmonton Public School Board. In their new setting, ECS teachers felt an urgent need to more deeply understand, and more consistently implement, the school's vision to offer a distinctively Christian education. Director of Curriculum and Instruction Doug Monsma, high school principal Peter Buisman, and junior high teacher Brian Doornenbal led the way in this endeavor.

In keeping with their Neo-Calvinist tradition, vision renewal for Monsma, Buisman, and Doornenbal started with thinking about the structure and meaning of curricular content.[205] They did not, however, resort to their legacy's established habit of first writing thematic statements, then constructing comprehensive unit and lesson plans that reflected these themes. Instead, they adopted a fresh approach, what Wiggins and McTighe called "backward design."[206] They flipped the traditional, linear theory-to-practice method of planning on its head. Rather than add learning goals at the end of the curriculum planning process, understanding by design (UBD) required educators to first identify the desired outcomes, then plan curriculum that met those goals. A key component in the UBD approach was the essential question.[207]

The work of Monsma, Buisman, and Doornenbal at ECS in conjunction with a few colleagues from two other Christian schools eventually piqued the interest of Elco Vandergrift, the executive director of the Prairie Association of Christian Schools (PACS). He was concerned about the general health of PACS member schools because they operated as individual silos of learning. Among other things, this isolation stifled collaboration on curriculum reform. As a result, the gap between the rhetoric of vision statements and actual practice had grown unacceptably wide. A popular cliché at the time summarized the big PACS picture: teachers could talk the talk but not walk the walk.

In a strategic move, Vandergrift set up an ad hoc committee that included himself, Monsma and Buisman from ECS, Gayle Monsma and Collette Hayes from Covenant Christian School in Leduc, and Carolyn

Stolte and Rob Molzahn from Gateway Christian School in Red Deer. Like the CDC mothers who launched *Joy in Learning* in the late 1960s, this committee of seven embraced the two beautiful daughters of hope. They shared a righteous anger, or holy discontent, as Doornenbal likes to say, over the state of Christian education in their tradition, and they possessed the courage to change the situation. The fact that everyone on Vandergrift's committee came from an alternative program Christian school is significant. As a result of their partnerships with public school boards, these schools had the resources to support the committee's work in ways that were never possible when the schools were independent.

The committee directed critical questions toward their historic vision of education for a Christian perspective. This deep dive into the soul of their tradition led to a subtle but significant shift in approach. They no longer treated the creation-fall-redemption-restoration meta-narrative of Scripture as a theme that somehow had to be integrated into every subject area. Instead, they adopted it as *God's story*. The purpose of Christian education changed from giving students a worldview to providing them with an understanding and experience of the way their own stories fit into this bigger narrative. To implement their new interpretation of Christian education, the committee had to come up with a different approach to curriculum design, pedagogy, and classroom practice. According to Doornenbal, the process was messy; teachers struggled to let go of their traditional teacher role and linear approach to curriculum planning. After a couple of years of testing ideas in their own classrooms, the committee eventually developed a fairly unified approach and named it Teaching for Transformation (TfT) because once we know our place in God's story, we will be changed.

Doug Monsma was the acknowledged leader of TfT, first in his role at ECS and later in 2011when he became the director of learning the Prairie Centre for Christian Education. He and the other co-creators of TfT shared many foundational beliefs, and the following two were particularly formative: 1) alignment with God's story means living a life of service and 2) students learn to serve best by serving. Their vision of education was captured by the phrase "learning TO serve and learning BY serving."

The key question they had to answer was, how can students learn to serve in a classroom setting? This question echoed the conundrum that frustrated the advocates of education for discipleship a decade or so earlier. In response, the TfT developers searched the Scriptures and identified ten traits of discipleship, such as justice-seeker, community-builder, and earth-keeper.[208] A life of service, they surmised, was sure to emerge when students embodied combinations of these traits. The more students took ownership of these discipleship traits or "habits of righteousness," the more clearly they would see themselves (personally and as a group) as "peculiar people."[209] Within the TfT framework, service learning was not an occasional key "add on" to the curriculum. If God's story is what made sense of and gave relevance to the "stuff" of the curriculum, service was the context within which students most fully grasped the meaning of the story.

Monsma and company avoided many mistakes that hampered earlier efforts to refocus CSC's Neo-Calvinist legacy. They understood that the development of TfT would take years rather than months, it had to be tested in real classrooms, and teachers committed to TfT required constant support via workshops, classroom consulting, and a mechanism for sharing their successes and failures.

At a certain point, Monsma and his team of committed developers acknowledged that the TfT units they posted on a shared website looked good on paper but did not impact classroom practice. Their plans were rich in "God talk," especially at the beginning and end of units, but these units did not achieve their goal for students to "see the story, enter the story." The team decided they needed a fundamental shift in approach. From the beginning they had pictured TfT as a template for writing curriculum, but what they actually needed was a framework for changing classroom practice. This realization eventually led to their development of three core practices named storyline, through lines, and the formational learning experience.

Tragically, Monsma died in 2018 after a fierce battle with cancer. At about the same time, Doornenbal was forced into retirement by a debilitating disease. Buisman and Vandergrift reached retirement age at around that time as well. Despite these losses, TfT continued to thrive in

Alberta. It also spread to the other CSC regions, the United States and further abroad.

Today, TfT has a presence in every Prairie Centre of Christian Education (PCCE) school, thanks largely to the diligent and visionary efforts of Monsma's sister, Gayle Monsma, and Jeremy Horlings, who now serve as the PCCE's executive director and associate executive director, respectively. Darryl DeBoer, the director of learning at Surrey Christian School in British Columbia, worked closely with Doug Monsma for a number of years and continues to play a key role in the development of TfT. Because of his leadership, TfT not only has a presence in the SCSBC but has taken off in the United States, where the PCCE established a relationship with the Centre for the Advancement of Christian Education (CACE), an outreach arm of the education department at Dordt University. As the director of learning for the CACE, DeBoer currently works with roughly fifty American schools in their efforts to implement TfT. Justin Cook, director of learning for Edvance, promotes TfT's development in Ontario. Edudeo, an organization committed to providing Christian education to children in the developing world, now uses TfT in several schools in Zambia. TfT is also making an impact in the Neo-Calvinist school movement in Australia.

TfT: What Is It, Really?

According to Jeremy Horlings, TfT is all of the following: a journey, a pedagogy, and an education for cultural engagement. TfT interprets the goal of Christian education as an invitation to students and teachers to enter a story that is bigger than their own by engaging in real work that meets the real needs of real people.

This TfT vision of Christian education represents a significant course correction for the Neo-Calvinist tradition of education. Writ large, TfT embodies an education for hope on multiple levels. It rekindles a flickering flame of righteous anger among CSC's regional leaders over the gap that separates rhetoric from reality in Christian education and encourages them to promote practices that bridge this gap. TfT nurtures in teachers a righteous anger over their inability to teach in ways that make the biggest and most enduring differences in their students' lives, and it enables them to replace their traditional approach to teaching and learning with classroom practices that authentically connect thinking with doing. It also fosters in students a righteous anger over the problems that plague people in their local community and the world at large and empowers them to meaningfully address some of them in their learning.

The specifics of the TfT approach are depicted in its literature by a chart of three concentric circles. The circle in the centre represents the school's "deep hope," a statement that expresses the purpose of Christian education. This vision functions as the school's point of orientation. The next circle out from the centre describes the three *Core Practices* that bring the vision to life: *Storyline*, *Throughlines*, and *Formational Learning Experiences* (FLEx). These core practices represent a serious challenge to the deep structure that upholds the traditional classroom.[210] They not only replace the traditional roles of teacher, student, and curriculum but also the assumptions that justify them.

The purpose of the storyline is to connect learning and learners to God's story of making all things new. This strategy undermines the established practice of students doing assignments for the sole purpose of meeting a particular standard and achieving a grade-point average. These assignments typically deal in content meant to inform and have virtually nothing to do with any lived reality. TfT believes in education that is forming rather than informing. In an article published in the *Christian Educators Journal* in 2018, DeBoer and Cook observe:

> There are many stories at work within a school—the story of being socially accepted, the story of achieving good grades, the story of handing in your school work on time, the stories of compliance and engagement. And, for good and bad, participating in these stories shapes us and deeply roots what we value and desire in our lives.[211]

The TfT approach challenges teachers and students to adopt a class storyline expressed in age-appropriate language. Examples from DeBoer's school in Surrey, BC, include: "instruments of change," "risk your status quo," and "nourish to flourish." The teacher's task is to place the content that normally serves the mastery of knowledge or a technical skill into the context of God's story. Without this story, DeBoer and Cook argue, things like measuring pollutants in streams, studying wars, stars, and trees, writing poetry and music, and playing a game of dodgeball in PE is "simply stuff."

Throughlines were initially understood as biblical themes that could be woven into the fabric of the whole curriculum. Unfortunately, they functioned as "labels" of discipleship, or ten more things to teach. When TfT transitioned from a curriculum template to a framework for classroom practice, the throughlines were reimagined as "who lines" or different ways to engage culture, namely, the practices of discipleship. These practices include "God worshipper," "idolatry-discerner/prophetic-speaker," "earth keeper," "beauty-creator," "justice seeker," "creation-enjoyer," "servant-worker," "community-builder," "image-reflector," and "order-discoverer." When these practices become habits in the lives of students and teachers, they redefine their unique roles as persons or a community in God's story.

Formational Learning Experiences (FLEx) serve as the third core practice in TfT. These experiences "provide students with opportunities to practice living in God's story by doing real work that meets the real needs of real people."[212] When done well, FLEx engages students in work that forms them and shapes the world. This kind of learning is difficult to imagine for anyone steeped in traditional forms of educating. DeBoer and Cook provide three snapshots of this kind of experience:

> While learning about visual art and language, grade one students in Edmonton, Alberta created thank-you cards and sent them to the city's snowplow drivers. In gratitude, the city workers brought their large trucks to the school to visit the students.
>
> While learning about literature and slavery, grade five and six students in Georgetown, Ontario, published a book of slave narratives and donated the proceeds to International Justice Mission Canada "to change history and free slaves today," as student Amelia shared with me.
>
> While learning biology, grade eleven students in Surrey, British Columbia, developed their knowledge of

flora and fauna as curious gardeners, caring for a local urban forest (Tynehead Regional Park and salmon hatchery) and leading tours for others to experience and care for the park too.[213]

The outer circle in the chart identifies nine *Essential Practices*. These practices address curriculum planning, assessment, pedagogy, and classroom community building. They function like throughlines for teachers, the desirable habits and practices that reform teachers and transform their classrooms. The descriptions of these essential practices are minimal in TfT literature, but their importance is fairly obvious. With respect to curriculum planning, TfT teachers use *Storyboards* because students need a constant visual reminder of their learning journey within God's story. Lessons need to be *Transformational Lessons*; that is, the kind that invite, nurture, and empower students. Lessons must encourage *Reflection*, repeated opportunities for students to extend their learning and make connections with other learning experiences.

Two of the nine essential practices support community building. TfT teachers use *Opening and Closing Circles* to foster belonging among learners. They also employ *Celebrations of Learning* to empower students to share the journey with their community. The three practices that pertain to pedagogy include cultivating the kind of *Habits of Learning* in students that nurture deeper learning, *Learning Targets*, and *Protocols* that promote collaboration. The last essential practice is *Formative Assessment*, which gives students clear feedback on their learning journey.

The TfT circle chart portrays an alternative orientation to teaching that is rooted in deep hope and comes to expression in actual classroom practices. Where it is consistently implemented, it takes students and their teachers on a journey that redefines what it means to be human and what the good life looks like.

Is TfT What We Have Been Looking For?

For those who have been searching for a way to redirect the Neo-Calvinist tradition of education while remaining true to its founding principles, the answer is a resounding *yes*. TfT educators no longer consider worldview to be the end game for Christian education because they know it is not the catalyst that changes lives. However, they acknowledge the importance of worldview because teachers and students need the lens of Scripture to interpret, critique, and imagine alternatives to the spirits that rule the age. TfT is not education for discipleship, although it comes close. Its advocates realize the futility of initiating students into a way of life that their own communities do not consistently model. Instead, TfT focuses on forming the habits of a radical Christian life in students through meaningful learning experiences. This merging of one's personal and communal stories into the larger narrative of God's story is a direction-setting, formative process. Ultimately, it is all about who or what we are committed to serve.

Where TfT is implemented, the school cannot help but be a dissident and transformative social institution. It directs teachers and students away from a status quo education and its priorities and instead invites teachers and students to enter a counter-cultural story, a story that engages them in the real struggles of real people.

TfT has great potential to educate for hope because it invites teachers and students to embrace hope's beautiful daughters of righteous anger (over what is broken in the world) and courage (to see things do not remain that way). Those who find this an exciting possibility must never overlook the fact that embracing hope comes with a cost; it purposely draws its participants into the experience of those who suffer, and to meaningfully act in their space requires sacrifice.

As is so often the case, a "yes" must be followed with a "but." TfT is what many teachers have been looking for, but few who try to implement it will likely succeed. The majority will lose their battle with the deep structure of schooling, just as so many did who tried to implement *Joy in Learning*. After some noble attempts to implement TfT's classroom practices, some teachers will predictably fall back into their traditional teaching routines. These outcomes are bound to happen, history teaches us, unless the regional associations are committed to providing all the resources that teachers need to sustain such a radical approach to education in their classrooms over the long haul! The TfT approach will only stick where it truly redefines the deep structure of schooling.

Cross-country Checkup

So, what is the status of TfT in the various regions of CSC today? The short answer is, it has a good foothold in all three, but the majority of schools are not fully committed to implementing it. The role that TfT plays in each region varies, and this is largely due to the different paths the regional organizations and their schools have chosen to follow, particularly over the past two decades. To get some insight into the current situation within each region, I contacted leaders from the Prairie Centre of Christian Education (PCCE), the Society of Christian Schools in British Columbia (SCSBC), and the Edvance Christian Schools Association (Edvance). The following brief regional sketches emerged from these exchanges.

The Prairie Centre of Christian Education is by far the smallest and most homogeneous of CSC's three regions, with nineteen member schools that serve approximately 6,500 students. All nineteen schools still identify with the Neo-Calvinist tradition of education. Most of them operate as alternative programs in their respective public school boards, a status unlikely to be duplicated in the other two regions. The association was initially divided over the Edmonton Society for Christian Education's decision to sign an agreement with the Edmonton Public School Board. As more and more schools followed Edmonton's lead, this rift appears to have narrowed or closed altogether. The fact that the alternative program schools maintained their commitments to the PCCE has been vital to the organization's survival and subsequent maturity.

Due to their full public funding, alternative program schools do not struggle financially. However, some of the independent members of the association do. Over the past two decades most school leaders have been administrators first and visionaries second, but this situation is improving. By contrast, the PCCE executive has consistently delivered strong visionary leadership.

With respect to school vision, many PCCE schools continue to struggle with this perennial question: what does it mean to be distinctively Christian? The answer largely depends upon the local community's perception of their school: is it only for the benefit of their community, or is it a gift to share with others? This is a contemporary way to express the historic struggle between the protectionist mentality rooted in the Afscheiding and the Kuyperian push for cultural transformation.[214]

The PCCE has distinguished itself as a champion of vision growth and implementation. As noted above, it led the way in the development of Teaching for Transformation. Remarkably, every member school today has a TfT leader on staff who encourages the implementation of this initiative. The most optimistic forecast predicts a situation where PCCE schools are united around a radically different approach to teaching. At this point in time, however, many schools are struggling to implement TfT's core practices. Their teachers are more comfortable visualizing TfT as a template for curriculum reform rather than as a framework for teaching.

The SCSBC currently supports forty schools with a total enrolment of 15,400 students. Although the majority of these schools still identify as members of the Neo-Calvinist tradition of education, a significant number do not. The strong presence of schools from various denominational backgrounds is due to the SCSBC's strategy of inclusion. This openness to diversity allows different traditions of Christian education to learn from each other, but it presents a unique set of challenges for the SCSBC's leadership. The most significant of these concerns vision.

Presently, there is no dominant vision of Christian education that animates the SCSBC. In fact, different spectra of visions overlap, and this contributes to a fluid situation. Within the core member schools, some educators locate themselves along a spectrum bounded by the historic vision of worldview education and education for discipleship. Others in the association see the endpoints of the spectrum as covenantal (Neo-Calvinist) priorities and missional (Evangelical) priorities.

SCSBC executive director Ed Noot does not interpret this widespread struggle to own a vision as messy but rather as an opportunity for teachers from all denominational backgrounds to move beyond a naïve acceptance of an inherited vision based on assumptions no one in the school holds to anymore. Nevertheless, he identifies four challenges that the organization's leaders must overcome if the SCSBC is to be vibrant and healthy. School leaders must find ways to prevent the tyranny of the urgent from sidetracking their efforts to implement a culturally engaging form of learning. School leaders and their staffs must also overcome the urge to wait and see what approach to teaching and learning has the most currency and relevance and instead position themselves on the frontlines of change. Schools must adhere to a vision that is strong enough to stand up to the well-meaning but very vocal members of the community who champion single-issue agendas. Finally, school communities must decide if their schools are to act as a bubble of protection from the negative influences of culture or a bridge for engagement that gives students opportunities to make culture in relevant ways.

On the bright side, there is a growing desire in a variety of schools to make the shift from a traditional education that primarily informs students to an education that forms them through encounters with deeper learning. This shift is primarily due to the increased popularity of TfT, project-based learning, and the SCSBC's own Experiencing Christ in the Classroom initiative (ECC).

Under the capable leadership of Darren Spyksma, director of learning for the SCSBC, Experiencing Christ in the Classroom is a professional-development program that encourages teachers to "examine how they teach" and "imagine how they ought to teach," so they can be more intentionally formational. The program places participating teachers into small cohorts that meet for four days at the beginning of the year to determine a set of personal goals and four days at the end of the year to take stock of their progress and plan for the future. During the ten intervening months of the school year, the cohort meets regularly to keep members accountable and to offer mutual support.

The Residency is another encouraging professional development opportunity for SCSBC teachers and administrators. The Residency is a collaborative effort involving the SCSBC, the Institute for Christian Studies, and Dordt University. It provides two tracks of professional development that lead to Christian deeper learning. The Professional Learning Track culminates in a master's degree from either the Institute for Christian Studies or Dordt University. The Covenantal Partnership Track promotes long-term professional development for SCSBC teachers in the areas of worldview, project-based learning, and Teaching for Transformation.

The diversity of schools that now populates the SCSBC makes the promotion of TfT more challenging, but Spyksma has played a key role in transforming his own K-12 school, Surrey Christian, into an exemplary TfT school.

The complexity of the situations in Alberta and British Columbia pales in comparison to the scene in Ontario. One of the most significant changes that has recently taken place there is the dissolution of the OACS (school boards), Edifide (teachers), and OCSAA (administrators) organizations in 2018 and the formation and subsequent development of the Edvance Christian Schools Association (Edvance). Edvance provides many of the services formerly delivered by these three defunct organizations, but it is not simply the product of folding three organizations into one. It is more accurate to say that the three disbanded organizations had fulfilled their purposes, and the time had come to replace them with an organization driven by new thinking, some visionary and some pragmatic.

This new thinking shows up in two significant shifts. One marks the move away from the tradition's historic emphasis on curriculum reform to a priority for innovative pedagogy and changed classroom practices. This shift already began in 2013 when the OACS replaced the position of curriculum coordinator with a director of learning. When Edvance decided to discontinue the printing of curriculum units developed by teachers, whatever remained of the region's historic teacher-led curriculum reform movement effectively ended. After decades of neglect, pedagogy became the organization's top priority. A similar shift has also taken place within the PCCE and the SCSBC.

The other, more pragmatic shift concerns membership in the association. Edvance seeks to expand the tent of Christian education by adding schools from diverse traditions of education. The origins of this initiative can also be traced back to the OACS. When that organization was shut down in 2018, it had sixty-nine member schools, and roughly one third of them did not identify with Neo-Calvinism. Edvance has added nineteen more, for a total of eighty-eight member schools, and most of these new additions also do not have roots in Neo-Calvinism. The total enrolment for all Edvance schools is 13,100.

Today it no longer makes sense to identify Edvance as a Neo-Calvinist organization. The diversity of schools belonging to Edvance also makes talk of a course correction for the Neo-Calvinist tradition of education in that association less meaningful. However, this tradition remains the guiding light for Edvance and its greatest source of hope.

When it comes to educational vision, Edvance faces a situation similar to the one that the SCSBC leaders encounter: its schools pursue a variety of educational visions and with different degrees of enthusiasm and success. One can now find schools that offer classical studies education, character development education, mastery of knowledge and technical skills education, and education that emphasizes deeper learning. Cutting across this spectrum are school staffs who believe they are engaged in "Christian education" but are in fact "Christians educating" (just like others in the status quo do).[215]

Edvance is still relatively new, and nearly half of its brief existence has been complicated by COVID-19. It faces a unique set of challenges, some with long histories and some brand new. The biggest of these challenges concerns vision: should Edvance take ownership of a particular vision of Christian education and invite its member schools, regardless of their diverse philosophies of education, to follow its lead? If this is its preferred strategy, what vision will it promote? If it is not, two other options come to mind: Edvance will not promote a vision, and/or it will function as a broker of multiple visions.

The second challenge is closely tied to the first. If Edvance officially adopts an educational vision, will everyone get on board? Throughout its history, the Ontario region of CSC has been plagued by the "old Dutch disease" that resulted in debilitating divisions over the decades (see the "rival community" as discussed in chapter 3). Will the new generation of Edvance educators overcome this bad habit?

The next two challenges are also connected at the hip. In the past, classroom teachers who committed to non-traditional approaches to teaching and learning, discovered rather quickly that they were either unable or unwilling to change. The resistance they faced from parents, colleagues, principals, and even their own habits proved to be too much to overcome. Is Edvance prepared to run interference for the implementation of non-traditional visions of the classroom?

The original designers of Teaching for Transformation understood the magnitude of the task to change a traditional classroom into one that put student learning at the centre and engaged them in culture making. Teachers typically require years, not months, to make this switch. Along the way they need a variety of supports, such as classroom consulting, regular PD opportunities, and collaboration with like-minded teachers, not to mention the full support of their school leaders. A Christian Teacher Academy already exists and provides some of these services. Similarly, the new iteration of the annual fall teacher's convention encourages professional development. Is Edvance prepared to implement and sustain all of the resources required to develop this radical approach to teaching over the long haul?

Finally, will Edvance and its schools commit to curricular reform as well as pedagogical reform? For many decades the Neo-Calvinist movement pursued curriculum reform to the neglect of pedagogical reform, even though the importance of the latter was never questioned. This strategy led to lots of talk and little action. In light of this legacy, it is completely understandable that the proponents of innovative classroom practices are tempted to neglect curriculum reform. However, this strategy will prove equally fatal if it prevails.

The desire to break away from the traditional classroom structure with its corresponding roles for administrators, teachers, and students has a long, shared history in all three CSC regions. It began in earnest with the *Joy in Learning* curriculum, reappeared in the consulting work that Agnes Struik did for the Curriculum Development Centre, and showed up again in the *Man in Society* curriculum. All of these early forays into changing classroom practice were curriculum driven, which turned out to be a mixed blessing. The integrality of curriculum design and pedagogy was never questioned, but pedagogy always took a back seat. In the end only a few teachers who tried to implement one or another of the curricular innovations just mentioned, did so in a non-traditional classroom setting.

The first flickers of change in Ontario appeared on the horizon when visionary principal Ren Siebenga initiated a different tactic in the late 1990s and early 2000s. He put classroom practice in the driver's seat. To the amazement of many, he did it in a high school. Inspired by a visit to High Tech High in San Diego, which promoted the project-based learning approach, Siebenga systematically changed the structure of learning at Toronto District Christian High School. This required altering the established roles of teachers, students, and the curriculum. He did not have to change the role of school leaders; he already was a visionary administrator, rather than an administrator who dabbled in vision. Teachers at his school became designers of learning instead of stand-and-deliver experts who exercised all of the decision-making authority in the classroom. Students were no longer treated as empty heads on sticks who needed to be filled with knowledge and kept under control. They became self-forming learners empowered to make decisions and engage in meaningful acts of culture making.

Nathan Siebenga followed his father's example a few years later when he led a transformation of the association's oldest high school, Hamilton District Christian High. He and his staff were instrumental in the establishment of the Christian Teacher Academy, which promoted the project-based learning approach developed by PBL Works, formerly known as the Buck Institute for Education. The Christian Teacher Academy was set up to introduce teachers to the PBL approach and support them in their implementation of it in their classrooms over the long haul. Under the capable leadership of executive director Harry Blyleven, the academy now has sufficient credibility to become an official player of teacher development in Edvance.

One of the visionary young teachers who helped set up the academy, Justin Cook, was appointed as the director of learning when Edvance was created. His strategic appointment also signaled that a long-awaited course correction was in the making. Cook is a thoughtful, inspiring leader and the perfect person for this critically important post. He maintains important ties with leaders in the SCSBC and the PCCE and also seeks to be a visionary leader for Edvance schools from every background. In addition to project-based learning, the Christian Teacher Academy also draws on the Dimensions of Learning, developed by the Expeditionary Education movement (now known as EL learning) and the core practices promoted by the Teaching for Transformation approach.

The pedagogy-first movement within Edvance has remained relatively small, but it flourishes here and there for several important reasons. Conceptual frameworks are available for teachers to use to transform their classroom practices. Teachers can also now draw on various resources to support their development as non-traditional teachers. Most importantly, strong leadership is popping up in various locations. Ray Hendriks, recently retired director of support services at Edvance, emphasized the importance of this last factor. If the movement to change classroom practice is going to flourish, entire school staffs need to get on board rather than a few keener teachers in an otherwise traditional school. A noteworthy example, said Hendriks, is the Halton Hills Christian School staff, under the leadership of Marianne Vangoor.

Deep Hope, Deeper Learning

Reform-minded educators across CSC currently draw upon three main sources of inspiration: Teaching for Transformation, Project-Based Learning, and Expeditionary Learning. The degree of influence of these approaches varies in each region.

Within the PCCE, TfT provides the framework for reform and elements of PBL and El are incorporated. PBL serves as one kind of FLEx experience, a particularly effective one. EL supplies the rhetoric of "Deeper Learning" and some key learning protocols.

When asked about TfT's significance relative to that of PBL and EL, Darren Spyksma, the director of learning for the SCSBC, identified three groups of schools within the association. Some school staffs fully subscribe to TfT as their communal structure for learning. It drives their planning and thinking, and in some cases, it is so embedded that it impacts structural decisions with scheduling and so on. Spyksma reports that many other school staffs have heard of TfT and EL, but rather than fully commit to one or the other, they incorporate those pieces of good practice that align with their own vision. Another large group of schools incorporates aspects of PBL, and some within that group do so extensively.

TfT, PBL, and El play prominent roles among reformers in Edvance. After a slow start, TfT has gained sufficient momentum in the association that Justin Cook sometimes refers to it and PBL as "beautiful siblings." As was the case in the SCSBC, we can find schools that primarily look to one of these approaches and/or draw from all three.

As elements from these three sources of pedagogical reform increasingly get stitched together to form a composite approach, the terms *deep hope* and *deeper learning* are gaining prominence as overarching themes. Both terms resonate with the Neo-Calvinist tradition. However, each one also raises concerns. This chapter ends with a quick look at the positive and negative connotations of deep hope and deeper learning.

Earlier in the chapter, we saw that deep hope defines the innermost circle of the TfT framework chart. There it refers to a school's "statement of purpose and calling" or a school's "North Star," as TfT educators like to say. Used this way, deep hope primarily functions as a category, that is, a type or level of hope. Here deep hope does not appear to refer to a specific hope or vision! In fact, the very opposite seems to be the case. If deep hope stands for whatever purpose or vision a school happens to pursue, this is problematic, for clearly not all visions of education will lead to a biblically informed deep hope. In other contexts, TfT uses deep hope to describe its own educational goal, "the formation of a peculiar people." This is a more compelling use of the term because living into God's story truly provides a deep hope.

When "deep hope" refers to the formation of a peculiar people in the TfT frame of reference, it connects teachers and students to God's promises. It also underscores their longing to find their coveted place in God's story. What the term "deep hope" needs to communicate, however, is what peculiar people are expected to do once they are in the story. By joining their story to God's story, teachers and students take responsibility for bringing hope to a despairing world that desperately awaits the fulfillment of God's promises. Here is where the notion of deep hope can benefit from St. Augustine's notion of the two beautiful daughters of hope.

I wholeheartedly agree with DeBoer's desire to connect the deep hope of living in God's story with deeper learning. However, deeper learning is used in two very different ways. Deeper learning is a concept borrowed from the Expeditionary Learning Program and its sponsor, the Hewlett Packard Foundation. In its original setting, deeper learning refers to learning by doing. It is based on research and experience that concludes students know most fully when they are engaged. Holistic or engaged knowledge is a worthy pursuit in its own right, as the EL movement can attest, and it is horribly lacking in our North American education system. However, "more holistic" or "more engaged" is not the same thing as "deeper." Deeper knowledge implies meaning, purpose, and direction. Deeper knowledge has more to do with a way of life and narrative than engagement.

Ren Siebenga once told me that he did not care if a teacher had a worldview, then he immediately said, "Actually, I do." He went on to describe a memory from his visit to High Tech High where he observed a group of students who had done an extensive project on revolutions.

> The kids were really into revolutions. I have never seen anyone dig into revolutions better. It fit their teenage story so well! If you saw what they read and what they thought they needed to know in order to answer their questions, it was just unbelievable. What did they come up with? What they produced was so dark and hopeless. So, then you say, man, if they only had some worldview.[216]

Deep learning within EL comes closest to expressing a worldview or narrative in the Hewlett Packard Foundation's promotion of twenty-first-century learning competencies. The competencies are not problematic in themselves, but they are used to shape students into successful competitors in the global economy.

DeBoer and Cook understand that the Hewlett Packard Foundation's use of "deeper learning" is incompatible with their own. They observe: "While the deeper learning goals described by the Hewlett Foundation (to ensure 'students compete globally and become engaged citizens at home') are consistent with the hopes of our students and parents, they fail to recognize the epic purpose and story we are part of."[217]

To sum up, "deep hope" for Christian education is not just any hope or vision that a school happens to cling to. Deeper knowing is not simply a matter of knowing more experientially rather than analytically. Deep hope and deeper knowing emerge from the biblical narrative that reveals what it means to be human and what constitutes the good life. To make TfT's vision of "see the story, live the story" go deep, CSC educators must not only seek to change the regularities of the traditional classroom, they need to replace the deep structure assumptions that validate them.

CHAPTER 10
Teacher Preparation at The King's University

Timeline

1981– 1994	Education courses are offered at The King's College.
1994	The King's University College BEd (Elementary) After-Degree Program is approved by Alberta Education
1995	The BEd (Elementary) After-Degree Program is inaugurated at TKUC
2007	The TKUC BEd (Secondary) After-Degree Program is approved.
	The Association of Alberta Deans of Education (AADE) is formed.
2009	The BEd (Secondary) After-Degree Program Inaugurated at TKUC.
2012	The Alberta Teachers Association (ATA) formally recognizes TKUC's education degrees

Expectations and Intentions

The long-term health of the Neo-Calvinist tradition of education in Canada depends in part on the presence of compatible teacher-preparation programs in Canada. The King's University in Edmonton, Alberta,[218] and Redeemer University[219] in Ancaster, Ontario, have provided this essential service since 1995 and 2003, respectively. Ironically, the very existence of these faith-based programs hinges on their approval by provincial governments and their commitment to prepare teachers for the larger world of public-school education. This chapter looks at the unique, trailblazing teacher-preparation programs offered at The King's. Someone who is intimately acquainted with Redeemer will have to tell that school's important story.

Like teacher-preparation programs everywhere, the elementary and secondary programs offered by The King's were shaped to some extent by the expectations of various stakeholders in education—in this instance, the Alberta government, Edmonton-area public school administrators, CSC communities, and the students who enrolled in these programs. Unlike education faculties that chart a zig-zag course somewhere between their stakeholder expectations and the latest research findings, the people who conceived, birthed, and nurtured teacher preparation at The King's had their own vision-driven intentions for their programs. The interactions between these intentions and what others expected from The King's BEd programs provide the backdrop to our investigation. Before we dive in, a review of these expectations is in order.

The Alberta government accredits all BEd degrees in the province. Its expectations for The King's were identical to those of the other teacher-preparation institutions. The government wanted graduates who were well along in embodying its list of KSAs (different types of knowledge, skills, and attributes). This "ideal teacher" was expected to teach the Alberta program of studies (POS) to students who upon graduation from the K-12 school system would emerge as "engaged" thinkers and "ethical" citizens with an "entrepreneurial" spirit (i.e., the 3-E graduate).

The King's education faculty was not alone in its recognition of inherent problems with the government's understanding of the ideal teacher, curriculum, and student. Colleagues from the other Alberta Universities as well as leaders of the Alberta Teacher's Association (ATA) found this eclectic set of nineteen KSAs problematic for at least two reasons. First, the sheer number of criteria in this list and the lack of any order of priority made it cumbersome as a standard for assessing teacher quality. Second, because the items in the list were drawn from all three streams of progressivism in education, they were not completely compatible.[220] The POS was a hodgepodge of units rather than a comprehensive, coherent body of knowledge. Parts of it were brand new while others had not been revised for a decade or more. The curriculum emphasized breadth over depth and lacked a clear sense of purpose. Teachers were free to go beyond its boundaries, but an overabundance of content provided little time for this. The 3-E model of the ideal student was equally controversial because it was so narrow in scope. An educated person was simply someone who easily fit into the workforce and accepted the social status quo.

Public school principals were obligated to hire the kind of teachers the government expected the universities to produce because their students had to demonstrate acceptable levels of understanding the POS and little else. What many principals most wanted, particularly in first-year teachers, was someone who needed minimal support for classroom management. From experience, they knew such teachers had to be capable planners and effective instructors. Some exceptional principals looked for thoughtful preservice teachers who had the desire and the ability to utilize non-traditional methods of instruction and unit planning. Most high school principals were content with knowledgeable, traditional teachers.

For CSC communities and their principals, the ideal preservice teacher understood the importance of a biblical worldview and could already demonstrate how this perspective shaped their approach to teaching and understanding of Christian education. Many elementary principals also wanted a teacher who knew how to use student-centred teaching strategies and could construct thematic units. A few looked for someone who could implement the Teaching for Transformation (TfT) approach and realize the goal of cultural engagement in their school. Secondary school principals consistently favoured a more traditional view of teaching.

The students who enrolled in The King's elementary and secondary education programs had many expectations. One of the most difficult to address had to do with their assumptions about teacher preparation. They pictured it as the acquisition and mastery of a set of specific skills. They expected the faculty to "show them how it's done," so they could do it. In a word, teaching was reduced to *technique*. Essentially, what these students expected from The King's education programs was what the government and many school principals also wanted: an education that churned out skilled traditional teachers.

Given these expectations it is reasonable to conclude that The King's education faculty felt pressured to pursue one or more of the following possible goals: 1) graduate a quality traditional teacher who uncritically teaches the provincial program of studies; 2) graduate a better version of the traditional teacher, someone who is student focused and reflective and can critically evaluate the provincial program of studies; 3) graduate the best version of a traditional teacher, one who occasionally utilizes non-traditional approaches to curriculum planning and instruction in the service of a robust, biblical worldview; or 4) graduate a visionary teacher whose nontraditional approach to teaching and learning not only reflects a biblical worldview but also presents students with opportunities to engage culture.

Blazing a Trail in Alberta (1981–1994)

Plans to offer teacher education at The King's began almost immediately after its inception in 1979 as The King's College. Bob Bruinsma was hired in 1981 to teach education courses in the areas of reading and language arts within the social sciences division of the faculty and to take the lead in developing an accredited bachelor of education degree. This proved to be a monumental task because in Alberta teacher preparation was the sole domain of three large provincial universities: the University of Alberta, the University of Calgary, and the University of Lethbridge.

The primary impetus to offer teacher education at The King's was to serve the needs of the Alberta and British Columbia regions of the Dutch Neo-Calvinist school movement, which were organized as Districts 11 and 12 of Christian Schools International. These schools employed several hundred teachers, who typically received their BEd degrees either from a secular Canadian university or an American faith-based school like Calvin College. At that time, there was no Canadian teacher-preparation institution committed to a biblical worldview. A teacher-preparation program at The King's would fill this critical void and also address the needs of other Christian school traditions. Everyone associated with the acquisition of a BEd program at The King's understood, if only vaguely, that if and when this program was approved, it would also have to prepare teachers for the public and Catholic school boards. However, the consequences of this additional responsibility for the education faculty were not well understood for many years.

Bruinsma pursued two strategies. The long-term goal was to get government approval for a BEd degree at The King's. To meet the immediate needs of students who wanted to become teachers, he explored ways to collaborate with Calvin College in Grand Rapids, MI. The objective here was to help students transfer to Calvin College for their third and fourth years to get their BEd and Michigan teacher certification. A similar arrangement with the University of Alberta was easier to arrange but much less desirable.

Bruinsma received considerable help to develop both strategies from sessional instructor Alyce Oosterhuis, who taught educational psychology. She took the lead, for example, in developing and coordinating a curriculum survey course that students from The King's needed to transfer to Calvin College. This course focused on curriculum issues in a variety of elementary subject areas. The King's did not have faculty expertise in most of these areas. To solve this problem, Oosterhuis solicited help from local in-service master teachers. Her unorthodox but brilliant strategy eventually became the most innovative component of teacher education at The King's. During the late 1980s and early 1990s, however, only a handful of students actually transferred to either Calvin College or the University of Alberta to complete their BEd degree.

In the 1980s, Alberta's three universities had virtual autonomy over their programs and degrees. By contrast, "private" institutions of higher learning, such as The King's, had to play by a different set of rules. Their programs and degrees had to be vetted through the Private College Accreditation Board (PCAB). The provincial government mandated this board to establish the criteria that private colleges had to meet to offer three- and four-year baccalaureate degrees in arts and sciences. Once these criteria were met, the PCAB would recommend that the Minister of Advanced Education approve the degree.

The King's application to offer a BEd degree in elementary education was particularly long and arduous because it was the first college to do so. The process was complicated by the fact that in addition to the PCAB, The King's had to negotiate with two government ministries: the Ministry of

Advanced Education, which oversaw the granting of education degrees, and the Ministry of Education, which was responsible for teacher certification. The King's lobbying was, in fact, the initiative that triggered the PCAB's development of guidelines for approving BEd degrees. These guidelines were finalized in March 1992, and The King's submitted its application that fall.[221]

In keeping with government policy, the PCAB required The King's to share its BEd program application with, and solicit responses from, the three public universities, the Alberta Teachers Association (ATA), and the College of Alberta School Superintendents (CASS). The motivation behind this stipulation was likely purely political. The government did not need the permission of these other stakeholders to approve programs, especially not from the ATA, which generally maintained an adversarial stance toward the government. The policy allowed the government to cover its political butt in times of controversy; it could always fall back on the fact that it "had consulted" other players prior to making a decision.

Bruinsma dutifully shared The King's application for an elementary BEd degree with the aforementioned bodies. The results ranged from indifference to outraged opposition. The two universities in southern Alberta did not respond; they either could not be bothered and/or they were not threatened by The King's offering a BEd. The University of Alberta replied that another program in Edmonton was redundant; the U of A had the capacity to prepare all the teachers that the region required. Furthermore, it argued that preservice teachers were best prepared in a setting where they rubbed shoulders with students from other professional programs, like nursing. The ATA was adamantly against private institutions preparing teachers for public schools. They felt private colleges were biased, lacked the appropriate academic resources, and should not receive public funding. These views were communicated indirectly because the union refused to validate the request with a response. CASS was noncommittal; it believed the application was more relevant for school boards to consider.

The lack of positive support from the consulted stakeholders did not prevent the PCAB from recommending approval of The King's application. The King's received formal government approval to offer a BEd degree in 1994. The government's green lighting of The King's teacher preparation program was both historic and controversial.

The King's program was a two-year "after-degree" program in elementary education rather than the more popular four-year BEd. Bruinsma favoured the two-year degree, to the chagrin of some at The King's, because he understood its potential for creative program planning. Innovations like the master teacher modules and a twelve-week practicum would have been impossible to schedule in a four-year degree. The fact that students had to first complete a three-year or four-year degree prior to their entry into a two-year education program was a deterrent for some students. They felt it was too expensive and time consuming. However, those who enrolled in it experienced both short- and long-term benefits. Not only were they much better prepared to teach, their extra year(s) of university education placed them one or two steps higher on the teacher salary scale throughout their careers.

On The Edge of Viability

Alberta Education wisely gave The King's five years to establish its education program before it conducted a full review that would determine whether The King's could continue to offer the degree. In fact, the review did not take place until year seven, my first year as chair of the faculty of education. The seven-year window was fortuitous because the viability of the program did not always look good in its formative years. For example, our faculty was always one person shy of the mandated staffing model. Throughout our probation period, Bruinsma, Oosterhuis, and I were the only full-time members of the education faculty. All of us taught courses, worked on putting the finishing touches to the program design and supervised student practicums. Bruinsma also served as the administrative head, a role that included the arrangement of student placements for practice teaching. We had some sessional and administrative help, but the workload was heavy and unsustainable for a faculty of three.

Our faculty's qualifications looked good on paper; we all had a doctorate degree in education, and we collectively had thirty-four years of teaching experience. We also had weak areas to overcome before we could effectively prepare students to teach in Alberta. Oosterhuis had taught for eight years at the elementary level, but in Holland. Bruinsma had seven years of teaching experience in British Columbia and Alberta, five at the grade 9–12 level, and only two years at elementary, including a principalship. I had taught a variety of subjects in Ontario over a nineteen-year career but all at the high school level. Alberta Education would likely not have acknowledged my teaching certificate from the Ontario Alliance of Christian Schools had anyone thought to check it. I had never taken an education course at the undergraduate level, but I was about to teach some. The three of us had much to learn about preparing teachers for elementary classrooms in both Christian and public schools. To address my lack of elementary school experience and credentials, Bruinsma arranged for me to spend three months in a grade five classroom taught by master teacher Andy Renema at the West campus of Edmonton Christian School. I learned a great deal about elementary-level education while observing and teaching in his classroom. The experience also gave me an opportunity to design our major practicum manual and do the observation exercises myself.

Our first cohort consisted of twenty-six students, which was a respectable number. We would have struggled to handle the program cap of thirty-five. Only eight students showed up the second year, and cohort sizes hovered around twenty for a few years after that. These numbers did not bode well for the program's future. To add to our enrollment woes, Edmonton's Concordia University College was granted permission to launch an elementary program a year after we did. Right from the start, they ran two cohorts of thirty to thirty-five students. Students interested in teacher education at a faith-based institution either did not know about our program, or they preferred to enroll at Concordia, which had a much longer history and did not take the intentional stance to integrate faith and learning as The King's did.

Although we received polite acceptance from our university colleagues in the province, our presence on the big stage of teacher preparation was questioned by some and outright opposed by others. As noted earlier, the powerful Alberta Teachers Association was particularly antagonistic. When it learned that the BEd proposal from Concordia University College of Alberta had also been approved, it proposed to take drastic action at its 1995 annual Area Representatives Assembly. The ATA published a resolutions bulletin in advance of this assembly to help the area representatives prepare. All policy statements that would be up for a vote were listed in the bulletin, including the provincial executive council's recommendation that "members of the ATA should participate only in practicum programs of the faculties of education of Alberta Universities and/or approved transfer programs."[222] Lest any ATA member not understand the intent of this proposed policy, an accompanying note made it clear that the executive was urging member teachers not to accept students from private-college teacher-education programs into their classrooms for practicum purposes.

Bruinsma and Bernie Potvin, the head of the newly approved BEd program at Concordia, decided to rent a hospitality suite in the Westin Hotel where the ATA meetings were to be held. Their strategy was to team up and dialogue with as many delegates as possible in an effort to get them to vote against the motion that would block private college students from practice teaching in public and Catholic classrooms. Somehow, a high-ranking ATA official, Charles Hyman, got wind of their intentions, and he phoned Bruinsma. Bruinsma recalls that it was one of the most unusual "out of the blue" calls he ever received. Hyman told Bruinsma that no matter how the ATA vote turned out, BEd programs offered by private colleges had protection under the law, and it would be a waste of time and money for Potvin and him to lobby ATA members at the hotel. He advised Bruinsma to look up Section 46[4] of the Education Act of the Province of Alberta, which clearly states that Alberta school boards are required to make classrooms available for practice teachers who are enrolled in ministerially approved programs. With this unexpected act of civility, Hyman discreetly signaled that the ATA's proposed policy encouraged its members to break the law.

The ATA delegates voted in favour of the motion, and this policy remained on the ATA books for many years without challenge from the government. As a consequence, The King's faculty regularly encountered teachers who refused to serve as mentors for our practicum students. Nevertheless, school principals were always able to find willing teachers to take students from The King's. Ironically, The King's program gained so much respect that, within a decade, teachers regularly informed us that they only wanted to mentor students from our program because they were so well prepared.

On the Cutting Edge

Despite its shaky beginnings, our program flourished. Bruinsma, Oosterhuis, and I developed it into one of the most innovative elementary teacher-preparation programs in Canada. Our program design was, in part, shaped by circumstance and government requirements, but our vision of teacher education was its deep driver. The program's design and small size prevented us from doing some of the things that big university education faculties were capable of. For example, we could not offer teaching specialties in areas like literacy, differentiated education, and technology. Neither could we deliver an intact program for Aboriginal or foreign-language students. However, we did establish a reputation for graduating the most well-prepared pre-service teachers in the province. Our small size was vital to this reputation, but not all small programs are innovative and alternative.

The three of us in the education faculty consciously pursued a common vision. The fact that we did made our program unique because university faculties, regardless of their size, rarely commit to a single vision. We managed this because Bruinsma, Oosterhuis, and I identified with the Reformational Movement within the Dutch Neo-Calvinist community in Canada. We did not share an explicit philosophy of education per se. Rather, we applied our individual, intuitive understandings of a Reformed biblical worldview to our courses. Evidence that we held to a common vision came to clearest expression in our mutual understandings of the ideal elementary education graduate, our roles as education faculty, and our program's design and priorities.

Our notion of the ideal graduate was identical to the kind of teacher we thought should teach in the Christian elementary schools that belonged to CSC. This meant we were not interested in educating some version of the traditional teacher. We wanted our graduates to be more than effective instructors, curriculum planners, and classroom managers. We intended them to have a biblical perspective on education and all of life. To capture what we envisioned as the ideal teacher, we borrowed and deepened the meaning of a then-popular term, the *reflective practitioner.*

We promoted the common understanding of a reflective teacher as one who analyzes and responds to the teaching/learning process as it happens in the classroom, to enhance student learning and their own effectiveness as teachers. To model this approach we constantly challenged our students to step back and reflect on what we as instructors had just done in class, what motivated our choices, and how the lesson could have been improved.

Our vision of the reflective practitioner went beyond its normal connotations. We wanted our students to be cognizant of the deep drivers of schooling and the ways they jockey for dominance as they jointly shape the curriculum, teaching strategies, assessment, and so on. We also challenged them to take a stand on all manner of perennial issues in education and to develop compelling reasons for their stance.

Furthermore, we expected our students to understand that their criteria for making wise judgments in the classroom came from a knowledge framework rooted in both philosophical thought and experience. We helped them develop a framework more by modelling our own and less by articulating the fine points of an educational philosophy. Our framework was unapologetically rooted in the biblical narrative.

Of course, we had to consider that not all of our students planned to teach in a CSC school, and a few in every cohort did not identify as Christians. Therefore, we could not in good conscience expect these students to adopt our framework, but they did have to try it on for size until they had the maturity and insight to assemble one of their own. We believed this was a critical step in every student's journey to clarify who they wanted to be as teachers. It was not lost on us that our strategy of teacher formation required a context of mutual respect and trust, and here is where the need for community was particularly acute.

Folk wisdom says it takes a village to raise a child. We believed it took a learning community to prepare a teacher. Community building was another key component of our vision. Our efforts to build a community of learning went beyond the nurturing of familiarity, respect, and care within the student ranks and between students and faculty. We wove community formation into the very fabric of the program. For example, we insisted that first- and second-year students take some key courses together. Later, when the secondary education program was added, we also grouped elementary and secondary education students together in some courses. Our faculty's approach to pedagogy also promoted community; we utilized team teaching, group work, group projects, and peer feedback as much as possible.

The implementation of our vision required a faculty that exhibited pedagogical expertise. We could not get away with explaining what good teaching looked like; we had to model it. This meant lecturing had to be minimized. Specifically, our challenge was to teach university students using methods that were effective at the elementary and secondary levels. As it turned out, these methods were equally effective with our own students.

Exemplary teaching included student practicum supervision. We supervised as many students as we could. Not only did our involvement in supervision provide us with some of our best teaching moments with our students, our constant exposure to a variety of classrooms informed and improved our own teaching. Based on conversations I had with other deans of education in Western Canada, I learned that their tenured faculty rarely supervised practicums. I never understood why an educator of teachers would see this task as a burden or a distraction. We saw it as an integral part of teacher preparation and our personal growth as educators.

Our vision for faculty members went well beyond the expectation that we had to be exemplary teachers. The university required each of us to pursue a research agenda. We accepted this responsibility, but we did not want our new knowledge to be hidden away in academic journals to be read by a few dozen specialized scholars. We were interested in research that could be meaningfully shared with our students and in-service classroom teachers, as well as with university colleagues.

Lastly, all faculty members at The King's were expected to engage in service. Service sometimes involved working with individuals or groups outside of the university. It always included administrative duties within the university generally as well as in one's own faculty. Throughout my career at The King's, every member of the education faculty was involved in program planning. This included responsibility for structural changes as well as personal course development. The former was not the sole responsibility of the dean, neither was the latter the autonomous domain of the professor.

Program design was a major component in our vision. We only had two years to prepare our students, so we had to make every moment count. We developed a four-semester sequence of preparation, integration, extension, and completion. Our intent was for terms one and three to prioritize practice driven theory and for terms two and four to accentuate theory informed practice.

The first semester was designed to get students to start thinking like teachers. They took six courses on campus, four of which were required. The required courses introduced students to foundational issues in learning theory, curriculum planning, language arts, mathematics, and so on. These courses incorporated a variety of opportunities to apply foundational knowledge, such as labs, and classroom-based assignments and projects.

The integration semester required students to take what they learned in the first semester and see how it came to life in a real classroom. Students spent the last six weeks of this second term observing and practice teaching in an area school. In this first practicum, they were expected to teach approximately twenty to twenty-five hours. Their performance in this practicum determined whether they could enter year two of the program.

The weeks leading up to this practicum represented the most unique element in The King's program. In the elementary education program, we offered eight to nine one-week modules that either focused on a specific subject area or a current topic, such as First Nations, Metis, and Inuit cultural awareness, differentiated learning, and assessment. We only had time to offer topical modules in the secondary program. Most of these modules were taught by in-service master teachers under the supervision of a faculty member.

The master teacher modules debunked a long-standing assumption that classroom teachers lack the intellectual wherewithal to contribute to teacher education beyond the mentoring of students in their practicums. In fact, they had more credibility than we did as faculty when they demonstrated various teaching strategies and explained why these strategies worked. Education students always paid close attention to the master teachers' stories about teaching the most challenging children or resolving tense classroom scenarios and the outcomes of their actions.

We described the third term of the program as one of extension, or the continuation and deepening of the theory and experience gained in year one. Students again took six courses on campus, the key courses dealing with curriculum planning and child exceptionalities. These courses also involved projects that required students to conduct observations in local classrooms.

The completion term consisted of a major twelve-week practicum. Our total of eighteen weeks of practicum far surpassed the provincial requirement of twelve weeks, which most universities met with two six-week experiences in their four-year degrees. The length and timing of our major practicum was as important as the total number of weeks our students spent in the classroom. Our extended twelve-week practicum put more demands upon the classroom mentor teachers, but it was a critical final step in the preparation of our students. We discovered that in most instances our students needed roughly six weeks to develop a firm bond with the students they had to teach. By week eight they were ready to assume the full teaching load of their mentor teacher. Those who could carry this full load of teaching for three to four weeks were truly ready to enter the teaching profession.

We saw both the six-week and the twelve-week practicums as opportunities for reflection and community building. Students were required to engage in several observation assignments, which the faculty supervisor evaluated. We also set up periodic call-back seminars on campus where students shared their experiences with each other. Our students regularly complained about the "extra" workload associated with these assignments. They would remind us that the U of A students practice teaching in their schools did not have to do any reflective assignments. At the same time, they let us know that they preferred to be in our demanding program because they could see it was preparing them to be better teachers.

Our students received a grade for the long practicum. We based it on their teaching performance (seventy percent) and their reflective assignments (thirty percent). They needed a passing mark in both categories to receive credit for the practicum. The teaching mark was correlated to one of five paragraphs that described their performance anecdotally. We knew that practicums were marked on a pass/fail basis, by the classroom teacher, in all the other programs in the province. We choose not to follow suit for two reasons. A pass could mean everything from a "hold your nose" pass to an excellent performance. For students in other programs, the quality of the pass they earned had to be deciphered from their classroom teacher's written evaluation. These teachers tried to be as positive as possible in their anecdotal comments. This was laudable, but it meant a hiring principal had to read between the lines to figure out how capable a student actually was in the classroom. Second, at The King's, we always consulted with the classroom mentoring teacher, but we felt it was our responsibility as faculty supervisors to determine a student's practicum grade. We had far more experience in assessing practicum performances, and we had the program's reputation to maintain.

Periodically, we called all the students from a cohort to return to campus for a seminar. One of our call-back seminars for the major practicum evolved into another innovative program component that we named the Mock Interviews. Students signed up for three twenty-minute practice interviews with current and past principals from a variety of school jurisdictions. It was the job interview equivalent of speed dating. Students not only honed their interviewing skills, they also learned how to articulate their own philosophy of teaching. The event was particularly rewarding for some principals; not a year went by without at least one of them hiring a student whom they first met in a mock interview.

The vision just outlined defined us as an education faculty and shaped our program's reputation, but it could not guarantee every student's success. Anyone intimately involved with teacher preparation knows that the most important factor for a student's success is the mentoring teacher in their major practicum. I have seen struggling students in our program blossom into effective teachers because the classroom teacher in their major practicum was not only an excellent teacher but also a patient, compassionate, and capable mentor. Unfortunately, I have also witnessed stellar students come undone because their mentor teacher was ill suited to the task.

Frieda Maaskant, an experienced teacher, served as our first field-placement coordinator, and she understood all of this. She transformed her job into a mission of service. For many years she made extraordinary efforts to get to know our students personally, so she could pair them with the right mentor teachers. I have no doubt that her matchmaking was critical to the high success rate of our students.

The Two Shall Become One

Our small faculty confronted many challenges, but none had greater importance than the addition of a secondary education program. In the absence of this program, The King's aspirations to prepare teachers for Christian Schools Canada and other faith-based education traditions remained unfulfilled. The preparation of secondary teachers was especially significant for me personally. My primary motivation to get a doctorate and leave high school teaching was to land a job in a teacher-preparation program. I wanted to spend my second career educating a different kind of high school teacher, one who was committed to radically changing the way students experience high school. That dream had all but died by 2007. At that time the elementary education program at The King's was entering its thirteenth year and the education faculty was undergoing a major transition. My colleagues, Oosterhuis and Bruinsma, had both retired, and one of the two new faculty members had just informed me that he was leaving. This left two of us in the faculty, with two vacant positions to fill. As the administrative head of the faculty, I was preoccupied with maintaining the quality of the elementary program; there was no time to dream about secondary education.

My colleague, Bob Bruinsma, temporarily left his teaching position in the education faculty in 2003 to serve as the university's associate vice-president academic. Among many other things, he started to work on a secondary education proposal. By this time the Private College Accreditation Board had been replaced by Campus Alberta Quality Council. This new body reviewed for approval program applications from all undergraduate institutions, public and private. I had no idea how complicated Bob's task was nor how far along he was in developing a proposal.

How could an education faculty as small as ours possibly deliver both an elementary and a secondary program? I could not picture this myself, so I conducted my own search of all the small colleges and universities in North America to find the ones that offered both programs. I thought that perhaps we could mimic their program designs. After many hours of searching, I discovered that the minimum enrollment for schools that offered both problems hovered around 1,500. This did not bode well for The King's, whose enrollment was well below 1,000. I also noticed that in every example where a small school offered both elementary and secondary education degrees, teacher preparation was the school's primary mission, and all the academic departments provided faculty support for education. Enrollment issues aside, I knew this model would be impossible to replicate at The King's, given its institutional history.

I was taken by surprise in the fall of 2007 when The King's announced that its foundation had accumulated enough money to launch a secondary education program and pay its budget for the first five years. Equally unexpected was the news that we had an application before the CAQC. When the program was approved, we were immediately thrust into a hiring frenzy. We needed to add three new faculty members prior to the launch of the program in the 2009–2010 academic year and one more before we offered the second year of the new program. This task seemed particularly daunting because in the past we had great difficulty finding suitable applicants; that is, people with teaching experience, a doctorate degree, and most of all, familiarity with the Dutch Neo-Calvinist tradition of education. Preparations moved along incredibly fast and remarkably smooth. Quality applicants were magically appearing and accepting our contract offers. Then the wheels fell off.

On March 28, 2008, I suffered a stroke and was forced to take an extended medical leave. My colleague, Bob Bruinsma, was called out of his two-month-old retirement to fill in as dean until I could return to work. He joined three other faculty members, all recent hires. One of them offered to take the lead role in guiding the faculty's efforts to flesh out the details of the secondary education program design and to oversee its implementation.

The fall of 2008 was a nightmare. I returned to work much too early; I only had enough mental and physical energy to work five-hour days, and that was with the benefit of a nap after lunch. Everyone in the faculty was overloaded and working hard at teaching new courses. In late October it became clear that the person responsible for leading us in the modification and implementation of our secondary education program had accomplished virtually nothing in six months. Sorting out this mess was a painful experience for everyone involved. To everyone's relief, our colleague resigned in January. Due to the hard work of new faculty members Bernice Stieva and Wendy Stienstra, we still managed to launch the secondary education program on time in the fall of 2009.

The King's was able to offer a secondary education degree because it, too, was a two-year (after degree) program. Students had to have both their major and minor concentrations virtually completed before they entered the program. The two-year format allowed us to piggyback the secondary program onto the elementary program. Required courses in the elementary program, such as curriculum planning, school administration, and learning theory, also had to be taken by secondary students. By overlapping the two programs, we did not have to add a whole slate of additional courses and the faculty to teach them. This strategy proved to be more than practically beneficial. Grouping elementary and secondary students together in these courses greatly enhanced their learning.

We still had to figure out how to offer methods of instruction for a variety of majors and minors. We did not have the personnel to do this in the usual way, so we ran two streams of methodology instruction, one for English and social studies majors/minors and one for science and math majors/minors. To accommodate students who majored in areas like physical education, music, or art, we set up individual tutorials with master teachers in a local school.

To overcome our limitations of disciplinary breadth, we had to be as creative as possible. We had no way of knowing if our strategy to merge our two programs rather than keep them separate would prove effective; no one had ever done anything like that before, at least as far as we knew. After several years we had our answer. Major practicum mentor teachers were unanimous in their praise; our secondary education students were, on average, better prepared than those from the big universities.

The Unexpected Costs of Advancing the Vision

The remarkable implementation of a secondary-education program brought about more than the major program changes mentioned above; it redefined the student body and the faculty itself. These changes presented our faculty with significant challenges, and our failure to resolve them meaningfully put the faculty's vision at risk.

No one anticipated how much the addition of secondary-education students would alter the character of our elementary student learning community that had evolved over the previous fourteen years. Secondary students, we discovered, were different from elementary students in significant ways. Most notably, they identified as subject specialists (I am a math teacher!). When they imagined themselves in the classroom, they were lecturing. They tended to focus more on content and were more comfortable analyzing foundational issues. By contrast, our elementary education students thought of themselves as teachers of children. In general, they gave more priority to forming relationships and teaching with projects. Teaching content vs. teaching kids sometimes emerged as conflicting priorities, but overall, the students in both programs saw the importance of balancing these two tendencies.

The addition of secondary-education students brought about a more significant change, one that proved difficult to address. When the faculty only offered an elementary program, most students desired to teach in a Christian school, if possible. No one questioned the need to embody a biblical worldview with one's approach to teaching. Virtually everyone bought into the faculty's vision of teaching that emphasized student-centred instructional strategies and a theme-based/project-oriented approach to curriculum planning. The majority of our secondary-education students, however, anticipated a future in the public school system. A surprising number of them were either unsure of their faith or claimed to have no faith at all. Many saw the value of teaching from a unified worldview, but a good number did not. They all aspired to be creative and able to use a variety of instructional strategies, but most balked at implementing a thematic approach to teaching their discipline.

The most significant transition pertained to the faculty. The doubling of programs led to a near doubling of our faculty. Not only were there more of us, everyone in the faculty was new, except for me. As dean, my top priority was team building, and the key to our unity had to be a shared vision. I did not expect my new colleagues to unquestioningly adopt the original vision that Bruinsma, Oosterhuis, and I had implemented, although in principle, they had committed to take ownership of it in their hiring interviews. We were obliged, I believed, to build on that founding vision. To that end I came up with a strategy that not only gave my colleagues an opportunity to share their own philosophies of teaching but also provided everyone with an overview of our program and how each of us contributed to it.

This strategy consisted of everyone sharing a *professor portrait* and a set of *course portraits*. The first amounted to constructing one's self-image as a teacher/educator. The other provided a detailed picture for each course that a faculty member taught. (The templates for both types of portraits are provided in Appendix 5.) The completion of these portraits required considerable time and energy, more than my colleagues had to spare during the school year. Consequently, we shared these portraits at our August retreats.

It did not take long for everyone in the education faculty to figure out that four members were committed to carrying forward the faculty's original vision and two were not. One of our colleagues regularly withdrew from us of us in mistrust while the other one consistently followed the beat of a different drummer. As a result we were never able to establish the unified, trusting, and respectful community of learning that the original faculty had experienced. With vision development derailed, the important work of moving the faculty forward as a leader in teacher preparation, especially for faith-based traditions of education, stalled out.

Taking Stock

What did the education faculty at The King's accomplish from 1995 to 2020? The list is long and impressive, but I will only name what I consider to be the three most significant achievements, and in no particular order. The

King's education faculty led the way in making faith-based teacher education respectable in Alberta. Before its ground-breaking efforts, the reality of a private school offering a government-approved teacher-preparation program was not only undesirable but also unfathomable. To the surprise of many, our education faculty demonstrated that it could prepare teachers for any jurisdiction as well as, if not better than, the big universities.

Second, our faculty developed a revolutionary new way to prepare teachers. For example, its programs effectively utilized innovations like in-service master teachers to deliver methods instruction. The elementary and secondary programs overlapped at key junctures that greatly enhanced the learning for students in both programs. The major practicum was a whopping three months long, and by virtue of that fact alone, it truly tested a student's readiness to have a classroom of their own.

The King's education faculty also reimagined what the ideal teacher looks like. It rejected the traditional notions of the teacher as the one who knows and the student as the one who needs to know. The program had no interest in training automatons who gave little thought to the nature of schooling and the roles of teachers and students within it and uncritically taught a prescribed curriculum. Instead, the faculty was in the business of forming reflective teachers who facilitated student learning. Preservice teachers at The King's were encouraged to think of themselves as curriculum makers who were ultimately responsible for what was or was not taught. Most importantly, the faculty challenged their students to reflect on what it means to be human and how we ought to live on this planet with all other creatures and teach their students in ways that would empower them to become such people.

In counterpoint to everything it has accomplished, the education faculty has unfinished business to attend to as it moves into its second twenty-five years. Topping the list is the recalibration of its founding vision. This assumes, of course, that the current faculty is committed to the pursuit of a common vision. If it is, the faculty must determine how the original vision can be moved forward. This is a profound undertaking because it involves nothing less than the faculty's demonstration of how the biblical narrative shapes their understanding of education and the respective roles of teachers and students.

On a related front, the faculty must learn how to effectively communicate its vision to students who either do not identify as Christians or are persons of other faiths. Past faculty members understood the importance of articulating and modelling how their faith-rooted worldview shaped their answers to foundational questions, which in turn became their criteria for deciding what and how to teach. However, the lingo we typically used was too laden with inhouse rhetoric for some students. To maintain this crucial element of our approach to teacher preparation, the education faculty will have to learn to "speak in different tongues."

Lastly, but most importantly, the education faculty missed an opportunity to help CSC schools make a much-needed course correction. This happened when we gave up on the Teaching for Transformation initiative. As outlined in the previous chapter, the faculty took some initial steps to coordinate our efforts to transform teaching and learning with those of the Prairie Centre of Christian Education, but we let that relationship slip away. We did not see how TfT could be formative for both CSC and public-school-bound preservice teachers. Although TfT is not perfect, it represents the best avenue for BEd graduates from the King's to take what they have learned and make the biggest and most enduring difference in the lives of elementary and secondary students in any jurisdiction.

To conclude this section, let us return to the comparison of expectations and intentions. As stated earlier, most beneficiaries of The King's teacher-preparation program expected it to produce a variant of the traditional teacher: the teacher as technician (standard), the reflective technician (better), or faith-inspired, reflective technician (best). All three permutations of the traditional educator could flourish in public school and CSC classrooms. A few CSC communities expected an altogether different kind of graduate; they wanted a visionary teacher who could transcend traditional curriculum planning and teaching practices and work at the implementation of a biblical educational vision that invited students to engage culture. This expectation eventually became synonymous with someone who could teach in a school committed to TfT.

The kind of graduate The King's education faculty intended to produce was the visionary teacher. By graduation, most of our students turned out to be traditional teachers, usually of the "better" and "best" varieties. A few visionary pre-service teachers graduated every year, but most ended up teaching in schools that were not prepared to turn them loose. There were some notable exceptions, however. The reality is, the biggest influence on a new teacher is the culture of their first school. To cultivate and implement a vision acquired from a university teacher preparation program is incredibly difficult, because in most schools this means swimming against the current of traditional teaching. However, neither this reality, nor the expectations of external stakeholders persuaded the original education faculty to settle for a lesser vision.

The education faculty at The King's during its first twenty years had to answer several challenging questions. Is it good enough if our grads meet or exceed the expectations of the main beneficiaries of our program? If we aspire to graduate the "visionary teacher," should we not form partnerships with those schools where such a teacher can thrive? If the TfT approach is deemed unsuitable for the preparation of most education students at The Kings, what are the consequences for the faculty's intent to graduate visionary teachers?

The Future Looks Bright

The King's education faculty went through a difficult time from 2015 to 2019. A division that had its beginnings at the end of my stint as dean deepened and split the full-time faculty in two. To everyone's credit, the quality of the program remained largely intact.

The fall of 2022 represents the twenty-eighth year that The King's has been involved in teacher preparation. The future looks promising for the current education faculty. The climate of division is gone, and the faculty has entered a new era. All faculty positions are filled, and both programs are fully subscribed with students. The dean and four faculty members are new, but they join Wendy Stienstra and Margie Patrick, who have been towers of strength since launching of the secondary education program. These two veterans will undoubtedly play key roles as this group charts its own course into the future.

Hopefully, the current faculty does not believe the pursuit of a common vision is too risky. Whether they decide to pursue the original faculty's vision or one of their own, they too must determine what their role is regarding the long-term health of CSC schools in Alberta and British Columbia? If they stand by program's historic vision, their primary task is the preparation of visionary teachers. Today this means graduating teachers who understand and are capable of implementing TfT's core practices. This expectation has significant implications and raises more questions for the faculty to resolve. If, however, the current faculty does not feel any obligation to these schools, it must clarify and justify this significant change in the faculty's identity.

Exit Slip #3: Clinging to Hope

As the Dutch Neo-Calvinist tradition of education in Canada enters its eighth decade and its families pass the Christian school baton to the third and fourth generations, it faces a vision crisis that has been brewing for some time. The original expression of its vision, to educate for a Christian perspective, transformed many minds but proved insufficient to transform individual lives, much less Canadian culture. For a time, some believed education for discipleship was the better way to express the vision, but it proved to be so far out of reach that it too was ineffective in setting a meaningful course for the movement. The problems associated with both expressions of the vision calls into question the tradition's long-standing interpretation of the biblical cultural mandate as a directive for cultural transformation.

The tradition is in serious need of a course correction. It requires a new way to express its vision that remains true to its biblical understanding of what it means to be human, what defines the good life, and provides it with a meaningful path forward. I believe there is a visionary "sweet spot" where we can educate for more than a worldview but less than a full-blown way of life. Teaching for Transformation's "see the story, live the story" creates such a space. It shifts the focus of education away from cultural transformation to "an identity in a story." It encourages cultural engagement for the purpose of reconciling relationships.

Cultural engagement is a risky educational goal. Harro Van Brummelen once said, "If you engage culture hoping to change it, in the end, it will change you." This thinking animates many CSC communities who take a protectionist stance: "our school serves us." But, it is also true that our authentic engagement with culture often makes a positive difference in our communities.

Nicholas Wolterstorff reminds us that any time we engage in culture, we interact with a fallen culture, but there is always something of God's order that remains. We do well to keep our eyes open for this order and advocate for it. If we do not, we will be tempted to equate our human preferences with God's order, and this almost always leads to idolatry. Kristin Kobes DuMez's recent book powerfully demonstrates this nasty outcome with her analysis of the Christian Right's promotion of a militant masculinity and patriarchal authority ideology.[223]

TFT embodies education for hope. If education for hope is to become the preferred way for CSC (or any other school jurisdiction) to express its educational vision, then local administrators, teachers, and community supporters must learn from this tradition's past successes and not repeat old mistakes. These lessons quickly come to mind.

1. Tft extends the profile of a Neo-Calvinist school as a dissident and transforming social institution into the present situation. To "see God's story" and "live into it," teachers and students at every age level must swim against the main current of North American education, which educates for a much different purpose. To experience what it means to be part of God's story, teachers and students need to embrace the daughter of Hope named Righteous Anger (to name and not accept what is broken in our world) and take hold of the daughter named Courage (to bring about reconciliation and restoration.)
2. Righteous anger is better directed toward the sources of brokenness in our world than at opposing viewpoints within the community. Let us put to death that "old Dutch disease" of in-fighting.
3. The antithesis of good and evil runs through us all; it does not distinguish between people, religions, institutions or cultures. Learn to work shoulder to shoulder with diverse peoples to address local issues of injustice, prejudice and violence. These problems are too big for any group to tackle alone, and to deny this is to be naïve and arrogant.

4. To change the purpose of education and its preferred way of life, educators must reimagine the traditional classroom: its personality, practices, and the deep structure beliefs that rationalize it all. This goal requires curricular and pedagogical reform. To engage in one and not the other ultimately leads to failure.
5. The formation of a nontraditional teacher and the implementation of alternative classroom practices require significant supports (administrative leadership, professional development, regular contact with classroom consultants, and opportunities for collaboration) and years, not months to unfold.
6. The long-term health of CSC and the teacher preparation programs at The King's University and Redeemer University hinge on their shared advancement of the Neo-Calvinist tradition of education. Although the worlds of classroom teachers and teacher preparation professors are different, they should not exist as two solitudes.
7. Schools typically mirror the priorities of society and prepare students to enter into that society's preferred way of life. True substantive school reform goes hand in hand with the initiation of students into an alternative way of life.

Endnotes

193 Gloria Goris Stronks, Doug Blomberg, eds., *A Vision with a Task: Christian Schooling for Responsive Discipleship*. (Grand Rapids, MI: Baker Books, 1993).

194 James K. A. Smith, "Is There Room for Martyrs in our Church?" Chapel homily (Indiana Wesleyan University, Marion, IN, October 18, 2009) http://forsclavigera.blogspot.com/2009/11/room-for-martyrs.html.

195 Robert Koole, "Curriculum and Cultural Engagement: Do Christian High Schools Enhance Students' Cultural Engagement?" *Christian Educators Journal* (December 2011) 25-28.

196 Koole, "Curriculum," 26.

197 Andy Crouch. *Culture-Making: Recovering Our Creative Calling* (Downers Grove, IL: Intervarsity Press Books, 2008).

198 John Hull, open letter from the ESCE board chair to the members and supporters of Edmonton Christian School, Edmonton, AB, February 26, 1999.

199 The jigsaw pedagogy first divides a class into a set of "home groups" that consist of roughly five students each. . The teacher then distributes a set of tasks equal to the number of home group members. Each home group assigns one of its members to tackle one of the tasks. All of the students assigned to task one become an "expert group." Those assigned to task two become a different expert group. When the expert groups have finished their work, they disband and students return to their home group. Now, each home group has an expert on each of the tasks, and these experts take turns sharing what they know with the other members of their home group.

200 Kevin Steel, "It Pays to Go Public: Three private Edmonton Christian schools join the godless government system," *Alberta Report*, June 21, 1999: 40.

201 Kevin Steel, "It Pays," 40.

202 Van Ginhoven graciously shared his views with me in a brief interview conducted via email.

203 The text that follows is paraphrased from an email exchange with Buisman.

204 This opening section is based on the firsthand account of the TfT story, graciously provided to me by Brian Doornenbal with input from Gayle Monsma.

205 Similar endeavors were taking place in Covenant Christian School in Leduc under the leadership of Gayle Monsma and in Gateway Christian school in Red Deer, led by Rob Molzahn. Both schools followed the lead of Edmonton Christian School and had become alternative programs in their local public school boards.

206 Grant Wiggins, Jay McTighe. *Understanding by Design* (Alexandria, VA: ASCD, 1998).

207 Grant Wiggins, Jay McTighe. *Essential Questions: Opening Doors to Student Understanding* (Alexandria, VA: ASCD, 2004).

208 The development of throughlines built on the earlier work of Robert Koole, who worked at the SCSBC.

209 A reference to 1 Peter 2:9, "But you are a chosen race, a royal priesthood, a holy nation, God's own people, in order that you may proclaim the mighty acts of him who called you out of darkness into his marvelous light."

210 The deep structure of schooling is described in "Dig Deeper," Topic 4.

211 Darryl DeBoer, Justin Cook, "Deeper Learning in Christian Education: Deeper Learning into What? https://www.cejonline.com/article/deeper-learning-in-christian-educaion-deeper-learning-into-what/.

212 Prairie Centre for Christian Education, "Teaching for Transformation." Online brochure, https://pcce.ca/resources/. Documents/PCCE-Educators-Documents/TfT/2017-18%20TfT%20Brochure.pdf.

213 cejonline.deeper-learning

214 This polarity of educational visions is described in chapter 1.

215 I first made this comparison in John Hull, "Aiming for Christian Education, Settling for Christians Educating: The Christian School's Replication of a Public School Paradigm," *Christian Scholars Review* XXXII, no. 2 (Winter 2003): 203-224.

216 Interview with Ren Siebenga, May 29, 2014, Hamilton, ON.

217 Darryl DeBoer, Justin Cook.

218 The school was originally named The King's College in 1979 and later was renamed The King's University College in 1993. The school received university status in 2015. For the sake of convenience, I refer to the school as The King's throughout this chapter.

219 Redeemer College was established in 1986 and renamed Redeemer University College in 2000. Redeemer received university status in 2020.

220 See "Dig Deeper," Topic 4.

221 The details of this application process can be found in Henk Van Andel's *A Step at a Time: A History of the First 25 Years of the King's University* (Edmonton, Alberta: The King's University Press, 2019).

222 Resolution 24/95, Resolution Bulletin of the Alberta Teachers Association, May 20-22, 1995.

223 Kristen Kobes Du Mez. *Jesus and John Wayne: How White Evangelicals Corrupted a Faith and Fractured a Nation* (New York, NY: Liveright Publishing Corp., 2020).

DIG DEEPER

Topic 1: Curriculum Babble

Conceptions, Orientations, or Ideologies

We use many terms to describe the different ways in which we design and implement the curriculum. For example, we recognize various *approaches*, *conceptions*, *orientations*, *ideologies*, *visions*, and *cultures* of curriculum.

Does it really matter which of these terms we use? "Yes."

Are not these terms synonyms, more or less? "No."

Are the exemplars of these categories of greater importance than the name we give to the category? "Yes."

Is the argument over which is the better term, just another theoretical tempest in a scholarly teapot? To that I say, "Sometimes."

The recognition and naming of these categories started around 1974 when the field of curriculum theory was relatively young. In that year, Eisner and Vallance published a landmark text titled *Conflicting Conceptions of Curriculum*.[224] After they surveyed the research that constituted this new field of study, they identified five more or less defined positions. These positions overlapped at times, but Eisner and Vallance made the case that they were sufficiently different to warrant their own names. They also observed that these positions held conflicting views in key areas. They called these different positions "conceptions of curriculum." Each one, they argued, was a conceptual model for the design and implementation of a curriculum.

Eighteen years later, Philip Jackson[225] took issue with Eisner and Vallance's use of the term "curriculum conception." Using that term has serious limitations, Jackson believed, because at best, it implies a theory. He also questioned whether these curriculum conceptions had the significance for teachers that Eisner and Vallance attributed to them. In the opening chapter of the *Handbook of Research on Curriculum,* Jackson offers no less than seven shortcomings of curriculum conceptions. Even if there are such things as curriculum conceptions, he says no one is exactly sure how many there are. Furthermore, none of these conceptions are as pure, comprehensive, and as contending as they are made out to be. Eisner and Vallance leave us with the impression, he notes, that many educators have chosen one curriculum conception as their own, so the rest of us ought to as well. Jackson claims that no one identifies with just one curriculum conception, and it's not necessary that anyone should feel pressured to do so. In fact, Jackson argues, teachers tend to combine the elements from several conceptions, even though they tend to favour one over the others. This happens, Jackson goes on to explain, because teachers typically lack the criteria required to select the best elements from the various conceptions, and they do not know how to assemble the pieces they do choose into a coherent approach. Lastly, Jackson observes there are important elements of these conceptions that are impossible to combine because they are mutually exclusive. The expectation that teachers should decide which curriculum model best suits them or make up their own if none of the available ones are suitable is unrealistic. In Jackson's experience, most teachers inherit a curriculum and cannot do much to change it. They usually teach the way they were taught, and rarely does any teacher conclude that, "I need a whole new curriculum perspective."

The impact of Jackson's argument is hard to gauge, but it probably has something to do with the fact that, after 1992, the term "curriculum conception" rarely shows up in the literature of curriculum theory. Jackson does not offer an alternative way to describe what curriculum conceptions signified, but he hints at a better way to understand curriculum formation, particularly if curriculum reform was the goal. Rather than think of these approaches as mental constructs, he suggests curriculum emerges in the context of *interpretive communities* and their distinctive ways of life. In one brief reference, Jackson acknowledges a fundamental connection between a community's way of life, intellectual tradition, and social networks.

In later editions of their work, Eisner and Vallance substitute the term "curriculum orientation" for "curriculum conception," likely to prevent readers from reducing these approaches to theoretical constructs. Later still, Eisner prefers the term "curriculum ideology" to accentuate the fact that these various approaches are rooted in beliefs about what schools should teach and for what purposes.

Van Brummelen[226] uses the term "curriculum orientation" for similar reasons. Curriculum conceptions, he says, are fixed theories; therefore, they are insufficient to inspire reform. In his last publication gift to Christian school educators, titled *Steppingstones to Curriculum: A Biblical Path*,[227] Van Brummelen is determined to outline a fully developed Christian orientation to curriculum. An *orientation* is superior to a *conception*, he believes, because it implies a place where one stands and a direction toward which one intends to move. For Van Brummelen, an orientation offers a vision that intends to "galvanize, motivate and provide a compass for the curriculum journey." He goes so far as to give it a biblical connotation when he says an orientation provides "a light for our path."

Let us consider what the term "orientation" connotes that the term "conception" does not. Eisner and Vallance said curriculum conceptions address all of the following: what content should be taught, how the content is to be organized, the reasons for deciding what goes in and what stays out, (i.e., the criteria, goals, or standards), and the conceptual biases or assumptions that rationalize all curriculum choices (a worldview?). For Van Brummelen, curriculum orientations include all of these elements, plus it gives a better account of what Eisner and Vallance meant by conceptual biases and assumptions. Like Van Brummelen, I prefer the term "orientation" because it implies that the acts of designing and implementing a curriculum are rooted in a set of assumptions that direct education toward a particular destination.

Whatever term one uses to indicate the differences in curriculum organization and delivery that have evolved in North American education, it should direct our attention to the *criteria* we use to determine what goes in or is left out of the curriculum, how best to organize what is selected, what knowledge is of greatest worth, and what is the purpose of education.

Without question, the design and implementation of a comprehensive and coherent theory of curriculum is one of the most crucial tasks for an educator to engage in. If Jackson is correct, then most teachers have done very little thinking about this. As a result, we are not as intentional about curriculum planning as we ought to be.

Finally, we should remember that theoretical knowledge is only one of the deep drivers that shape curriculum, whether these are simple theories about content organization or the most complex curriculum models. Jackson intuitively understood this, and so does the Neo-Calvinist tradition. What other deep drivers are there? Jamie Smith makes a case for the *desires of the heart*.[228] What we "know" in our hearts gives rise to our commitments, which in turn, drives our decision-making. We teach what we most love, he argues. *Experience* is another acknowledged deep driver. All teachers understand the formative power of classroom experience. What we learn from teaching determines how we plan and implement the curriculum. I suspect there may be other deep drivers as well.

As useful as it is for us to properly categorize the different ways educators design and implement the curriculum, the ultimate challenge in curriculum reform is to achieve coherence between our classroom practice, our conceptual understanding, and the deep drivers that propel them both.

Topic 2: Integration and Integrality

To Talk about Faith and Learning in the Same Breath

Historically, educators in the Neo-Calvinist tradition have been sloppy in their use of *integration* and *integrality*. We use the term "integration" the way most educators do if we talk about combining content from different subject disciplines. Unfortunately, we are in the habit of mostly using this term to refer to the relationship between learning and faith. If one assumes as Neo-Calvinists do, that there is such a thing as Christian education, then it makes more sense to talk about the integrality of faith and learning, for all of the reasons outlined below.

The term "integration" in mainstream education has three historic meanings. For many decades the term primarily referred to racial integration in schools. We have also used "integration" to mean the introduction of students with special needs into the regular classroom. This initiative has expanded significantly over time, and we now refer to it as "inclusive education." The third and most common meaning of integration, at least in discussions around programs of study, refers to a curriculum that consciously connects and/or unifies the content that students ordinarily study in separate subject disciplines. When taken to the extreme, the integration of content from various subjects culminates in a thematic approach to curricular organization.

In the past, content integration has been a major concern in the pedagogical progressivist's opposition to the traditional liberal arts and sciences curriculum. However, Drake and Burns[229] point out that progressivists as diverse as Dewey, Tyler, and Bloom all shared an appreciation for curriculum integration. Collectively, the proponents of subject integration seek a more holistic kind of knowledge, which they feel cannot be obtained from any of the traditional subject disciplines on their own.

Drake and Burns identify several types or degrees of integrated curriculums. In *intra* and *multidisciplinary* curriculums, integration is minimal, and the subject disciplines remain largely intact. As an example of an intradisciplinary integrated curriculum, students would study a topic like trees from the perspectives found in the sub-disciplines within natural science, such as biology, chemistry, physics, and environmental studies. Alternatively, in a multidisciplinary integrated study of trees, students would acquire knowledge from a combination of natural science, economic, social, aesthetic, and literary perspectives.

As we move across the integration spectrum, we next encounter interdisciplinary and trans-disciplinary curricula where the distinctions between subject disciplines gradually disappear altogether. The skills we associate with particular disciplines often remain important, but students develop them in the service of a theme, project, essential question, or current issue that cannot be adequately understood from any one disciplinary point of view. The push to provide students with a more integrated curriculum has typically coincided with demands for more project-based learning and student-centred pedagogy.

Bracketing the spectrum just described, curricula are organized around the traditional academic subjects at one end and by themes at the other. Regardless of their position on this spectrum, educators rarely talk about the integrality of the curriculum. Recently, some educators have expressed concerns about *curriculum fidelity*, but they do so only in the context of program evaluation.

In contrast, when CSC educators talk about integration, they seldom have the Drake-Burns spectrum of curriculum integration in mind. Teaching a theme-based or interdisciplinary curriculum has not been a top priority for most educators in the tradition. What most interests Neo-Calvinist educators is the harmony, unity, and consistency between a faith perspective and learning. In fact, the hallmark characteristic of this tradition is the assumption that all learning is shaped by a worldview, which is, in turn, rooted in a set of foundational beliefs.

CSC educators' habit of using integration to refer to a relationship between faith and learning creates unnecessary confusion, particularly if they want to communicate with educators outside of their tradition. They unwittingly imply there are two kinds of knowledge that need to be unified, the knowledge of a faith perspective and the knowledge of the disciplines. Often, this mistake has led to the conclusion that there are two kinds of science, two kinds of social studies, and so on. The one kind is saturated with a biblical perspective, and the other is not. Intuitively, they know something is wrong with that picture, but just what it is eludes them. The term "integrality" better expresses the Neo-Calvinist assumption that an authentic curriculum exhibits coherence with a worldview/faith position. In short, integrality pertains to curricular meaning and direction, whereas integration refers to curricular structure and organization.

The matter doesn't end there, however. The criteria that teachers use to decide what to include or exclude in the curriculum are themselves biased toward a seemingly set-in-stone organizational structure. That is to say the criteria assume a curriculum organized around the subject disciplines as defined by the scientific establishment and rooted in the curricular organization of the medieval university. This bias reflects that establishment's belief that the disciplines embody the structural principles that govern reality.

This status quo bias posed a serious problem for the Neo-Calvinist educators who worked at the Curriculum Development Centre[230] because they believed a curriculum organized around the subject disciplines offered students a fragmented picture of reality. They believed an interdisciplinary/transdisciplinary curriculum better matched a biblical worldview and most accurately reflects our experience of reality. Van Brummelen, the undisputed spokesperson for the Neo-Calvinist school movement in Canada in his day, took a different position. Throughout his career he remained loyal to the primacy of the subject disciplines, even though he also promoted the use of thematic units.[231]

In an effort to clarify the confusion surrounding the use of integration by CSC educators, Van Brummelen once observed that integrated learning should refer to the integration of learning with a) sound biblical perspective, b) the call for students to make a commitment to Jesus to engage the life of discipleship, and c) a holistic understanding of creation and life.

According to him, integration simultaneously refers to the curriculum's source of inspiration, its ultimate purpose, and its principle of content organization. By overloading the meaning of the term, Van Brummelen made integration even more confusing. Ironically, he faulted the CDC for doing the same thing in its vision statement.[232]

The term "integrality" more accurately connotes what Van Brummelen and the CSC tradition sought to achieve, which was the unity, harmony, and consistency between their faith, worldview, educational philosophy, curriculum orientation, classroom practice, and way of life. In his book, *Steppingstones to Curriculum*, Van Brummelen offered a helpful insight when he said *an integral unit* exhibited internal unity, external consistency, and natural connections with concepts from other subject disciplines.[233]

Robert Sweetman recently published a book that both expands and deepens this discussion.[234] He begins by asking this foundational question: is there such a thing as Christian scholarship? If the answer is yes, then he next asks what distinguishes it from other kinds of scholarship. Since the notion of Christian education is predicated on the reality of Christian scholarship in the Neo-Calvinist tradition, we can substitute the term "education" for "scholarship" in Sweetman's argument with impunity.

Sweetman says Christians imagine scholarship to be Christian in several ways. For some, scholarship is Christian when it connects with or confirms the scholar's faith claims. For others, scholarship is Christian if it is conducted by a scholar who demonstrates a Christian character and calling in life. In both examples, the scholarly work is not fundamentally different from that conducted by non-Christians, but it is considered to be Christian by virtue of its alignment with orthodox Christian morality and theology. A third group believes the scholarship itself is somehow Christian. This understanding is the most controversial by far.

To imagine there is such a thing as distinctively Christian scholarship, one must somehow account for the integrality of faith and scholarship. Sweetman identifies three historic ways Christians have understood this relationship. He calls them *complimentarist, integrationist,* and *holist*.

The complimentarist account is rooted in the thinking of St. Bonaventure, Etienne Gilson, and Pope John Paul II. For them, faith is an expression of religion. As such, it remains separate from scholarship in every discipline except theology. Christian scholarship occurs whenever faith enables the scholar "to judge claims and methods as believer rather than scholar with regard to their Christian appropriateness."[235]

Sweetman associates the integrationist account with Alvin Plantinga and George Marsden. They speak of the possibility and desirability of the integration of faith and scholarship in all disciplines. Christian scholarship conducted in any discipline "need not give a place to faith . . . faith need not be excluded . . . either."[236] Sweetman then summarizes the individual arguments that Plantinga and Marsden make in support of the assumption that "Christian faith can and often does play an immediate and intrinsic role in the constitution of all academic disciplines."[237]

The holist account insists on the inseparability of faith and scholarship. Sweetman links this view to Herman Dooyeweerd and Evan Runner. They believed that, like all socio-cultural endeavors, learning bears witness to some religion; i.e., all scholars start from a position of faith. In their view the Western notion that science presents us with an unbiased description of reality, is itself a bias rooted in our faith (that is, trust) in reason.

CSC has embraced all three approaches just described, which more or less align with Van Brummelen's categories of monist, dualist, and integrationist. The integrationist or holist approach represents the most radical interpretation and expression of the Neo-Calvinist agenda. Where educators struggled to imagine or implement it, they settled for something more in line with the complimentarist (monist) and integrationist (dualist) approaches. Sweetman affirms the validity and relevance of all three even though he personally identifies with the holist approach. He likens them all to folk recipes: the dish is the same, but the chef and the cultural context vary.

Sweetman then makes a helpful observation. All these historic efforts to define Christian scholarship do so within Aristotle's framework for making distinctions. Within this framework, scholarship is a genus, and Christian scholarship is one of its species. As such we should expect to find "stable differences" associated with scholarly methods and claims that constitute each species. As a "conceptual figure" or exemplar in this framework, Christian scholarship gives rise to two embarrassments.

The first embarrassment arises when Christian scholarship must "use the same words and phrases to articulate its claims about the world" that secular scholarship uses. The second one rears its ugly head when Christian scholarship cannot define those concrete and available methods or claims that distinguish it from other kinds of scholarship.

Sweetman makes a compelling case that the Gordian knot of curriculum reform as conceived by many in the Neo-Calvinist tradition was ill conceived because if we finally figured out how to integrate Christian perspective into each subject discipline, we would bring about a reformation of the sciences. Curriculum integrality makes little sense, he argues, as long we try to describe it within a genus/species framework. Sweetman's solution is to "identify the integrality of Christian scholarship with its animating spirit or ethos, rather than with delimited features intrinsic to its methods and claims."[238] What distinguishes Christian scholarship is its "sense of direction or purpose" and its commitments and priorities. It is a question of which master scholarship serves. Ditto for education.

Topic 3: The Calvin College Factor

Introduction

By 1950, Calvin College (now University) was a robust institution of higher learning. Over the next two decades, a handful of Calvin professors seriously engaged the issues of curriculum reform at both the school and university levels. Some of them taught in the education faculty, as one would expect, but others belonged to departments as diverse as philosophy and English. These professors contributed to the education of many students who would become teachers in NUCS schools in Canada and the United States. Outside of the classroom they spoke at meetings where teachers and administrators gathered, and they published articles in both the magazine and journal published by NUCS.

The following discussion draws heavily on three sources: Peter De Boer's 1983 monograph, *Shifts in Curriculum Theory for Christian Education*;[239] a valuable collection of writings called *Voices from the Past: Reformed Educators*,[240] edited by Donald Oppewal; and a compilation of Wolterstorff's major writings and speeches on education, entitled *Educating for Life: Reflections on Christian Teaching and Learning*, edited by Gloria Stronks and Clarence Joldersma.[241]

My short summaries below do not capture the full force of what these educators believed or contributed to the Neo-Calvinist movement of Christian education. A book could be written about the accomplishments of each of them. My intention is to isolate some key elements in their positions that I believe are relevant, either because they show up in the way American and Canadian NUCS educators interpreted and expressed their educational vision or because they were dismissed by them.

Peter De Boer[242] observes that American Neo-Calvinist educators at both the college and school levels were consistently grounded in a rich theological tradition based on three historic creeds: the Heidelberg Catechism, the Belgic Confession, and the Canons of Dordt. This shared theological tradition was married to an educational tradition that drew from St. Augustine, John Calvin, Abraham Kuyper, Herman Bavinck, and the Dutch schoolmasters who implemented Bavinck's pedagogical principles in the classroom. They also shared the assumption that what made an education Christian was its distinctive curriculum. However, educators at both levels of education disagreed strongly about the meaning of curriculum reform.

De Boer developed a schema of the major philosophical camps that existed at Calvin College from 1950 to approximately 1980. His list of the dominant "traditionalists" included professors William Jellema, Henry Zylstra, Lambert Flokstra, and George Stob. The lone wolf "progressivist" was Cornelius Jaarsma. Jellema and Jaarsma embodied the two polar positions in the curriculum discussions that animated Calvin College during the 1950s and 1960s. The Jellema-Jaarsma debate, as some historians refer to it, mirrored the larger public dispute in education at that time, but it was distinguished by its Neo-Calvinist content.

DeBoer also identified a third group of educators, which he labelled the "revisionists." However, he portrayed this camp as a synthesis position that tried to bridge the traditional and progressive viewpoints. In this category he placed Nicholas Wolterstorff and Henry Beversluis, along with two educators who did not teach at Calvin but had prominence in Neo-Calvinist education circles, Canadian teacher Harro Van Brummelen and educator Geraldine Steensma, who happened to be Jaarsma's daughter. Based on my investigations, Beversluis is the only one of these four who advocated for a consensus position.

One could only lump Wolterstorff, Van Brummelen, and Steensma into a revisionist camp, if that term implied a change in direction. All three wanted their tradition to alter its course and reclaim its original mandate to educate for a Christian way of life. Given the curriculum debates of their day, they were the only ones who stood with at least one foot outside of the paradigm that dominated North American education.

The five Calvin College professors who most impacted NUCS educators at that time, either by their engagement with matters pertaining to the nature of Christian education generally or with curriculum reform in particular, were William Jellema, Cornelius Jaarsma, Nicholas Wolterstorff, Nicholas Beversluis, and H. Evan Runner.

In the discussion to follow we will take a cursory look at the contributions of the first four just named. Runner's influence is addressed in chapter 2. The contributions of Van Brummelen and Steensma are summarized in part II of this book.

William Jellema

Jellema was the first philosophy professor hired by Calvin College. He taught at Calvin twice from 1920 to 1936 and again from 1948 to 1963. Bratt[243] is not alone in his belief that Jellema was the greatest teacher Calvin College has ever had. Ironically, Jellema rarely published in his field. Oppewal[244] observes that he preferred to apply his keen mind to social, political, and educational matters instead.

Jellema's manner of expressing the Neo-Calvinist educational vision was coloured by his commitment to the classical liberal arts curriculum orientation. He was an ardent follower of Kuyper, yet his philosophy had unmistakable Platonic overtones. His position assumed that society is made up of spiritual kingdoms and cities (civitates). He was aware, of course, that individuals and institutions populate a society, but these "spiritual kingdoms" were the most formative social phenomena.

A second assumption in Jellema's position defined the function of education. Ultimately, education is always "by" and "for" citizenship in a kingdom. In other words, "education is always the manifestation of the life of a kingdom and an initiation into that life."[245] Upon the back of these two assumptions, Neo-Calvinist educators established their central claim that public school education and Christian education are fundamentally different. They must be different because they manifest the way of life and community experience of two different kingdoms.

Jellema also believed *mind* was determinative of every faith community. Furthermore, determinative of every mind is the community's answer to the question: who or what is divine? Individuals and communities answer this question with the whole of their lives in the kingdom, not just with words. According to Jellema, education, and everything else humans do, is ultimately a religious act of kingdom service.

What exactly does Jellema mean by the mind? Clearly, the mind is abstract, something we need to make concrete in our living. It refers to a *way of thinking and understanding* or a *set of ideas*, what we more commonly refer to as a worldview. He distinguishes between our "subjective individual minds" and the major "objective minds of Western culture," as in the classical Greek pagan mind, the medieval Catholic mind, the Reformation mind, and the modern mind. In order for individuals to adopt the "right mind," they require an education that both explores and provides an understanding of the inner workings of each major mind.

> Far more important than *what* the individual happens to think about this or that is the *mind with which* he thinks, the mind to which he is religiously committed. And for intelligent commitment and articulation, the individual needs acquaintance *from the inside* with what are by this time three or four objective, well-articulated, major minds.[246]

Jellema also fervently believed that the Christian mind or way of thinking is antithetical to all the other major objective minds.

Wolterstorff clarifies another key, but highly problematic, element in Jellema's thinking, namely, his notion that "human existence, both personal and social, has the fundamental characteristic of expression."[247] According to this borrowed view from the Romantic tradition, individuals and faith communities "give social and cultural expression to their inward mind, and that in turn is the expression of an identification with God."[248] This component in Jellema's educational vision fortifies his conviction "that it could reasonably be expected that students who thought with the Christian mind would then express that mind in their specific cultural and social situation."[249]

Most CSC educators shared Jellema's belief that an education that fostered in students a knowledge of, and a commitment to, a Christian worldview would naturally result in students expressing that worldview in every aspect of their lives as individuals and, more importantly, as members of a faith community.

In Jellema's view both curriculum reform and his vision of education are best served by what we have come to know as the academic rationalist curriculum orientation. Calvin College published his curriculum blueprint for a liberal arts education in 1958.[250] In that document, Jellema opens with the observation that the curriculum taught at Calvin in his day had been borrowed from the University of Michigan some five decades earlier when Calvin College was just starting up. What matters most about a curriculum design for Jellema is the "intrinsic idea" that justifies it. This intrinsic idea reveals what counts as "wisdom" in a curriculum. He contends that the intrinsic idea that rationalized Calvin College's copied curriculum design was incompatible with its aspiration to offer a Christian program of studies. This plagiarized wisdom, Jellema says, "consists, very simply, in the ability so to use nature as to achieve position in a society devoted to mastery over nature."[251] The intrinsic idea buried inside this borrowed curriculum model was a wisdom that reflected nature and its laws. The aim of this truncated form of liberal education was to "think like nature would think, could it think."[252]

Jellema vehemently rejected this modern notion of wisdom, yet he remained steadfast in his commitment to the intrinsic idea propagated by the liberal tradition of education rooted in classical Greek culture. In fact, he strongly held to the view that his college's ability to offer a Christian education hinged on its efforts to implement a truly liberal education, not the watered-down version it inherited from the state university. Curriculum reform, as he imagined it, not only required the implementation of a different "intrinsic idea" but a wholesale shift in programming choices. His vision for curriculum reform hinged on two central concepts: the "mind," which we explored above and "the man." In his development of both terms, he reveals his blind spot for infusing Platonic meaning into his Christian framework.

Jellema believed a Christian liberal education should aim at "the man" in the individual and not concern itself with individual differences, as progressive educators were wont to do. By "the man" Jellema means "human nature," or to use his phrase, "man intellectual and moral."[253] Jellema claims a liberal education cultivates in the individual the human ability "to think" and "to judge," but he recognized it did not go far enough. In addition to knowing "that the aim of liberal education is 'the man' in the individual, we must further know that 'the man is the man of God completely furnished.'"[254] This "furnishing process" is what ultimately distinguishes a liberal education offered at a Christian institution like Calvin College from a liberal education obtained at a secular university. The details pertaining to this process are vague in Jellema's thinking, but the outcome is not: a Christian liberal education furnishes students with an understanding of, and a commitment to, God and His Kingdom.

Jellema advocated for a program of liberal education at the high school level of education as well, but what he envisioned for the elementary curriculum is unclear. Van Brummelen reports that the only two textbooks NUCS managed to produce under the leadership of John Van Bruggen, who directed NUCS in the 1950s, reflect the academic rationalist emphasis on the "cultural storehouse" of knowledge. There is no evidence that directly links Jellema to the contents of these textbooks, but it is obvious that the head office at NUCS held the same overall view that Jellema espoused. According to Van Brummelen, this academic approach to high school curriculum at NUCS was short lived because schools became less elitist and needed to "provide teachable programs for an ever-increasing percentage of students finishing high school."[255]

In a 1984 speech presented to Canadian Neo-Calvinist educators, Nicholas Wolterstorff[256] claimed that Jellema had articulated the Neo-Calvinist vision of education better than anyone else. It was also Wolterstorff's view that most Neo-Calvinist educators on either side of the forty-ninth parallel more or less held to Jellema's point of view that the aim of Christian education culminated in the cultivation of a Christian mind, or perspective.

There is no reason to doubt either of Wolterstorff's claims. CSC educators, however, disagreed over how to cultivate this perspective in their students. Those influenced by the Reformational Movement believed the working out involved making major curricular and pedagogical changes. The majority took the position that they could teach this perspective without making major adjustments to the organizational structure of what or how they taught.

Cornelius Jaarsma

Cornelius Jaarsma was a professor of education at Calvin College and a contemporary of William Jellema. In his introduction of Jaarsma, Oppewal tells us the man was a prolific writer and speaker. He addressed his fellow scholars at Calvin as well as NUCS teachers and administrators in at least seventy-five articles over a forty-year career that ended in the early 1960s. Like Jellema, Jaarsma was wholeheartedly dedicated to Christian education from kindergarten to university, and a serious scholar who developed the philosophical and historical foundations of his curriculum theory. Both men addressed fundamental questions such as, what does it mean to be human? They also situated their own position relative to the major currents in Western thought. However, despite similarities in approach, their views on curriculum reform were diametrically opposed.

Jaarsma envisioned a uniquely Christian curriculum orientation that addressed the "whole person." His approach did not rely on the thinking of Rousseau, Dewey, or Rogers but on the work of Dutch educators Bavinck and Waterink. Whereas Jellema believed we are "minds," Jaarsma argued the human "heart" defines us as creatures. Jellema placed himself in the context of the four major objective minds that characterize the West, and his vision of Christian education stood on the shoulders of the classical liberal arts tradition. In contrast, Jaarsma identifies four "historic end goals" or destinations that justify all human activity.[257]

The classical world gave us two of these end goals: the *natural* end goal is achieved through "the fulfillment of man's natural propensities" (naturalism), and the *ideal* end goal comes about with "the realization of the ideal life of reason" (idealism). The third end goal he identified arose out of the Hebrew-Christian tradition, which "finds the justification of all human activity in the *glory of the Creator*." The Renaissance produced the fourth end goal. In this context the cultural activity of humans has no final purpose other than *to meet human needs* (pragmatism). Jaarsma positions himself in the Hebrew-Christian tradition when he declares that "education is distinctively Christian when the authority of Christ and the realization of his authority in the lives of men is the justification of all educational activity."[258]

Jaarsma was a scholar who was well ahead of his time. In his *Fundamentals of Christian Education,* published in 1953, he recognizes four major "curriculum concepts." They are remarkably like the curriculum conceptions identified by Eisner and Vallance in their ground-breaking text published almost twenty-five years later.[259] Two of the four concepts come from ancient times. Jaarsma describes them as an information or *knowledge-getting concept* rooted in philosophical essentialism and a *disciplinary concept* representative of philosophical perennialism that values knowledge that transcends time and develops critical minds. The remaining two come from the modern era: a *social concept* that he associates with the social reconstruction side of Dewey's philosophy and the *creative concept* born of the child-centred, humanist side of progressivism. Jaarsma believed the two modern concepts held sway over the educational world of his day.[260]

To Jaarsma's way of thinking, none of the popular curriculum concepts were appropriate for Calvin or for NUCS. He reached this conclusion by following a remarkable path, one that should not go unnoticed by current CSC educators or by school reformers from any other tradition. Typically, initiatives calling for reform are judged, then summarily rejected, or significantly modified, based on criteria supplied by the status quo paradigm. Jaarsma reversed this pattern. He appraised each of the four major curriculum concepts using the alternative criteria of a "Christian view" to determine which one, if any, could serve as the curricular context for a Christian education.

The first step in Jaarsma's process to develop a Christian approach to curriculum from scratch entailed drawing up this list of four requirements a curriculum with a Christian view must meet:

- First, the curriculum must treat the person as a whole being, not simply as a mind.
- Second, it must recognize that the soul which bears God's image as a whole person does this all of the time, not just during acts of worship. Therefore, "education is a process of man-making, not merely a training of the intellect . . ."
- Third, a Christian curriculum must acknowledge Scripture's grand narrative of creation-fall-redemption-restoration.

- Finally, it must help students learn how to live in this world without succumbing to worldly ways.

In step two, Jaarsma used these criteria to test the four major curriculum orientations. In each instance the orientation got at least one thing right, but beyond that, it failed miserably. For example, the knowledge-getting curriculum concept recognizes there is a "pre-existent truth to be apprehended," but it fails to see that a person is more than just a mind. The discipline concept is right insofar as it calls attention to the fact that we achieve mental discipline when we think according to the patterns embedded in the academic disciplines, but it fails to understand that a well-disciplined mind cannot produce wisdom any more than a mind full of knowledge can reflect it. The social concept is right to recognize the importance of a person's wider social life, but the implementation of social adjustments to the curriculum does not, of itself, lead to an understanding of the truth. The creative approach is right to "highlight the ability to reorganize past experience into new knowledge for the present," but objective truth is lost when each individual determines what knowledge and/or the curriculum will be.[261]

Jaarsma not only rejected each of the major curriculum orientations as a suitable crucible for developing a Christian approach to curriculum, he also scrapped the notion that some creative combination of these concepts would suffice. Jaarsma believed that no manner of rejigging the conceptual contours of these orientations would change their misguided assumptions about human nature, the divine, and our purpose on Earth. An eclectic or additive approach to curriculum design is simply not an option for the Christian educator.

Jaarsma's thinking led him to the following unavoidable conclusion: the only way Christian educators can fulfill the four criteria of a Christian education is to develop their own curriculum orientation. He did not have one in his back pocket that he could pull out, but he did construct a blueprint for building one. To begin, educators must answer three critical questions:

1. What materials are available to us for educational purposes?
2. What end or destiny must they serve?
3. How shall we select curriculum materials?"[262]

With his first question, Jaarsma is not asking which published materials may teachers bring into the classroom. Rather, he wants to know what "subject matter domains" the curriculum will explore. For Jaarsma, there are three fundamental domains of curricular content: the natural world, the world of human culture-making, and the divine. The second question addresses the meaning, interrelationships, purpose, and direction that apply to these domains. Jaarsma's answer to this question is core to the whole Christian life: the justification of all we do in education has one common end: "that the authority of Christ may be realized and manifest."

The following graphic organizer (Figure 1) depicts Jaarsma's understanding of the fundamental relationships that Christian education must address: God to creation, human to human, human to God, and human to creation. In Jaarsma's understanding of the domains for study, the divine resides outside of the natural order as its creator and the relationship between creator and humanity provides the purpose and meaning of all the interrelationships that exist within the creation I to I, (self image), I to God, I to neighbour, neighbour to God, and we to the natural world.

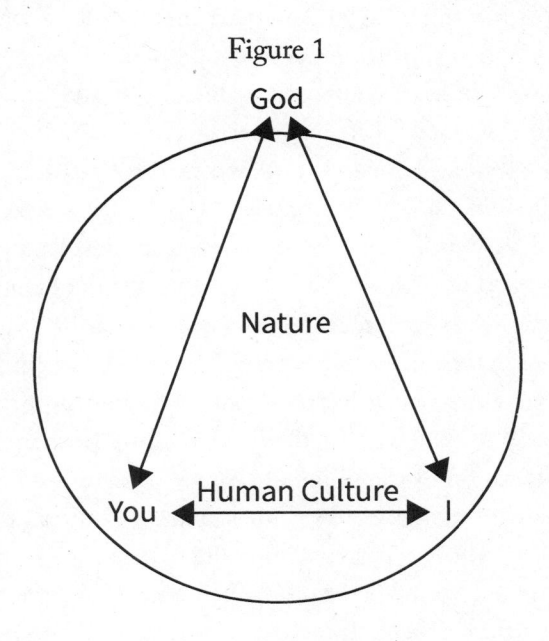

Figure 1

God

Nature

You ← Human Culture → I

If the ultimate end of learning is meant to acknowledge the Lordship of Christ and to celebrate the establishment of His Kingdom, then the final critical question asks: how do we select materials that will fulfill these criteria and keep education on track? This process of selecting and organizing curriculum materials for any level of Christian education requires educators to answer three additional questions based on the above criteria:

> First, what is needed on this level to have the learner face God and God's claim upon his life? Second, what is needed to have the learner discern the cultural products and cultural activities of humanity with reference to his heavenly citizenship? Third, what is needed to have the learner face the call of service as a worker?[263]

Based on the documents provided by Oppewal and others, it is clear that Jaarsma proposed two things. He advocated for a uniquely Christian curriculum orientation, and he devised a process for constructing one. He did both as well as anyone in the Neo-Calvinist tradition who lived before, during, or after his time. To be sure, his methodology lacked concrete examples and stopped short of providing a fleshed-out philosophy of education and a universe of discourse that educators could use to design and implement a distinctively Christian curriculum.

On the positive side, he clearly outlined the first steps of a curriculum-planning methodology. Van Brummelen and Wolterstorff contend that Jaarsma exerted very little influence on curriculum development in NUCS, even though he authored several key documents for the organization. Why NUCS educators failed to appreciate Jaarsma's ideas is unclear. Wolterstorff kindly speculates that he may have been perceived to be too individualistic or pietistic in his views. Perhaps what most sidelined him was the intensity with which he objected to the more popular notion that Christian education was all about the education of the mind. Or it may be, as more than one of my contemporaries who took a course from Jaarsma will attest, that his quirky behaviours and overly pious persona limited his influence.

Much of what Jaarsma failed to achieve in curricular reform was accomplished by his daughter Geraldine Steensma, who championed key elements of his approach in her career as an educator, author and consultant.[264]

It is rather remarkable that Jellema and Jaarsma could simultaneously share a common faith and commitment to Christian education and yet hold to such contradictory views about how best to fulfill its purpose. Jellema believed the ultimate aim of Christian education was the knowledge of and commitment to a life appropriate for the Kingdom of God. Jaarsma meant basically the same thing when he defined the aim of education as living in the world without being worldly. The adoption of a "life in the Kingdom of God" for Jellema depended upon the community's understanding of and commitment to a Christian worldview. The Christian life for Jaarsma hinged on the *manifestations* of our relationships with Christ, neighbour, and the rest of creation. For Jellema, education was an exercise of the mind, while for Jaarsma it was an expression of the heart.

Nicholas Wolterstorff

Nicholas Wolterstorff graduated from Calvin College in 1953. After receiving a master's and doctorate from Harvard University, Wolterstorff returned to Calvin in the mid-1960s, where he taught philosophy for the next thirty years. It is safe to say that Wolterstorff, more than anyone else, has been the philosopher laureate of Christian education in the Reformed tradition.

In 1966 when Wolterstorff was a young professor at the beginning of his academic career, he delivered one of his most memorable speeches to an annual gathering of NUCS principals. The speech, entitled "Curriculum: By What Standard?" served as a wake-up call to the established leadership. At the time of this speech, NUCS had been in existence for over forty-five years, and the Neo-Calvinist school movement in America was over one hundred years old. Strangely, in all this time, NUCS had generated relatively little in the way of Christian curriculum materials. It also lacked a clearly defined philosophy of education and conceptual framework to guide curriculum design. Even though the Canadian schools were much younger, by the mid-1960s, they were far more eager to engage in curriculum development than their American counterparts. In this historic speech, Wolterstorff does not advocate for the curriculum orientation that is best suited to the educational aims of Christian educators. Instead, he begins by clarifying what the aim of a Christian education actually is before determining how best to achieve this aim. Wolterstorff's approach is like Jaarsma's in that each of them defined the criteria for curriculum reform by drawing upon their own Christian tradition. This unique entry point into curriculum reform alone makes his speech remarkable. On the down side, Wolterstorff's speech is vague about what happens after the criteria are identified.

At the outset of this speech, we see evidence of Wolterstorff's trademark capacity to lay out a clear, concise, and compelling case. He begins, as many of his speeches do, by asking a primary question: what criterion shall we use to map a curriculum for the Christian school? He immediately follows with a stripped-down definition of curriculum making: curriculum making, he says, is ultimately the process of deciding what goes in and what stays out. Then he raises the embarrassing fact that "what often happens in schools is that nothing deserving the title 'decision' is made on such matters at all."[265] In actuality, teachers are quite passive when it comes to their curriculum choices. Teachers too often teach as they were taught, teach what is of greatest interest to themselves, or they simply teach what is provided to them in prescribed teaching materials where some unknown person(s) decided beforehand what is in and what stays out.

These unreflective habits, Wolterstorff declares, are unworthy of the NUCS tradition, which holds to a much richer view of the human person and to a larger vision of education. To give better focus to this curriculum decision-making process, Wolterstorff says the curriculum must consider the needs of the child. This reorientation has two major implications. First, the child is a whole person and not merely a student. Second, the child has a life outside the school as well as inside. Thus, a Christian school curriculum must deal with the whole person and with all of life. In an oft-quoted passage, Wolterstorff says, "The aim for school, I have suggested, must be to equip the child for life—for life outside the school as well as inside, for life in the future as well as the present."[266]

The problem is, he observes, not everyone agrees on what a human life should be. Therefore, it makes no sense to engage in a discussion about curriculum in general because we can only discuss curriculum "appropriate to this, or that, perception of authentic human existence." The upshot of this introduction to Wolterstorff's speech confronts the audience with an unsettling fact: because NUCS members do not share a common understanding about the Christian life, they lack the primary criteria required to decide what to teach or not teach in the curriculum. The prior curriculum issue, he argues, is coming to grips with the foundational question: what does it mean to be human?

In the rest of the speech, Wolterstorff offered his own vision of the Christian life as "the standard" NUCS needs to design its curriculum. As he developed the five principal features of this Christian life, Wolterstorff also addressed what he understood to be the movement's Achilles heel: its habit of intellectualizing education. With his bigger vision of life, he hoped to call NUCS back to its Kuyperian roots to educate beyond mere "thinking about" life.

To begin, Wolterstorff stated, "The Christian life . . . is the life of the person, a human person." He used this seemingly obvious statement as a vehicle to dismiss several commonly held misconceptions that characterized the anthropologies of the general population:

> The Christian life is not the life of a pure spiritual soul that happens, for some God-alone-known reason, to be attached to a body. It is not the life of a mind, a rational-moral principle that happens to be imprisoned in a chunk of flesh. Rather it is the life of creatures who are body and soul, inner person and outer person, conscious being and biological being.[267]

The second feature of the Christian life is this: "it is a life of faith, by which I mean not that it is a life that includes faith, but that as a whole it is the life of faith." Here Wolterstorff addressed another fundamental dualism popular among Christians of all backgrounds.

> The object of faith is not propositions. It is rather a personal God. To have faith in this personal God is not to believe various propositions about God. It is rather to give God one's loyalty, one's allegiance, one's service, one's confidence, one's trust, one's obedience. The call to faith

is the call to be trusting, loyal, devoted, obedient servants of God.[268]

Wolterstorff was convinced that to believe in God is to become one of his disciples. In his development of this second feature of the Christian life, we find one of the most often quoted passages from Wolterstorff's writings:

> Insofar, then, as Christian education fails to educate for comprehensive faith, insofar as it fails to educate for life discipleship, it fails to be fully Christian education. Insofar, for example, as it educates for the passive contemplation of God rather than the active service of God, it fails of its true end. Insofar as it confines its Christian content to separate courses in the curriculum rather than putting everything in Christian perspective, it fails of its true end. It is not faith added to understanding that we are after. It is not faith seeking understanding that we are after. Rather, it is faith realized in life.[269]

The third feature of the Christian life is its communal aspect. Although individual Christians are undeniably disciples of Christ, Christian education must equip them to function as members of the community of believers. Wolterstorff then developed five features of this community. First, it is in this context that we develop our fundamental human relationships: I to God and I to neighbour. In later years, Wolterstorff made a point of adding we to creation. Second, the bonds that unite this community are faith bonds, not bonds of ethnicity, social status, or friendship. Third, during this time between Christ's two comings on Earth, the community of faith fulfills its various purposes—being a light for a darkened world, a healing balm to the socially marginalized, and a witness to the new life in Christ—by trying to live that renewed life.[270]

Wolterstorff's fourth feature of the Christian life reveals that "it is a life that is to be lived in the midst of ordinary human society."[271] Here Wolterstorff dismissed the world flight mentality of the *Afscheiding* tradition. The pietist tradition was too inward and self-serving. The community of believers is not meant to live solely for itself but to serve the needs of others, particularly the needs of the socially marginalized.

Finally, Wolterstorff said, "the Christian life is a life engaged in helping carry out the task of cultural domination." This feature of the Christian life means the legitimate tasks of the Christian community go far beyond the space reserved for faith within secular society, such as acts of worship, devotion, and charity. The whole realm of human culture is the domain within which the community of faith must live the Christian life.

The concluding words of this speech summarize his thesis and they too are often quoted:

> Today, I have made but one point. It is this: The curriculum of a Christian education is for Christian life. It is not for the training of theological sophisticates, not for the continuation of the evangelical churches, not for the preservation of Christian enclaves, not for getting to heaven not for service to the state, not for defeating the communists, not for preserving the United States or Canada, not for life adjustment, not for cultivating the life of the mind, not for producing learned and cultured people. Christian education is for Christian life.[272]

As far as I know, this early speech of Wolterstorff's is the first time anyone clearly refers to Neo-Calvinist education as "education for discipleship." This is not a life of cultural accommodation or escaping the world but a life of cultural engagement. Christian education must be education that aims for social change, and to accomplish this the curriculum must engage students with this life. This is not a revisionist position that combines Neo-Calvinist reformulations of popular curriculum orientations. Neither is it a compromise position that cleverly resolves the tension between Jellema and Jaarsma. It is a radical call to change course for a tradition that had gradually lost its bearings. Wolterstorff provided NUCS with a new compass heading, which is what a good philosopher should do. It was up to the educators to navigate the new course.

Nicholas Beversluis

Nicholas Beversluis taught in the education faculty at Calvin College. After a long and distinguished career, which included teaching and administrative duties at both the secondary and university levels, he retired from Calvin College in 1979. Oppewal notes that Beversluis was highly educated, holding a seminary degree and a doctorate in philosophy of education.[273] In 1970, the NUCS board of directors commissioned Beversluis to build on Wolterstorff's 1966 speech and formulate a philosophy of Christian education that would speak to every level of the Neo-Calvinist community and beyond: to parents, administrators, teachers, and curriculum coordinators. The board further requested

> that the formulation be positive, not basically a refutation of other philosophies; that its language, insofar as possible, be non-technical; that a consideration for the nature of the child be an essential ingredient; and that the document integrates the two-pronged emphasis: the involvement in culture and the pursuit of Godliness.[274]

To construct a comprehensive philosophy of education is a daunting challenge, but to write one that could simultaneously speak to laymen and professionals made the task especially difficult. When the board added in the impossible requirement that he also reconcile the Kuyperian and pietist approaches, one wonders why Beversluis ever imagined he, or anyone else, could deliver the prescribed product. However, in the forward to the document published in 1971, the board confirms that Beversluis had satisfactorily met all their conditions. Their endorsement rings hollow, however, because the document itself included a set of notes at the back where Beversluis responds to twelve critical questions raised by educators who were given advance copies of the text. The nature of their questions tells us the respondents had serious misgivings about the usefulness of Beversluis's eclectic document.

To his credit, Beversluis chose to construct a Christian philosophy of education by initially addressing three "first-order questions": what should be the school's religious vision? What should be its major learning goals?

What should be its core required studies? Given the fact that Wolterstorff's speech only dealt with the first of these questions, questions two and three represented the logical next steps for the Neo-Calvinist tradition to take. However, by taking this high-altitude approach, Beversluis was destined to produce a document that still did not address the specific tasks of curriculum design.

In defense of his decision to stick to the more foundational issues, Beversluis offered a checklist of "readings" or "indicators" that school officials could use in a self-evaluation process while they also engaged his foundational questions. This list attempted to bridge the theoretical and the practical aspects of curriculum development, a task it failed to do well. It does, however, provided us with interesting insights into the NUCS of Beversluis' day.

He suggested that the first question about religious vision can help NUCS schools sort issues like the following:
1. Does the school lean more toward pragmatism or fundamentalism?
2. Is religion in the school limited to creedal/ceremonial/personal expressions or a comprehensive world and life view?
3. How well does the school address the needs of the child as an image bearer of God?
4. Does the school address faith development as well as how to live obediently in the world?
5. Does the school address the religious differences among Reformed people?

Likewise, the second question about learning goals should help clarify these concerns:
1. Does the school accept a comprehensive vision of the Christian life? Is this vision fleshed out?
2. Does the school go beyond the normal concerns for social, psychological, and physical growth to prepare students to both know about and be committed to the Kingdom of God?
3. Does the school face the issue of different educational aims among NUCS schools?

Finally, the third question about curriculum requirements drew attention to these indicators:
1. As a consequence of having a religious vision and major goals, are these expressed in the curriculum?
2. Does the school require a core program that all students must take?
3. Does the school address the differences in curriculum theory among NUCS schools?[275]

In addition to this introductory chapter, the document contained three more chapters. Readers would naturally expect that each of these would develop a response to one of the first-order questions. Chapter two conformed to this expectation insofar as it addressed the question of religious vision. However, on this front Beversluis went no further than to simply restate the educational vision that Wolterstorff articulated in his 1966 speech. He reiterated Wolterstorff's claim that what it means to be human ultimately comes to expression in living as a disciple of Christ, but he provided no additional insights or its implications for curriculum design. Consequently, NUCS educators were still left with a vision of Christian discipleship that lacked curricular directives.

Rather than proceed to an analysis of the second first-order question that dealt with appropriate learning goals, the next chapter took an unexpected turn with the introduction of a fourth first-order question: "How must the educational vision come to control the decision-making in the school's educational program?" Or, to rephrase the question slightly, how does the Christian life of discipleship function as criteria when we decide what is or is not included in the curriculum? Why Beversluis did not include this important question with the three others he named in his introduction remains a mystery. Nevertheless, it is a critical question, for in asking it he picked up exactly where Wolterstorff left off in his 1966 speech.

Unfortunately, it is also precisely at this point where Beversluis got sidetracked by the mandate from NUCS. Rather than demonstrate how the life of Christian discipleship actually makes a difference in the curriculum-design process, Beversluis attempted to resolve divisive positions that were prevalent within the ranks of Christian educators.

First, he tried to harmonize two conflicting educational priorities: "what is learned" (curriculum content) and "who is learning" (the learner). This false dichotomy between object and subject epitomized the curriculum debate at Calvin College, and Beversluis was loath to choose one over the other. After a tip of the hat to the legacies of Jellema and Jaarsma, Beversluis dismissed each of them when he said, "The Christian school's model should not be the reductions born of teacher preferences or philosophical systems but the Bible's view of God and man in relationship."[276] So far, so good, but his decision to not take sides did not result in an alternative third way. With relative ease and no compelling logic to substantiate his position, Beversluis simply stated that "subject matter will find its place in the school as the indispensable means to human growth in education."[277]

Beversluis's weak effort to transcend the conflict over education's first priority is followed by an even less compelling attempt when he addressed the first-order question about major learning goals. He began by sorting all learning goals into three broad categories. To the traditional categories of "cognitive growth" and "moral growth" he added Wolterstorff's category of "creativity." By utilizing these three categories Beversluis believed he could incorporate the major themes promoted by Jellema, Jaarsma, and Wolterstorff. However, this attempt to unify diverse points of view had serious flaws. In the first place, these categories do not account for the full spectrum of human functioning, so Beversluis was still left with a truncated view of the person as God's image bearer. Second, the categories of cognitive and moral development had a long history of holding the middle ground between the false dichotomy of faith and practice. Despite his efforts to smooth out these past polarities, Beversluis's work restated the traditional gaps in Western thinking that divide faith from reason, theory from practice, and religion from living.[278]

As NUCS moved into the 1970s, it finally had a philosophical framework document, flawed as it was. The document did not inspire the organization to take up the gauntlet that Wolterstorff had laid down in 1966. Instead, the document reflected the NUCS board's view that the main challenge for Christian educators at that time was to accommodate rather than choose between the two nagging polarities in the tradition: the rift between traditional and modern approaches to curriculum development rooted in the Jellema vs. Jaarsma debate and the older split between pietist and Kuyperian interpretations of faith-learning integration.

The achievement of philosophical consensus seemed both plausible and appropriate to the American leadership at NUCS since virtually everyone in the NUCS movement shared the same theological foundations and more or less agreed that Christian education must ultimately result in Christian living. What Beversluis and the NUCS board failed to understand is both polarities just mentioned are rooted in conflicting assumptions that could not be dismissed with so many strokes of the pen. In the end, Beversluis' philosophy had a little something for everyone but satisfied no one. His document failed to provide a clear answer to the all-important question of what it means to employ a biblical vision of humanity as the standard for making all crucial curriculum decisions. This standard remained up for grabs, and in short order it was filled by something altogether different.

Not long after Beversluis submitted his statement of philosophy, the document underwent two telling transformations. Initially, it was reworked into a document called "Principles into Practice." This document, in turn, morphed into the scientific curriculum framework document written by NUCS curriculum coordinator Henry Triezenberg, whose primary inspiration came from the dominant curriculum-as-technology orientation.[279]

In the beginning, the aspirations of NUCS staff to finally adopt a philosophical statement that could drive policy and guide curriculum-writing projects seemed motivated by Wolterstorff and his profound understanding of the Neo-Calvinist legacy of education. What they received from Beversluis was a statement that tried to reconcile the differences between Wolterstorff's compelling vision and the other main voices currently active within the Neo-Calvinist educational movement. By the time Triezenberg had finished with Beversluis's submission, what NUCS ended up with was no philosophy at all but a means-ends, technical approach to curriculum development that embodied the dominant administrative progressivist approach.

Conclusion

To recapitulate, the closest circle of Christian thought to surround NUCS and CSC at this time emanated from Calvin College. The key contributors in this intellectual circle all laid claim to the same Neo-Calvinist theological and philosophical tradition and its assumption that the ultimate aim of Christian education is the Christian life. However, as each scholar departed from this common starting point, he embarked upon a different path in the effort to articulate the distinctive nature of Christian education. Jellema remained entrenched in a Christian liberal arts orientation that pursued the formation of a Christian mind through the study of classical texts. Jaarsma argued for an education aimed at the heart rather than the mind. His holistic approach to curriculum design rejected all four major curriculum conceptions in favour of a set of biblical criteria. Wolterstorff also preferred an education that aimed at the heart instead of the mind. However, his contribution to curriculum design was solely focussed on the purpose of education, which for him was the life of discipleship. Beversluis reiterated Wolterstorff's position but failed to advance it in his effort to develop a philosophy of curriculum that encompassed all the major voices that populated the Neo-Calvinist tradition.

The upside for NUCS teachers, including those teaching in CSC, was their close affiliation to Calvin College and the opportunities they had to engage in and learn from academic conversations about the meaning of curriculum reform. Despite these advantages, in 1970 NUCS still only possessed the vaguest of educational philosophies. I have already alluded to the fact that in this philosophical vacuum, NUCS adopted the dominant curriculum-as-technology approach.

Topic 4: The Paradigm of Progressive Education

Naming the Big Box

Educators who aspire to be innovative often say they need to "teach outside of the box." This phrase is not simply a metaphor that stands in for the habits that define a local school setting. If the vast body of literature on school reform that we have accumulated over the past sixty years has clarified anything, it is the fact that there really is a rigid structure that determines how life in the classroom unfolds across North America. I referred to this in chapter 3 as the "invisible American context." The "box" that walls in North American education writ large is the *paradigm of progressivism* in education. The business of this discussion is to unpack the contents of this paradigm to assess how it has influenced the way CSC educators interpret and express their educational vision.

What do we find when we peer inside this enormous box? We see our culture's signature assumptions about what it means to be human and what constitutes the good life. We notice that liberalism, progressivism, and the democratization of society function as the ideological lungs that breathe life into this space. We also discover that the various expressions of progressivism have coalesced to form a paradigm for educating; that is to say, the three major streams of thought and action rooted in progressivism have determined, and continue to determine, the trajectory of American and Canadian systems of education.

To equate the big box with progressivism in education may seem antiquated because the term "progressive education" has been absent from our discourse about school reform for many years. It is likely that most educators today know very little about progressive education, and those who do probably believe it died in 1955. However, well-respected researchers make a compelling case that a progressive education paradigm still functions as the proverbial "box" that resists change, and I believe they are right.

The analysis that follows is divided into four sections. In the first we investigate the deep structure of schooling and its relationship to classroom practice. This analysis gives us insight into the raw materials that fill the big box, what binds them together, and the target at which educators must aim their reforms if they hope to teach outside this box. The next section traces the evolution of the big box by highlighting the interior conflicts that define its nature. Here we must revise our thinking about traditional and non-traditional approaches to education and better understand the patterns that characterize life inside the big box. The third section describes two ways that CSC educators were influenced by the paradigm of progressivism. In the concluding section, we analyze how well CSC has stood up to its encounter with this American context.

Coherence Inside the Big Box

For many years I have made extensive use of Barbara Benham Tye's[280] heuristic device for analyzing change and resistance to change in a school setting. She distinguishes between *the deep structure* and *the personality* of a school. For Tye, a school's deep structure refers to that mostly invisible, subterranean world of foundational values, beliefs, and assumptions that rationalize what has been called the *regularities of schooling*. These regularities refer to well-established practices in the visible classroom, such as frontal teaching, direct instruction, streaming students, standardized curriculum, a bell schedule, and the summative evaluation of student work derived primarily from paper-and-pencil tests with achievement expressed as a quantity. My main interest in Tye's research is the relationship between the deep structure and these regularities of classroom/school life.

In Tye's schematic, a school's personality refers to the individual and distinctive ways that teachers and students execute the regularities of schooling. To the extent that a school's personality and the deep structure are two separate entities, I find her categories problematic. Even though schools do have different personalities or cultures, it seems more likely that they, too, are intrinsically linked to the deep structure

From Tye's perspective, certain established practices are undesirable, and the assumptions that sustain them are unacceptable. For example, frontal teaching and streaming are perpetuated by the ill-informed belief that students of a given age and ability level all need to learn the same things and can learn them at the same rate. Presuppositions like these, Tye argues, are shaped by deeper beliefs like those associated with conventional wisdom (quiet, controlled classrooms are better than noisy loose ones), tradition (education refers to transmitted knowledge from an expert), vested interests (teacher autonomy in the classroom is normative), and institutional inertia (the school is the best learning environment).

Tye is not critical of all classroom regularities, nor does she reject all educational assumptions, but she clearly opposes teaching habits that optimize control and a classroom habitat which maximizes confinement. Tye's biases against traditional classroom perspectives and practices will not resonate with all educators, but hopefully, everyone can appreciate the significance of her key conclusion that "the regularities of schooling are value-laden," which in her schematic means they are fundamentally tied to the deep structure of schooling. Her analysis builds on this insight, and she persuasively argues that anyone who desires to make significant changes to the regularities of schooling must also change the deep structure of assumptions and beliefs that nourish them.

Tye concludes that most school reforms fail because they only target the school's personality; consequently, the school's deep structure remains untouched. Her investigation helps us understand why reforms such as developmentally appropriate curriculum, project-based learning, individualized instruction, recognition of multiple intelligences, and greater student voice do not stick. It is not enough for innovations like these to dominate the rhetoric of educational vision statements and/or temporarily add strategies to a teacher's pedagogical toolbox. They are only sustainable when the requisite beliefs and assumptions that sustain them take up permanent residence in the school's *deep structure*. Conversely, we are also mistaken if we assume the regularities of the classroom are arbitrarily chosen, neutral techniques. On the contrary, they embody entrenched beliefs and assumptions. Regrettably, Tye neither offers suggestions about what we should add to the deep structure nor a strategy for implementing such changes.

Bosco[281] is one of the rare commentators on school reform who offers a convincing explanation of why school reformers habitually overlook the fact that classroom practice is closely coupled to the deep structure of schooling, or what he calls the school's *rational mythology*. This mythology, he argues, provides the I-beams and girders of schooling. Put another way, it is the cognitive sinew that binds individuals together as a community. In this capacity the truth or falsity of these myths is irrelevant.[282] These myths are rational, he says, in the sense that "they identify specific social purposes and then specify in a rule-like manner what activities are to be carried out (or what types of actors must be employed) to achieve them."[283]

Bosco makes two additional astute points about these deep structure myths. He says they define a social consensus about what the school is supposed "to be." This agreed-upon purpose of the school evolves out of the school's *institutional context*. He also traces the origins of these myths to the mid-nineteenth century during the first great reformation of American education. In keeping with the Enlightenment ideals of that time, we quickly adopted the following ideas as unquestionable truths: the school is a social institution designed to create a more perfect society, schooling is the way to educate the young, as the educational instrument of society the school equips the young for success in life, school is the safe place for children during the day, and the school provides the social and economic passports for social mobility.[284]

Bosco distinguishes between the school's institutional context and its *technical context*, which defines the school in terms of what it is expected "to do." The normal juxtaposition of these two contexts creates the Gordian knot of public education. The social consensus about what the school is meant "to be" breaks down at the operational level of the school. At this level, people disagree frequently, and at times vehemently, about the specifics of program, curriculum, and pedagogy. This presents the school with a dilemma: how can it "maintain the consensus which pertains to the institutional nature of the school (i.e., the myths) . . . in the face of a situation where there is little consensus on the specifics of the most critical aspects of the operation of the schools (i.e., curriculum and instruction)."[285]

School reforms fail, Bosco believes, because we decouple the rational myths from the operational context. That is, we allow them to live separate lives. This decoupling, he concludes, has become an elegant solution to an organizational problem. In other words, decoupling allows us to believe we only have to change what the school does, not what it is meant to be. Unfortunately, Bosco does not build on his perceptive observations about decoupling. Like Tye, he neither has any alternative myths to offer, nor does he suggest how they can be implemented.

Tye and Bosco give voice to important realities about school reform that have puzzled school reformers from all philosophical perspectives. Both recognize the existence of foundational beliefs/assumptions/theories and their inherent connection to what we practice in the classroom. They believe that school reform typically fails because reformers do not primarily target this deep structure. Instead, they wrongly assume school reform takes place at the operational level where we experience the regularities of schooling. Tye and Bosco also acknowledge this foundational world has evolved over time, but they pay little attention to this important insight. Tye links the regularities of schooling with well-established traditional practices, but she does not identify or evaluate their origins. Bosco says the rational myths were born of the Enlightenment, but he fails to be more specific.

The most important lesson to be learned from scholars like Tye and Bosco is their recognition that what regularly happens in the visible classroom is deeply rooted in a mostly invisible foundation of beliefs and assumptions. Reformers who recognize this know that real and sustainable school reform must target both classroom practices and the beliefs that rationalize them.

At times Tye and Bosco ascribe terms like "unity" and "coherence" to the deep structure or rational mythology of schooling. This leaves the impression that the foundational substructure of the school is internally coherent and consistent. The fact that the regularities of schooling have been around for such a long time also connotes permanence at the deep structure level. There is evidence that suggests the deep structure of schooling is driven by a singular purpose, but this is not the whole story. In the next section, we will not only name this unifying vision but also uncover serious fractures within the "deep structure/regularities of schooling" edifice.

Conflict Inside the Big Box

The most celebrated texts that have been published on school reform are virtually unanimous in their belief that the American context for education consists of four contending approaches to education. What is less well known is that they arose from the liberal arts tradition and three streams of progressivism in education. Figure 2 below offers a sampling of perspectives that we can cull from these texts.

Figure 2

Major Approaches	The Liberal Arts Tradition	Administrative Progressivism	Social Reform Progressivism	Pedagogical Progressivism
Missions of Democratic Education*	Academic Training	Vocational training	Citizenship training	Self-actualization
Educational Philosophies	Perennialism	Essentialism Behaviourism	Social Reconstructionism	Humanism Existentialism
Concepts of Excellence**	The Rational	The Technical	The Social	The Personal
Curriculum Conceptions***	Academic Rationalism	Curriculum as Technology	Social Reconstruction	Self-Actualization
Educational Ideals	Culture	Science	Social Reform	Personal Relevance

* Ernest L Boyer, "America's Schools: The Mission," in *Education on Trial: Strategies for the Future*, ed. William J. Johnston (San Francisco, CA: Institute for Contemporary Studies Press, 1985), 301-320.

** Madhu Suri Prakash, Leonard J. Waks, "Four Conceptions of Excellence," *Teachers College Record* Vol. 87, no. 1 (September 1985): 79-101.

*** Eisner and Vallence, *Conflicts*. They identified five curriculum conceptions, but the one they called "cognitive process" does not have equivalents in other lists. My only explanation for this is to suggest its agenda was adopted by a revised liberal arts tradition when, as a consequence of being pummeled by all three streams of progressivism in education, it exchanged its historical quest for enduring principles and wisdom to the process of inquiry.

Although the vested interests promoted by these four major approaches often overlap or run parallel to each other, their educational priorities differ substantially, and are at times, mutually exclusive. These approaches have not been equally developed as conceptual frameworks, but each has carved out its own relatively permanent space inside the big box. That is to say, each one makes a unique contribution to the regularities of schooling and the deep structure assumptions that sustain them. Let us take a quick tour of these four "corners" of the big box and review their relative strengths.

The oldest approach to choosing content and organizing a curriculum is, of course, the liberal arts tradition, whose roots we can trace back to ancient Greece. In curriculum theory circles, this approach is known as academic rationalism or the academic scholar approach. The liberal arts tradition accentuates the training of the mind and the cultivation of virtue. Education is viewed primarily as a process of cultural transmission from expert teacher to neophyte students through the study of established academic disciplines. What is most worth knowing is contained in our culture's great books. Teachers are most concerned about conserving and passing along humanity's collective wisdom. For this reason their teaching strategies focus on principles rather than skills. The educational philosophy known as perennialism best expresses the vision of a liberal education. Robert Maynard Hutchins[286] was a chief spokesperson for the liberal arts tradition. In the 1950s he strongly advocated for a curriculum that accentuated our common humanity rather than one that indulged our individuality, as the "progressivists" were wont to do.

In what specific ways has the liberal arts tradition taken up permanent residence inside the big box? Its lasting legacy can be seen in the persistence of a curriculum organized around a set of academic disciplines at virtually all levels of education. The lingering perception that teaching essentially means to explain and transmit knowledge to passive students also speaks to the longevity of this tradition.

Pedagogical progressivism has always been highly critical of the liberal arts approach to education. The most well-known pedagogical progressives were Francis Parker, G. Stanley Hall, William Kilpatrick, George Counts, Harold Rugg, Boyd Bode, and, of course, John Dewey, the "father of progressive education." Many of these educators were leaders of the Progressive Education Association, which flourished from 1919 to 1955.

Philosophically, pedagogical progressivism draws on humanist and existentialist perspectives. In particular, followers of this approach take inspiration from Rousseau's romantic view of the child and from the psychological research of developmental and humanist thinkers like Piaget, Rogers, and Holt. From these sources pedagogical progressives hold to the belief that human nature is innately good, and children should be allowed to develop naturally, away from the external and corrupting interference of civilization. The purpose of education in pedagogical progressivism is to enhance the growth, freedom, and creativity of the individual child. Consistent with this vision, the curriculum should provide personally satisfying and relevant experiences to each individual student. The self-actualization of the individual takes precedence over all other educational goals.

Despite its high profile, pedagogical progressivism has carved out surprisingly little space for itself within the big box. While it is responsible for generating almost all of the pedagogical innovations that educators have attempted to implement over the last century, particularly those that put children at the centre of the educational enterprise, most of these have not endured. While it has failed rather miserably to influence what we do in schools, pedagogical progressivism has succeeded in shaping how we talk about schools.[287]

Like pedagogical progressivism, administrative progressivism opposes the liberal arts approach to education. This approach looks to science and technology to achieve its goal of human emancipation through social efficiency. In the spirit of Frederick Taylor,[288] whose time-motion studies standardized factory work, the administrative progressives brought technological order to bear upon schools, particularly high schools. They proposed a "more useful, efficient, and centralized system of public education based on vertically integrated bureaucracies, curricular differentiation, and mass testing."[289] Those who significantly contributed to development of this wing of progressivism include John Franklin Bobbitt,[290] E. D. Hirsch[291], Edward Thorndike,[292] Ralph Tyler,[293] and Benjamin Bloom.[294]

This approach is concerned with the "how" rather than the "what" of education. The purpose of the curriculum is to find efficient means to a set of predefined ends. "It is concerned not with the processes of knowing or learning, but with the technology by which knowledge is communicated and 'learning' is facilitated."[295] The educational philosophies of essentialism and behaviourism are most compatible with this approach.

Administrative progressivism has left a huge and indelible mark upon the big box. All the following hallmark features of our school system have their origins in the administrative progressive movement: a centralized school administration, the differentiation of the curriculum into tracks and the segregation of students into those tracks, intelligence testing, the standardization and quantification of educational goals, and a dependence upon summative assessment instruments.

Social reform progressivism places the role of the school and the curriculum within the larger societal context, which means the school is supposed to engage society with the intention of reforming it, not simply mirroring it. In this approach the needs of society outweigh those of individual students. Schools must constantly adjust the curriculum to address the social issues of the day. Of all the major approaches, this one has received the least support. Even so, it has found a small but significant place to flourish within the big box. We see its enduring presence where our educational goals still express the expectation that education can remove a litany of nagging social problems, such as poverty, crime, ignorance, and racism.

From this set of short summaries, it is not hard to imagine how an educational context made up of this combination of approaches will be pulled in several directions at once. Researchers who work in the field of curriculum theory have provided us with most of our knowledge about the determinative patterns that characterize the interactions between these various approaches. Most often they simply depict the formative unfolding of the big box as a tug of war between traditional and non-traditional approaches to education. This struggle started around the mid-nineteenth century when the progressive education movement seriously challenged the supremacy of a liberal arts education. Ever since that time, we typically associate the liberal arts approach with the traditional pole of education and a learner-centred education with the non-traditional pole.

The meaning of traditional and non-traditional in education is not as straightforward as we might think. Every decade or so we conjure up new terms to define what we mean by a traditional or a non-traditional approach to education. To add to the confusion, educators at both ends of the philosophical spectrum often jump on the same bandwagon for school reform and claim it as their own. To cite a recent example, educators representing a wide variety of viewpoints have all advocated for "twenty-first century learning" and its emphasis on a constructivist pedagogy.

My characterization of the big box as a paradigm of progressivism hangs upon the clarification of two major misunderstandings about the polarity between traditional and non-traditional forms of education. First, we should remember that *pedagogical progressivism* was only one expression of progressivism in education. Due to the popularity of the Progressive Education Association and its exaggerated emphasis on child-centred education, it is easy to understand why we lost track of the other two historic expressions of progressivism. Second, we must account for the major shift that took place in the status quo of Canadian and American education systems many decades ago. The highly visible debate waged between the advocates of the liberal arts tradition and those who championed pedagogical progressivism was short lived, and the liberal arts tradition was the biggest loser, although it is still the dominant orientation in elite private schools, whose graduates continue to occupy key positions in Canadian society. Pedagogical progressivism was not exactly the victor, however. While the supporters of these two approaches argued over which of their educational visions should have priority, the administrative progressives effectively took control of education, and in doing so, their stream of progressivism in education became the new status quo. Therefore, the polarity between traditional and non-traditional approaches to education morphed into a confrontation between two expressions of progressivism in education: progressivism through social efficiency vs. progressivism through personal relevance. See Figure 3 for a graphic organizer of the main conflicts that define the big box.

Figure 3: Conflicting Approaches Inside the Big Box
*box size indicates overall influence in the paradigm;
arrow size indicates prominence of polarities

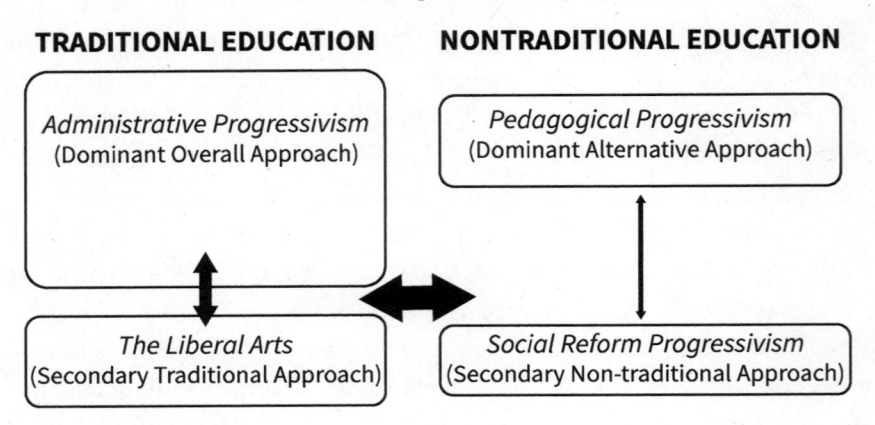

TRADITIONAL EDUCATION   **NONTRADITIONAL EDUCATION**

Administrative Progressivism (Dominant Overall Approach) ⇕ *The Liberal Arts* (Secondary Traditional Approach) ⟷ *Pedagogical Progressivism* (Dominant Alternative Approach) ⇕ *Social Reform Progressivism* (Secondary Non-traditional Approach)

Since the distinction between traditional and non-traditional approaches to education actually refers to a polarity between two wings of the progressive movement in education, we need a quick refresher about the social movement called progressivism that aimed to liberate modern society from all traditional political and ecclesiastical structures. The best insights into this movement can be found in the writings of Cremin,[296] Tyack,[297] Kliebard,[298] and Labaree.[299] Cremin describes progressivism this way:

> ... [it] began as a part of a vast humanitarian effort to apply the promise of American life—the ideal of government by, of and for the people—to the puzzling new urban-industrial civilization that came into being during the latter half of the nineteenth century ... In effect, progressive education began as Progressivism in education: a many-sided effort to use the schools to improve the lives of individuals. In the minds of the Progressivists this meant several things.
>
> First, it meant broadening the program and function of the school to include direct concern for health, vocation, and the quality of family and community life.

Second, it meant applying in the classroom the pedagogical principles derived from new scientific research in psychology and the social sciences.

Third, it meant tailoring instruction more and more to the different kinds and classes of children who were being brought within the purview of the school.

Finally, Progressivism implied the radical faith that culture could be democratized without being vulgarized, the faith that everyone could share not only in the benefits of the new sciences but in the pursuits of the arts as well.[300]

Over the next one hundred years, progressivism meant all the following: a vast social reform movement, a general philosophy of education, John Dewey's philosophy of education, a brand of schooling shaped by scientifically derived principles of business management, and a child-centred pedagogy based on developmental principles. Eventually, progressivism in education solidified into the three distinct streams described above. As pointed out earlier, the most dominant of these streams exaggerated the role of science and technology. The most vocal stream overstated the significance of the individual, while the most neglected one prioritized the importance of social reform. At times these three expressions of progressivism appear to be so diverse as to be virtually incompatible. These differences should not, however, distract us from the fact that all three pursued the same liberal dream of building a strong, unified yet diverse, scientifically organized, democratic society filled with virtuous, educated, and free individuals all living up to their human potentialities.

It is important to understand the pattern that defines the relationship between the administrative and pedagogical streams of progressivism. The pattern is quite simple; administrative progressivism consistently shapes our school system, and pedagogical progressivism repeatedly fails to, even though it generates the most substantive reform initiatives. The reason this happens will help us understand how well CSC stood up to its American context.

Within the first two decades of the twentieth century, the administrative progressives had already centralized and bureaucratized the organization of the American school system and established a top-down curriculum that was first spelled out in a historic 1918 document entitled "The Cardinal Principles of Secondary Education." With this document, the administrative progressives forever transformed "traditional disciplinary subjects (such as math, science, history and English) into a form that was less narrowly academic and more broadly aligned with the diffuse social efficiency aims of Cardinal Principles."[301]

Within administrative progressivism, curriculum making has been understood as a technological process. Ralph Tyler designed the quintessential prototype of a scientific approach to curriculum design. The key to the longevity and supremacy of Tyler's model lies in its ability to appear as if it is not a distinct approach to developing curriculum but simply a technique involving four simple steps. When curriculum designers utilize Tyler's model, the curriculum effectively achieves whatever policy makers demand. Tyler did not intend for his method to be a lock-step process. However, after Benjamin Bloom and his team produced a comprehensive taxonomy of measurable learning objectives, the vision of education as rational production was firmly established. Education became reduced to the "efficient adjustment of productive means to determinate measurable ends."[302] The nature of these ends is particularly significant. They are conceived as "cognitive competencies;" that is, pieces of information and mental skills that can be measured by standardized tests. From that point onward, excellence in education has been defined by the primary values of mental proficiency and problem-solving routines.

Curriculum as technology has dominated the way we develop curriculum for decades. In the beginning it absorbed the academic rationalist approach and redefined traditional education in its own image. When that happened, the educational centre of gravity shifted away from the past as something to emulate to a study of the classic disciplines for their insight into the "structures of thought." The administrative progressives were interested in why the traditional divisions of knowledge had held up for so long, not what great thinkers had said through them in the past. The perennialist concern for "content" gave way to the essentialist interest in the rational "process." Thinking was reconceptualized as problem solving, and the disciplines of study were expected to generate new kinds of problems requiring higher-order analytical, creative, and imaginative abilities. Learners were responsible for inventing the rules for solving the most interesting and important problems.

Long criticized for its promotion of an instrumental rather than a relational brand of education, the "curriculum as technology" approach has maintained its dominance over the other deep structure approaches to this day. It's shaping influence in the classroom is most evident in the way we imagine knowledge as measurable outcomes and through our unyielding commitment to summative forms of classroom assessments, standardized testing to determine student achievement, and quantified grades to symbolically represent student learning. Our faith in the assessment establishment is so deep, it has been said that quantified student assessment is the tail that wags the curriculum dog. Van Brummelen noted in his description of administrative progressivism that its curriculum-as-technology approach fulfills Jacque Ellul's prophetic warning that the down side of technology is its suppression of meaning. The "technical orientation so concerns us with how we teach, and how students learn that we lose sight of why we live and what we want our students to become."[303]

By contrast, the pedagogical progressives focus on experience-based teaching and learning that puts the child at the centre. To this day:

> It means basing instruction on the needs, interests and developmental stage of the child; it means teaching students the skills they need in order to learn any subject, instead of focusing on transmitting a particular subject; it means promoting discovery and self-directed learning by the student through active engagement; it means having students work on projects that express student purposes and that integrate the disciplines around socially relevant themes; and it means promoting values of community, cooperation, tolerance, justice and democratic equality. In the shorthand of educational jargon, this adds up to 'child-centred instruction,' 'discovery learning' and 'learning how to learn.' And in the current language of American education schools there is a single label that captures this entire approach to education: constructivism.[304]

Labaree describes the primary pattern within progressivism this way: administrative progressivism structures the school and its curriculum in ways that are impervious to substantive reform. In contrast, pedagogical progressivism vehemently objects and proposes leaner-centred alternatives. In the end, however, pedagogical progressivism fails to do little more than influence the way we talk about teaching and learning. The rhetorical entrenchment of pedagogical progressivism within the halls of teacher-preparation institutions and in the minds of many teachers has "posed no serious threat to the accomplishments of the administrative progressives." Within the larger progressive education movement, these two approaches "divided the territory between themselves, with one taking the ground and the other taking the air."[305]

Labaree's spatial metaphor reminds me of Raphael's famous 1511 painting of Plato and Aristotle walking across the pavement of the School of Athens where the teacher and his prized student make contrasting arm gestures to signify their respective philosophical orientations: Plato points upward toward the ethereal domain of the Ideals while Aristotle points down toward concrete reality (See Fig. 4).

Figure 4

Just as Aristotle, rather than Plato, eventually became the father of science, administrative progressivism, not pedagogical progressivism, set the trajectory for our education systems in Canada and the United States. Labaree summarizes the struggle between traditional and non-traditional approaches to education inside the big box with a single graphic phrase: administrative progressivism has pummeled pedagogical progressivism. Why has pedagogical progressivism been so inept at school reform? According to researchers like Tye and Bosco, it fails because it does not impact the deep structure of schooling.

There is at least one other way to account for this recurring pattern. Years ago I came across the concept of the *latent paradigm syndrome* while reading an article by Yvonna Lincoln.[306] Lincoln struggled to understand why the concerted efforts of scholars like herself to popularize a "naturalistic approach to inquiry" always failed. She finally realized their alternative method of inquiry lacked staying power because the criteria used to evaluate its worth belonged to the reigning paradigm. Lincoln discovered this important truth about paradigm change: it is not enough to champion an alternative approach; if you want your reform to take hold, you must also introduce new and compatible criteria to assess its merits. Paradigms persist, she learned, because their established standards carry over to judge alternative proposals when they arise, and invariably, these standards find the alternatives wanting.

The latent paradigm syndrome shows up repeatedly. Consider this one example: the research-based, alternative notion that student learning improves when teachers modify instruction in ways that take into account student diversity and their different learning styles flourishes for a time, but as soon as teachers are unable to cover the required curriculum and/or student achievement scores start to sag, various educational stakeholders call for an end to these learner-centred strategies and revert back to a more traditional pedagogy. Scenarios like this happen repeatedly because the big-box criteria for academic excellence is high test scores, not personal relevance. Learner-centred instruction will only take hold long term when its merits are judged by a correspondingly new understanding of educational success. The implementation of this new criteria is, of course, a deep structure matter, because these criteria are themselves rooted in foundational beliefs.

There is one other pattern that characterizes the big box as a paradigm of progressivism. I call it the *additive approach to teaching*. Just like industrial chemists strive to make the perfect synthetic motor oil by mixing the right additives, teachers pursue excellence by combining multiple approaches to teaching, even when they serve conflicting goals. For example, teachers feel compelled to simultaneously cover increasingly more curriculum content, motivate students to achieve minimum academic standards in a variety of subject disciplines, teach to the various learning styles in their student population, encourage students to take responsibility for their own learning, and provide students with opportunities to cultivate social responsibility. The big-box vision of teacher excellence reminds me of the family game *Twister*, where players have to contort their bodies to touch different coloured circles on a plastic sheet all at the same time, only to eventually fall into a heap.

To quickly recap, the American context/big box paradigm of progressive education expresses itself in the following patterns. Pattern one: the regularities of schooling—which includes established classroom practices—are inherently linked to a deep structure of belief. This deep structure of belief defines the purpose of education, rationalizes the way we teach, and creates the criteria we use to judge excellence for teachers, students, and the education system itself. When educators fail to acknowledge the integral bonds that tie the regularities of schooling to this deep structure of belief, they mistakenly perceive the regularities of schooling to be value free. This failure also hinders their capacity to understand how the Enlightenment ideologies of liberalism, progressivism, and the democratization of society continue to function as deep drivers of education.

Pattern two: four educational visions have shaped the evolution of the interface between the regularities and the deep structure of schooling. Administrative progressivism has dominated this formative process while its chief rival, pedagogical progressivism, has generated a repository of school reform rhetoric, but no long lasting school reforms. Pattern three: serious efforts to reform school goals, teaching, the curriculum, student assessment, and so on fail to stick because their merits are judged by unfriendly, established criteria. Pattern four: standards of teacher excellence require teachers to straddle the boundaries that separate the four historical approaches to education even though some priorities promoted by these approaches are mutually exclusive. In reality, teaching methodology must serve the agenda set by administrative progressivism. Pattern five: educators fail to teach outside of the big box because they are either unable and/or unwilling to alter the deep structure of belief.

Topic 5: The Curriculum Development Centre's

Failed Partnerships

Scenario 1:

This section of "Dig Deeper" delves into the details of the Curriculum Development Centre's (CDC's) inability to establish significant partnerships. These missed opportunities are significant not only for the consequences they had on the CDC's ability to pursue its vision but also for their impact on the history of curriculum development among Canadian Neo-Calvinist School (CSC) communities. The two scenarios investigated below bring to light flaws in key players on both sides of the negotiating table, but these weaknesses are not the main focus of the investigation. These scenarios provide us with a rare opportunity to see how a shared vision for education can be expressed in conflicting ways to the detriment of a tradition of education.

As outlined in chapter 5 of this book, the CDC began as a legal entity, so four women could more easily publish and distribute a major curriculum text entitled *Joy in Learning*. *JIL* was the first book of a nine-volume program of studies that these women, and many other CSC teachers, imagined for the K-12 Christian school movement in the early nineteen seventies. It is important to remember that every aspect of curriculum development at that time was left up to the teachers in CSC because their school system lacked the necessary leadership and the administrative structure to carry out curriculum reform, even though this was a centrepiece of their educational vision.

When the Association for the Advancement of Christian Scholarship (AACS) agreed to take ownership of the CDC and make it an actual centre for the purpose of developing and publishing the alternative program of studies imagined by these women, it not only filled a visionary and administrative void, it also set up shop on turf that many felt solely belonged to the National Union of Christian Schools (NUCS).

There was little likelihood that the CDC could have formed a meaningful relationship with NUCS due to their different understanding of curriculum reform. However, it was well within the realm of possibility for the CDC to form partnerships with district administrators or major donors in Canada. The most obvious potential partner was the Ontario Alliance of Christian Schools (OACS), but its leaders lacked the vision to boldly move ahead with curriculum reform. The only partnerships that had any immediate chance of success were those made with private benefactors.

As chapter 5 makes clear, the CDC was perpetually on the brink of financial collapse. Even when it was operated by the AACS, CDC staff had fundraising responsibilities that inhibited their research and writing. The CDC needed partners with money just to survive. It also needed partners to enhance its credibility in the larger Neo-Calvinist education movement in Canada. CDC staff were particularly inept at cultivating such partnerships, and they mismanaged the one that fell into their laps at the beginning of the CDC's history.

A few months after the AACS announced that it had adopted the CDC as a project, it received $25,000 ($166,500 in today's money) from an anonymous donor who had a heart for Christian education. The donor was actually a small group of entrepreneurial businessmen, who ran Birchwood Builders. They were sympathetic with the Reformational Movement[307] generally and were ardent supporters of certain leaders within that movement but sceptical of others. They were motivated to give money to the CDC because they appreciated the importance of homegrown texts like *Joy in Learning* for their school system, although it is doubtful that any of them had actually read it or understood the extensive reforms it contained. Did they trust the CDC? Not completely, which explains why their money came with strings attached. The CDC had to provide monthly financial statements and project progress reports to the donors. Both reports were to be vetted through an educational expert appointed by the donors to serve as an advisor. This advisor was a trusted friend of the donors and also happened to be a CSC educator.

In June 1975, just a couple of months into the relationship with their benefactor, the CDC's director, Arnold De Graaf received a draft of the advisor's first report to the donors. The Birchwood advisor wanted De Graaf's feedback before he submitted the final draft of this report. The CDC archives reveal that De Graaf and the adisvor disagreed on just about everything stated in the report, as well as the assumptions written into the report's introduction.

The advisor introduced his report by saying, "within the context of support for curriculum development from a Christian perspective, this report singles out critical areas that need close attention if the Centre is to serve a large section of Christian Schools in Ontario." His assumption about the CDC's role within the CSC context, particularly in Ontario, was the first of many contentious points in his exchange with De Graaf. He assumed that the purpose of the CDC was to serve the needs of the Neo-Calvinist school movement, and none of these was more critical than the development of an alternative curriculum integrated with a Christian worldview. This was a perfectly natural assumption to make. Many CDC supporters, including me, held this assumption for years. We never knew that while De Graaf agreed that the CDC's purpose was to develop an alternative curriculum model, he saw obligations to organizations like the OACS as impediments to this purpose.

The tone of the draft report was not mean spirited, but the advisor expressed genuine concerns over the CDC's lack of interest in being a service organization for the Neo-Calvinist movement, particularly in Ontario. His report cited multiple concerns about the CDC's organizational structure and its overall program, and it raised specific questions regarding the three volumes that CDC staff were currently developing.

The CDC's organizational structure was problematic in the following ways. As a corporate body, the CDC had a closed membership of ten people with no clear rules about who could be a member and how members were selected. The CDC also lacked connections with the Ontario Christian School Teachers Association, the principals' group, and the association of school societies, the Ontario Alliance of Christian Schools. The CDC staff appointed its own members and was practically autonomous with respect to project decisions. This last point was particularly disconcerting because the advisor, who was himself a school administrator, felt the staff council's independence from the AACS board set a bad precedent and could incite teachers within CSC to seek similar autonomy from their administrators.

The report also had plenty to say about the CDC's proposed curriculum program. The CDC seemed unsure about what kind of product it was producing. Was it published research, teacher resources, or a program of studies? The danger this lack of clarity posed, the report said, was the probability that the CDC's products would not be particularly useful for teachers or as a defined program of studies.

Additionally, the advisor found that nowhere did the CDC offer a plan that would assist principals and teachers when they had to make practical decisions with respect to a program of study. Examples of these questions include: how do we distinguish between core content and optional content? What content should be taught at each grade level? What is the scope and sequence of this content? The CDC's program was also criticized for being totally geared to "open education," meaning a theme-based curriculum coupled with lots of student choice. According to the advisor, the CDC's "open approach" only had a limited place in a regular class setting.

The report then addressed the three curriculum volumes that the CDC staff were working on at the time. Roughly half of the advisor's comments were complimentary, but he also raised a couple of serious concerns. First, he observed that in two of the three projects, the content did not match the age level it was meant to serve. Second, the content did not have an obvious place within the curriculum currently being taught in the schools.

The two summary questions at the end of the report got to the heart of the CDC's legacy. The first question asked to what extent the CDC was willing to address the needs of the general learning community, meaning the Ontario district of CSC, when it decided what projects to publish and how to design them. Second, was the CDC willing to primarily write curriculum suited to the more structured, formal classrooms that prevailed in CSC schools, or would it insist on preparing curriculum suited to an open, informal, integrated classroom structure that did not exist in most schools?

The tone of De Graaf's lengthy response to the advisor was also friendly. He acknowledged that the two of them were equally committed to Christian education. He also felt that even though they had very different understandings about the nature of Christian education, they should be able to work together. This was wishful thinking at best, for both De Graaf and the advisor shared an assumption commonly held among Neo-Calvinist educators, that a disagreement at the level of worldview foundations would necessarily play out everywhere the worldview was expressed. This belief often led people to adopt an all-or-nothing posture whenever serious disagreements occurred, and this often killed any hope for collaboration

In his response to the report's multiple concerns over the CDC's curriculum projects, De Graaf appealed to a concept known as the "latent paradigm syndrome," which is discussed in topic 5 of "Dig Deeper." De Graaf told the advisor that he could not accept his critique "at face value, since it is entirely written from out of your point of view." In other words, the criteria the advisor used to find fault with the CDC's program were unacceptable because they were biased toward an approach to education that the CDC had consciously chosen not to follow. The use of hostile criteria was bound to find any program wanting that did not try to meet its demands. De Graaf's argument was valid, but it did not magically erase the weaknesses that plagued the CDC's curriculum.

De Graaf also addressed the central question of the CDC's role as a service organization. He was unwilling to make the CDC accountable to either the district teachers' organization, the principals' organization, or the OACS's parent organization, NUCS, because all of them were rife with division. The dysfunctional character of these organizations is what gave rise to the CDC in the first place. Furthermore, De Graaf argued, the CDC already served those teachers and principals within CSC who agreed with its approach to curriculum. This, he assumed, was the most anyone could hope for in the current climate.

There is one additional point in De Graaf's response that is worth mentioning. In reply to the criticism that the CDC's program lacked a sense of direction and an organizational plan for developing projects, De Graaf did not deny these "weaknesses." In fact, he argued that what the advisor hoped to get from the CDC was simply unrealistic at that point in its development of a distinctively Christian approach. What he was looking for could not be achieved until the CDC staff had first understood and articulated the philosophical and anthropological underpinnings of their curriculum approach. This groundwork was both challenging and time consuming, De Graaf explained. Here De Graaf articulated a fundamental assumption that many CSC educators understand; before we can meaningfully reform the curriculum, all of our worldview ducks must be properly aligned. Right or wrong, De Graaf and his colleagues believed this foundational thinking could only happen in the abstract, disconnected from any actual classroom situation.

The archives do not contain the final draft of the advisor's first (and as far as I can tell, only) report or how the donors responded to it, but there can be no doubt that it raised concerns. These concerns were surely amplified when, around mid-July, the donors received a progress report from the AACS liaison person but written by CDC staff member Ann Tuininga. This update focused on the Kenya segment of volume 2 of the program of study. Essentially, the report said that a lot of writing had been completed, but much more still needed to be done. The donors had provided the CDC with the money it said was needed to produce the complete cultural studies volume, but six months later, the project was still far from completion.

In early September, the donors invited a delegation from the AACS to meet them in their company office. The stated purpose of the meeting was to explore the CDC's vision and mission. De Graaf came to the meeting accompanied by the AACS liaison person, Harry Houtman, and its executive director, Robert VanderVennen. The donors were joined by their advisor, and two other invited guests, a prominent educator in their community and a local pastor. The presence of a pastor is indicative of the general Calvinist belief that the source of perspectival disagreements was ultimately theological in nature.

Based on the meeting notes prepared the following day by the AACS executive director at the behest of the donors, the meeting resembled an inquisition, and De Graaf was the person under examination. The donors wanted to know what he believed about such things as the "integrated approach" and its relation to the "open classroom," the nature of the learning process, the nature of the child, the meaning of authority in the classroom, and the effects of sin on a child's eagerness to learn.

Throughout the meeting the donors and their supporters expressed concern that CDC materials were biased toward an "integrated learning approach" appropriate for the "open classroom." De Graaf did not deny this, but according to VanderVennen's notes, he tried to assure the donors that he wanted CDC materials to serve schools that used a more conventional approach as well as those experimenting with a more open approach. He also pointed out that *Joy in Learning* was currently being used in conventional classrooms.

Considerable time was also given to the donors' concerns over the lack of diversity on the CDC's board of advisors. These meeting notes offer no evidence that De Graaf assuaged his inquisitors' concerns. One outcome of this meeting is rather clear now: no one in that room came away believing that the CDC had a future as a major curriculum provider for CSC.

There is no record of communication between the CDC and the donors for the next eight months. What accounts for this long silence is unknown, but it surely signifies a lack of collegiality, if not trust. Then, in late April 1976, the AACS liaison, Harry Houtman wrote a letter to one of the donors to describe how the AACS had spent the $25,000 ($160,000) donation. In an almost flippant paragraph, Houtman writes, "If your donation given in January of 1975 was exclusively meant to fund Vol. 2, then $8,000 ($51,200) was applied to the first six months of 1976. If it was used for whatever in 1975, then the money actually helped produce Bible curriculum." Houtman attached a copy of this project to his report.

This is an odd report on several fronts, and it could only have further confused and/or disappointed the donors. CDC records clearly show that the donors gave their money so the CDC could publish volume 2, so why did Houtman suggest the purpose of the donation was unclear? We know from other files that $8,000 ($51,200) was taken out of the donation to cover the AACS's portion of an expanded budget. It seems the AACS applied this $8,000 ($51,000) to one fiscal budget and the remainder of the donation to another. At best, Houtman was not fully disclosing what might be called creative accounting. At worst, he was trying to pacify the donors' desire to see some concrete results for volume 2 when there were none.

About a month later, on May 19, the liaison submitted a lengthy six-page update with a two-page letter attached. This update reported on the seventeen months since the donation had been given. By then all the money had been spent, so it was time to disclose what had been accomplished. There are oddities about this communique as well. The report includes the bios of De Graaf, Jean Olthuis, and Anne Tuininga, the CDC staff members assigned to the cultural studies volume. Why would a declaration of qualifications and experience as curriculum writers be shared with the donors at this late date? Perhaps the liaison was worried the donors would think the CDC staff were incompetent when the truth came out that they had not completed the volume. The report also describes the hard work these writers had put into the development of an original philosophical/anthropological framework, which they said was needed in order to write the Kenya and Japan units, which by then had both grown to the size of textbooks. On page three the liaison finally addresses the ultimate question: "What did your $25,000 ($160,000) accomplish for Christian education?" His answer: "You paid for a lot of groundwork for which there are no tangible results." In the end the donation essentially paid the salaries provided to Olthuis and Tuininga, which included a month to prepare for and give presentations at a conference.

The report clearly states that the CDC staff did not meet their own expectations because they overestimated the number of projects they could work on at one time. They also underestimated the enormity and difficulty of writing cultural studies. The Japan and Kenya units were basically finished, he said, but not yet ready to be published. Houtman said nothing about why the CDC staff chose to start work on cultures like Japan and Kenya instead of first completing the Canada unit, which had been partially written prior to the CDC's existence.

Houtman also argued that the donation allowed the CDC staff to do the hard work of foundational studies, namely researching and testing the assumption that "culture expresses a religious belief." This argument may have pacified the donors, but in hindsight it lacks credibility. The seven pages that introduce pedagogical considerations in the Kenya curriculum, for example, draw heavily from the *Joy in Learning* binder published years earlier. The section on patterns of culture that addresses anthropological foundations also runs a mere seven pages.

In a two-page letter attached to his report, Houtman described the CDC staff's agenda for the upcoming fiscal year, July 1976 to June 1977. They planned to publish the Japan and Kenya units, write six hundred pages of text for the Canada study, complete four Bible study books, and if funding allowed, complete the grades 1-8 mathematics project. This agenda was obviously included in the report to encourage the donors to give another gift in the new fiscal year. No written record tells us what the donors thought of Houtman's update and the not-so-subtle hint for a second donation, but their actions speak louder than words, for no additional money was forthcoming.

A few weeks later, in mid-June, Houtman again contacted the donors. He told them that the AACS had set the CDC's budget at $70,000 ($448,000), and it hoped to attract a couple of major donations to help meet this target. He also requested a meeting to discuss the possibility of a second donation. In response, the donors told Houtman that they no longer donated directly to fund curriculum projects. Instead, they now distributed their donations through an intermediary. This intermediary body just happened to be a new committee set up by the National Union for Christian Schools (NUCS) to channel funds collected from its Canadian schools to deserving curriculum projects. The fact that one of the donors sat on this committee is a clear indication that the donors had made a strategic decision to shut the donation door on the CDC and only fund projects vetted by NUCS.

This failed relationship is tragic on several levels. The CDC could have learned much from the donors and their advisors, but they were not open to criticism. To their credit, the CDC staff pursued curriculum reform on three levels: the development of a new model, the articulation of the principles that rationalized the model, and the actual writing of curriculum content using the model. Because they chose to work in the abstract with no clear audience in mind for their cultural studies volume, they incorporated their work at all three levels into their projects. This not only led to overly complicated texts but also a curriculum that was not age appropriate and not applicable to a regular social studies program. Events could have turned out differently had they been willing to take the advisor's criticisms seriously.

Looking back, one wonders why the CDC staff decided to start three projects prior to doing this groundwork if, as De Graaf observed, they needed time and resources to develop a conceptual framework prior to writing the curricular content for the cultural studies volume? If, as he believed, partnerships with existing CSC entities were not possible because of disagreements about educational vision and direction, why not put more effort into cultivating a partnership with the donors?

The donors were equally narrow minded. They expressed great concern about the dangers of the "open classroom," yet they ended up committing their money to an organization that had adopted the Tyler model of curriculum writing, which had equally unacceptable views of the child.

This brief partnership between Birchwood Builders and the CDC failed for many reasons, and both sides must share the blame for its demise. With the benefit of hindsight, we can see that this failed partnership was a harbinger of curriculum reform in CSC. Both sides assumed there was only one approach to curriculum design and one best way to teach, and neither was willing to find common ground. Both sides believed the pursuit of an ideal superseded the cultivation of a relationship. For CDC staff, the all-important goal was to be right philosophically, which meant writing a curriculum that was free of dualisms. Incredibly, it also meant being disconnected from real teachers and students in actual classrooms. For the donors, theological orthodoxy was primary; however, their understanding of authority, knowledge, and human nature was most compatible with the Tyler model of curriculum design that NUCS had adopted.

The partnership also failed because the CDC staff made a series of questionable decisions regarding the cultural studies volume. Taken together, these decisions made the curriculum less useful and impossible to finish on time. It also appears that the CDC staff were too cavalier toward the donors' expectations. They took an entitled approach to their development of volume 2, and they used the money under the pretense that they were writing a curriculum that CSC teachers needed.

Personalities also got in the way. De Graaf was definitely a charismatic leader who could articulate a faith-infused approach to curriculum better than most of his contemporaries in the Neo-Calvinist tradition, but he was not a gifted negotiator. Too often in CSC circles, people objected to the person bearing an idea more than they did to the idea itself.

Finally, the CSC was the biggest loser in this failed relationship. Had the CDC staff and the donors made the sustainability of their relationship a high priority for the sake of curriculum reform, by the time CSC administrative bodies were ready to coordinate the efforts of their teacher-led curriculum reform movement, the Neo-Calvinist movement in Canada would have had a curriculum development think tank available to guide it.

Scenario Two[308]

In 1978 the new intermediary committee mentioned above evolved into a standing committee named the Canadian Curriculum Council (CCC). The purpose of this committee was fourfold: long-range planning, project development, coordination of curriculum work, and diffusion of materials. This committee partially filled the leadership void that plagued the teacher-led curriculum development movement that had been underway in CSC for more than a decade. According to Harry Fernhout in a report he wrote in 1984, the CDC staff had hoped the third function of the committee would "coordinate the work of Christian Schools International (CSI, formally NUCS) with that of other groups, including CDC."

In September 1978, the CDC sent a congratulatory letter to the CCC on its formation. The letter also expressed the CDC's hope that the relationship between the CCC and the CDC would be one of mutual respect and cooperation. Two months later, representatives from the CDC met with the CCC. They encouraged the CCC to be open-minded, meaning they support a diversity of approaches to curriculum development within CSI schools. The CDC representatives also asked the CCC for advice about the submission of project proposals. These initiatives suggest the CDC staff had softened their position about forming partnerships. Although they still clung to their distinctive approach, they seemed more willing to develop curriculum that the schools actually needed.

In December of that year, the CCC responded positively but tentatively. They did not want to enter into any "structural" relationship, but they would pursue a "consultative" one with the CDC. The CCC also informed the CDC that they saw its approach to curriculum design as one of three in use among CSI schools, although they failed to identify the other two.

Fernhout reports that in the spring of 1979, the CDC submitted some partially finished material in the area of social studies to the CCC, at its request. Although the report does not name the material, it was likely drafts of the Japan and Kenya units. The CDC also asked the CCC to fund the revision of some biblical studies curriculum that SPICE[309] teachers had written in 1970. The CCC said Bible curriculum was not one of its current priorities, but it would conduct a survey of teachers to assess the need. Up to this point, the relationship between the CCC and the CDC seemed open, cordial, and respectful. That would soon change.

One year later, in June 1980 the CCC asked the CDC to submit the units on Japan and Kenya for review for possible publication by CSI. The CDC informed the CCC that the Japan unit had already been published, and the Kenya unit was in the advanced stages of being published as well. The CCC refused the CDC's suggestion that it help fund the publication of the Kenya unit.

In March 1981, the CDC approached the CCC with a proposal that they co-publish *Canada: A Way of Life*. At that time, Peter Enneson was the administrative head of the CDC and the point person in communications with the CCC. Sometime in April, the CCC rejected the CDC's proposal. For reasons unknown, CCC's secretary, did not write a letter to inform the CDC staff until May 27. The CDC received that letter on May 31. In the meantime, the CCC's decision was made public through the newsletter of the Society of Christian Schools in British Columbia (SCSBC), the BC equivalent of the OACS.

The CCC's lack of professional courtesy is also evident in the less than subtle, critical tone of its secretary's letter. His lack of tact made it more difficult for the CDC staff to hear the CCC's reasons for rejecting their proposal. The CCC said only part of *Canada: A Way of Life* was applicable to the grades 4–6 social studies program, and its conceptual level was well beyond students of that age. Furthermore, the material already seemed ready for publication, too late for serious revisions. These weaknesses lead to the CCC's view that "a responsible discharge of curriculum coordination requires more precision and planning than you have been able to evidence to this point."

The CDC staff took great umbrage over both the tone and the contents of this letter. The belittling tone was unnecessary, but the specific criticisms of the CCC should not have been that surprising. On April 11, just days after the CDC submitted their proposal for the Canada module to the CCC, the CDC staff told its own board that the project had been a challenging one for them in terms of the massive amount of material, its controversial message, and the need for pedagogical coherence.

On June 19, roughly three weeks after it received the CCC's letter, the CDC's board of directors instructed Enneson to draft a letter of response to the CCC's letter expressing disappointment and challenging its criticisms. The CDC's board finally received and accepted Enneson's draft of a letter on September 18. Three months seem like an unusually long time to produce a reply to an urgent matter. The letter not only responded to each of the CCC's points of criticism, it also expressed the CDC's hurt at having to hear the news first via a third party newsletter. Enneson also challenged the legitimacy of the CCC's judgments since two of its members had informed CDC staff person Agnes Struik that they had insufficient time to give the material serious consideration.

Enneson's letter acknowledged that the materials were not provided to the CCC on time, an administrative blunder that likely contributed to the CCC's view that the CDC was administratively challenged. His letter reinforced this notion when he claimed that the CCC never provided the CDC with an official response. This was not true. He should have said that the CCC's response came so late that the CDC found out about their decision via a newsletter.

In December 1981, the CDC submitted a new proposal to the CCC, suggesting that the CDC and the CCC co-publish the "Transportation" section of *Canada: A Way of Life*. As a show of good faith, the CDC said it welcomed editorial input from the CCC. In February of the next year, the CCC responded positively, informing the CDC that one of its members would discuss possible publication arrangements with them. That meeting took place in March. The memo prepared by the CCC representative addressed the meeting's two main outcomes, possible publication arrangements, and the CDC staff's demonstrated flexibility.

Two months later, the CCC rejected the CDC's proposal regarding the "Transportation" manuscript. According to the CCC, this material shared some of the same flaws as the Japan and Kenya units. Only parts of it were applicable to the grades 4–6 social studies curriculum, and conceptually, it was better suited to junior or senior high school students. Additionally, the learning activities did not address a balance of learning types. Specifically, it did not promote "precision learning," which likely meant factual recall.

The response also informed the CDC of a motion that the CCC had adopted. With this new ruling, the CCC set in stone what had been rather obvious all along: the CCC wanted no part of the CDC's approach to curriculum design. The motion read as follows:

> That the Canadian Curriculum Council invite the C.D.C. to indicate its willingness to cooperate in the development of regional studies of Canada as designated by the C.C.C., as subject to the following conditions:
> a. that the structure as outlined by C.C.C. and approved by C.S.I. would be adhered to;
> b. that in-service teachers would be involved in the development and evaluation of the unit, including pedagogical concerns; and
> c. that the C.D.C. would present to the C.C.C. a draft copy of resulting materials for approval before submission to C.S.I.

The CDC responded to the CCC in July. In addition to expressing its disappointment in the CCC's decision, it also asked the CCC to explain how its new motion would have applied to the "Transportation" unit. The CCC met in August, but it did not reply to CDC's inquiry.

The CDC eventually received a letter from the CCC in January 1983. The CCC apologized for not inviting CDC representatives to its November meeting. In response to the CDC's question, raised in July of the previous year, the CCC simply said they had already given the CDC an answer in earlier correspondence. The message from the CCC to the

CDC was this: the CSI had already developed the model for cultural studies, and if the CDC was willing to use it under the CCC's supervision, they could write a unit on Egypt or Mexico for them. Nothing further was communicated by either side until April 1984 when the CDC asked the CCC to return its manuscripts of the "Transportation" unit.

The inability of the CDC and the CCC to form a working partnership failed for a variety of reasons, most of them identical to the ones that kept the CDC from developing a meaningful relationship with a major donor. Differences in personality and educational vision were certainly major factors. Unfortunately, no one seemed to understand that the CDC was a vital player for the overall health of CSC.

The CDC was the keeper of the most profound expression of a Neo-Calvinist vision of education, yet it became a liability to that vision because of its decision to work on a theoretical model in isolation from the very teacher-led curriculum reform movement that gave birth to the CDC. CSC administrative bodies rejected the CDC primarily because they perceived it to be a renegade organization. Instead, they chose to remain loyal to their parent organization, CSI, even though its approach to curriculum was even more out of step with the Canadian districts.

Topic 6: The "Ordering Principle"

The concept of an *ordering principle* for the curriculum is one of several important insights that the Curriculum Development Centre (CDC) gave to the Neo-Calvinist tradition of education specifically and to the larger world of curriculum reform. Tom Malcolm coined the term in the first issue of the CDC's *Joy in Learning* newsletter, published in 1978. The term "ordering principle" refers to the deep driver that determines the design of the curriculum.

The logical structure of the traditional subject disciplines has served as the ordering principle of the curriculum throughout the history of mass education in North America. Its status has gone largely unchallenged because most everyone assumes the best education is a science-based education, and the internal structures of the disciplines are thought to reflect the structure of nature itself. The need for a different ordering principle only makes sense to those who want to implement a radically different vision of education, like the people who worked at the CDC.

Malcolm explained why the CDC's approach to curriculum depended upon an alternative ordering principle. Arnold De Graaf first unpacked the CDC's approach to curriculum design in the *Joy in Learning* curriculum in 1973.[310] He replaced the dominant assumptions just mentioned with biblical alternatives. The aim of education, he believed, must be rooted in the biblical definition of what it means to be human, not the logical structure of the disciplines. For De Graaf, *the ordering principle for the curriculum is a way of life, not a way to organize knowledge.* Few people within or without the Neo-Calvinist tradition of education have understood the significance of this shift.

De Graaf's argument unfolds like this: Scripture reveals that God called humans into being for one purpose, which is to live a particular way in relationship to their Creator, their fellow humans, and the rest of creation. The Bible variously depicts this way of life with totality words like love, service, mercy, peace, hope, and justice. The best blueprint of this life is the one that Jesus modeled for his disciples.

Education for this alternative way of life must take child development into account. De Graaf believed the primary function of the curriculum is to help students at every stage of their growth "take up their common tasks" in contemporary society as followers of Christ.

At this critical juncture, De Graaf, and those who carried on his work at the CDC, failed to follow through on their radical new approach. Rather than explore what a curriculum designed to help students take up their tasks actually looks like, they felt compelled to pick sides in the perennial debate over disciplinary vs. interdisciplinary designed curricula.

Why did the CDC staff get sidetracked by a debate over which type of knowledge should have priority in education when the more fundamental issue was what vision or way of life should education serve? Hindsight offers an explanation. De Graaf said that an education shaped by a vision of the Christian life urges us to see everything in its deepest and fullest meaning. He believed the CDC staff did not yet possess the alternative framework of knowledge they needed to plumb that level of meaning. This assumption dovetailed into the staff's acceptance of the traditional view that theory precedes practice. The need to get all their conceptual ducks properly aligned delayed the CDC's implementation of an alternative ordering principle.

In the absence of an alternative conceptual framework, the CDC staff latched on to the best the paradigm of progressivism had to offer, which was the interdisciplinary curriculum. The interdisciplinary unit, they believed, provided the deeper meaning their new ordering principle demanded. In the end, interdisciplinary studies failed to fulfill the CDC's expectations. In the first place, the CDC's own examples of interdisciplinary units were rarely thematic or transdisciplinary in nature; they were multidisciplinary. That is, rather than explore a more holistic level of knowing, these units rotated through a variety of disciplinary perspectives on one topic. Second, and more importantly, no matter how holistic interdisciplinary knowledge is, it remains head knowledge. To "think about" taking up the appropriate common tasks of life at any given age is not the same as "engaging" these tasks.

The CDC's preference for interdisciplinary studies and its rejection of the fragmented knowledge siloed in pseudo-autonomous disciplines put it at odds with the views of Harro Van Brummelen and Geraldine Steensma, which permeated their influential book, *Shaping School Curriculum: A Biblical View*, published in 1977.[311] Steensma and Brummelen agreed with many of the assumptions expressed in *Joy in Learning*, including the all-important belief that the purpose of Christian education is to educate for a life of response to the Creator. They did not, however, see the need to make this way of life the ordering principle of the curriculum. Instead, they adopted Philip Phenix's approach, which emphasized the unity of meaning in the disciplines.

Harry Fernhout[312] characterized this reliance on Phenix as a momentary but critical departure from their otherwise consistent efforts to build a curriculum framework that is rooted in biblical principles and leads to a Christian way of life. Fernhout said he would not be so concerned if *Shaping* merely exhibited similarities to Phenix's view; the problem is, the book's framework actually depended on Phenix at the critical point where it determined how to order subject matter.

To select meaningful curriculum content, Phenix articulates four principles for curriculum specialists to follow. These principles are of particular interest, Fernhout argues, because they are prominent in *Shaping*.

- The first principle says, "all material for instruction must be drawn from the scholarly disciplines," which implies that the curriculum will be organized around distinct subjects.
- The second principle states that "content should be chosen to exemplify representative ideas of the discipline." Thus, students come to a key understanding of the discipline even when not all its content is studied.
- The next principle says that "content should be chosen to exemplify the methods of inquiry of the discipline."

- Lastly, "content selection should arouse imagination." For Phenix, "imagination is essential for self-actualization and attainment of the highest human good, namely, the fulfillment of meaning."[313]

Fernhout was initially puzzled about why Phenix's "self-actualization model, with its lofty phrases about human fulfillment, ended up in a rigorous treatment of academic disciplines and a reductionistic view of knowledge," until he understood that Phenix never breaks free from the rationalist paradigm. Fernhout then expressed his difficulty in understanding why Steensma and Van Brummelen gave such prominence to the academic disciplines as the organizer of content, and why they felt obligated to adopt Phenix's principles of content selection. [314]

Throughout the 1970s and 1980s, the leading lights for curriculum reform within the Canadian Neo-Calvinist tradition of education promoted a biblical way of life as an alternative purpose for education. De Graaf and Fernhout believed this way of life should be the ordering principle of the curriculum, and Van Brummelen and Steensma did not. For different reasons, both teams got sidetracked from their main objective of educating for a way of life by defending a position in the academic disciplines vs. the interdisciplinary studies debate within the paradigm of progressive education.

The CDC's recognition of an ordering principle for the curriculum remains a big deal, even if they failed to get much mileage out of it. The concept identifies the exact location where a shift in educational paradigms should begin. At this important juncture, educators must not rely on the paradigm of progressivism to supply a replacement. As De Graaf and others at the CDC found out, the interdisciplinary unit did not hold the key to implementing an education for a way of life. Van Brummelen and Steensma discovered that the same was true for a curriculum shaped by the academic disciplines.

In the early 2000s, the architects of Teaching for Transformation (TFT), led by Doug Monsma, Peter Buisman, and Brian Doonenbal, faced virtually the same challenge that De Graaf/Fernhout and Van Brummelen/Steensma did. They, too, believed Christian education must promote an alternative way of life. They did not have the term "ordering principle for the curriculum" in their academic vocabulary, but they intuitively understood their curriculum had to be designed differently in order for them to successfully implement their educational goal, which was to *help students understand and experience how their stories fit into God's story.*

At the critical point where De Graaf/Fernout and Van Brummelen/Steensma got sidetracked by the perennial debate over disciplinary or interdisciplinary curriculum design, TfT managed to implement a new ordering principle: see the story, live the story. How did they accomplish this? First, they employed the "understanding by design" (UBD) approach to curriculum planning created by Wiggins and McTighe.[315] In this approach the goal of education (entering God's story) shapes the curriculum and the core practices of teaching, not the other way around. Second, they were not content with an education that stressed head knowledge only; this kind of learning was ill suited to their purpose. They pursued the integrality of head, heart, and hand knowledge (HHH). This holistic kind of knowledge would have surely benefited the advocates of education for discipleship.

At a key point in the development of TfT, its creators realized they needed to focus on pedagogical reform even more than curricular reform.[316] Curricular reform is crucial to "see" and "understand" how one's own story can merge into God's bigger story, but, they realized, pedagogical reform—how classroom practices are carried out—is vital if students are going to "live" into the story.

The challenge for reform-minded CSC educators today is naming and committing to an ordering principle for curriculum design and classroom practice alike. They may well discover there is one principle for both.

Endnotes

224 E. Eisner and E. Vallance (eds.), *Conflicting Conceptions of the Curriculum.* (Berkeley, CA: *McCutchan*, 1974), 2.

225 Philip Jackson, "Conceptions of Curriculum and Curriculum Specialists," in *Handbook of Research on Curriculum: A Project of the American Educational Research Association*, ed. Philip Jackson (New York: Macmillan Publishing Co., 1992).

226 Harro Van Brummelen, rejoinder to John E. Hull, "Education for Discipleship: A Curriculum Orientation for Christian Educators," *The Journal of Education and Christian Belief* (Autumn 2009): 169-176.

227 Harro Van Brummelen, *Steppingstones to Curriculum: A Biblical Path*, 2nd Ed. (Colorado Springs, CO: Purposeful Design, 2002).

228 Jamie Smith, *Desiring the Kingdom: Worship, Worldview, and Cultural Formation* (Grand Rapids, MI: Baker Academic, 2009).

229 Susan Drake and Rebecca Burns, *Meeting Standards Through Integrated Curriculum* (Association for Supervision and Curriculum Development, 2004).

230 The CDC's story is presented in chapter 5.

231 See the discussion of Van Brummelen's curriculum theory in chapter 7.

232 See the last section in chapter 6.

233 Van Brummelen, *Steppingstones*, 169f.

234 Robert Sweetman, *Tracing the Lines: Spiritual Exercise and the Gesture of Christian Scholarship* (Eugene, OR: WIPF & Stock, 2016).

235 Sweetman, 8.

236 Sweetman, 66.

237 Sweetman, 80.

238 Sweetman, 10.

239 Peter DeBoer, *Shifts in Curriculum Theory for Christian Education* (Grand Rapids, MI: Calvin College Monograph, 1983).

240 Donald Oppewal, ed., *Voices from the Past: Reformed Educators* (Langham, ML: University Press of America, Inc, 1997).

241 Gloria Stronks, Clarence Joldersma, eds., *Educating for Life: Reflections on Christian Teaching and Learning* (Grand Rapids, MI, Baker Academic, 2002).

242 Peter DeBoer, "Shifts."

243 James Bratt, "Dutch Calvinism."

244 Oppewal, "Voices."

245 Nicolas Wolterstorff, "Beyond 1984 in Philosophy of Christian Education," in *Educating for Life: Reflections on Christian Teaching and Learning*, eds. Gloria Stronks and Clarence Joldersma (Grand Rapids, MI: Baker Academic, 2002) 66.

246 Wolterstorff, 21.

247 Wolterstorff, 69. Also discussed in chapter 5, "Publish and then Perish."

248 Wolterstorff, 69.

249 Wolterstorff, 70.

250 Oppewal, "Voices."

251 William Jellema, "The Curriculum in a Liberal Arts College," in *Voices from the Past: Reformed Educators*, ed. Donald Oppewal (Langham, ML: University Press of America, Inc, 1997), 5.

252 Jellema, 5.

253 Jellema, 11.

254 Jellema, 12-13.

255 Van Brummelen, "Telling," 178.

256 Nicolas Wolterstorff, "Beyond 1984," 63-83. An analysis of this speech appears in chapter 7.

257 Oppewal, "Voices," 184.

258 Oppewal, 184.

259 Oppewal, 184.

260 Oppewal, 185.

261 Oppewal, 190.

262 Oppewal, 191.

263 Oppewal, 195.

264 See the discussion of Steensma's contributions in chapter 7

265 Nicolas Wolterstorff, "Curriculum: By What Standard?" in *Educating for Life: Reflections on Christian Teaching and Learning*, eds. Gloria Stronks and Clarence Joldersma (Grand Rapids, MI: Baker Academic, 2002), 19.

266 Wolterstorff, 22.

267 Wolterstorff, 23.

268 Wolterstorff, 25.

269 Wolterstorff, 26.

270 Wolterstorff, 27.

271 Wolterstorff, 28.

272 Wolterstorff, 31.

273 Oppewal, "Voices," 121.

274 Nicholas Beversluis, *Christian Philosophy of Education* (Grand Rapids, MI: The National Union of Christian Schools, 1971), 3.

275 Beversluis, 15-16.

276 Beversluis, 36.

277 Beversluis, 36.

278 John Van Dyk has written a concise and clear analysis of these gaps in an article entitled "The Relation Between Faith and Action: An Introduction," *Pro Rege* X, 4, 1982, 207.

279 This approach is described in Dig Deeper, Topic V.

280 Barbara Benham Tye, "The Deep Structure of Schooling," *Phi Delta Kappan* (December 1987): 281-284.

281 James Bosco, "Is It Possible to Reform Schools?: Toward Solving the Riddle." Paper presented at the *9th International Conference on Technology and Education*, Paris France (Kalamazoo MI: Western Michigan University, Merze Tate Center for Research and Information Processing, 1992).

282 Bosco, "Is It Possible," 7.

283 Bosco.

284 Bosco. 10-15.

285 Bosco. 16.

286 Robert Maynard Hutchins died in 1977 at age 88. He served as dean of Yale Law School and chancellor of the University of Chicago, where he oversaw the implementation of a new approach to pedagogy in the undergraduate College of the University of Chicago. This new approach featured a curriculum based on the Great Books, the Socratic method of inquiry, and comprehensive exams. Hutchins was a leading advocate of secular perennialism.

287 David F. Labaree, "Progressivism, Schools and Schools of Education: An American Romance, *Paedagogica Historica*, Vol. 41, 1&2 (February 2005): 276.

288 Frederick Taylor, *The Principles of Scientific Management* (New York, 1911).

289 "Progressive Education," *Encyclopedia of Children and Childhood in History and Society*, Encyclopedia.com. (February 13, 2019), 5.

290 John Franklin Bobbit, *The Curriculum: a Summary of the Development Concerning the Theory of Curriculum* (New York: Houghton Mifflin Company, 1918).

291 Founder of the Core Knowledge Foundation, an organization dedicated to increasing the factual knowledge of elementary school children.

292 Edward L. Thorndike, "The Nature, Purposes, and General Methods of Measurements of Educational Products," *Seventeenth Yearbook, Part II* (Bloomington, IL: National Society for the Study of Education, 1918).

293 Ralph W. Tyler, *Basic Principles of Curriculum and Instruction* (Chicago, IL: University of Chicago Press, 1949).

294 Benjamin S. Bloom, *Taxonomy of Educational Objectives, Handbook I: Cognitive Domain* (New York: David McKay, 1956).

295 Eisner and Vallance, 7.

296 Lawrence Cremin, *The Transformation of the School: Progressivism in American Education, 1876–1957* (New York: Vintage Books, 1961).

297 David Tyack and Elisabeth Hansot, *Managers of Virtue: Public school Leadership in America, 1820–1980* (New York: Basic Books, 1982).

298 Herbert Kliebard, *The Struggle for the American Curriculum, 1893–1958* (New York: Routledge & Kegan Paul, 1986).

299 David Labaree, "Progressivism," 275-288.

300 Cremin, "The Transformation," viii-ix.

301 Labaree, 282.

302 Madhu Suri Prakash and Leonard Waks, "Four Conceptions," 4.

303 Harro Van Brummelen, *Steppingstones*, 9.

304 Labaree, "Progressivism," 277.

305 Labaree, 287.

306 Yvonna Lincoln, "The Making of a Constructivist: A Remembrance of Transformations Past," in *The Paradigm Dialogue, ed. E. G. Guba (Los Angeles: Sage, 1990),* 67-87.

307 See chapter 3 for details.

308 The information for this scenario comes from two main sources: a file in the CDC's archives contained the correspondence between Peter Enneson and the CCC. Harry Fernhout submitted an undated summary report, probably to the CDC board of directors, in mid to late 1984 titled: Chronological Summary of the CDC's interaction with the CCC.

309 SPICE stands for Summer Program in Christian Education. These were curriculum-writing workshops offered by the Association for the Advancement of Christian Scholarship and also, at times, the Ontario Alliance of Christian Schools.

310 See chapter 5, "What *Joy* was meant to Be," for an analysis of *JIL*.

311 Geraldine Steensma and Harro Van Brummelen, eds., *Shaping School Curriculum: A Biblical View* (Terre Haute, IN: Signal, 1977), 67-87.

312 Harry Fernhout, "Summary of Critique of *Shaping School Curriculum*," in *Shaping Christian Schools: A Conference* (Surrey, BC: Society of Christian Schools in British Columbia, 1981).

313 Fernhout, 5.

314 Fernhout, 6.

315 Grant Wiggins, Jay McTighe, *Understanding by Design* (Alexandria, VA: ASCD, 1998).

316 See chapter 9 for a more detailed account.

MEMOIR OF AN EDUCATOR

THE MAKING OF A REFORMATIONAL EDUCATOR (1947–1970)

Bob Dylan once recorded a song entitled "Gotta Serve Somebody."[317] He understood that the key question of our identity is not "Who are you?" but "Who owns you?" Which master we choose to serve is arguably the most important decision we ever make. It is a choice that comes with weighty consequences. It determines, for example, where and to whom we belong, and whether our hearts will be at peace, indifferent, or at war. In another song on the same album, Dylan says that our natural inclination is to "satisfy our wandering desires." In other words, we prefer to "be our own master." However, a life focused on serving oneself is a futile life. Dylan knew it, and so have all wise men and women.

The Bible tells us that God calls us into being (and expects us to be) human. Humans naturally participate in four natural relationships: with our creator, with fellow humans, with creation, and with ourselves (self-image). The authenticity of our humanity and the quality of our lives hinge on our engagement in these relationships; everything boils down to who is master, who is servant, and the integrity of the servant's service. Now that I am suddenly seventy-five, I more frequently reflect on my life generally and my career as a live-long educator. There are myriad ways to assess how well or poorly I served in my career as an educator. In this brief memoir, I mainly addressed two questions: "How well did my wandering desires overlap with my creaturely service to God?" and "Are their parallels between my own narrative to educate for hope and the larger story of the Neo-Calvinist tradition of education?"

My purpose for including this memoir, was to put a human face to a tradition of education that I hold dear, a tradition that has so much to offer to its advocates and those from other traditions who also desire a substantially different education for their children. Although we identify traditions of education with their stated visions, we experience them through our encounters with the teachers who are committed to these visions.

Nebraska – My Place of Orientation

At the same time that the Neo-Calvinist school system emerged in Canada, I lived out my youth and adolescence many miles away in the United States. No one could have predicted that a tradition which originated in the Netherlands more than a hundred years before my birth and was transplanted to Canadian soil after World War II would find me and dramatically reorient me to a different worldview, a foreign country, another community, and a new career path. Prior to that life-altering encounter, my life was shaped by my hometown experience.

Sutton, Nebraska, has had a constant population of 1,500 people for as long as anyone can remember. The town was founded in the mid-1800s by pioneer farmers just a few years after all the Great Plains bison were shot, and a remnant "Indian" population was resettled on reserves. Sutton prospered because two major transportation arteries that connected Chicago, Omaha, Lincoln, and Denver ran right through it, the Burlington Railroad and US Hwy. 6.

My hometown was an insular community where virtually everyone shared a common worldview. In that universe people went to church, voted Republican, and believed the United States was God's model for society, while the Soviet Union embodied evil. We deified the Nebraska Cornhuskers football team and despised the Oklahoma Sooners. The German immigrants who farmed north of town and attended a country church where sermons from a long-deceased pastor were read in German (still true today) were known to be good farmers but maligned as inbred, backward, social misfits. The Germans who lived in town, even if they were related to the Germans in the country, as I was, largely avoided these stigmas.

In Sutton everyone was white. It was socially acceptable to tell and laugh at jokes about "n***ers," "spicks," and "kikes." If we had known about homosexuals, we would have slandered them as well. We practiced a "soft racism," if there is such a thing. There were no visible victims of our racism because racial minorities did not live in or anywhere near Sutton. I never saw an African-American until I was in my mid-teens, and I never shared my personal space with a person of colour until I went to college. Friendships with people we now associate with LGBTQIA+ only emerged in my thirties. In my privileged, white, narrow-minded world, Indigenous people only existed as ignorant, painted warriors in Hollywood Western movies. We assumed, as most white Americans did, that we had killed them all decades ago.

Everyone in Sutton went to the public school. All but the last two years of my K-12 education took place in the old factory-style, two-storey brick box erected in 1912. My class was the second to graduate from the new, round school building built on the edge of town in 1964. I experienced joy in my learning prior to grade three and very little afterward. I quickly learned that the point of assignments was to complete them and then move on to the next one. The primary purpose of learning was to pass to the next grade level. Along the way I had several good teachers, a few incompetent ones, and many who were mediocre. No matter what level of competence they possessed, my teachers did not pursue relationships with their students; we lived in two solitudes within the same building.

I admired two of my teachers in high school. Our one-armed math teacher, Mr. Schaal, was an effective teacher, but it was his stories that made him special. On occasion we could coerce him into telling us about his high school and college days. He was the only teacher who ever made himself vulnerable to us by revealing aspects of his personal life, like how he lost his left arm in a car crash. Mr. Vreeland was a quirky English teacher who would leave us spell-bound with his readings of Edger Allen Poe. I remember how he pounded out a heartbeat on the podium when he read the *Tell-Tale Heart* and the time he climbed up on his desk and jumped onto the silver radiators that heated our classroom while reciting "The Raven." This feat was particularly remarkable because Mr. Vreeland was a short, paunchy, unathletic fellow who always came to school dressed in a dark, sweat-stained suit.

My ethnic origins are best described as "American mongrel." My pedigree is a combination of German and English ancestry from my father and German and Welsh from my mother. My relatives were predominantly poor, uneducated, and often coarse, especially on my father's side. My family exerted the greatest impact on my formation, but even now I am unable to explain the breadth and depth of it. In this memoir I will only focus briefly on my parents.

My father missed nearly all the important events in my life in Sutton because he was a long-distance trucker providing for our family the best way he knew how. Dad was the oldest child in a dysfunctional sharecropper family. He fought in WWII as a Sherman tank driver. He rarely told me and my four younger brothers his war stories, but we knew the experience was a formative one in his life. My dad loved to hunt and fish, but he rarely found the opportunity to do either; the times he took me along I can count on one hand. He did teach me about hunting safety: "A shotgun in the car is never loaded, you and your gun don't pass through a fence at the same time, the safety stays on until the moment before you pull the trigger, and always be aware of your surroundings before shooting."

My mother was a hairdresser who worked out of our home for a time. She also took shifts as a night cook preparing the next day's meals at the local nursing home. We lived from paycheque to paycheque all the years that I lived at home. We existed on the poor side of middle class, but my brothers and I never knew that. My mother single-handedly raised us. For the first thirty-five years of her married life, she lived for the weekends when my dad would come home from the road. Long after I moved out, my dad finally landed jobs that allowed him to be home every night.

I was close to my mother. As her oldest child, she expected a lot from me. Mom and I often engaged in serious talks. Whenever I came home from a game or a date, I had to pass by her bedroom door on my way to the older boys' room. She always called me to her bedside, so we could chat for a while about my date or my game. I learned many things from my mother. She taught me practical stuff like how to dance, iron shirts, match the colours of my clothes, mow the grass, and identify weeds. Most significant of all, she was instrumental in my faith development. I also inherited some unfortunate biases and behaviours from my mother. Like her, I avoided conflict at all costs, and it took me years to learn how to fight fair and resolve differences with those I loved. For a time I shared her beliefs that reputation (appearances) means everything and Roman Catholics are not real Christians, even if they are decent people. My mother kept a tight rein on me. I needed her permission to do almost anything social until I was eighteen. I wanted to please her, so I did not rebel against her control. She held me to a high moral standard, and I credit her for the fact that I entered marriage still a virgin.

My parents modelled love, commitment, and faithfulness to each other throughout their sixty years of marriage. I was not surprised by the last three words my seventy-eight-year-old mother spoke to my father when we stood beside his open coffin just before I ushered her into the church sanctuary for his funeral. "Goodbye, my lover," she said. How does one calculate the positive influence that parents who are deeply committed to each other have on their children?

For as long as I can remember, I have identified as a Christian. It was my maternal grandma, Asta Wiard, and my mother who oriented me to the Christian faith as a young child. Grandma Asta's people were German Calvinists who immigrated to America in the early 1900s after farming in Russia for a hundred years. The two Reformed churches they established in Sutton belonged to a small denomination named the Reformed Church in the United States (RCUS). Growing up in that church, I equated Christianity with the memorization of the Heidelberg Catechism. From age five to my confirmation at age thirteen, I spent many hours memorizing and reciting this catechism. At the time of my confirmation, I could recite all 129 questions and answers from memory, a process that took nearly an hour to complete. Ironically, I cannot recite any of it today! Throughout my childhood and adolescence, what most motivated my Christian convictions was not a love of Jesus but a fear of going to Hell. Contrary to the message of the first question and answer in the catechism, my only comfort in life did not come from knowing that I belonged, body and soul, to my faithful Saviour but from knowing that what my church believed was the true version of Christianity.

To have the right beliefs defined my understanding of Christianity for too many years of my life. The church failed to instill in me any responsibility to act justly and mercifully toward those in need. I was born into what Richard Rohr calls a "transactional Christianity." I was taught that if we believe the right things, say the right prayer, and practice the right rituals, things will go right for us in the divine courtroom. During my adolescence my transactional faith manifested itself most clearly when I engaged in "religious discussions" with my Catholic classmates. In these one-sided conversations, I not only informed them what Catholics believed, I also adroitly explained to them why it was wrong. Through such behaviours, I developed a reputation among my classmates as the "religious person."

My favourite Old Testament figure wasn't Noah, Moses, or David, but Solomon. When Solomon was given the opportunity by God to have anything he wanted, he chose wisdom. God granted his wish and rewarded Solomon with prosperity as well. Since my childhood, I, too, prayed that I might be wise, and I can honestly say, I did so not because I expected wealth to follow on its heels. Wisdom was clearly the better gift. Initially, I equated wisdom with believing the right things, but eventually, my transactional Christianity gave way to a more compassionate Christianity. Marking this process of change, my list of absolute truths has steadily diminished. I am now down to one: Jesus is who he said he was. My great regret as a person of faith is how long it took me to become a true servant of wisdom.

Years later I realized that my faith orientation back in Sutton was actually not so different from most other Christians who lived in the American Midwest at the time. We all identified as Americans first, Christians second, and Republicans third. This image of ourselves was never problematic because these identities were virtually synonymous in our worldview vocabulary.

The biggest question I ever had to answer in my youth confronted me at the end of grade 12: what happens after high school graduation? My world presented me with three options: go fight in Vietnam, get married, or attend college. As a fledgling forced to leave the nest, I felt ill prepared to fly in any of these directions. Of course, attending a college was the only sensible choice among those available. My pastor, Peter Grossman, told my parents and me about a Christian liberal arts college in Iowa that he thought would be the perfect place for me to get the pre-seminary education I desired. The school had been started by Dutch Calvinists associated with the Christian Reformed Church, and it bore the odd name of Dordt College (now University).

I already knew in grade ten that I would be among the fifty percent of each graduating class that did not end up living in Sutton for life. There was no farm or family business for me to work at and eventually take over. Despite knowing this, I was not prepared when the time came to leave home, and I "heard" this unspoken message from my parents: "You are well loved and always welcome here, but after you graduate from high school, you are basically on your own." I had to find my own way at college as every freshman must, but I also had to find a new home. I started to feel alone and afraid before I ever left town.

I was the first male on either side of my family to go to college. I only had the vaguest idea about my future. In retrospect I understand that while growing up in Sutton I was oriented to two visions for my life, one public and the other private. The public vision was the American dream of success and consumption; it was a way of life that my family pursued but struggled to attain. The private, Christian vision amounted to holding the right theological views and living a good moral life. At that time, I had no inkling of how incompatible this pairing of visions was with the life of service that Jesus actually calls his followers to take up. But that was about to change.

Iowa – A Place of Disorientation and Reorientation

Any confidence I might have had about who I was, what I believed, where I belonged in the world, and where I was headed and why soon evaporated at Dordt College. I experienced culture shock when I moved to Sioux Center, Iowa, even though it was a mere 300 miles from home. The theological differences between the German Calvinism of my Reformed Church in the US and the Dutch Calvinism of the Christian Reformed Church were negligible. However, the ethnic idiosyncrasies and customs of the two faith traditions were significantly different. It puzzled me why CRC people had to pray before and after a meal or go to church twice on Sunday and not attend Wednesday night Bible study. There was enough cachet in the "just joking" slogan, "If you aren't Dutch, you aren't much," that I often found myself on the margins of Dordt's campus life. My first two years at Dordt College were marked by loneliness and a nagging question. What had I gotten myself into?

Despite all my efforts to be a good student during my first two years at Dordt, I did not fare well in the classroom. The pre-seminary course of study required me to take two years of Greek and a semester of Latin. Because I planned to serve churches where many older folks spoke German as their first language, I also decided to take two years of German. My abysmal performance in high school Spanish should have alerted me to the challenges I would encounter learning multiple languages simultaneously, even with the aid of good professors.

My disorientation at Dordt College reached its zenith during my second year. My life plan was in disarray. Nothing in the pre-seminary program of study inspired me. I struggled to maintain a C+ GPA. Never had my grades been so poor, or my interest in learning so low. Life outside the classroom was no better. I systematically struck out with the few women that I found attractive until I met a girl with stunning blue eyes sometime in November of my second year. My relationship with Sandy, was as immature as my one high school "going steady" experience with Jacque. We used each other to distract ourselves from the pressing issues that burdened our individual lives. My life quest to be just like my pastor, Peter, imperceptibly eroded away. I became a person without a plan, and I was in desperate need of hope.

Everything changed for the better during the fall term of my third year. Three new people entered my life, and because of them, I was never the same. On the first day of classes, one of my roommates introduced me to a freshman named Glenda, who hailed from his hometown. I was immediately smitten by her beauty and personality. She has been my heart's desire ever since. Somehow, we managed to successfully navigate the landmines of our small-town America dating cultures over the next two years, and we eventually married. As I write this, we have moved past our fiftieth wedding anniversary. To quote John Prine, "She is my everything."

That fall I also became best friends with Bob Vander Plaats. He was a year behind me and also in the pre-seminary program. Bob was a brilliant person who infected me with a love for philosophy and the fun of singing folk music. He taught me how to write research papers, and I took him fishing. We shared many adventures over the next two years.

That third fall term at Dordt College, I still needed a couple of philosophy courses to fulfil the requirements for the pre-seminary program. I took these courses from a new philosophy/theology professor from Canada named John Vander Stelt. He impacted my life more than all of my other teachers combined! He also made a large and lasting difference in the lives of dozens of other students at that time and throughout his long and illustrious career. Students like Bob and me felt liberated by Vander Stelt's lectures and inspired by the intensity, urgency, and passion of his persona.

I can recall many examples that demonstrate how Vander Stelt impacted my life, but I will cite just three. Vander Stelt and his wife, Sandy, opened up their home to us students. We were regularly invited over to engage in conversations about world events while sipping coffee and eating baked goods. No other professor invested so much of themselves in us.

Glenda and I once told Vander Stelt about a problem that we were having. After giving us some wise counsel, he said, "I will pray for you," as we parted. I knew this was not a cheap promise. If Vander Stelt said he would pray for you, it likely meant bringing your case before the Almighty at some length and with considerable passion. The thing is, no one had ever said they would pray for me before, not even my mother, though I know she did regularly. I can still remember how loved those five words made us feel.

Vander Stelt's teaching was rooted in the Reformational philosophy he learned from Herman Dooyeweerd and D. H. Th. Vollenhoven, who taught at the Free University of Amsterdam. Reformational philosophy, or Dooyeweerdian philosophy, as it was often called, offered Christian scholars an alternative way to account for the coherence of reality rooted in what they called law structures. The key feature of Dooyeweerd's philosophy was his theory of modalities or recognizable ways of being in the world. For his part, Vollenhoven designed an elaborate system for cataloguing all of the major philosophical positions that made up the history of Western thought. His Problem-Historical method assumed all the schools of philosophical thought that belonged to the timeline of the Western intellectual tradition were embedded in a particular "time-current" and addressed a basic set of bifurcating ontological problems in particular ways. He devised a complex method that cross-referenced each philosophy in terms of its contemporary current of thought and its type of ontology.

The scope of Vander Stelt's teaching went beyond his elucidation of the fine points of Reformational philosophy. He unpacked for us the biblical worldview that inspired this philosophy and the vision of cultural transformation that gave it legs. His efforts, combined with those of a few other professors like John Van Dyk and Hugh Cook, led to a small but controversial movement. Adherents, sympathizers, and opponents all referred to this sea change of Christian thought as the Reformational Movement. Many students on Dordt's campus were oblivious to the movement's existence. Some were intrigued by its message, but only a handful of professors and a few dozen students, including me, identified with it. What united us was a common commitment to deepen our understanding of a biblical worldview and incorporate it into our lives. Given the degree of concern over this movement that arose among some faculty and students, one would have thought the Reformational Movement numbered in the hundreds and threatened to take over the campus.

Many people inside and outside the Reformational Movement at Dordt College thought of it as an intellectual movement, and it was for the most part. However, what Vander Stelt shared with us was more than a philosophy or a theology; it was a desire to reclaim every chunk of culture for the Kingdom of God. At its heart it was a movement that reoriented Christians to a life characterized by acts of justice, mercy, and peace, especially toward those on the margins of society. I was intrigued by the philosophy, but what challenged me most was his vision of the Christian life.

Midway through my junior year, I found myself at a crossroad. Would I continue to pursue the pre-seminary program and my goal to "be like Peter," my hometown pastor, or would I reorient myself to the Reformational Movement that was beginning to catch fire?

In December of my third year, I dropped out of the pre-seminary program. My parents and others from my home church were shocked when they eventually learned that I no longer planned to become a minister in our denomination. Their disappointment weighed on my conscience, but I felt a much greater burden had been lifted from me. For the first time in two and a half years, I enjoyed my studies. I finally found my groove as a student.

The decision to drop the pre-seminary course of study meant I had to choose a new major. I chose philosophy, not because I imagined myself a philosopher but because philosophy was the epicentre of the Reformational Movement on campus.

My reorientation to a more expansive vision of Christianity did not take place overnight, nor did it reach its climax at Dordt College. I seriously pursued my studies in philosophy during my last two years at Dordt College, but I remained a young man who could be easily distracted.

It was inevitable, I suppose, that my new trajectory would bring me into conflict with my home denomination. My parents accepted my decision not to become a pastor, but they struggled to understand and/or agree with my views about the church and the need for a second Protestant Reformation. When I visited home, we talked about such matters without generating too much emotional heat. My friend, Pastor Peter, never expressed any concerns about my decision. By this time he had moved to a church in another state and was having marital difficulties. The conflict arose unexpectedly in early November 1970, just weeks before I finished my studies at Dordt, and Glenda and I got married.

I received a letter from the minister of a South Dakota congregation in my home denomination, a man whom I had met for the first time some weeks earlier when he had visited campus to check up on some students from his congregation. I had no idea why he would send me a letter, but it did not take long to find out that what I held in my hands was the only "pastoral letter" I have ever received. The letter expressed two concerns that this minister had about our recent and brief conversation, a discussion that I only vaguely remembered. To begin, the pastor shared his concern over my view that the instituted church in general, and the RCUS in particular, was irrelevant. He was also concerned that I believed the historic creeds of the church needed updating.

He was right about the fact that I held these views. I believed the instituted church was generally unresponsive to the people on the margins of society who pleaded for justice and mercy. I also thought it was time the church developed a new creed that would address its life in our current time.

As I read deeper into the letter, I came face to face with the vision that animated the RCUS tradition: the church is society's theological gatekeeper, the Bible is a set of logical propositions, and RCUS ministers understand these propositions better than anyone else. My suspicion that my home denomination had lost sight of the central tenet of Christ's ministry, which is to care for the most vulnerable in society, was confirmed by this letter. The tradition had become so focused on staring into the light of Scripture, it had become too blind to see the path that that light was meant to illuminate.

After signing off with a "warm regards in Christ," he unloaded on me in a postscript. There at the bottom of the page, he said that he had just received news that I was "trying to get men to leave the RCUS." He didn't reveal the source of this accusation, and he was quick to say that this might not actually be true, but he informed me that the matter was causing enough confusion that he had asked the governing body of our church to investigate the matter. His accusations and actions were so outrageous that I did not take him seriously.

As fall turned to winter in December 1970, my plans for the future were not well developed, but I knew the general direction I wanted to follow. Vander Stelt had sketched out the broad outlines of a scenario for his students just as Professor Runner at Calvin College had done for him, and I sought a place in that grand scheme. He told us there was a critical weakness in the edifice of Reformed Christian education and scholarship in North America. Dutch Calvinists in the United States had been building this tradition of education since the late 1800s, and over the past twenty-five years, Canadian Neo-Calvinists had added dozens of Christian elementary and secondary schools to this school system. Dutch Neo-Calvinists in the United States had also established three liberal arts colleges: Calvin College, Dordt College, and Trinity Christian College. These colleges prepared most of the teachers who taught in the system's high schools and elementary schools. They also educated many more students from the Dutch immigrant community to engage the spirits of the age in other areas of culture. The problem was that the college professors at these institutions of higher learning were themselves educated at secular universities where they obtained their master's degrees and doctorates. This dependency on graduate programs framed by secular worldviews put the philosophical purity of the Reformed tradition of Christian education at risk. Removing this dependency upon secular institutions was critical, Vander Stelt believed, and the only institution in North America dedicated to that cause was the newly established Institute for Christian Studies (ICS) in Toronto. Convinced that I had a role to play in this scenario, my first step away from Dordt College was to move to Toronto and study philosophy at the ICS. I finally found a cause to live for. Where this first step would eventually take Glenda and me, we had no idea, but at the time this was not a big concern.

After we were married in December 1970, Glenda and I had seven months to save as much money as we could before we moved to Canada.

There was a major obstacle in our way, however: the Vietnam war. My birthday lottery number for the draft was low, and I had passed my army physical. I was days away from being drafted. I had already decided that I was not going to war, even if it meant fleeing to Canada. An official letter from the ICS, which stated that I was enrolled in their program "to study for the Lord's service," turned out to be sufficient evidence for my draft board to grant me a theological deferment. By means of this not exactly factual expression of the truth, I avoided the Vietnam war without becoming a draft dodger.

To wrap up this segment of my story, I feel it is important to report how my interpretation of my time at Dordt College has changed over time. My initial, say, ten-year old memory of that experience is reflected by the title I chose for this section: I understood it as a time of dis-orientation moving toward reorientation. When I became disenchanted with my pre-seminary program, I felt lost, homeless, and disconnected. My participation in the Reformational Movement, by contrast, invigorated and enlarged my Christian perspective. In that movement I found a new sense of direction, purpose, and community.

At around age forty, it dawned on me that my reorientation at Dordt College was not as radical as I had always imagined it. As liberating as Reformational thinking was for me at the time, I realized later that it had been little more than a reincarnation of the misguided belief that I had inherited from my own denomination. At home I had reduced the Christian faith to holding the right theological views. As a participant in the Reformational Movement, I had simply substituted having the right philosophy. I never regretted trading in a suspect theology for a sophisticated philosophy, but I am sorry that it took me so long to move beyond an intellectualized Christianity. I did not fault Vander Stelt for this outcome then, nor do I now. He never reduced Christianity to Reformational thinking. Even though he was a career academic who taught with passion in both theology and philosophy departments—a vocation that required him to spend most of his waking hours thinking about foundational issues in both disciplines—he advocated for, and lived, a life of selfless service.

I am less critical of those days now, for I see something else that I missed before. I have considered the possibility that I am conjuring up a memory, but I believe my new understanding is still rooted in that past reality. As I now recall that time and set it within the context of the life I have lived since, I believe the Reformational Movement set me on a life path of hope. In the preface of this book, I acknowledged that it was my friend, Roy Berkenbosch, who alerted me to St. Augustine's observation that Hope has two beautiful daughters named Anger and Courage: anger at how things are and courage to see they do not remain the same.

The Reformational perspective that I received from Professors Vander Stelt, Van Dyk, and others, levelled a devastating critique at the spirits of the age, not only those powers and principalities that directed our culture and rationalized the good life of material consumption but also those within the church that allowed Christianity to become a civic religion that accommodated our indulgent American Dream way of life. The more this critique resonated within me, the more I embraced the angry daughter of Hope. I remember that I was righteously angry about the injustices of the Vietnam war, the plight of African Americans, the materialist lifestyle of the white middle class, and the reluctance of the institutional church to address the social injustices experienced by the marginalized in society. The daughter named Courage was more elusive, however, and it took many years before I embraced her. Now when I think back to my reorientation at Dordt College, this new image comes to mind: I am walking down the path of hope between its two beautiful daughters. I have one arm wrapped around righteous Anger, but the arm next to the daughter named Courage remains close to my side, its hand jammed inside my pocket.

THE REMAKING OF A REFORMATIONAL EDUCATOR (1971–1995)

In early July 1971, Glenda and I left my parents' home, where we had been living rent free for the previous six months to save money. We set out for Canada, driving a partially-paid-for 1965 Chevy Caprice that pulled a tarped, two-wheeled homemade trailer full of mostly unopened wedding gifts. We had my student visa that would get us across the border and approximately $500 in cash to set up our new lives in Toronto. My inexperience at packing a trailer partially depleted our meager savings and led to some anxious moments on our trip. Due to the excessive weight on the trailer's tongue, the hitch broke loose from the car in the middle of a rainy night on Interstate 80. The safety chains averted a major disaster. We spent that night sleeping in our car outside a welding shop in a small town somewhere in western Illinois.

With a welded hitch and a rearranged load in our trailer, we reached the Canadian border, crossing between Detroit and Windsor in the early afternoon of our second day on the road. Our entry into Canada was the first of many eventful border crossings that we experienced over the next five years. On this occasion we had to declare all the goods that we were bringing into Canada, which meant writing out a description and serial number for each item in our trailer on the appropriate form. While Glenda patiently waited inside the air-conditioned customs building, I sat amongst our trailer's contents under a sweltering sun, dutifully opening boxes and recording serial numbers. After about an hour, I slipped over to the dark side and started to make up the remaining serial numbers, so we could get on our way. Fortunately, my lapse in judgment never came back to bite us.

Toronto – Fantasy Meets Reality

I am still not sure if we were brave, naïve, or just plain foolish when we rolled into Toronto in the early evening with only the address and phone number of the Institute for Christian Studies (ICS) in hand. At that time the ICS was illegally located on the ground floor of a large two-storey brick home in an older but stately residential neighbourhood just north of the city centre. We finally found the house, and the young couple, John and Jenny Hultink, who lived on the second floor told us about a reception for new students that was taking place downtown at the Newman Centre near the University of Toronto. The reception was over by the time we arrived, but we met some people we knew, including our best friend, Bob, and his new wife, Nancy. The next two nights the four of us crashed on the living room floor of an apartment that belonged to some ICS supporters who we met that at the reception.

Within two days Bob, Nancy, Glenda, and I had rented an unfurnished two-bedroom second-floor apartment about a twenty-minute walk from the ICS. We furnished our new home with second-hand furniture that cost us a total of one hundred dollars. The following week, Glenda found a job at a dry cleaner's shop in the wealthy Forest Hills area. The owners were willing to pay her wages in cash, and it was just enough to cover the rent and food. Classes at the ICS were set to begin in a few weeks, and I was so ready.

Life in Toronto that fall was full of surprises, some trivial, some instructive, some delightful, and one that was incredibly painful. We quickly discovered that we did not need a car; we could easily traverse the city using its amazing transit system. This was fortuitous because our car was repossessed at Christmas due to our inability to make the remaining monthly payments. I learned that I had no stomach for smoking a pipe, so I abandoned that romantic image of a scholar. We had no illusions about our ability to experience Toronto's extensive arts, theatre, and music scenes, but we managed to scratch enough money together to see a Crosby, Stills, Nash, and Young concert at Massey Hall in October.

From what we had heard about the ICS, we expected to find a vibrant Reformational community in Toronto just waiting to take us in, but the ICS had no capacity to function as the organizational hub of a community, and it was unrealistic for us to think it could, despite what we had heard. I had two encounters with the larger but dispersed Reformational community that existed in Ontario at the time, and both happened before I attended my first class. In late July, Bob and I often "helped around the house" to get the ICS ready for classes, which were set to start the day after Labour Day. One day we met Gerald Vande Zande, who worked for the Christian Labour Association of Canada (CLAC). Gerald was a wise man and a saint. In fact, he was awarded the Order of Canada in 2001.

When Gerald met Bob and me, he insisted that we join him downtown later that week. He promised that we would see firsthand the struggle to bring about the Kingdom of God in Canadian society. I am sure he was so insistent that we come because he feared ICS students would spend too much time thinking and not enough time engaging the real world.

On the appointed day, we met Gerald on the fourteenth floor of a high-rise office building on University Avenue in the heart of Toronto. He took us into a hearing room of the Ontario Labour Relations Board. What Bob and I experienced at that hearing highlights some of the challenges and ironies that the Reformational community encountered as it tried to incarnate a biblical worldview into a secular society. In this hearing, Gerald represented a General Motors worker named Ted, who wanted the board to grant him the option to donate his United Auto Workers union dues to a charity. Ted's case was built on the premise that he had to be a member of the United Auto Workers to work at GM, even though the union's worldview and adversarial negotiation practices conflicted with his Christian faith. Gerald argued that Ted's situation was unjust and a violation of his beliefs. The option to pay his dues to a charity was presented as a reasonable compromise. The UAW cleverly countered by bringing forward the shop steward who oversaw the area on the assembly line where Ted worked. Like Ted, this man was of Dutch ethnicity and a member of the Christian Reformed Church. Unlike Ted, he saw no conflict between his Christian faith and paying dues to the UAW.

Gerald wanted us to see a living example of worldviews in conflict, albeit between two white guys with good paying jobs. This experience is particularly memorable for me because a few years later the shop steward and I lived on the same street eighty kilometers away, and all three of Ted's children took their turn as students in my high school classroom.

The second experience took place a few days later and a couple of hours' drive outside the city when we attended the annual family conference sponsored by the Association for the Advancement of Christian Scholarship (AACS). This annual event was held on the August civic holiday weekend at the campus of Niagara Christian College, which was situated on the Niagara River, just upstream from the falls. The conference featured academic lectures, singing, and worship times, as well as wall-to-wall camping on the campus lawn and at Miller's Creek Campground next door. Nearly a thousand Reformational-minded people from Dutch Christian Reformed Church communities scattered across Ontario gathered there each year to deepen their biblical perspective on life; experience a more informal, authentic worship; meet old friends; make new ones; and camp out in their tents or small trailers. This was the community that we had heard about and longed to join but could not find in Toronto. In reality, this community did not belong to any single location; it came together once every year when its scattered members met at that conference. Like most attendees, we felt the weekend experience was a little taste of heaven.

Studying at the ICS that fall was a one-of-a-kind experience because the institute had no academic programs and offered no degrees. The senior members offered lecture and seminar courses each term. The lecture courses attracted both the serious and the not-so-serious students. They dealt with a combination of foundational and current topics in one or more of the following areas: systematic philosophy, theology, ethics, aesthetics, psychology, history, and the history of philosophy. As I recall, the lecture courses were partially designed to meet the perceived needs of students.

In contrast, the content of the seminar courses was directly linked to the research of a senior member and was geared to the most serious students like Bob and me. Since we considered ourselves to be philosophers in the making, we took the seminar offered by Hendrik Hart, the senior member in systematic philosophy. He was in the midst of writing his big book on epistemology, and that fall he happened to be focused on the rise of theory in the Middle Ages. Consequently, I spent many hours in the St. Michael's College library on the University of Toronto campus researching the rise of the university in medieval Europe. I enjoyed this work, but I never thought much about its relevance for my own future as an academic. I was never encouraged to pick an area of research that I wanted to pursue while I was at the ICS. Had that happened, I do not think I would have known what to choose.

The evolution of a worship community was the most delightful surprise for us that fall. Rev. Morris Greidanus was the Christian Reformed chaplain on the University of Toronto campus at that time. He held Sunday morning Bible study/prayer services in the stately Hart House building. This gathering was seen as an alternative to going to a mainline church for many people floating around the ICS. Over the next two years, this Bible study morphed into a vibrant worship community. The authentic worship and relationships we experienced there reminded us of our informal Followers of the Way services led by John Vander Stelt back in Iowa.

The biggest surprise of that fall was also the most devastating. Glenda and I were aware that Bob and Nancy had started to smoke dope and regularly met with Bob's older brother, Dave, and his friend, Albert, to discuss Marxist writings. What we did not anticipate was how divisive their new interests would become. By late November it was painfully clear that Bob and Nancy had acquired views and a lifestyle that conflicted with ours. We felt pressured to either join them or part company. We chose to part ways. The loss of our good friend Bob broke our hearts.

Glenda and I found a furnished basement apartment in a predominantly Jewish neighbourhood located at Lawrence and Bathurst. When we moved in at the beginning of December, our lease required us to pay for the first and last months' rent. Even though the rent for our new apartment was only ninety-five dollars per month, our hand-to-mouth budget was maxed out. We paid Mrs. Cohen, then ate oatmeal for a week until Glenda got paid again.

We rebooted our life in Toronto in January 1972, and our situation was much improved in several key ways. We continued to mourn the loss of Bob and Nancy, but for the first time in our married lives we had a home to ourselves. We also had neighbours. Three other married couples who had ICS connections lived within walking distance of us, and a fourth couple resided a short bus ride away. Over the next eighteen months we became a tightly knit group. We gathered almost weekly to socialize, play games, and drink cheap Mateus rosé, which was all any of us could afford.

In the early summer of 1972, we decided to become landed immigrants, so both of us could work legally. It is unthinkable now, but at that time it was possible to apply for, and receive, landed immigrant status at any border crossing. To qualify we needed a certain number of points, and points were awarded for things like years of education, age, marital status, good health, and, most importantly, the guarantee of a job. We did not know how many points we actually needed or how many we could muster, but we believed we qualified. I had in hand the all-important job-offer from a Dutch construction contractor named John Veldman. Veldman was a strong supporter of the ICS, and he hired ICS students to work for him when he needed extra help. For most of April, May, and June, I helped him build a restroom facility two hours away on the shores of Georgian Bay in Penetanguishene. We drove up on Mondays and returned on Saturday mornings. During the week we slept in a motel and ate all three daily meals in the local Chinese restaurant. There was plenty of time for conversation, and by late June Veldman knew vastly more about my beliefs and aspirations than my parents did. In return, I understood much about the Dutch immigration experience and why a builder with a limited formal education felt so strongly about Christian higher education. Veldman felt no guilt about offering me a job that he knew I would never take, just so we could immigrate to Canada.

Our plan to immigrate was simple but incredibly risky. We rented a car with some friends who hailed from Chicago and then drove with them to the windy city for the July long weekend, so we could visit some old friends we knew who lived there. The plan was for us to apply for landed immigrant status at our favourite Windsor border crossing on our way back to Toronto. Incredibly, we had no back-up plan if our application was declined. Since we had to turn in our student visas as part of our application to become landed immigrants, we would not be able to live in Canada if we failed to qualify.

The customs officer who interviewed us was clearly having a bad day. He appeared agitated and under extreme stress. He did not seem to like us very much, and as the interview progressed, we began to worry that we were not going to get our status. About midway into our interview, he abruptly got up and left. At that point we were very concerned about our situation. When fifteen minutes passed, and the officer still had not returned, another officer stopped by and inquired if we were being helped. We explained the situation to him, and he disappeared to check on our missing officer. The second officer returned a few minutes later with our paperwork and resumed our interview. He finished asking us the remaining questions and made some notes, but he did not tell us our score. To this day we don't know if we actually had enough points, but our hearts rejoiced when he smiled at us, apologized for what had happened, and handed us our landed immigrant cards.

On July 13, 1973, God gave us a healthy, beautiful son, whom we named Christopher. In August we moved out of our tiny basement apartment into the High Park area, where we rented a large house that we shared with three single ICS students. Two other couples in our Lawrence and Bathurst group also moved; one left town, and the other separated. We rebooted for the third time in two years.

I entered my third year of studies at the ICS as a part-time student because I needed to work to support our family of three. That year the ICS made some important strides as an institution. Faculty and students worked together to map out programs of study and degree requirements. The degrees would not be recognized by any accrediting agency, but at least students who had taken courses for the past several years had some idea of what they needed to "graduate." I was a little more than halfway finished with the newly minted MPhil degree.

Thirteen months later, Glenda and I faced the greatest test of our lives. Christopher fell into a campfire and severely burned both of his hands.

He spent the next six months in Sick Kids Hospital. Glenda saw him every day. During a lengthy transit strike, she had to hitchhike back and forth. Over the next three years, our young son endured many skin graft operations, and we did our best to take care of each other and not lose our faith. I am forever grateful for Dr. Hugh Thompson's pioneering work in skin grafting, for Glenda's great capacity to care for our son during that time and for Christopher's amazing resilience. As often happens when tragedy rears its ugly head, we were buoyed up by countless acts of loving support from the people around us as well as from people we did not know but who knew of us through the Reformational Movement's communication grapevine

As we entered our fourth year of living in Toronto, the demands to provide for a family and complete my studies were overwhelming. I did all that I could to finish the MPhil degree in systematic philosophy in time to participate in the first-ever ICS graduation in the fall of 1975. My prospects did not look promising at the beginning of that academic year because my mentor was away on a leave of absence. To complete the program, I had to take my two remaining courses with Al Wolters, who was the senior member in the history of philosophy, then somehow, write a thesis in systematic philosophy without a mentor. To their credit, the ICS faculty proposed that I combine the major papers required for the two courses in ancient philosophy to serve as my thesis. I gratefully accepted their offer, but there were serious problems inherent in this plan. I had not studied ancient philosophy at the ICS; all of my work had focused on the theory of knowledge and the rise of the university in the Middle Ages. The thesis I would have to write and defend would not be the thesis that I was prepared to write.

As problematic as this arrangement was, I embraced the opportunity to finish my ICS degree in the 1974–75 academic year. I was motivated in part by the prospect of being in the first graduating class at the ICS. In reality, I had no choice. I had already spent three years at the ICS working on the MPhil degree. My slow pace was directly tied to my need to work part time. Glenda and I had struggled just to pay our bills. Our bare-bones lifestyle had to end soon. Thankfully, Ontario's provincial health plan paid for all of Christopher's surgeries. It was in the midst of this desperate situation that I took Wolter's two courses in ancient philosophy, wrote a master's thesis on the Greek Stoics, and delivered furniture for the T. Eaton Co.

Forty-seven years have passed since I graduated from the ICS as a member of its first graduating class. I have sometimes wondered why I was so committed to the ICS while I studied there. Was I a dreamer, a committed believer in a vision, or naïve to the point of being foolish? I found truth in all three answers when I discovered an interview that was published in the spring 1975 issue of the ICS *Perspective* newsletter. That issue featured a conversation between the editor and three students, one being me. The interviewer asked me how it felt investing so much time and energy into obtaining a degree that no one recognized and would not, in all probability, qualify me for any academic position that I might pursue in the future. I acknowledged that this was the stark reality for those of us who were about to graduate, but I said all the sacrifices that I had made over the past four years to study at the ICS were my way of paying back AACS supporters (people like John Veldman) who had also sacrificed much to establish the institute. I went on to say that my dedication to the ICS was integral to my pursuit of a Christian academic vocation. I hoped that my determination and commitment would be recognized and rewarded somehow. I trusted that somewhere in the Christian community there was a place for me to serve as an academic. There it was in print, the cause that animated my life in my twenties. Was I a dreamer, a visionary, or a fool? Yes!

What I failed to mention in the interview was my aspiration to continue with my studies at the ICS and pursue the doctorate degree which the ICS was planning to offer in conjunction with the Free University in Amsterdam. Neither did I bring up the fact that I anticipated receiving one of the substantial grants that the ICS was planning to offer to one or two students in the coming year. These grants were the first that the institute offered to help students in need. I felt confident that my unwavering dedication to the institute put me at the front of the line to receive one of these grants. I quietly and eagerly looked forward to a situation where I could study full time.

My fantasy bubble burst at my thesis defense a short time after that interview. I was unable to adequately address many of the questions put to me, especially those that focused on ancient philosophy. When the defense was over, the faculty examiners deliberated for roughly thirty minutes before calling me back into the room. They informed me that I had passed my exam and I would receive the MPhil degree, but my joy at hearing those words quickly evaporated when they told me that I should forget about pursuing a doctorate. Their message was clear: they did not believe I had the intellectual wherewithal to attain a doctorate. My time at the ICS had come to an abrupt and painful end!

As I walked down College Street to the subway station, I was in a state of shock and fighting back tears. What had just happened to me? What could I say to Glenda? I was deeply hurt, confused, and not a little angry. I felt misunderstood and betrayed by people who I had studied under for four years at great personal cost. I felt cheated because I had to demonstrate my ability on a topic that was not an integral part of my program of study. I was angry that no one had alerted me to my shortcomings before or had offered to help me prepare for the defense. But, deep in my heart, I also felt the sting of self-doubt. I felt foolish for thinking that I was a scholar all this time.

In the spring of 1975, I lost my lucrative part-time job delivering furniture for Eaton's when it shut down its mail-order catalogue. For the next year I drove a rendering truck for the Darling Company. We finally had some money, even enough to buy a used 1972 VW Super Beetle! In July of 1975, God gave us a healthy, beautiful daughter, whom we named Jessica. We were very happy to have a boy and a girl, but our birth-control methods were clearly flawed.

Not knowing what else I could do, I applied for teaching jobs at several elementary and secondary Christian schools in various Neo-Calvinist communities around Ontario. When I landed a temporary one-year contract at Durham Christian High School in Bowmanville for the 1976–77 school year, we were happy to shake Toronto's dust off our feet and move to a large town an hour away to raise our children. We would miss our fellowship at Hart House church, but, like many others we knew, we needed to get away from Toronto and our ICS experience.

I was twenty-eight years old when we left Toronto. Up to that point, my life had followed a disturbing pattern—not that I was consciously aware of it at the time. After graduating from high school, I left home and attended Dordt College because I wanted to be a pastor like Peter Grossman. It took two and a half years for me to decide that I was not cut out for that calling. Newly married, I left home a second time to attend the Institute for Christian Studies because I aspired to be a philosopher like John Vander Stelt. After four years at the ICS, I discovered that I was not suited for that calling either. What had my life amounted to in the ten years since I left home? Had I pursued and failed to satisfy a series of "wandering desires," or was my life a bumpy journey of faith in search of wisdom? It turned out to be an odd combination of both.

Bowmanville – Fantasy Becomes Reality

In the 1970s it was still possible to teach in a school like Durham Christian High School (DCHS) without a provincial teaching certificate. My interview with the DCHS society board was my third attempt at getting hired by a Christian school that spring. By then I knew what to expect. As before, I was seated at one end of a long table and asked questions by the school principal and a half dozen parents who formed the board's interview committee. Unlike my previous interviews, this time the questioners did not focus on my lack of teaching experience or what I would do in certain scenarios that required disciplinary action. Led by Principal Ren Siebenga, this group was more interested in my biblical perspective on life, my passion for teaching, and my dedication to the cause of Christian education. They saw enough potential in me to offer me a one-year contract to teach Bible and English. The most skeptical among them probably figured, how much damage could I do in ten months? Had they posed that question to the students I taught that year, some of them would likely have answered, "Quite a lot, actually!"

As a matter of fact, I made many mistakes that year, everything from picking an overly complex novel for grade 11 English to being too intimidated to write on the chalkboard until mid-November, to standing toe to toe with a student much bigger than I was to resolve a confrontation. By far my most regrettable mistake was one that would get me fired in a heartbeat if it happened in a classroom today: I slapped a student! The fact that she had just lit her desk on fire did not justify my response.

The teaching staff at "Durham," as we affectionately referred to the school, met briefly at the end of each day to debrief, and on many afternoons the conversation was prolonged after I shared what had happened in my classroom that day. On those occasions, several of my colleagues would hang around to advise me on how I might have better handled the situation. My on-the-job teacher preparation was humbling but also very enabling.

Despite my lack of experience and lapses in judgment, students let me know—as only they can—that they generally liked being in my classes. I especially bonded with my small grade 11 homeroom class. In addition to the boring stuff I taught, we shared serious discussions about life and some hilarious moments. I will never forget the time a burly student named Isaac somehow used his thick fingers to tie a strand of his long hair around the leg of a lazy housefly while I was leading a discussion in English class. Eventually, we all stood spellbound around his desk to watch the tethered insect fly in circles above his thumb and finger, which pinched the other end of the hair. We also shared profound moments of vulnerability, none more poignant than the time all seventeen of us were huddled together in a tent at our year-end wilderness campout to share stories and memories. After most people had shared something, a timid, beautiful girl named Louise told us why she always wore pants to school and never swam when her PE class went to the pool. Louise revealed that when she was a young girl, her dress caught on fire out in the hayfield as her parents burned off an old stand of stubble. Before anyone could catch her and extinguish the flames, her legs were badly burned and horribly scarred. Most of her classmates didn't know this about her, and they expressed their gratitude that she had trusted them enough to share this horrific experience with them.

When the teacher whose position I temporarily held decided not to return from his leave of absence, I had the job for keeps if I wanted it. And I did! My second year was as memorable as the first, but for very different reasons. We began the year in a new building. Prior to that year, the school was housed in five round portables. Four served as classrooms, and one contained the administration offices, teacher's lounge, and a small workroom. Once upon a time these buildings had been chicken coops, but an enterprising local school supporter saw their potential as a school. He bought them cheap and had them "renovated" and moved onto the property of the Christian elementary school. The portables were not well insulated, and they only had a narrow row of five single-pane windows to let in outside light. The electric baseboard heaters fought a losing battle to keep the rooms warm during the winter months. The coat hooks that lined one section of the wall were superfluous because our students never took their coats off.

The new school building was a very basic and barely functional two-storey rectangle, but it was so much better than the portables. On the flip side, the building was a huge investment for a relatively small group of parents who wanted their children to have an alternative Christian education. We started that year a few days late because the building was not ready on time. In fact, several teachers, including me, spent Labour Day painting our classrooms. I hesitate to mention that I painted a feature wall in my room bright orange. It did not contribute to a calming atmosphere, but it did match the orange carpet that covered the floors in every room and the hallway upstairs. Someone in the community had found a deal on the carpet!

A local school supporter and contractor named Peter Vogel had erected the new building, with plenty of advice from those in the community who had the time to stop by and watch. Peter was a well-respected man in the Christian Reformed community, both for his character and the quality of his work. Because his crew had worked nonstop for eighteen months to build the school, no one in the community objected when he took his family on a weeklong holiday to Arizona once the school was up and running. Tragically, a late-night collision with a drunk driver took the lives of Peter and his daughter, Elsa, who was in my grade 12 homeroom. The crash left his wife and two youngest sons damaged but alive. Elsa's death was the first of two student deaths that the school community had to work through during my time there. I was deeply impacted by both. Some years later, a student named Gabby, who often babysat our children, died in a car crash just minutes after leaving our home. The experience of these deaths and other tragedies at the school, as well as the many occasions we had to celebrate life, remain constant reminders to me that the essence of education is rooted in relationships.

We came to Bowmanville hoping to find a community. We were not disappointed, but the experience was complicated. The parent society that operated Durham Christian High School drew its members from the two Christian Reformed churches in Bowmanville as well as from CRC churches in seven surrounding communities. Each of these outlying communities had established an elementary school but lacked the resources to also operate a high school. Some members of this amalgamated DCHS community found themselves at odds with fellow church members who held one or more of these opinions: a Christian elementary education was sufficient for their children; the tuition for two schools was unaffordable; the principal and teachers at DCHS were too liberal and they supported the Association for the Advancement of Christian Scholarship, which regularly criticized the church.

I encountered this division in the community before I taught my first class. The two Bowmanville CRC churches held a combined picnic in Orono Park every Labour Day. The day was filled with good food, jovial conversation, and lots of games. An outsider like me would never have guessed that the picnickers attended two different churches with two distinct reputations until the end of the day when a serious soccer match took place. It was the one event that day when people took sides.

Sometime between lunch and the soccer game, I was approached by two glowing fourteen-year-old girls. They introduced themselves as Henrietta and Silvia. In short order I found out that they had been lifelong friends and had recently graduated from the Christian elementary school. They now faced a crisis. Henrietta's parents had enrolled her at Durham, but Silvia's father insisted that she attend a huge public high school. The two friends wanted me, the new teacher, to talk with Silvia's father and try to change his mind. I naively said I would see what I could do.

I told my principal, Ren, about this conversation and asked if he thought I should talk with Silva's father. Not one to miss a teachable moment, Ren encouraged me to go have a chat with the fellow. The next afternoon I met Silvia's father in his barn as he prepared to milk his handful of dairy cows. I talked more than I should have, but my talking/listening ratio really did not matter in that instance, for Silvia's father had made up his mind already, and nothing would change it. As best as I could tell, he refused to send his children to Durham because he did not want them to be influenced by a principal and teachers who liberally interpreted the Bible, just like those professors who taught at the Institute for Christian Studies.

He was unable to provide me with any concrete examples of their bad exegesis, but that did not seem to matter. When I asked him if he was not even more concerned about his children coming under the influence of non-Christian teachers at the public school, he simply replied, to my utter amazement, that he was confident his children would be good witnesses at the public school.

The parents who sent their children to DCHS functioned like an interpretive community[318] even though they lived in different towns. They believed in cultural transformation, and they expected Durham to not only provide their children with a biblical perspective on life but also to set them on a path to live that life. Some parents could articulate the school's vision better than others, but they all trusted their principal, Ren Siebenga, and the staff he had assembled. They assumed that whatever we were doing at Durham must be good because their children were happy and learning. The longer I taught at DCHS, the more I felt connected to this scattered community. Ren encouraged his staff to develop relationships with the parents, especially those who lived in the outlying towns. On various occasions I travelled to these towns to meet with parents, give a talk, or share a Sunday dinner. As my ties with parents deepened, I saw more clearly the significant sacrifices they were making to send their children to a Christian elementary school and a Christian high school.

In Bowmanville, some people who only supported the elementary school openly criticized those who sent their children to both schools. The rivalry between these two groups was ignited and kept burning by local Christian Reformed pastors. As members of one or the other local churches, my colleagues and I had no trouble figuring out who in the pews or pulpit respected us as educators and who did not. The pro-Durham/anti-Durham rivalry was a flashpoint for a deeper divide in the Christian Reformed community over issues of faith. Durham staff were caught in the middle of it; people were either respectful of or fearful and angry over what they assumed we stood for. I will never forget my painful encounter with contractor Peter's wife after church one Sunday, about ten years after their horrific car crash. Poisoned by a new pastor who believed the Durham staff taught students a perverse understanding of the Bible, she confronted me in the foyer of the church one Sunday morning and angrily blurted out that if her husband were still alive, he would regret that he had built the school!

Despite all the rivalry, Glenda and I embraced the local Christian Reformed community. We learned some Dutch lingo, ate meatball soup on Sundays, and incorporated Sinterklass into our family traditions. We had our third and last child, Jonathan at that time. He was the only one we planned and the only one born at home. Like his older brother and sister, he grew up to identify as Dutch.

Our most intimate community experience evolved through our relationships with six other couples from Durham's teaching staff. We were drawn together for a variety of reasons. Although we were highly regarded by the parents of our students and considered part of the immigrant community, we remained outsiders in some respects. Seven of us were Americans whose circuitous routes to Durham all involved studying at the Institute for Christian Studies. Our closest family members lived more than a thousand kilometers away, so we gravitated toward each other for socializing, friendship, and the need for family. Our children referred to the adults in the group as aunts and uncles and still do to this day.

Our school principal, Ren Siebenga, was a visionary educator who knew how to assemble and nurture a staff. He wanted teachers who had a big vision of the Christian life, who had a passion for students, and who would give their all to the task at hand. He did not look first of all, for teachers with experience or even pedagogical expertise; he believed the staff and students at Durham could make teachers out of people with the right potential. He was right about this with most of his hires, including me.

My colleagues and I constantly thought and talked about our educational vision and its challenges. We were committed to interpreting curricular content from a Reformational Christian perspective and educating students to live a Christian life. Our most immediate priority, however, was to "get these kids through their high school years intact," which was more or less the way Ren would say it. Above all else, this meant developing meaningful and affirming relationships between staff and students and within each of those groups. Some people in the Ontario Alliance of Christian Schools (OACS) mistakenly thought we were a "feel good" school that downplayed academics. Many disagreed with our belief that students learned best when their school environment was nurturing and encouraging.

All the OACS educators that I knew thought curriculum reform was critical for our school movement's success. Textbooks posed the biggest problem for us; the only available ones were written from a secular perspective. Neither the Ontario Alliance of Christian Schools nor our American parent organization, the National Union of Christian Schools, had published alternative texts. It was up to us as individual teachers to decide what materials our students would study, what content we would or would not teach, and what interpretations of important issues we would affirm or critique. None of us had been prepared for this kind of decision-making. Our choices mainly relied on our intuition because we lacked clear criteria to guide our curriculum choices.

At Durham I discovered my scholarly niche was curriculum theory, not systematic philosophy. At the end of my second year, Ren assigned me to attend a Canada-wide curriculum-writing team that had already been meeting for a couple of summers to create a new perspective course called *Man in Society*. This course would serve as the capstone to the Bible curriculum throughout the CSC system. My tenure on this team made me aware of CSC's extensive teacher-led curriculum reform movement and the importance it placed on the development of a distinctively Christian perspective of reality. I also discovered that curriculum reform was challenging work on many levels, not the least of which was the limited time we had to work on major projects. These tasks were much too demanding to tackle during the school year when daily preparations consumed us, so we had to accomplish most of our curriculum-writing work during a couple of weeks in July.

My analysis of the *Man in Society* project appears in chapter 7, but one story is worth telling here because it illustrates the kind of obstacles we faced and our vulnerability as curriculum reformers. To wrap up our multi-year development of *Man in Society*, we assigned specific units of the course to different team members. Each writer or group of writers had to review all of the old drafts and any notes or new material we had accumulated, then construct the penultimate draft of the unit and bring it to Edmonton, Alberta, the following July, where we would finalize the text for publication. For reasons that I can no longer recall, I had to write two of the eight units by myself.

Keep in mind that the 1970s belonged to the pre-computer age. Without the aid of a computer on which to create and store our documents, we had to type our work and retype our revisions; we never had more than one hard copy of a draft. The materials we brought to our meetings mainly consisted of typed pages of text and paste-up pages where we manually spliced together text, pictures, cartoons, and other adornments. To make copies for the other team members, we had to "burn" mimeograph stencils and run them off on Gestetner machines with hand cranks, a process that was both time consuming and expensive, not to mention messy.

My two units included many illustrations and pictures from resources that I had ordered and received permission to use. I worked on these units as often as I could throughout the school year, but work still needed to be done in early July before our team was scheduled to meet in Edmonton later in the month. Even though I was worn down by the year-end events of graduation and a four-day, all-school wilderness campout, I poured myself into finalizing the manuscripts for the two units I had to write up.

Disaster struck one week before I packed up my family and our camping gear into our old station wagon to make the long drive out to Edmonton. I took my box of roughly one hundred pages of completed material to Toronto so my friend, Harry Fernhout, could look them over and give me feedback. I was buoyed up by his positive response to my work, but two hours later at home I was emotionally crushed when I figured out that I had absent-mindedly left the box on my car's roof so I could unlock the door. Somehow, I also failed to notice when the box blew off the roof, scattering my work across College Street. For the second time in my life, College Street became my personal roadway of tears.

I had just five days to reconstruct my units from memory and with the aid of some discarded pages still in my office garbage can. I was able to reorder and receive some of my resources before we had to leave for Edmonton, but I had no time to incorporate them. When we left Edmonton for my week of editorial meetings, I had managed to roughly reconstruct about half of my lost work. In Edmonton I sequestered myself in a classroom for four grueling days of working alone while the rest of the team shared their units with each other. On Friday I reluctantly presented my two units to the larger group. What I submitted was not nearly as good as the material that ended up in Toronto's landfill, but there was nothing I could do except endure the humiliation of the experience.

During the 1970s and 1980s, the Ontario Alliance of Christian Schools included eleven high schools. Those of us who taught in them tried to implement our alternative educational vision in a traditional high school setting. Some of us were cognizant of the barriers that traditional forms of teaching and learning presented to our vision, but most were not. Those of us who saw the danger struggled to change the way we organized our curriculum and taught it. We shared everyone's concern for the cultivation of a Christian worldview, but we wanted our students to be engaged with real issues, not just understand them differently. At Durham we took major strides toward offering an education whose quality would be determined by lifestyle rather than grade-point average.

My colleagues and I addressed the problem best at an institutional level. We tinkered with scheduling and added some innovative elements to the curriculum like cooperative learning modules and a weekly activity period, where, for example, six students and I learned how to throw pots on a potter's wheel at a local potter's studio. The two most extreme examples of alternative learning that we devised for our students was Special Emphasis Week and the year-end campout.

Special Emphasis Week was a collaborative effort to implement a transdisciplinary, project-based curriculum in a traditional high school setting. During this week all regular classes were suspended, and students from all grade levels were mixed together. Students attended workshops, listened to guest speakers, took field trips, and engaged in other activities, all focused on a single topic such as food, the Middle East conflict, work, family celebrations, or waste and the environment. A committee of two or three teachers spent a year planning this week. The committee invited dozens of presenters, constructed a major multimedia presentation to kick off the week, and designed a variety of appropriate activities. The public was also invited to participate in this event, and many parents attended.

These special weeks made lasting impressions on our students. For this reason, we continued to plan them, even though they taxed the staff's energy, especially those who served on the planning committee. Despite our hard work, our dependence upon a traditional approach to education prevented us from making the most of these weeks. For example, we failed to involve senior students in the planning of these weeks. Neither did we use our individual courses as contexts to prepare or debrief our students about the theme of our week. Worst of all, we were unable to provide opportunities for our students to actually engage the issue.

The year-end campout was hands down the most impactful event of our school year. We took our whole school to Algonquin Provincial Park for four days. Four or five dedicated community members joined us, and without them we could not have pulled off such a demanding event. The experience was predominately recreational, but students learned many valuable lessons, such as paddling a canoe using the J-stroke, recognizing and treating black fly bites, packing the proper gear, setting up a tent correctly, respecting the quiet bedtime curfew, doing one's share of the work on a meal crew, and passing the water-safety test. The nightly campfires were bonding events structured around themes of remembrance and mutual recognition of gifts. After the last fire, the graduating class filed past the rest of us for farewell hugs and handshakes. It was affectionately known as the "rejection line." It was a bookend to the "reception line" that grade nine students experienced on their first day of school when they filed by all the older students and staff for personal welcomes.

On May 6, 2017, I attended Durham's fiftieth anniversary, a date that also marked twenty-five years since I had taught there. Throughout the two days of celebrations, I met many of my former students and their aging parents. Without fail, each student at some point in our conversation mentioned the impact that the campout had on them, both at the time and later in their adult lives. When I asked them to explain further, the answer was always the same; the campout epitomized their school experience at Durham where they felt personally affirmed and valued. They were forever grateful that their teachers had expended so much time and energy just to hang out with them in a black-fly-infested wilderness for four days and three nights.

Toward the end of my tenure at Durham, some of us seriously tried to change our traditional approaches to teaching and organizing our content. Ren brought in Agnes Struik, a consultant who worked with the Curriculum Development Centre in Toronto. With her help, we planned ways to recast our curriculum into a more thematic approach and to make our teaching strategies more student-centred. We found it challenging to implement these curricular and pedagogical reforms. At that time, we knew such structural changes were necessary if we wanted to better implement our vision, but we did not clearly understand why this was so difficult.

Throughout my high school teaching career, I pursued my own quest for learning. Within seven years I had earned a master's degree in education at the prestigious Ontario Institute for Studies in Education at the University of Toronto. I chose to work in the department of history and philosophy of education, and I wrote a thesis on student evaluation. My years at the ICS started to pay some unexpected dividends. The OISE dropped the number of required courses by two in lieu of my MPhil. I also discovered that my ability to engage in foundational issues was far superior to that of most other students, and my professors took notice.

About fifteen years into my career at Durham, I decided to get my doctorate degree. I was motivated to do this for two reasons. The first was a matter of survival. By this time, I was an effective high school teacher, but I did not think I could sustain that degree of engagement for another twenty years. The second, and more compelling reason was my desire to take up a variation of Vander Stelt's gauntlet and cut out the secular influences that shaped teacher education in the Neo-Calvinist tradition. Everything that I had experienced and learned as a high school teacher convinced me that we had to fundamentally change the way we educated high school students. My colleagues and I had worked hard to implement those changes at Durham. However, our inability to give up our traditional approach to teaching and learning posed the biggest obstacle to our efforts at change. I thought if I got a doctorate, I could teach in a teacher-preparation program at a Christian college or university and, God willing, prepare teachers to plan curriculum more holistically and teach in more effective, non-traditional ways right from the start.

My doctoral program proved to be an exhilarating experience. The seminars were challenging, and I was able to do the research that I wanted to do. My thesis on the deep structure of schooling was well received by my professors. More importantly, I realized that my ability to be a reformational scholar was no longer a fantasy but a reality. I was not a philosopher, and I never would be, but I understood the foundations of education and why school reform is such a daunting endeavor. It took me four years of studying at the Institute for Christian Studies to discover that I was not meant to be the reformational educator that I aspired to be after I graduated from Dordt College. Eighteen years of reflective teaching at Durham and a doctorate at the University of Toronto turned me into a reformational educator of a different kind.

THE UNMAKING OF A REFORMATIONAL EDUCATOR (1995-2022)

Edmonton: Culture Making

As noted earlier, this memoir is focused on my journey as an educator. I recalled that my hometown experience shaped me into a person who desired to be wise, morally upright, and Heaven bound. In those days I imagined my future as a pastor in an obscure corner of Calvinist Christianity in America's heartland. My faith was dominated by theology and limited to familiar churchly activities. As a white, privileged, working-class American male, I was oblivious to those who lived in a world of despair. I had little personal need for hope because the American dream remained a reality for me. When I left home, I had no concern for what was broken in the world, and if I had, I certainly lacked the courage to do anything about it.

My time at college reoriented me to a career in Christian education. I was tempted to equate my Christian discipleship with scholarship. I desired to become a philosopher who understood everything from a biblical worldview. I imagined myself rethinking the foundations of learning as a member of the Reformational movement launched by Dutch Neo-Calvinist scholars Dooyeweerd and Vollenhoven and transplanted in North America by professors like Runner, Vander Stelt, and others. At the tender age of twenty-four, I was eager to take on the spirits of the age intellectually. I began to nurture a righteous anger over the plight of the suffering, disadvantaged and marginalized, but I lacked the courage to engage injustice in concrete situations. I did, however, risk moving to Canada to serve a cause greater than myself.

My identity as a Reformational scholar sprouted briefly, then shrivelled up and died during my four years at the Institute for Christian Studies. Over the next twenty years, I evolved into a Reformational educator of a different sort. I worked as a high school teacher dedicated to cultivating relationships with students and sharing with them a biblical perspective on life. In the classroom I tried to implement a pedagogy and a curriculum that harmonized with a Reformational worldview of culture transformation. As a scholar I investigated the foundations of curriculum design and contributed to the development of an alternative Christian curriculum orientation. Throughout most of this period I remained committed to worldview education. However, along with other like-minded Neo-Calvinist educators, I eventually reached two disturbing conclusions. We finally acknowledged that worldview education on its own had no chance of transforming culture. Second, initiating students into an alternative way of life in a school setting is elusive, if not impossible.

My time at Durham Christian High School taught me a central truth about education: relationships lie at the heart of authentic learning. I also learned that with the right mix of leadership and vision, it is possible to cultivate a hope-filled community of learning and sustain it for a while.

My move to Edmonton in 1995 to teach in the education faculty at The King's University provided me with an opportunity to develop an alternative approach to teaching and curriculum making at the level of teacher preparation. (Chapter 10 provides the details about The King's teacher-preparation program.) It also revived my aspirations to be the scholar I was unable to be at the Institute for Christian Studies. Little did I know that my career as an academic would actually cause me to let go of my ambition to be a Reformational educator. I eventually accepted the fact that the Neo-Calvinist aspiration for cultural transformation, not only claimed too much for itself but wrongly assumed its devotees could achieve this goal while working in isolation from almost everyone else.

In his ground-breaking book, *Culture Making: Recovering Our Creative Calling*, Andy Crouch defines culture as what we make of the world. "It is a name for our relentless, restless human effort to take the world as it is given to us and make something of it." When "what we make of it" heals brokenness and fosters love, we bring hope into the world. During my tenure as a professor at The King's University, I was involved in three formative situations of hopeful culture making outside of the classroom. In each instance I participated as an agent of change rather than a disengaged academic. In all three cases, I had no preconceived notions about making a difference in the lives of real people or institutions, and I was mostly unaware that I was undergoing a significant personal transformation in the process.

The first situation arose out of my obligations as a professor at The King's University. Faculty positions there consist of three components: teaching, research, and service. My first year and a half as a professor were consumed with the teaching of new courses and launching the new elementary school BEd program. Consequently, I gave little thought to service inside or outside of the university. When I could no longer say I was new on the job, my colleague, Alyce Oosterhuis, suggested that I fulfill my service obligation by letting my name stand for election to the board for the Edmonton Society of Christian Education (ECSC), a parent-run organization that operated the elementary and secondary campuses that comprised Edmonton Christian School. She reminded me that my youngest child, Jonathan, would attend Edmonton Christian High School for another couple of years, so the timing was right for me to serve on this board. Besides, she reasoned, being a member of this board would draw me into a school community that was vitally important to our teacher-preparation program.

As Alyce predicted, I was elected to the board. Two years later I agreed to serve as the board chair. I had no idea that my tenure as chair would coincide with arguably the most critical time in the society's history. This period was dominated by our board's negotiations with the Edmonton Public School Board over the possibility of Edmonton Christian School becoming an alternative program within its jurisdiction.[319] The stakes could not have been higher. The community had to decide whether or not the future flourishing of Edmonton Christian School hinged upon giving up control of their school to a public board. Throughout its existence, the society would never have taken such a scenario seriously because it would have appeared to contradict the educational vision that the society had worked so long and hard to implement.

As chair of the ESCE board and its negotiating team, I was primarily responsible for sharing the results of our negotiations with our society members, which I did through several open letters. Fielding questions from our school administrators and teachers about the motives guiding both sets of negotiators also usually fell to me. It was also my job to communicate our school's vision of education to ESPB negotiators and to members of the press. When I look back on that time, I think that I navigated these challenges as well as I did because of my previous experiences as a teacher and scholar. I also benefitted greatly from the wisdom and support of my fellow board members.

My experience as the ECSC board chair taught me some important lessons, and I will limit myself to naming two of them. My leadership was inspired and informed by the Reformational worldview that I had been striving to understand theoretically since I was a college student. I learned firsthand that when this way of thinking was applied to a challenging social issue, it could effectively guide a community's decision-making process. Second, I understood that the ongoing fulfillment of the society's aspirations to offer an alternative Christian education required working with partners who stood outside the Neo-Calvinist tradition, people we had always assumed were on the other side. In brief, I learned that for the Reformational worldview to have legs, it had to be applied in a real-life situation and be meaningfully shared with others.

A second Edmonton experience also thrust me upon a big stage, the public platform of higher education. After chairing the education faculty for its first six years, my colleague, Bob Bruinsma, stepped down and redirected his administrative talents to other areas of the university. I replaced him as chair for no other reason than it was my turn. For the next thirteen years, I served as the head of the faculty of education, first as its chair then as the dean when the university restructured its governance model. Prior to the addition of a secondary education program, I also taught courses in the fall term and supervised practicum students in the winter term. Once the secondary education program was launched, the job of dean became a full-time administrative position.

The most intimidating part of being the education faculty dean for me was attending the semi-annual stakeholder meetings sponsored by the Alberta Ministry of Education. The meetings were chaired by the deputy minister, who was supported by his personal secretary, the registrar who oversaw teacher certification, and a small contingent of ministry researchers. The provincial stakeholders included the deans of education from Alberta's government-approved teacher-preparation programs (six in the beginning and ten eventually) and representatives from the Alberta Teachers Association (ATA), the public and Catholic school boards from Calgary and Edmonton, the Alberta School Boards Association, the Association of Charter Schools, and the Association of Independent Schools and Colleges of Alberta.

For reasons that I never fully understood, only the deans were expected to report to this body and take questions at every meeting. This level of scrutiny was a routine matter for the deans of the four major university programs, but reporting on the status of our programs was a dicey business for the deans from Concordia and The King's, the recently approved faith-based programs. Many people around the table privately wondered about the quality of faith-based teacher-preparation programs. The ATA, for its part, publicly denounced our programs and discouraged teachers from supervising our students.

This provincial stakeholder group is unique to Alberta, I believe, and, unfortunately, the vitality and personality it exhibited from 2010 to 2015 no longer exists. Throughout most of my time as dean, Kerry Henke was the deputy minister of Alberta Education, and he cultivated an atmosphere of mutual respect among the stakeholders. He also encouraged cooperative endeavors to develop and carry out ministry policy. These included initiatives regarding teacher quality standards and curriculum reform.

I gradually became less intimidated at these meetings. It helped that I had become friends with the other education faculty deans. Besides our two annual meetings with the stakeholder group, all of the Alberta deans met once a year with the deans of education from British Columbia, Saskatchewan, and Manitoba. In both of these settings, The King's program was by far the smallest, yet I was always respected and treated as an equal. To put this differential into perspective, the University of Alberta's teacher-preparation program is bigger than all the other Alberta programs combined. There are more professors in the U of A education faculty than all of the students, faculty, and staff at The King's University.

The six Alberta deans eventually formed an organization called the Association of Alberta Deans of Education (AADE). I can't imagine another provincial jurisdiction where the dean of a small, faith-based program would have been given the responsibility to draft the association's constitution or serve as its chair for a time, with the U of A's dean sitting as the vice chair.

I have many fond memories of those early AADE days. We always met for supper the day prior to the stakeholder meetings to strategize about the agenda and to decide who should speak for the group on a given agenda item. When we needed someone to validate the AADE, we typically looked to Jane O'Dea from Lethbridge, our cheerleader. If an issue required the voice of authority, we looked to Fern Snart from the University of Alberta. We deferred to Concordia's Mark Swanson on matters of policy, and we could always count on Mark Arnal of Campus Saint-Jean to tackle controversial issues. The group looked to me to offer big picture perspective. The ADDE became a united front in the arena of stakeholders. It influenced government policy making and put an end to programs standing alone to advocate for or defend a position.

We also had fun as a group. Jane O'Dea often got us laughing, especially when she embellished stories, like the time she and Fern Snart decided to ride in my 2001 Ford pickup instead of taking a cab or a limo from Calgary's McDougall Centre to the Fairmont Palliser Hotel. It didn't matter that they were dressed in their smart business suits; they squished beside me in the front seat of my small cab, and we laughed at ourselves the whole way across the city.

Even the vindictive ATA eventually acknowledged the high quality of our program and invited us to sign a memorandum of agreement with them. No one was more shocked than I was at my retirement when our academic vice president quoted from a congratulatory email sent to him by Gordon Thomas, the ATA's adversarial executive director. What he said still shocks me: "Dr. Hull could provide several other deans with a tutorial on teacher education." He then compared our program's commitment to quality teacher education to that of Meyer Horowitz, the legendary former dean of education and president of the University of Alberta.

My experience as a dean affirmed what I learned as the ESCE chair. First, the Reformational worldview made a significant impact when it was drawn upon to interpret real-life situations. Second, making culture that addresses fixing what is broken requires working shoulder to shoulder with people who stand outside of the Neo-Calvinist tradition.

The third experience of culture making I want to describe falls outside the realm of formal education, but the reasons why I believe it belongs in this memoir will soon be apparent. Encouraged by Gary Garrison, the Edmonton coordinator of the Man to Man, Woman to Woman (M2W2) program sponsored by the Mennonite Central Committee, I agreed to become a prison visitor in the fall of 2005. For years, I had challenged high school and university students to trade in the American dream of personal success for a life of discipleship that served the most marginalized groups in society, but I had never been seriously involved with those on Jesus's short list of the most vulnerable and in need of care, justice, and hope (Matt. 25:35–36). My involvement with prison inmates taught me many things, some which I knew already. One of the most important of those lessons was to practice what I preach. My experience of walking alongside prisoners also gave authenticity to my alternative philosophy of education when I shared it with my students. I regret that it took me so long to act on that knowledge.

Over the next fifteen years, I often visited inmates at the Edmonton Institution, a maximum-security prison. Typically, five or six of us met a dozen inmates for an evening of sharing, snacking, and playing games. Each month we met prisoners from a different cell range. Given the size of the prison, we rarely met a prisoner more than twice in a year. For this reason, on five different occasions, I met separately and developed relationships with individual inmates. Over the years, I talked with dozens of inmates who were willing to share parts of their story, and in every instance their trajectory into crime was triggered by their own victimization by family members and/or some other dysfunctional segment of society. It was also plain to see that Canadian prisons were designed to dehumanize prisoners rather than rehabilitate them. The system methodically chipped away at a person's hope. Our society will not only be remembered for our degradation of the environment and our disrespect for the elderly, Indigenous peoples and the mentally ill but also for the way we mistreat people while they serve time in prison.

EDUCATION FOR HOPE

What follows is the story of my ten-year relationship with Martin Pincus. For the first six months, I met Marty every other week. Then he was transferred to the medium-security prison in Drumheller, a three-hour drive away. This move significantly improved Marty's life behind bars, but it greatly reduced our visits over the next nine years. Nevertheless, through letters and my periodic trips to Drumheller, we steadily deepened our friendship.

Marty is one of the most remarkable persons I have ever known, because he embraced both daughters of hope. When I met Marty, he was thirty-nine years old and nearly two decades into a life sentence. He had just committed his life to Jesus, but he only had the faintest idea of what that meant. What motivated him at that time was a desire to turn his life around and get paroled within a few years. By then Marty had already kicked his drug addiction but remained dependent on heavy doses of methadone. He wanted to get weaned off this drug too and also quit smoking. He managed to do both during the time I knew him. If you think overcoming a narcotic or nicotine addiction is extremely difficult, imagine doing it while in a prison environment that encourages addictions. Marty also desperately wanted to control his temper. This goal proved to be just out of his reach because his anger and proclivity to violence had been his saviour for most of his life.

Marty was one of the youngest in a family of seven boys and two girls. His parents lacked most parenting skills. His father was an alcoholic who regularly beat his wife and children. Marty grew up hating his father. He was further burdened by anger and guilt over his inability to protect his mother and his two younger sisters from his father's fury.

Marty grew up in a household of petty criminals. When he was six years old, Marty's brothers involved him in his first break-and-enter burglary. They put him through a small window, so he could unlock the door and give them access to the building. Marty and his two sisters were also sexually abused by a relative and a friend of one of his brothers, but he felt powerless to report these episodes. His father was very clear; he would beat senseless anyone in his family who ratted on someone. In his addled mind, ratting on someone was worse than sexual abuse.

Marty developed a survival strategy that proved effective in his dysfunctional home and violent Ottawa neighbourhood. He purposely picked fights with older, bigger kids. He knew he would get beat up, but he learned that if he fought like a wild dog and inflicted some damage on the other guy, everyone would eventually leave him alone. His message got out on the street soon enough: do not mess with Marty, it is not worth it. Marty learned early that his anger and wildcat fighting kept him strong and safe. However, this behaviour also got him kicked out of school. At the tender age of eleven, Marty was sent to a reform school, where his teachers often used physical force to subdue the students.

At age seventeen, Marty got caught robbing a home, and he served four years in prison as a result. When he returned home after doing his time, he discovered that his beloved younger sister, Lori, was being pimped by a friend of one of his brothers, the same guy who had sexually abused Marty and his sister when they were children. No one in the family seemed to care about what was happening to Lori. Marty believed the only way he could rescue his sister was to take out her pimp, which he did.

The judge at Marty's trial was empathetic; he convicted Marty of manslaughter rather than murder and gave him a relatively light sentence. While in prison this time, Marty got hooked on drugs, and to get his drugs, he became a member of a gang. When he got out of prison, the deck of life was stacked against him. He had no family or community to support him, he had a limited education and no job skills, and he was addicted to drugs and obligated to a gang. In very short order, Marty got mixed up in a robbery that went bad, and he killed an innocent man. This time around, Marty got life in prison. He was twenty-two years old.

By the time I met Marty, he had served time in numerous maximum-security prisons across Canada and had earned a reputation as one the most volatile, angry, and fight-prone inmates in the system. He only stood five feet, six inches tall, but he packed two hundred pounds of muscle. He was not a person that anyone wanted to mess with. The survival strategy that Marty had honed on the street proved to be just as effective inside the prison; fight like a crazy man, and people will leave you alone. But Marty was not that person anymore when I met him. His new problem was that few people on the inside recognized his change of heart.

The soft Marty, the Marty who deeply cared about his mother and sisters, had already started to emerge about seven years prior to my meeting him. He implemented a vision of hope that only makes sense in a twisted environment like prison. When he described what he did to help new prisoners navigate prison life and why, I immediately thought of Holden Caulfield, the main character of Salinger's controversial novel, *The Catcher in the Rye*. Caulfield is a misunderstood, struggling teenager who imagines a scenario of children playing in a field of rye next to a cliff. His role is to protect the children and catch any of them who wander too close to the edge. He was their "catcher," i.e., saviour. Marty was not a catcher in a dream world; he did his saving work in a real world of perpetual revenge and violence. When new and often young men came onto the range, they inevitably transgressed the unspoken rules of prisoner conduct. This usually resulted in a severe beating or knifing. Marty let it be known that he would be the enforcer in such matters, and because of his reputation, no one objected. However, Marty's intention was to give the offending inmate a minor roughing up, thus preventing him from suffering a serious injury or even death. Marty's strategy helped many newcomers adjust to prison life with minimal consequences, but it hurt his own desire to be paroled one day. Prison officials misunderstood Marty's fighting. They assumed he was still taking out his rage on other inmates.

A few years prior to our meeting, Marty had decided to stop fighting. If he was ever to qualify for parole, he would have to stop "helping" others and do what was best for Marty. His vision of hope shifted to a new agenda. Among other things, he wanted to write a book about his life. His target audience would be parents. He believed that if they read his life story, they would not raise their children the way he was brought up. Their children would not live the life he had to live, nor would they end up in jail. He often talked about taking his book on a speaking tour when he got out of prison. This was his dream. I offered to edit his book, but only once did he ever muster the courage to send me something he had written.

Even though Marty was able to spend a year in an anger-management program while serving time in Drumheller, he periodically got into altercations that would set him back in his bid to be paroled. He tried so hard to be good. He was off drugs, off methadone, and off cigarettes. To avoid encounters where he would be offered a banned substance or get into a petty quarrel, he quit taking meals in the mess hall. He preferred the companionship of a baby gopher or a bird, both of which he was known to keep in his cell.

One morning while I was reading the paper at breakfast, I happened to see the headline of a one-paragraph news item about two older inmates who had been found dead in their cells that week in the Drumheller Institution. One of them was Marty. Thanks to the efforts of the local M2W2 coordinator and the two chaplains at the Drumheller Institution, I was allowed to attend the memorial service held for Marty and the other inmate. It was one of the most moving experiences that I have ever had. "The brothers" granted me permission to share what I knew about Marty. After the service, one of the chaplains told me this was an honour rarely extended to someone from the outside. This was further testimony to Marty's positive influence on those around him. I also learned from one of the inmates that, contrary to the official news release, Marty had actually been in "the hole" (solitary confinement) when he ended his life, not his cell. I never learned why Marty had been sent to the hole. The chaplains told me that Marty had become very depressed because he believed the people who controlled his fate had decided he would never get parole. This news helped clarify for me why Marty had not replied to my letters for several months.

Marty often told me that I was the only person in the world who loved him. That was, and continues to be, one of my greatest rewards and sorrows in life. Since Marty never got to be a catcher on the outside by sharing his story in a book or on a speaking tour, the least I can do is share his story here. Who knows what hope Marty's story may yet generate?

Retired: Embracing Hope

The concept of retirement is a relatively new phenomenon in human history. Prior to the Industrial Revolution, most people did not live past the age of forty. They simply did not reach an age when they were too old to work. Over the past one hundred years, retirement has become popularized and institutionalized all over the world. Led by Chancellor Otto Von Bismarck, the Germans were the first to require people over sixty-five to retire from working and to pay them a pension.

Public pensions began showing up in various sectors of American society in the mid-1800s. Franklin D Roosevelt's Social Security Act of 1935 institutionalized the concept of workers paying for their own retirements. The reality of retirement because one was no longer able to work gradually shifted to retirement as a time to be free from work and enjoy the perks of life. However, various studies now reveal that significant numbers of retired people suffer from depression due to bereavement, divorce, failing health, boredom, and loneliness.

The question that burdens many people on the cusp of retirement is, "What do I do now?" Dylan's insight into the human condition that I cited earlier still applies; you have to serve somebody! Will I serve my wandering desires or causes other an my own, assuming of course, that I still have the physical and mental capacities to act?

I have been tempted to ask the wrong question in my early years of retirement: can I start indulging myself now? The question gains legitimacy the more I feel weary of fighting the good fight because in the end, I know we can't fix what is wrong in this world. This unhelpful question leaves me hanging somewhere between a messiah complex and despair. Recently, I heard some good news that gave me clarity when I listened to a recorded conversation between Roy Berkenbosch and Ruth Padilla-DeBorst, two visionaries who have given much of their lives to development work in the third world. What follows is my understanding of the most salient points in their conversation.

For those of us who believe we have to fix what is broken, then fall into despair when we discover that we can't, it is tempting to think of retirement as a time to finally let go of this burden and enjoy the good things in life. But embracing retirement as a time of well-deserved fun comes at a high price. The more self-serving our retirement, the more we become anesthetized to suffering and ecologically illiterate.

The better choice is to remain as active as possible in the human narrative, even though problems seem to be overwhelming and the powers that be so intractable. But how do we not give in to the temptation to spend our retirement checking off the items on our bucket list of desires? Hope is vital to the answer. Hope is preferable to failing as a messiah, giving in to despair, or draining the retirement savings plan nest egg travelling to exotic destinations. The acquisition of hope, however, requires us to honestly face up to how broken our world really is, and this is particularly challenging for privileged, educated white males like me.

Ruth Padilla-DeBorst believes the way to hope begins by seeing that "what is" is not "all there is." This beyond-the-horizon vision requires imagination and faith that God has not given up on this world. To acquire this kind of sight, we must accept the fact that we are all refugees in exile; we are stuck in a place where God's promises are so distant from the brokenness we experience. Yet, it is in this very space where we benefit from God's promises.

One of those promises is the gift of hope. Indeed, hope is a gift we receive from God, either directly or indirectly through selfless people like Marty. We cannot manufacture hope, but we can expect it to emerge in the context of unlikely relationships. So, while we wait for what is expected, we do not accommodate ourselves to the brokenness that is all around us, but we persevere and flourish where we are. Hopeful waiting is neither passive nor fatalistic, says DeBorst; hope is a commitment in the here and now in the midst of everything that conspires to kill hope.

After reading my almost-finished memoir, my friend and education faculty colleague, Bob Bruinsma, asked if I was going to address this common question: if you could relive your life, knowing what you know

now, would you follow the same path? It is a highly speculative question because we never have the benefit of hindsight. I suppose what the question is really after is a balance sheet of regrets and moments of happiness.

I have portrayed my life as an educator in three phases: my pursuit and failure to be a reformational philosopher, my relatively successful life as relational teacher and reformational curriculum theorist, and my second career as a teacher educator who waited too long to substitute my reformational agenda with education for hope. If I actually could to do it all over again, knowing what I now know, I would follow the same path. Yes, I experienced some hard knocks along the way, but I also encountered dozens of amazing men and women, and each one taught me important lessons about life inside and outside of the classroom.

The philosophical/theological scope of the Dutch Neo-Calvinist tradition is incredibly rich and empowering. If I had another go at my carer, I would want a better grasp of this intellectual tradition. For a brief moment, I thought I would have preferred to be part of the Teaching for Transformation movement[320] rather than a precursor of it. Then I remembered the challenges that my student teachers faced when I observed their practicums; I am not so sure that I would be as effective in the classrooms of today as I was in the 1980s.

Bob Dylan needs to write another song about service. This one should talk about the hope that comes to those who align their wandering desires with service to the Lord. There would be verses about righteous anger or holy dissatisfaction over the way things are and verses about the courage to see these things do not remain so. A chorus that celebrated *kenosis* (self-emptying love) as the context for hope would follow each verse. I believe this would be a fitting theme song for the Neo-Calvinist tradition of education and like-minded educators.

This memoire tells an important story, but it is only one strand of my life's narrative. Like Michael Coren, I committed my whole life to following the rebel Christ. This is a life filled with struggle, work, sacrifice and effort. Followers of the rebel Christ, he says, "follow out of love and out of belief, and we follow because it reaches the point where we can do no other…(it) is a daily challenge, because we're so often limited by our own experience and environment, by what we have known and with what we feel familiar."[321]

Endnotes

317 Bob Dylan, *Slow Train Coming*. Columbia Records, 1979.

318 The terms "interpretive community," "rival community," and "revival community" are defined in chapter 3.

319 See chapter 8 for my summary of this event.

320 See chapter 9 for my summary of this approach.

321 Michael Coren, *The Rebel Christ*, (Toronto, ON: Dundurn, Press, 2021) 134.

APPENDICES

APPENDIX 1

Acronyms

Dutch Neo-Calvinists have a fondness for forming committees, societies, associations, institutions, and organizations with long names. They also have a penchant for using acronyms when talking about these creations. Community insiders hardly notice this habit, but for outsiders, a conversation punctuated with these acronyms can quickly become confusing. This appendix is offered as a quick access guide to the abbreviated titles of the various bodies mentioned in this book.

AACS   The Association for the Advancement of Christian Scholarship. Formerly known as the Association for Reformed Scientific Studies. Created in 1967 as the parent organization of the Institute for Christian Studies, and for a short while, the Curriculum Development Centre. It ceased to exist in 1983 when the institute received a charter to grant a master's degree in philosophical foundations

AADE   The Alberta Association of Deans of Education. Formed in 2012, the association seeks to speak as a united body in provincial stakeholder meetings.

ARSS   The Association for Reformed Scientific Studies. Founded in 1956 to promote the development of Neo-Calvinist higher education. Later changed its name to the Association for the Advancement of Christian Scholarship.

ATA   The Alberta Teachers Association. A union representing all teachers in both the public and Catholic provincial school systems. The union strives to also function as the professional association for teachers, a role that includes teacher certification. Alberta Education refuses to relinquish its power to certify teachers to the ATA as long as it insists on combining union activities with professional responsibilities.

CASS   College of Alberta School Superintendents. A professional organization dating back to 1958 that oversees standards of practice for school superintendents.

CACE   Center for the Advancement of Christian education. A project of Dordt University and funded by the Sid & Carol Verdoorn Foundation for the purpose of sharing best practices in Christian education. Under the leadership of Darryl DeBoer, the CACE leads the development of Teaching for Transformation (TFT) in the United States.

CDC   The Curriculum Development and Training Centre. Created in 1973 as a legal entity to front the publication of *Joy in Learning*. In 1974 it became an actual centre with employees, operated by the Association for the Advancement of Christian Scholarship. The CDC became an independent curriculum developer/publisher/teacher consulting organization in 1976 and closed its doors in 1990.

CRC   The Christian Reformed Church. Emerged in 1857 when several churches split off from the Dutch Reformed Church (now known as the Reformed Church in America). Most members and supporters of Christian Schools Canada are members of the Christian Reformed Church.

CSC   Christian Schools Canada. Formed in 1999, as a loosely affiliated collection of three independent regional school associations. These associations were formerly known as

Districts 10, 11, & 12 of Christian Schools International. Currently, they are named Edvance (Ontario), the Prairie Center for Christian Education (Alberta) and the Society of Christian Schools in British Columbia. Even though CSC is not a parent organization, and the regional associations prefer to be known by their own names, CSC is the most accurate way to refer to them collectively.

CSI Christian Schools International. New name given to the National Union of Christian Schools in 1978 to reflect the fact that three of its twelve school districts were in Canada.

EDVANCE Edvance Christian Schools Association. In 2015 three groups that formerly represented school boards (OACS), teachers (OCSTA), and principles (OCSAA) in the Ontario region of the Neo-Calvinist school movement were dissolved. Edvance Christian Schools Association replaced them, and while it performed many of their respective duties, it was animated by a new vision to partner with Christian schools of other traditions.

EL Expeditionary Learning. This personalized approach to learning is based on the educational philosophy of Kurt Hahn, a German educator and founder of Outward Bound.

ESCE The Edmonton Society for Christian Education. A parent organization that launched its first school in 1949. In all, the society established three elementary schools and a high school. In 1999, the society negotiated an agreement with the Edmonton Public School Board that made its high school and elementary schools an alternative Christian program within the public school system. The society still partners with the public board to oversee its particular responsibilities.

EPSB The Edmonton Public School Board. The second-largest and most progressive public school board in Alberta.

HHH	Head, Heart, Hand knowledge. A biblical notion of knowledge that combines thinking, desiring and doing.
OACS	The Ontario Alliance of Christian Schools. Created in 1952 as an administrative body for District 10 of the National Union of Christian Schools to provide leadership particularly in the area of curriculum development. In 2015 the OACS was dissolved to make way for a new organization named Edvance. At that time the OACS represented sixty-nine schools. Edvance currently has 88 member schools, from a variety of backgrounds, with a total enrollment of 8,500 students.
OCSAA	The Ontario Christian School Administrators Association. Disbanded in 2015.
OCSTA	The Ontario Christian School Teachers Association. Organized in 1954 to promote the professionalism of Christian school teachers. In October 2011 the board changed the name to the Edifide Christian Educators Association. In 2015, Edifide was dissolved to make way for Edvance.
NUCS	The National Union of Christian Schools. Founded in 1920 as the centralized administration of a growing number of Neo-Calvinist schools in the United States. In 1978 the organization changed its name to Christian Schools International to reflect the fact that three of its twelve school districts were in Canada.
PBL	Project-based learning. Dating back to John Dewey, PBL is organized around open-ended questions that deal with real-world problems.
PCAB	The Private College Accreditation Board. Established in the 1980s by the Alberta government. This board established the

criteria that private (independent) colleges would have to meet to be eligible to offer three- and four-year baccalaureate degrees in arts and sciences or two-year after-degree programs in education. Once these criteria were met, the PCAB would recommend that the Minister of Advanced Education approve the program or degree.

PCCE The Prairie Centre for Christian Education. Established in 2011 as a unique combination of three former bodies that represented various stakeholders in District 11 of Christian Schools International: the Christian Educators Association (teachers), the Christian Principals Association (administrators), the Prairie Association of Christian schools (parent societies and school boards). The PCCE is one of the three organizations that make up Christian Schools Canada. Current numbers: 17 schools, 7,300 students.

SCSBC The Society for Christian Schools in British Columbia. Established in 1976 to serve the various parent-run school societies that operated the Christian schools in District 12 of Christian Schools International. In 1999, the SCSBC, along with its counterparts in Ontario, Alberta, and Manitoba, left Christian Schools International and formed Christian Schools Canada. Current numbers: 40 schools, 15,300 students.

TFT Teaching for Transformation. An alternative approach to organizing teaching and learning developed under the direction of the Prairie Centre for Christian Education in Alberta.

UBD Understanding by Design. A novel approach to curriculum developed by Grant Wiggins and Jay McTighe in 1998. The authors flipped the traditional approach on its head by first clarifying the educational goals, then planning activities that would address those goals.

APPENDIX 2
Curriculum Development Centre Publishing Chart

Published Texts

Vol. 1: *Joy in Learning*, Ed. Arnold De Graaff & Jean Olthuis   1973, reprint 1975

Vol. 3: *Reclaiming the Land: A Study of the Book of Joshua*, Don Sinnema   1977

Vol. 3: *Of Kings & Prophets: A Study of the Book of Kings*, Harry Fernhout   1979

Vol. 4: *The Number and Shape of Things*, Trudy Bakker, Cal Jongsma   1979

Teaching with Joy, Jean Olthuis   1979

Education and the Public Purpose, Lyle McBurney   1979

Vol. 2: *Japan: A Way of Life*, Arnold De Graaff, Jean Olthuis, Anne Tuininga   1980

Vol. 2: *Kenya: A Way of Life*, Arnold De Graaff, Jean Olthuis, Anne Tuininga   1981

Vol. 3: Promises Broken, Promises Kept: A Reader's Guide to I and II Samuel, Harry Fernhout   1986

Additional products

The Denendeh people study kit (written between 1981–1982)
Puppetry book (written circa 1983)
Concept for an integrated curriculum dealing with handicapped people

Newsletters Featuring Visionary Content (See chapter 6)

No. 1: Spring 1978: Education for Discipleship I – Staff
No. 2: Summer 1978: Education for Discipleship II – Staff
No. 3: Fall 1978: Education for Discipleship III – Staff
No. 4: Spring 1979: Looking to the Eighties – Nicholas Wolterstorff
No. 6: Fall 1980: Strategy for the Eighties – Geraldine Steensma
No. 15: Fall 1984: Reaffirming the Vision – Staff
No. 16: Winter 1985: A Dialogue on Christian Education – John Stronks, Clive Beck, Harro Van Brummelen, Aukje Masselink

APPENDIX 3
CDC Founding Members, Staff and Board Members

Founding Members

Anne Tuininga, Jean Olthuis, Debra Steele, Mary Gerritsma

CDC Employees

*Major figures in Italics

Staff – Researcher/Writer/Consultant

Arnold De Graaf: June 1974 – Jun 1976
Jean Olthuis: Sep 1973 – July 1982
Anne Tuininga Sep 1973 – Sep 1983;
Harry Fernhout June 1975 – Sep 78;
Agnes Struik Sep 1978 – June 1990
Don Sinnema
Trudy Bakker
Cal Jongsma
Don Vander Klock

Administration

Arnold De Graaf (ED): June 1974 – June 1976
Tom Malcolm (ED): Oct 1976 – Oct 1980
Anne Tuininga (Admin) 1982, Jun 1985 – Jun 1986

Harry Fernhout (ED) Sep 1983 – Mar 1986
Yael Barbour (ED) Oct 1980 – Nov 1980
Peter Enneson
Sally Armour-Wotton (ED) June 1982 – May 1984
Alan Engelstad
Marian Kits (Admin)
Linda Leenders (Admin)
Hilda Fernhout (Admin)
Amy Rowe (Admin)

People Who Served on the Board of Directors

Miki Beltman
Helen Breems
Gwendolyn Dekker
Alan Englestad
Peter Enneson
Henriette Fayer-Murphy
Karen Gerritsma
Chris Gort
Barbara Hudspith
John Hull
Jannake (Jenny) Koole
Linda Leenders
Henry Lise
Aukje Maaselink
John Olthuis

Debbie Marshall
Lyle McBurney
Thomas McIntyre
Jane Reitsma-Hoogendam
Hilda Roukema
Eric Schilperoort
Mary Siebenga
John Sneep
Geraldine Steensma
Harry Van Belle
Harro Van Brummelen
John Olthuis
George Vandezande
Tony Vyn

APPENDIX 4
CDC Timeline

1973 (Fall) Four women who have worked on the *Joy in Learning* project form an incorporated company called the Curriculum Development and Teacher Training Centre to expedite the development, financing, and distribution of the *Joy in Learning* manuscript.

1974 (June) The Association for the Advancement of Christian Scholarship (AACS) officially adopts the centre (known as the Curriculum Development Centre) as a project and hires Dr. Arnold De Graaf as a part-time executive director and Jean Olthuis, Anne Tuininga, and Harry Fernhout as part-time staff.

1975 (Jan.) The AACS receives a $25,000 grant from an anonymous donor to fund the development of a second volume of a planned curriculum writing project.

1976 (Spring) CDC staff raise concerns with the AACS board that their obligation to fundraise is impeding their curriculum development work. Arnold De Graaf is given an ultimatum: he cannot be a senior member of the Institute for Christian Studies and be executive director for the CDC. He chooses to remain at the ICS.

1976 (Oct.) The AACS board decides it can no longer operate the CDC due to limited finances. Tom Malcolm is hired as executive director. His task is to keep the CDC afloat long enough to publish all the finished projects in some usable form. The CDC changes its by-laws, so it can continue as an independent organization, administered by an elected board of governors from a body of dues-paying members.

1977	The CDC publishes a study on the book of Joshua, volume 3 of the Bible curriculum, its first product release since the publication of *Joy in Learning*.
1978 (Sept.)	Agnes Struik is hired as a half-time classroom teacher consultant.
1979–1981	The CDC publishes six texts. Only two projects planned for its four-volume program of study remain to be published. Overall, these texts do not generate a great deal of revenue because they are not readily applicable to most classrooms in Christian Schools Canada.
1981	The CDC seeks to develop co-publishing agreements with the Canadian Curriculum Council (an arm of Christian Schools International and with Signal publishing, but neither pans out. Agnes Struik is now employed four fifths of the time, and she is fast becoming the face of the CDC through her consulting work. Internal conflicts between the three women on staff impacts their work and personal well-being.
1982 (Jan.)	Donor support levels off to $35,000/year ($233,500 dollars in today's currency), which is not enough to support a staff of three.
1982 (June)	Sally Armor Wolton is hired as executive secretary.
1982 (Oct.)	Jean Olthuis takes a leave of absence that was supposed to last for a year; she does not return.

1982 (Fall)	Tensions in the office remain high between the three staff: Armor Wolton, Tuininga, and Struik.
1983 (Summer)	Staff are not paid in July and August due to the CDC's limited financial resources. Staff tensions come to a head.
1983 (Sept.)	Anne Tuininga, decides to leave the CDC. Sally Armor Wolton is released from her paid position and taken on as a freelance fundraiser, to be paid on a commission basis. Harry Fernhout (ex. dir.) and Linda Leenders (bookkeeping) are hired to part time-positions and join Agnes Struik on staff.
1984 (May)	Armor Wolton resigns from her fundraising position.
1984 (June)	Anne Tuininga is appointed to the CDC board.
1985 (June)	Anne Tuininga replaces Linda Leenders as a half-time administrator. Agnes Struik continues as a full-time consultant. Harry Fernhout remains as executive director at one fifth of the time.
1985 (Spring)	The seventeenth and last newsletter is published.
1986 (Jan.)	The board conducts a major review of the CDC's role and how it is perceived in the CSC community. A long-range plan is commissioned.
1986 (Mar.)	Harry Fernhout leaves to take up a position as senior member at The ICS. Agnes Struik considers leaving to either start a master's program or form her own consulting company.
1986 (June)	After years of delay, the final Bible curriculum text is published. This is the last text that the CDC publishes. The board adopts a new strategic plan. The CDC moves

	away from its vision to develop a thematic-integral approach to curriculum design and focuses instead on teacher development.
1986 (Sept.)	The CDC moves out of its office space provided by the AACS at 229 College St. All past and current documents are placed in boxes and stored at different people's homes.
1987	Agnes Struik continues working half-time as a consultant. She also takes on the task of rewriting the *Joy in Learning* manual.
1988	Agnes Struik continues her consulting work, but the lack of an address and a physical office curtail the sales of available curriculum stock
198	The function of the board and the administration seems to have faded away. Agnes Struik continues to do some consulting. Orders for materials are unfilled.
1990 (April)	Agnes Struik informs Harry Houtman of Christian Stewardship Services that the CDC is defunct, and it will pay its outstanding loan by June 30.
1990 (July–Dec.)	An inactive file contains text orders, inquiries about unfilled orders from all over the world, and a couple of uncashed cheques.

APPENDIX 5
The King's University Education Faculty Visioning Documents

From 2011 to 2015, the education faculty used two documents to further develop its vision for teacher education, the Professor Self-Portrait and the Course Portrait. Completing these documents took considerable time and energy. Typically, they were worked on over the summer and shared at the Education Faculty retreat, which was held in late August.

PROFESSOR SELF-PORTRAIT

INSTRUCTOR: _____
DATE: _____

The purpose of this " self-portrait" is to capture your own image as teacher in The King's B. Ed Programs. The template attempts to balance a common structure for our individual "images" as well as leave plenty of room for our distinctive personalities. In this format the portrait will be a composite of at least four image-features: pedagogy (teaching approach/strategies), curriculum orientation, assessment (approach/strategies) and metaphor (e.g., teacher as facilitator, etc.) Other features may be added as well. Each of the common features will take shape through a narrative sketch as well as a set of short-answer responses to selected items. Additional information may be added to each section, if desired.

Instructions:

Each feature below (excepting the final summary section) consists of two parts. The A parts require an essay response of at least 300 words (1 page). Add these responses to the end of the document as appendices. For example, Appendix 1 contains Feature 1, Part A, Appendix 2 contains Feature 2, Part A, and so on. The B Parts require short answers to the various items. Type in your answers after each item! You may want to italicize your responses so they stand out visually. After inserting all of your responses, save and rename this template file and email it to the dean.

FEATURE I: PEDAGOGY/TEACHING STRATEGIES

A. On a separate sheet, write a 300–700 word overview of your pedagogical approach. Describe your philosophy of teaching! Describe what it looks like in practice! What are your staple teaching strategies? Explain how your pedagogical approach evolved!

B. Short Answer items

1. 1. Which authors, educators, schools of pedagogy have shaped your way of teaching? Explain how you have modified/combined these influences into your singular style? Which positions do you consciously repudiate?

2. Explain what learning style(s) are most compatible with your teaching? (linear thinking, deductive, inductive, etc.)

3. Which elements of your approach to teaching do you find most challenging to implement? Explain why!

4. How do you justify your approach to teaching in your courses within the vision/mission statements of King's?

FEATURE II: CURRICULUM ORIENTATION

A. On a separate sheet, write a 300–700 word overview of your orientation to curriculum. Describe the typical design of your lessons, units and bigger chunks of content! Explain how your approach to curriculum planning evolved.

B. Short Answer items

1. Which authors, educators, curriculum orientations have shaped your way of organizing content and structuring the learning situation? Explain how you have modified/combined these influences into your singular style? Which positions do you consciously repudiate?

2. What are the most essential questions you ask your students?

3. What do you present to your students as "most worth knowing?"

4. Which elements of your approach to curriculum making do you find most challenging to implement? Explain why!

5. How do you model your approach to curriculum making in your courses at King's?

FEATURE III: ASSESSMENT

A. On a separate sheet, write a 300–700 word overview of your approach to assessment of student learning. Describe your philosophy of student assessment! Describe what it looks like in practice! What are your staple assessment strategies? Explain how your approach to student assessment evolved!

B. Short Answer items

1. Which authors, educators, schools of assessment have shaped your way of evaluating student progress? Explain how you have modified/combined these influences into your singular style.

2. Which elements of your approach to assessment do you find most challenging to implement? Explain why!

3. How do you model your approach to assessment in your courses at King's?

FEATURE IV: METAPHOR

A. On a separate sheet, write a 300–700 word overview of your favourite metaphor(s) for teaching. Deconstruct what each metaphor does or does not mean to you? Explain how you arrived to this point.

B. Common Set of Short Answer items

1. Which authors, educators, schools of pedagogy have shaped your metaphor for teaching? Explain how you have modified/combined these influences into your singular style? Which metaphors do you consciously repudiate?

2. Which aspects of your metaphor do you find most challenging to implement? Explain why!

3. How do you model your metaphor of teaching in your courses at King's?

FEATURE V: SUMMARY

A. On a separate sheet, write a summary statement that pulls together the various components sketched above. Focus on the connecting points; show how the components reflect/reinforce/complement each other. Explain how your teaching portrait bears the markings, traits, features of a Christian faith-based teacher preparation program.

COURSE PORTRAIT

COURSE # _____
INSTRUCTOR:_____
DATE:_____

SECTION A: THE CONCEPTUAL STATEMENT

Write a 300–700 word overview of the course that: i) outlines the boundaries and priorities of the content—<u>The What</u>, ii) describes the organizational principles employed—<u>The How</u>, iii) discloses the foundational framework—<u>The Why</u>.)

Also demonstrate how this course concept i) addresses the Education Faculty's Program Goals and the larger vision/mission of the university and ii) clarify how the *biblical themes and your Christian faith perspective shape your foundational stance vis a vis the other major positions associated with the topics covered in this course.*

*Spaces left on this form do not reflect the amount of text expected. Most sections do not have prescribed requirements or even approximations for length. The document is arranged so instructors can use it to construct their individual course portraits.

SECTION B: THE WHAT – BOUNDARIES AND PRIORITIES OF CONTENT

1. List of Essential Questions

Essential Questions are the most important questions that students should investigate in this course. EQs are open-ended queries raised by both teacher and student. A course built around Essential Questions presents itself to students as an experience of probing significant issues rather than achieving pre-set outcomes.

The Essential Questions typically raised in this course include the following:

2. List of Big Ideas

Big Ideas represent what the teacher most wants the students to remember from taking this course: the most significant, principles, conclusions, and guidelines encountered.

The Big Ideas typically presented in this course include the following:

3. List of Expected Student Outcomes

These outcomes reflect what the teacher expects students should be capable of as a consequence of taking this course. Expectations may apply to any or all of these categories: believing, understanding, speaking, writing, feeling, and doing.

Upon completing this course students should be able to:

4. Complete list of Class/Lecture titles or topics:

5. Alternative Method of Portraying the Boundaries and Priorities of Course Content: (Use this space to either supplement or replace any combination of items B 1-3 above.)

BIBLIOGRAPHY

Beck, Clive. "A Dialogue on Christian Education," *Joy in Learning*, no. 16 (Winter 1985): 2-3.

Beversluis, Nicholas. *Christian Philosophy of Education*. Grand Rapids, MI: The National Union of Christian Schools, 1971.

Blomberg, Doug. *Wisdom and Curriculum: Christian Schooling After Postmodernity*. Sioux Center. IA: Dordt College Press, 2007.

Bobbit, John Franklin. *The Curriculum: a Summary of the Development Concerning the Theory of Curriculum*. New York: Houghton Mifflin Company, 1918.

Bosco, James. "Is It Possible to Reform Schools?: Toward Solving the Riddle," a paper presented at the 9th International Conference on Technology and Education, Paris, France. Kalamazoo MI: Western Michigan University, Merze Tate Center for Research and Information Processing, 1992.

Boyer, Ernest L. "America's Schools: the mission." In *Education on Trial: Strategies for the Future*, edited by William J. Johnston, 301-320. San Francisco, CA: Institute for Contemporary Studies Press, 1985.

Blamires, Harry. *The Christian Mind*. London: S.P.C.K., 1963.

Blomberg, Doug. *Wisdom and Curriculum: Christian Schooling After Postmodernity.* Sioux Center. IA: Dordt College Press, 2007.

Bloom, Benjamin S. *Taxonomy of Educational Objectives, Handbook I: Cognitive Domain.* New York: David McKay, 1956.

Bratt, James. *Dutch Calvinism in Modern America: A History of a Conservative Subculture.* Grand Rapids, MI: W. B. Eerdmans Pub., 1984.

Curriculum Development Centre. "Reaffirming an educational vision," *Joy in Learning* Fall 1984: 1-6.

Cook, Justin and Darryl DeBoer. "Deeper Learning in Christian Education: Deeper Learning into What?" *Christian Educators Journal* 58, no. 1 (October 2018): 10-14.

Cremin, Lawrence A. *The Transformation of the School: Progressivism in American Education, 1876-1957.* New York: Vintage Books, 1961.

Crouch, Andy. *Culture Making: Recovering Our Creative Calling.* Downers Grove, IL: IVP Books, 2008.

De Boer, Peter et al. *Educating Christian Teachers for Responsive Discipleship.* Lanham, ML: University Press of America, 1993.

De Boer, Peter. *Shifts in Curricular Theory for Christian Education.* Grand Rapids, MI: Calvin College Monograph, 1983.

De Boer, Peter and Donald Oppewal. "American Calvinist Day Schools." In *Voices from the Past: Reformed Educators,* edited by Donald Oppewal, 267, Langham, MD: University Press of America, 1997.

De Graaff, Arnold. *The Educational Ministry of the Church: A Perspective.* Nutley, NJ: The Craig Press, 1968.

De Graaff, Arnold, and Jean Olthuis, eds. *Joy in Learning: An Integrated Curriculum for the Elementary School.* Toronto: Curriculum Development Centre, 1973.

De Graaff, Arnold, Jean Olthuis, and Anne Tuininga. *Kenya: A Way of Life*. Toronto: Joy in Learning Curriculum Development and Training Centre, 1981.

De Moor, Ary. "Curricular Concerns in the Eighties," in *Shaping Christian Schools, Conference Proceedings*. Surrey, BC: The Society for Christian Schools in British Columbia (April 8–10, 1981): 2.

De Moor, Ary. et al. *Man in Society*. Grand Rapids, MI: Christian Schools International Publications, 1980.

Dooyeweerd, Herman. *In The Twilight of Western Thought: Studies in the Pretended Autonomy of Philosophical Thought*. Nutley, NJ: The Craig Press, 1968.

Drake, Susan, and Rebecca Burns. *Meeting Standards Through Integrated Curriculum*. Association for Supervision and Curriculum Development. Alexandria, VA. 2004.

Eisner, E., and E. Vallance, eds. *Conflicting Conceptions of the Curriculum*. Berkeley, CA: McCutchan, 1974.

Encyclopedia of Children and Childhood in History and Society. "Progressive Education," (February 13, 2019): 5.

Fernhout, Harry. "Summary Critique of Shaping School Curriculum," in *Shaping Christian Schools Conference Proceedings*, Surrey, BC: Society for Christian Schools in British Columbia, (April 8–10, 1981).

Fernhout, Harry. "Reaffirming an Educational Vision," *Joy in Learning* no. 15 (Fall 1984): 1-6.

Gardner, Howard. *Multiple Intelligences: New Horizons*. New York: Basic Books, 1993.

Jellema, William. "The Curriculum in a Liberal Arts College," in *Voices from the Past: Reformed Educators*. Langham, ML: University Press of America, 1997, 5.

Hull, John. "Aiming for Christian Education, Settling for Christians Educating: The Christian School's Replication of a Public School Paradigm." *Christian Scholars Review* XXXII: 2 (Winter 2003): 203-224.

Hull, John. *Christian Education and the Deep Structure of Schooling*. Doctoral thesis. University of Toronto, 1993.

Hull, John. "Education for Discipleship: A Curriculum Orientation for Christian Educators." *The Journal of Education and Christian Belief* (Autumn 2009): 169-176.

Hunter, James Davison. *To Change the World: The Irony, Tragedy, and Possibility of Christianity in the Late Modern World*. Oxford University Press, 2010.

Jackson, Philip. "Conceptions of Curriculum and Curriculum Specialists," in *Handbook of Research on Curriculum*, edited by Philip Jackson, 3-40, New York: Macmillan Publishing Company, 1992.

Jellema, William. "The Curriculum in a Liberal Arts College," in *Voices from the Past: Reformed Educators*, ed. Donald Oppewal. Langham, ML: University Press of America, Inc, 1997.

Kliebard, H. *The Struggle of the American Curriculum 1893–1958*. New York: Routledge & Kegan Paul, 1986.

Kobes-Du Mez, Kristin. *Jesus and John Wayne: How White Evangelicals Corrupted a Faith and Fractured a Nation*. New York: Liveright Publishing Corp., 2020.

Kohn, Alfie. *The Schools our Children Deserve: Moving Beyond Traditional Classrooms and "Tougher Standards."* Boston, MA: Houghton Mifflin, 2000.

Konyndyk DeYoung, Rebecca. "Courage as a Christian Virtue," *Journal of Spiritual Formation and Soul Care* Vol. 6 (November 2013): 301-312.

Kornelis, Pat. "More Than a Pious Wish: Living into the Story," *Christian Educators Journal* Vol. 58, no. 1, (October 2018): 26-28.

Labaree, David F. "Progressivism, Schools and Schools of Education: An American Romance. *Paedagogica Historica* Vol. 41, 1 & 2 (February 2005): 275-288.

Lincoln, Yvonna. "The Making of a Constructivist: A Remembrance of Transformations Past." In *The Paradigm Dialogue*, edited by E. G. Guba, Los Angeles: Sage Publications, 1990, 67-87.

Masselink, Aukje. "A Dialogue on Christian Education," *Joy in Learning* no. 16 (Winter 1985): 5-6.

McIntire, C. T. "Herman Dooyeweerd in North America," in *Reformed Theology in America: A History of Its Modern Development*, ed. D. F. Wells, 172-186. Grand Rapids, MI: Eerdmans, 1985.

McNeil, John. *Curriculum: A Comprehensive Introduction*. Boston: Little, Brown, 1977.

Middleton, J. Richard. "A New Heaven and a New Earth: The Case for a Holistic Reading of the Biblical Story of Redemption," *Journal of Christian Theological Research* 11 (2006) 73-97.

Monsma, Gayle. "Listening for Echoes: Storylines in Teaching for Transformation," *Christian Educators Journal* Vol. 58, no.1, (October 2018) 15-17.

Newell, Ted and Ken Badley. "Caught Between Stories: A Narrative Approach to Worldview for Christian Professionals," in *Bridging the Gap: Connecting Christian Faith and Professional Practice*, edited by Bram De Muynck, Johan Hegeman, Peter Vos. Sioux Center, IA: Dordt College Press, 2011: 117-126.

Niebuhr, H. Richard. *Christ and Culture*, New York: Harper Torchbooks, 1951.

Olthuis, Jean. *Teaching with "Joy," Implementing Integrated Curriculum in the Classroom*. Toronto, ON: Curriculum Development Centre, 1979.

Olthuis, John. "Towards the 21st Century: Vision and Direction," *The Christian Vanguard* Vol. 10 (July 1970): 6-9.

Oppewal, Donald, ed. *Voices from the Past: Reformed Educators.* Lanham, ML: University Press of America, Inc., 1984.

Palmer, Parker. *The Courage to Teach: Honoring the Teachers Heart.* San Francisco, CA: Jossey-Bass, 2002.

Paterson, Katherine. *The Spying Heart: More Thoughts on Reading and Writing Books for Children.* New York: Lodestar Books, 1989.

Peetoom, Adrian. "From Mythology to Mythology: Dutch-Canadian Orthodox-Calvinist Immigrants and Their Schools." Master's Thesis, University of Toronto, 1993.

Phenix, Philip. *Realms of Meaning.* New York: McGraw-Hill Book Company, 1964.

Pinar, William, et al. *Understanding Curriculum: An Introduction to the Study of Historical and Contemporary Curriculum Discourses.* New York: Peter Lang, 1995.

Plantinga, Theodore. "The Paralysis of the Christian Student," *The Christian Vanguard* Vol. 10 (July 1970): 10-14.

Prakash, M. S. and L. J. Waks. "Four Conceptions of Excellence." *Teachers College Record* 87:1 (1985): 90-101.

Prinsen, Peter, "That Old Dutch Disease: The Roots of Dutch Calvinist's Education in Alberta," PhD diss., (University of Alberta, 2000).

Rohr, Richard. *Falling Upward: A Spirituality for the Two Halves of Life.* San Francisco, CA: Jossey- Bass, 2012.

Smith, James K. A. *Desiring the Kingdom: Worship, Worldview, and Cultural Formation.* Grand Rapids, MI: Baker Academic, 2009.

Smith, James K.A. "Is There Room for Martyrs in our Church?" Chapel homily. Indiana Wesleyan University, Marion, IN, October 18, 2009, http://forsclavigera.blogspot.com/2009/11/room-for-martyrs.html.

Smith, James K. A. *You Are What You Love: The Spiritual Power of Habit.* Grand Rapids, MI: Brazos Press, 2016.

Steensma, Geraldine J. *To Those Who Teach: Keys for Decision-Making.* Signal Mountain, TN: Signal, 1971.

Steensma, Geraldine J. "Strategy for the Eighties," *Joy in Learning* no.6, (Fall 1980):1-3, 6.

Steensma, Geraldine and Harro Van Brummelen, eds., *Shaping School Curriculum: A Biblical View.* Middleburg Heights, OH: Signal, 1977.

Stronks, G. and D. Blomberg, eds., *A Vision with a Task: Christian Schooling for Responsive Discipleship.* Grand Rapids, MI: Baker Books, 1993.

Stronks, John. "A Dialogue on Christian Education," *Joy in Learning* no. 16 (Winter 1985): 1-2.

Struik, Agnes. *The Life Story of CDC.* Unpublished.

Tanner, D., and L. Tanner. *Curriculum Development.* New York: Macmillan, 1980.

Taylor, Frederick. *The Principles of Scientific Management.* New York: Harper & Brothers, 1911.

Thorndike, Edward L. "The Nature, Purposes, and General Methods of Measurements of Educational Products," in *Seventeenth Yearbook, Part II.* Bloomington, IL: National Society for the Study of Education, 1918.

Tyack, David and Elisabeth Hansot. *Managers of Virtue: Public School Leadership in America 1820–1980.* New York: Basic Books, 1961.

Tye, Barbara Benham. "The Deep Structure of Schooling." *Phi Delta Kappan,* (December 1987): 281-284.

Tyler, Ralph. *Basic Principles of Curriculum and Instruction*. Chicago: University of Chicago Press, 1949.

Van Brummelen, Harro. "A Dialogue on Christian Education," *Joy in Learning* no. 16 (Winter 1985): 3-5.

Van Brummelen, Harro. "Rejoinder to John E. Hull, 'Education for Christian Discipleship: A Curriculum Orientation for Christian Educators.'" *The Journal of Education and Christian Belief*, (Autumn 2009): 169-176.

Van Brummelen, Harro. *Steppingstones to Curriculum: A Biblical Path*. Colorado Springs: Purposeful Design Publications, 2002.

Van Brummelen, Harro. *Telling the Next Generation: Educational Development in North American Calvinist Christian Schools*. Langham, MD: University Press of America, 1986.

Van Brummelen, Harro. *Walking with God in the Classroom: Christian Approaches to Learning and Teaching*. Seattle, WA: Alta Vista College Press, 1988.

Van Dyk, John. "The Relation Between Faith and Action: An Introduction." *Pro Rege*, X, 4, (1982): 2-7.

Vander Goot, Henry, ed. *H. Evan Runner*. St. Catherines, ON: Paideia Press. 1981.

Walsh, Brian J. "Transformation: Dynamic Worldview or Repressive Ideology," *Journal of Education and Christian Belief* 4, no. 2, (September 1, 2000): 101-114.

Walsh, Brian J and J. Richard Middleton. *The Transforming Vision: Shaping Christian World View*. Downers Grove, IL: Intervarsity Press, 1984.

Walsh, Brian J and J Richard Middleton. *Truth Is Stranger Than It Used to Be: Biblical Faith in a Postmodern Age*. Downers Grove, IL: Intervarsity Press, 1995.

Wiggins, Grant and Jay McTighe. *Essential Questions: Opening Doors to Student Understanding*. Alexandria, VA: ASCD, 2004.

Wiggins, Grant and Jay McTighe. *Understanding by Design*. Alexandria, VA: ASCD, 1998.

Wolters, Al. "Dutch Neo-Calvinism: Worldview, Philosophy and Rationality," in *Rationality in the Calvinian Tradition*, eds. H. Hart, J. van der Hoven, and Nicholas Wolterstorff. Toronto: UPA, 1983: 113-131.

Wolters, Al. *Creation Regained: Biblical Basics for a Reformational Worldview*, Grand Rapids: Wm. B Eerdmans Publishing Co., 1985, 2nd ed. 2005.

Wolters, Al. "The Importance of H. Evan Runner," *Comment*, 2003, https://www.cardus.ca/comment/article/the-importance-of-h-evan-runner/.

Wolterstorff, Nicholas P. "Beyond 1984 in Philosophy of Christian Education," in *Educating for Life: Reflections on Christian Teaching and Learning*, edited by Gloria Stronks and Clarence Joldersma, 63-83. Grand Rapids, MI: Baker Academic, 2002.

Wolterstorff, Nicholas P. "By What Standard?," in *Educating for Life: Reflections on Christian Teaching and Learning*, edited by Gloria Stronks & Clarence Joldersma, 17-31. Grand Rapids, MI: Baker Academic, 2002.

Wolterstorff, Nicholas P. *Educating for Responsible Action*. Grand Rapids: Eerdmans, 1980.

Wolterstorff, Nicholas P. "Looking to the Eighties: Do Christian Schools *in Learning* no. 4 (Spring 1979): 1-6.

Wolterstorff, Nicholas P. "Keeping Faith: Talks for a New Faculty." *Occasional Papers*. Calvin College, (1989): 9.

Zylstra, Bernard. "H. Evan Runner: An Assessment of His Mission," in *Life is Religion: Essays in Honor of H. Evan Runner*, edited by Henry Vander Goot. 1-14, St. Catherines, Ontario: Paideia Press, 198.

INDEX

additive approach to teaching 278, 307,
administrative progressives *See under* paradigm of progressivism
Alberta Teachers Association (ATA) 228-229, 233, 236, 382-383, 395
American dream 23, 62, 71, 344, 352, 378, 384
antithesis 196, 253
Association for the Advancement of Christian Scholarship (AACS) 28, 46, 68-69, 81-89, 96-97, 309-315, 394
Association for Calvinistic Philosophy 42
   (later known as Association for Reformational Philosophy)
Association for Reformed Scientific Studies (ARSS) 42-43, 46, 394
Association of Alberta Deans of Education (AADE) 228, 382, 394
Augustine xvii-xviii, 16-17, 49, 83, 271
   two daughters of hope xvii-xx, 17, 51, 64, 83, 87, 178, 211-214, 217, 253, 352

Berkenbosch, Roy xvii, xx, 352, 390
Beversluis, Nicholas 26, 271-272, 286-291
Blomberg, Doug xix, 99, 137
Bratt, James 12, 22
Bruinsma, Bob xx, 231-237, 243-244, 381, 390
Buisman, Peter 205-206, 210, 327

Calvin College (now University) 4, 18-20, 42-46, 138, 231-232, 270-276
Calvin, John x, 16, 49, 271
Calvin Seminary 18
Calvinist Contact (now *Christian Courier*) 28, 36
Campus Alberta Quality Council (CAQC) 244
CDC mothers. *See under* Curriculum Development Centre

Christian Labour Association of Canada (CLAC) 356
Christian mind xvi, 38, 44, 60-61, 141-142, 176, 273, 291
Christian Reformed Church (CRC) 18, 345, 368, 395
Christian School Herald 28, 35-38, 137
Christian Schools Canada (CSC) xiii, 5, 19, 58, 137, 164, 176, 203, 243, 395
    Educational vision x-xi, xvi, 5, 15, 49, 62,
    regional organizations xiii, 5-6, 48, 218
    communities
        as interpretive 32-33
        of rivals 32, 34-39
        of revival 32, 40-47
Christian Schools International (CSI)
    See NUCS
Christian Teacher Academy 223-234
conceptual statement 76, 160, 162, 166-167, 411, 463
Cook, Hugh 347
Cook, Justin xx, 213, 224-225
course portrait 247, 411-412
Crouch, Andy 158, 190, 379
cultural mandate xvi-xvii, 37, 149, 154, 160, 188-191, 252
culture transformation x, xvi-xvii, 13, 15, 40-41, 112, 176-177, 188-190, 252, 347, 379
curriculum
    conception 260-262, 277, 291, 297
    debates
        1950s and 1960s at Calvin College 18, 138, 231, 289
        among CSC educators 142
    dualist view of 36-38, 110
    integral 60, 65, 72-73, 81, 87, 206, 239, 267, 308, 362-363
    integrated 67, 76, 99, 118-119, 121-124, 127, 130-132, 265-269, 299, 314-315
    integrationist view of 36-38, 165, 267-268
    intrinsic idea in 274
    liberal arts 141, 264, 272, 276, 291, 297-302
    monastic view of 36-37, 39, 164
    orientation 50, 59, 62-64, 72-73, 165-166, 168, 176-177, 260-263, 379
    nontraditional 301-302
    ordering principle for 109-110, 127, 133, 162, 171, 324-328
    traditional 249, 301-302
Curriculum Development Centre (CDC)
    as a project of the AACS 86-95
    CDC mothers 82-91, 101-102, 118, 211
    educational vision 77, 89-90, 101-102, 106-107, 110, 117-124, 133-134
    key staff 96-101
    publications 101, 399-400
    strengths and weaknesses 80-81, 92, 103-105, 109, 324

curriculum reform xiv-xv, 20-25, 36-38, 80-81, 163-168, 221, 223, 270,
    teacher led 48, 50, 62-63, 65-68, 206

daughters of hope (Anger & Courage)
    See also Augustine
De Afscheiding 8, 12-13, 20, 36, 165, 219, 284
De Boer, Peter 20, 270-271
De Graaff, Arnold 68-69, 86-88, 90-94, 96-98
De Moor, Ary xix, 136, 171
DeBoer, Darryl 209, 213,
deep structure of schooling 116, 217, 293-296, 307-308
dissident social institution (the school as) 15, 35, 49, 51, 176, 188, 217, 253
Doleantie 8, 13-14
Doornenbal, Brian xx, 327
Dooyeweerd, Herman 28, 42-45, 69, 268, 347, 378
Dordt College (now University) 43, 46, 97, 213, 345
Dosdall, Emry 195, 199
dualism in philosophy 116, 128, 145, 147, 165, 178, 268,
Durham Christian High School (DCHS) 365-376
Dylan, Bob 146, 338, 381

Edmonton Christian School (ECS) 191, 193-195, 204, 210, 235, 380
Edmonton Public School Board (EPSB) 194-203
Edmonton Society for Christian Education (ESCE) 192, 196-200, 396
education for discipleship xvi, 60-63, 77, 1087, 113, 118, 178, 217, 252, 285, 328
education for hope xvii, 178, 191, 207, 213, 253, 391
Edvance xii, 5, 221-225, 396
Eisner, Elliott 33, 161, 260-262, 277, 297
Enlightenment 9-11, 110, 295, 308
expeditionary learning 209, 225-226, 396

Fernhout, Harry xix, 372
    roles at CDC 88, 97-98, 319
    author of CDC vision statement 106, 117-124
    critique of *Shaping Curriculum* 161, 326-327
foundational relationships
    See also Jaarsma, Cornelius

Gereformeerde Kerken 8, 13
Gordian Knot 24-26, 269, 295

Harari, Yuval Noah ix
Hart, Hendrik 358
head, heart, hands knowledge 328, 397

Hendriks, Ray 225
Hervormde Kerk 9, 13
Het Reveil 8, 10, 12
Hewlett Packard Foundation 226-227
Holland March Christian School x
Horlings, Jeremy xx, 213

Institute for Christian Studies (ICS) 46, 58, 68, 95, 350, 355-364
    See also AACS
integral. *See under* curriculum
integration. *See under* curriculum
integrationist. *See under* curriculum
interpretive community. *See under* community
intrinsic idea. *See under* curriculum

Jaarsma, Cornelius 38, 155, 271-272, 276-281, 289-290
    four foundational relationships 279
Jackson, Phillip 33, 260-263
Jaeger, Werner 44
Jellema, William 38, 141, 271-276, 281, 289-290
Joy in Learning
    as a program of learning 83-84
    the K-3 curriculum, Vol 1 65, 69
        educational vision of 70
        purpose, process, project 70-72
        ordering principle for *See under* curriculum
    the newsletter 63, 77, 97, 106, 111

Klapwyk, Ray 38
Koole, Robert 136-137, 190
Kuyper, Abraham x, 13-14, 20-22, 31, 41, 45, 196

latent paradigm syndrome 307, 313
liberal arts. *See under* curriculum
Lincoln, Yvonna 307

Maaskant, Frieda 242
Malcolm, Tom xix, 96-97, 107, 109-110, 324
Man in Society 84, 136, 169-175, 223, 371
Marcel, Gabriel xvii,
McTighe, Jay 210, 328, 398
Middleton, Richard 139-140, 142-148, 150-155
Modernity *See under* philosophy, modern
Monsma, Doug 210-213, 327

Monsma, Gayle xx, 210, 213

National Union of Christian Schools (NUCS) 23-24, 50
   (now Christian Schools International)
   curriculum development 26
      See also Triezenberg, Henry
   philosophy of education 26-27
      See also Beversluis, Nicholas
   relationship to CSC xii, 4, 34-35, 67
Neo-Calvinism 2, 32, 142, 188
Neo-Calvinist education
   as a legacy of hope 16
      See also Man in Society
   five formative features of 15-17, 23, 31, 49, 51
Noot, Ed xx, 219

old Dutch disease 34, 97. 222. 253
   See also Christian Schools Canada, community of rivals
Olthuis, Jean 69, 77-78, 82, 85-86, 96
Olthuis, Jim 97
Olthuis, John 40
Ontario Alliance of Christian Schools (OACS) xii, 28, 35-36, 38, 68, 81, 370, 397
Oosterhuis, Alyce xx, 196, 232, 380
Oppewal, Donald 14, 20, 23, 220, 280
ordering principle. *See under* curriculum

parable of the sower 51
paradigm of progressivism 5, 19, 292, 301, 327
   administrative progressives 21, 50, 127, 299, 301-304, 306
   pedagogical progressives 134, 298-299, 302, 305
   social reform progressives 297, 300, 302
Parker, Faye 196, 199, 201
Patrick, Margie 250
patterns within progressivism 308
pedagogical progressives *See under* paradigm of progressivism
Peetoom, Adrian xx, 6, 9, 30, 38
philosophy
   Ancient 147, 274, 277, 298, 361
   Medieval 16, 147, 273
   Modern 60, 108, 121, 141, 147, 150-152, 273, 277
   Postmodern 141, 150-153
   Romantic
      expressionism in 103, 273
Phenix, Philip 133, 155, 158, 161-162, 326-327

Prairie Centre of Christian Education (PCCE) xii, 209, 213, 218-219, 225
   (formerly Prairie Association of Christian Schools)
Prinsen, Peter 6, 14, 30, 34, 97
Private College Accreditation Board (PCAB) 232-233, 397
professor self-portrait 247, 407-410
project-based learning (PBL) 224-225, 397
program of learning 37, 75, 83, 90-91, 142

regularities of the classroom 73, 116, 168, 227, 293-294, 296, 308
reflective practitioner 238
Reformational movement 42-48, 85, 237, 275, 347-348, 351, 378
Reformational philosophy 42-44, 70, 90, 347
Reformed Church in the United States (RCUS) 342, 349
revival community. *See under* community
rival community. *See under* community
Rugg, Harold 59, 298
Runner, H. Evan 42-46, 68, 268, 35, 378

school society 7, 30, 95, 199, 204
   See also Edmonton Society for Christian Education
Scholte, H. 12, 20
Society of Christian Schools in British Columbia (SCSBC) xii, 209, 213, 219-220, 398
   The Residency 220
social reform progressives *See under* paradigm of progressivism
Shaping School Curriculum See under Steensma, Gerladine
Siebenga, Ren xix, 223, 227, 365, 369-370
Siebenga, Nathan 224
Spyksma, Darren xx, 209, 220, 225
Stienstra, Wendy 245, 250
Stieva, Bernice 245
Steensma, Geraldine 99, 133, 155
   "Strategy for the Eighties" 113-117
   keys for teaching 156-158
   Shaping School Curriculum 159-163
storyline *See under* Teaching for Transformation
Stronks, John 126-128
Struik, Agnes xix, 79, 93, 99-101, 103-105
Summer Program in Christian Education (SPICE) 28, 65-69, 83, 98, 169
Sweetman, Robert 267-269

Teaching with Joy 65, 76-77, 98, 399
Teaching for Transformation (TfT) xviii, 191, 206
    core practices 212, 214, 219, 224-225
    formational learning experiences 212, 214-215
    peculiar people 212, 226
    throughlines (known later as who lines) 212, 214-215
    storyline 214
The King's College (now University) xv, 98, 191, 228
    education faculty vision 237-239
    launch of teacher preparation 228-234
thematic statement
    See conceptual statement
Toronto District Christian High School 28, 39, 126, 170, 223
transforming social institution (the school as) 15, 51, 176, 188, 217, 253
transforming vision
    in Walsh and Middleton 136, 140, 143, 146
Triezenberg, Henry 26, 290
Tuininga, Anne xix, 77, 82, 85-86, 96
Tyler model (of curriculum design) 59, 67, 318

Understanding by design 210, 328, 398

Vallance, E.
    See also Eisner, Elliott
Van Brummelen, Harro
    critique of CDC's philosophy 129-131
    his legacy 138, 164-165, 167
    on curriculum orientations 165, 166-168
    on the history of American Neo-Calvinist education 20, 22, 24, 26
    on the history of Canadian Neo-Calvinist education 30-31, 36, 38-39
    on integrated units 67, 76, 166
    Shaping School Curriculum 159-160,
Vangoor, Marianne 225
Walsh, Brian 139-140, 142-148, 150-155
Wiggins, Grant 210, 328, 398

ABOUT THE AUTHOR

John E. Hull is an emeritus professor of education at The King's University in Edmonton, Alberta, where he taught courses in education foundations and curriculum theory/design. He also served as the education faculty dean for many years. He received his masters and doctorate degrees in the history and philosophy of education at the University of Toronto's Ontario Institute for Studies in Education. Prior to his academic career, he was a high school teacher for nineteen years. He has written curriculum for high school social studies and published articles on school reform. He is a founding member and former chair of the Association of Alberta Deans of Education. John and his wife Glenda live in Edmonton.